ADMINISTRATION OF ATHLETIC PROGRAMS

ADMINISTRATION OF ATHLETIC PROGRAMS

A Managerial Approach

J. FRANK BROYLES — *Athletic Director*

ROBERT D. HAY — *Professor of Management*

University of Arkansas, Fayetteville

PRENTICE-HALL, INC.
ENGLEWOOD CLIFFS, NEW JERSEY 07632

Library of Congress Cataloging in Publication Data

BROYLES, J. FRANK, 1924–
Administration of athletic programs.

Includes index.
1.–Sports—Organization and administration.
2.– Intramural sports—Management. I.–Hay, Robert D., joint author. II.–Title
GV713.B76 375'.796 78-25993
ISBN 0-13-005249-3

Printed in the United States of America

10 9 8 7 6 5 4 3 2 1

Editorial/production supervision and interior design by Cynthia Marione and Wendy Terryberry
Cover design by Jorge Hernandez
Manufacturing buyer: Harry P. Baisley

PRENTICE-HALL INTERNATIONAL, INC., *London*
PRENTICE-HALL OF AUSTRALIA PTY. LIMITED, *Sydney*
PRENTICE-HALL OF CANADA, LTD., *Toronto*
PRENTICE-HALL OF INDIA PRIVATE LIMITED, *New Delhi*
PRENTICE-HALL OF JAPAN, INC., *Tokyo*
PRENTICE-HALL OF SOUTHEAST ASIA PTE. LTD., *Singapore*
WHITEHALL BOOKS LIMITED, *Wellington, New Zealand*

CONTENTS

PREFACE

This book was written as a response to athletic directors who expressed the need for information concerning the administration of athletic programs. It is necessary for those who administer athletic programs to be truly professional administrators rather than nonprofessionals who use a hit-or-miss approach to athletic administration. They must recognize that the principles of administration are universal and can be applied to athletics. Finally, the administrators should view athletics as a form of entertainment subject to the same analyses as any business enterprise.

This is not a book about physical education or coaching. It is a book devoted to objectives, strategies, and policies regarding the administration of athletic programs. The reader will not find an outline of detailed procedures within the text; in this book, a general approach to athletic administration is stressed.

This book is distinctive because it is written as a professional approach to athletic administration. It stresses objectives, strategies and policies—universal principles and concepts applicable to sports at the high school, college, and professional levels. At the conclusion of each chapter, information can be applied to the case problems, situations similar to those faced by athletic administrators on the job. These cases often require the reader to assume the role of athletic director, to analyze hypothetical problems, and to make rational decisions.

It must be assumed that those interested in a book on general athletic administration have some background in athletics and physical education. Further, the reader should have some experience, knowledge, or background in other subject areas, such as statistics, accounting, personnel, marketing, coaching, and economics.

Obviously, there are differences in the administration of athletics in high schools, colleges, and professional sports. However, this book emphasizes the similarities in the administration of all levels of athletics. It is our assumption that the universal principles of administration will prove effective at all three levels of sports.

This book's audience includes those who have a vital interest in providing entertainment through athletics; those who are dedicated to serving the needs of fans, athletes, and administrators; those who hope to improve the quality of life through sports. Our readers are from the high school, college, and professional levels. In addition, this book should benefit those interested in participating in athletics because it reveals the problems facing an administrator of activities in which each participant—spectator as well as athlete—plays a role.

A special feature of the book is a management audit of the strengths and weaknesses of an athletic program, based on the concepts discussed in each chapter. Any athletic director could use the management audit as a tool when determining the strengths and weaknesses of his athletic program.

By way of acknowledgement, we would like to thank Thomas P. Sattler of the University of Illinois and Guy G. Reiff of the University of Michigan who reviewed our book. We would also like to express our appreciation to Dr. Lon Farrell, Assistant Athletic Director, University of Arkansas, who read every word of the manuscript before it was sent to the publisher.

J.F.B.
R.D.H.
Fayetteville, AK
March, 1979

Part I

Introduction

What is the value of competitive athletics? In the first chapter, values (benefits minus costs) are considered from several perspectives—from the point of view of the athlete, fan, coach, organization, and society.

1

THE VALUES OF COMPETITIVE ATHLETICS

Today, competitive athletic events are part of the entertainment business. Athletes are brought together to create a social event that is exciting and valuable to fans. These events are marketed to attract customers. They provide revenue so that an athletic program will remain in the black, break even, or receive a subsidy if it is in the red. Although athletes are often students as well, the emphasis in competitive athletics is placed on providing entertainment for paying customers who wish to view athletes in action. An athletic director hires coaches who serve as production coordinators by acquiring athletes, coaching them, and preparing them to produce a win on the day of the athletic event. The marketing coordinator determines the place for the event, directs its operation, promotes it, sets the prices for it, and provides a complete entertainment package for the fans to enjoy. Competitive athletics—in high schools, junior colleges, colleges, and professionals—provide entertainment by producing an athletic contest, marketing it to potential customers, and financing these contests to make money to support other forms of athletics.

The athletic administrator or coach will admit that a successful athletic program must win athletic events and produce gate receipts. The activities should be inexpensive enough for an athletic program to support itself, or receive a subsidy from another source. The athletic program's win-loss record, its attendance figures, its revenue and expenses, and its prestige provide the basic criteria for judging whether it is successful. These facts concern all athletic administrators. They realize that their positions will be secure only if they guide winning programs, produce results, and keep their programs financially sound. A glance at the sports page in any newspaper will support the preceding discussion.

THE VALUE OF ATHLETICS

Since athletic events have an economic value, at least from the spectator's point of view, it might be appropriate to examine the value of athletics to see if there is a future in athletic administration. Studies in business administration emphasize that products and services must have value before any organization will produce and market them. What is the value of athletics?

Value is a subjective judgment of a person of what a product or service is worth. Worth or value has two basic determinants: (1) the utilities, or benefits which accrue when the service is used, and (2) the costs, or what is sacrificed to acquire the service. The benefits and costs of athletics will provide a measure of its value. If we use a simple, descriptive model of the benefits of athletics minus the costs of acquiring those benefits, we can analyze the value of athletics from several points of view: those of the athlete, the customer, the organization, the coach and other personnel, and society.

Value of Athletics from the Athlete's Perspective

What are the benefits of athletics from the participant's point of view? First, it promotes a healthy body, which is necessary for a full life. Athletics helps to develop physical skills and stamina useful to the individual in a variety of circumstances. It further develops a discipline which is so vital in promoting the welfare of individuals in dealing with others. It also contributes to moral values of good ethics in dealing with fellow human beings. Because an athlete must constantly deal with other people, he learns to compete as well as cooperate—to become socially competent—through sports. Athletes gain recognition from other people. Finally, athletics opens the door to higher education for the athlete, and makes him aware of other financial opportunities. These are the benefits created by participation in athletics.

What are the costs incurred by participation in athletics? There is the possibility of injuries that might impair an athlete's physical prowess. Athletics may isolate the athlete from other members of the student body and society. The athlete may become emotionally "sick" if he does not win. In addition, he must sacrifice other activities to spend hours on sports. His grades in school are likely to suffer; so will his academic preparation for a career. The fun of athletics is replaced by the pressure to win at all costs. Coaches sometimes dehumanize athletes, treating them as machines, or chattel to be bought and sold. In addition, the successful athlete may lose his privacy; someone always wants to pry into the personal life of a star.

In summary form, let us add the benefits and subtract the costs to arrive at the value of athletics from an athlete's perspective:

+ *Benefits*	– *Costs*	= *Value*
+ Healthy body	– Injuries	
+ Physical skills and stamina	– Exclusiveness	
+ Discipline	– Emotional "sickness"	
+ Moral values	– Time	
+ Emotional maturity	– Low grades	?????
+ Social competence	– Poor academic preparation	
+ Competitiveness	– Dehumanization	
+ Cooperation	– Brutalization	
+ Opportunities	– Lack of fun	
+ Recognition	– Lack of personal privacy	

Do the pluses outweigh the minuses? This is the decision an athlete must make.

Statistical evidence of student-athlete participation in men's intercollegiate athletics sheds some light on the value of athletics in today's colleges (see table 1-1).

These statistics show that several thousands of male athletes participate in sports and find athletics valuable. It is also evident that the number of participants is steadily increasing.

The same type of statistical information about women's intercollegiate athletics is available (see table 1-2).

The annual NAIA Varsity Participation Survey shows that approximately 64,000 athletes from 555 colleges participate in 14 different sports (see table 1-3).

There is a spectacular student-athlete participation in intramural sports at the college level.

At the high school level approximately 4 million boys and 800,000 girls participate in interscholastic programs, according to the 1973 Sports Participation Survey issued by the National Federation of State High School Associations. The boys participated in 27 different sports, the girls in 20.

These figures indicate the growing number of student-athletes who find that the benefits of athletics outweigh the costs.

Table 1-1 Men's Intercollegiate Athletics of NCAA Schools
(Comparative number of student athletes and colleges participating in 1956–57, 1961–62, 1966–67, 1971–72 and 1976–77)

Sport	*1956–57*	*1961–62*	*1966–67*	*1971–72*	*1976–77*
Football	28,032 (384) *	30 519 (410)	36,799 (447)	42,187 (465)	41,551 (475)
Baseball	16,378 (431)	16,798 (497)	17,701 (527)	19,487 (616)	19,113 (654)
Track and field	16,441 (401)	18,180 (471)	18,967 (484)	19,190 (535)	20,063 (533)
Basketball	14,477 (467)	15,125 (536)	15,247 (576)	16,760 (658)	14,683 (715)
Soccer	6,120 (153)	8,270 (220)	10,370 (277)	12,024 (351)	13,458 (435)
Wrestling	5,720 (220)	7,630 (289)	7,889 (332)	9,437 (393)	8,712 (379)
Cross Country	4,828 (284)	6,047 (371)	6,281 (428)	9,194 (556)	8,810 (576)
Swimming	6,524 (233)	7,913 (292)	8,269 (312)	8,867 (382)	8,830 (394)
Tennis	6,062 (433)	6,936 (510)	7,155 (515)	7,445 (608)	7,635 (655)
Golf	4,778 (399)	5,440 (405)	6,160 (466)	6,795 (604)	6,713 (620)
Subtotals	109,360	122,858	134,838	151,386	149,568
Other sports	N.A.	20,920	19,341	21,061	20,816
Total	N.A.	143,778 (536)	154,179 (577)	172,447 (663)	170,384 (722)

* *Number of colleges in parentheses.*

Source: NCAA Report 1 (1956–57), 2 (1961–62), 3 (1966–67), 4 (1971–72), 5 (1976–77) on ***"The Sports and Recreational Programs of the Nation's Universities and Colleges,"*** *Shawnee Mission,* ***P.O.*** *Box 1906, Kansas. Reports available for two dollars for NCAA members and four dollars for non-members.*

Table 1-2 Women's Intercollegiate Athletics of NCAA Schools (Comparative number of student athletes and colleges participating in 1976–77, 1971–72 and 1966–67)

Sport	*1976–77*	*1971–72*	*1966–67*
Basketball	10,859 (649) *	6,176 (307)	4,253 (217)
Field Hockey	6,847 (290)	5,012 (191)	3,126 (137)
Volleyball	9,356 (544)	4,124 (208)	2,178 (114)
Softball	6,310 (317)	3,185 (147)	1,366 (60)
Tennis	7,127 (582)	3,071 (243)	1,361 (137)
Swimming	5,969 (338)	2,429 (140)	1,184 (68)
Gymnastics	2,722 (203)	1,855 (126)	579 (47)
Track & Field	5,831 (314)	1,389 (78)	309 (28)
Other			
Total	64,375	31,852	15,727
Source of Finance			
Intercollegiate Athletics	(404)	(120)	(50)
Student Fees	(122)	(89)	(94)
Physical Education Budget	(32)	(76)	(92)
General Budget	(219)	(65)	(92)
Others		(55)	(49)
Not Reported		(298)	(201)

* *Number of colleges in parentheses.*
Source: NCAA Reports 3, 4, and 5.

The Value of Athletics from the Organizational Perspective

Since high school and college athletic departments are part of a larger organization, it is best to analyze the benefits and costs of athletics from the larger, organizational perspective. Most administrators of schools would admit that athletics serve as a unifying and cohesive force for the school to provide links of cooperation among diverse groups within the organization. Social affairs before and after games bring together students and townspeople. Athletics may also smooth the way for hostile legislatures to become friendly toward the school. Facilities may be provided by a wealthy alumnus who enjoys a winning athletic program. A further benefit arises from the fact that the competitive value of athletics is consistent with academic values of high standards in the classrooms; competion in academics is consistent with competion in athletics. In many ways, a substantial athletic program is beneficial to the organization.

There are costs incurred from the organization's perspective as well. The raw professionalism of athletics is not compatible with the academic functions of a school. Schools can rationalize that student-athletes are a part of the system, but athletics today really functions as entertainment for the

Table 1-3 NAIA Varsity Participation Survey
(Comparative number of student athletes and colleges participating in 1970–71 to 1974–75)

Sport	*1970–71*	*1971–72*	*1972–73*	*1973–74*	*1974–75*
Football	11,680 (292) *	11,400 (285)	12,185 (273)	10,440 (261)	11,790 (262)
Baseball	10,164 (462)	10,296 (468)	10,142 (461)	9,834 (447)	9,878 (449)
Track & Field	9,048 (348)	10,192 (392)	9,436 (386)	9,282 (351)	9,438 (363)
Basketball	7,686 (549)	7,770 (555)	8,175 (545)	7,518 (537)	8,010 (534)
Golf	5,496 (458)	5,424 (542)	5,376 (448)	4,908 (409)	4,932 (411)
Soccer	4,272 (178)	4,368 (182)	4,440 (185)	4,440 (185)	4,464 (186)
Cross Country	4,104 (342)	4,080 (340)	3,960 (330)	3,660 (305)	3,684 (307)
Tennis	3,496 (437)	3,568 (446)	3,528 (441)	3,352 (419)	3,344 (418)
Others	—	—	—	—	—
Totals	64,166	65,350	65,565	61,301	63,323

** Number of colleges in parentheses.*

Source: National Association of Intercollegiate Athletics Varsity Participation Surveys; In 1975, 555 colleges in the United States and Canada were members.

fans who support it. Athletics is very costly for a few students who need physical training the most. Often, scandals erupt, damaging the reputation of the school. Finally, some administrators do not open the athletic programs's financial records to the public, violating the basic educational principles of light and search for truth.

In summary form, we can see the benefits and costs of athletics from the organizational point of view.

+ *Benefits*	– *Costs*	= *Value*
+ Unifying force	– Raw professionalism does not square with academics	
+ Cements relations between town and students	– Costly for a few students who need it the least	????
+ Soothes hostile legislatures	– Scandals	
+ Facilities provided	– "Closed book" finances violate academic principles of truth and light	
+ Competition is consistent with professional standards		

Table 1-4 Intramural Sports in NCAA Colleges
(Comparative number of men and women participating in 1956–57, 1961–62, 1965–66, 1971–72)

	1957	*1962*	*1967*	*1972*	*1977*
Women Participants	N.A.	N.A.	165,081	276,167	576,648
Men Participants	N.A.	N.A.	1,273,908	1,676,995	2,067,167
Total	679,402	1,160,843	1,438,989	1,953,162	2,643,805

Source: NCAA Reports, 1, 2, 3, 4, 5.

The school or college must weigh the benefits and costs of athletic programs to determine their value.

An athletic program has been deemed valuable by 722 NCAA colleges. They support the following athletic programs:

Class A - Division I basketball and Division I football	137
Class B - Division I basketball and Division II or III football	47
Class C - Division I basketball and no football	62
Class D - Division II basketball and CD II football	112
Class E - Division III basketball and CD III football	179
Class F - Division II basketball and no football	71
Class G - Division III basketball and no football	144
	*722

**Source: NCAA Report No. 5.*

The growth in NCAA institutions increased from 476 in 1957–58 to 536 in 1961–62, to 577 in 1966–67, to 663 in 1971–72, and to 722 in 1976–77.

These NCAA institutions also have spent millions of dollars in operating expenses each year and have billions of dollars invested in facilities.

Value of Athletics from the Customer's Perspective

In high schools and colleges, those who attend athletic events are usually students, faculty, and ticket-paying fans. What value do they see in athletics?

The benefits to customers are varied. First, they view athletics as providing entertainment that releases them from their daily routines. Athletics provides a useful, wholesome way for fans to spend their leisure time. Fans may meet old acquaintances and renew friendships at athletic events. Often spectators hope to gain some recognition from apparel that identifies them with a particular team. If the student, faculty member, or fan represents a winning team, peers might consider him/her a winner as well.

What are the costs? First, one must pay for the tickets and take the time

Table 1-5 Financial Operations and Facilities of NCAA Schools (Comparison during 1961–62, 1966–67, 1971–72, 1976–77)

	Operations (Yearly)	*Facilities (Value)*
1961–62	$100,299,042	Not Available
1966–67 (577 institutions)	190,393,993	$2,050,019,519
1971–72 (663 institutions)	329,625,420	1,545,917,580
1976–77 (722 institutions)	533,143,476	5,355,936,634

Source: NCAA Reports 3, 4 and 5.

to attend an athletic event. Out of town fans must finance the travel and lodging expenses when they attend an athletic event. Finally, the "win at all costs" attitude of some fans threatens to become a destructive force for competitive athletics.

The following is an outline of the benefits and costs from the customers' perspective:

+ *Benefits*	– *Costs*	= *Value*
+ Release from routines	– Ticket price	
+ Wholesome use of leisure time	– Opportunity time cost	
+ Meet their friends	– Travel costs	????
+ Apparel recognition	– "Win at all cost" attitude	
+ Identify as winners		

Each customer must weight the benefits against the costs when deciding whether to attend an event.

Evidence is available indicating how many customers value athletics enough to attend athletic events (see table 1-6). Attendance at most sports events is on the upswing. Americans are fascinated by athletics.

Value of Athletics from the Coach's Perspective

Most coaches are former athletes. Therefore, they understand why participants, as well as spectators, value athletics.

A coach derives numerous benefits from athletics. Coaching is his/her livelihood. Athletic events allow coaches to test their views of how a game should be played. Coaches learn to make careful decisions based on intuition, information about the opposing team, and experience. They become tacticians as well as strategists. Coaches gain a degree of recognition from fans, peers, and athletes. Finally, most coaches enjoy working with young people.

What are the costs? Coaches must spend a tremendous amount of time working with athletes. They must leave home and travel with their team. Coaches are constantly pressured by customers, athletes, parents, alumni, and administrators, to produce a winning team. Finally, the coach must accept the insecurity of his/her position.

Table 1-6 Attendance at Athletic Events

	1977	1974	1971	1968
Football				
Collegiate	32,905,178	31,234,855	30,455,442	27,025,846
NFL	11,018,632	10,236,322	10,076,035	8,517,851
Post season games	1,653,727	1,438,894	1,507,588	1,480,383
Totals	45,577,537	42,438,071	42,039,065	37,024,080
Baseball				
Major leagues	38,709,781	30,025,608	29,193,417	23,102,745
Minor leagues	13,481,355	11,031,918	11,443,489	10,033,142
Playoffs	831,005	604,881	619,239	379,670
Totals	53,004,141	41,662,407	41,256,145	33,515,557
Basketball				
Collegiate	29,041,337	24,629,718	23,965,090	21,161,490
NBA		5,910,023	5,583,974	3,649,511
ABA	10,705,515	2,319,214	2,247,568	1,330,000
Playoffs		924,142	806,402	—
Totals	39,746,852	33,785,097	32,603,034	26,141,001
Hockey				
NHL	9,210,169	9,241,420	7,965,310	5,301,354
WHL	4,025,419	2,764,506	—	—
Collegiate, etc.	7,745,911	9,380,281	9,056,880	—
Total	20,981,499	21,386,207	17,022,190	5,301,354
Horse Racing	79,455,828	78,799,936	76,954,288	68,899,989
Dog Racing	20,040,021	16,274,471	13,666,462	12,059,762
Boxing	3,899,420	2,674,504	2,341,116	1,987,400
Wrestling	4,864,415	5,783,874	3,892,014	3,420,000
Auto Racing	49,638,500	47,500,000	43,700,000	40,981,340
Soccer	6,935,986	5,631,460	4,794,020	4,049,139
Tennis	4,650,000	3,598,000	—	—

Source: Yearly Sports Survey on Attendance, Triangle Publications, Inc.

Whether the benefits outweigh the costs is the decision a coach must make. The following is a summary of the benefits minus the costs of coaching:

+ *Benefits*	– *Costs*	= *Value*
+ Means of livelihood	– Time	
+ Testing of their views	– Travel	
+ Decision makers	– Constant pressure to win	????
+ Recognition	– Lack of security	
+ Enjoyment with others		

Growth in the number of collegiate coaches indicates that coaches find athletics a valuable occupation (see table 1-7).

Table 1-7 Coaches in NCAA Colleges
(Years 1961–62, 1966–67, 1971–72, 1976–77)

Year	*Full time coaches*	*Part time coaches*	*Total*
1961–62	3,252	1,607	4,859
1966–67	4,293	1,600	5,893 (+21.3%)
1971–72	5,379	2,801	8,180 (+38.8%)
1976–77	6,786	5,485	12,271 (+50.0%)

Source: NCAA Reports 2, 3, 4 and 5.

Football has the highest average number of coaches per institution, approximately 4 per NCAA school. Basketball has approximately 2 per school. However, basketball has a ratio of one coach to 13 athletes compared to a 1 to 16 ratio in football.

Other athletic department employees also enjoy the benefits of athletics. Table 1-8 indicates a constant increase in the number of personnel employed in collegiate athletics. It appears that a growing number of coaches and other personnel find athletics important and worthwhile.

Table 1-8 Athletic Personnel Employed by NCAA Schools
(Years 1961–62, 1966–67, 1971–72, 1976–77)

Year	*Athletic Department*	*Intramurals*	*Physical Education*	*Clubs/ Recreation*	*Total*
1961–62	9,571	3,236	5,351	593	18,751
1966–67	13,155	3,121	6,371	1,013	23,660
1971–72	15,909	5,089	10,983	1,470	33,461
1976–77	21,591	7,609	13,123	4,160	46,483

Source: NCAA Reports 2, 3, 4 and 5.

Value of Athletics from Society's Perspective

We have analyzed the value of athletics from the perspectives of the athlete, coach, organization, and customer. It is time to consider athletics from the perspective of society.

Athletics acts as a unifying force for the city, the state, and the nation. The Olympic Games draw people of a nation together to support their team. Similarly, people become unified when supporting a particular state or local team. In this way, athletics serves as a cohesive force for society.

Athletics also serves as a vehicle for social mobility. Athletics has done more to advance the causes of minority groups than any other institution, except the federal government. It has helped to further the American goals of racial integration and equal rights for women. Through participation in athletics, minority group members are able to advance from the poorest to the richest social and economic classes.

Some sociologists contend that athletics helps people to forget the unpleasantness of modern society. There may be some truth in their contention because athletic events do bring people together. The old Roman view, "Give the masses bread and circuses," may also apply to our society.

Yet, in some ways athletic programs are detrimental to society. Many consider athletics to be society's new "religion." People often read the sports section of a newspaper before scanning the front page. The individual's overwhelming interest in athletics has superseded his/her concern for society's problems.

The athletes who are eliminated from the game because they are too slow or too weak to be "winners" often lose their self-respect. The "losers" suffer pain inflicted by athletic competition.

Furthermore, athletics encourages hostility toward the opposing team. Hostility does not promote a better society.

The following is a summary of the effects of athletics on society.

+ *Benefits*	– *Costs*	= *Value*
+ Unifying force	– "Religion" of athletics	
+ Vehicle for social mobility	– Pain and suffering to losers	????
+ Takes people's minds off problems	– Encourages hostility	

When deciding whether or not to support athletics, people must carefully weigh its benefits against its costs. They must determine how they feel society could profit from organized sports. One could easily analyze the motivation of everyone involved in athletics by considering the benefits and costs of their actions. However, the decision whether athletics is worthwhile depends exclusively on an individual's judgment of the benefits minus the costs.

CHAPTER SUMMARY

What is the value of competitive athletics? Value is determined by the benefits minus the costs of a product and service. From an athlete's perspective, the benefits must outweigh the costs of participation. This is a judgment the athlete must make. That there is an increasing number of athlete-participants indicates that many individuals consider athletics valuable. Similarly, the benefits of organized sports must outweigh the costs. If fans continue to pay the price of tickets, they must consider athletics worthwhile. Evidence suggests that the number of athletic organizations is increasing, and that fan attendance is on the upswing.

The increasing number of coaches indicates that coaching athletics is a worthwhile occupation. Since society supports competitive athletics, sports must benefit society to a certain degree. It is pointed out in this chapter, however, that one must consider the costs as well as the benefits of a product and service when measuring its value.

Case 1-1 DEAR ANN LANDERS

The following is a letter from a high school student to the noted columnist, Ann Landers:[1]

Dear Ann Landers: I am a senior in high school who has always enjoyed participating in athletic events. But I have a beef I'd like to air in your column.

Three coaches in our school act like high school sports are a business. If the team doesn't win, they chew out the players and make us feel as if we have let everyone down.

If a person is in sports for a living, I can see why winning might be a big deal, but why should high school competition be THAT important?

I enjoy sports, but I consider it healthy exercise, good competition and fun. I hate all the unbearable heat put on the players to win.

Please, Ann, tell the athletic directors that many guys like myself have been turned off by their attitude. I have participated in tournaments and meets outside of school and I've never felt the terrific pressure to win until I played on a high school team. Just sign me—A N.Y. Griper.

Dear Gripe: Of course you are right, but the coach who turns out winning teams gets support and praise from the alumni, the community and the press. He also enjoys victory dinners, plaques, and silver cups for the showcase. Often it means a salary increase.

It's unfair to hassle and put down a losing team that happens to be outclassed. I agree such coaches should be chopped down to size. But inherent in the American ethic is the importance of being a winner and I see nothing that suggests it's going to change.

QUESTIONS:

1. What is your reaction to the student's letter and to Ann Landers' reply?
2. From a student's point of view, what are the benefits of participating in competitive athletics? What are the costs? Is participation worthwhile?

Case 1-2 ATHLETIC ADMINISTRATORS—JOB SECURITY??

COLLEGIATE LEVEL

A recent newspaper article, "Does College Athletics Need Complete Overhaul?," analyzes collegiate athletics as follows:[2]

A widely respected athletic official feels that swift, sweeping changes must be made if intercollegiate athletics are to survive.

The problem is money, or the lack of it. Inflation has taken a brutal toll on the athletic budgets of many colleges across the country. Among those affected is the University of Texas-Arlington. U.T.A. President, Dr. Wendell Nedderman, states:

"Intercollegiate athletics across the nation are in financial difficulty. The inflationary spiral of increasing costs is having a devastating effect. . . . The results, even during the past 12 months, are significant. UTA, like many other institutions, is facing a financial crisis in its athletic program."

These words are not encouraging for the school's athletic program, directed by Chena Gilstrap, a widely respected former football coach. Gilstrap has given considerable thought to the program's economic problems. He suggests the following drastic procedures to lessen the financial burden:

1. Abolish all athletic scholarships (Gilstrap does not believe this will reduce the quality of football).
2. Reduce coaching staffs.
3. Cut recruiting expenditures.
4. Limit the size of traveling squads.

Can't Maintain

"What I'm suggesting," Gilstrap said, "is that intercollegiate athletics has been living at a level it can't maintain. We may be at the end of an era. You'd be surprised at some of the schools with reputations for success that are really strapped for money. I bet there are fewer than fifty colleges that show a profit in athletics."

Gilstrap's superior, Dr. Nedderman, recently rejected a student advisory committee's recommendation that football be abolished. He chose to commit UTA to a football program through 1975. Nedderman's only comment: "We have the situation in constant review; we're taking the issue a year at a time."

The advisory committee hoped to allocate the program's $300,000 to other needy areas.

Although many of U.T.A.'s problems are similar to those of other universities, some aspects of its case are unique. The school has enjoyed some success in football, but last year lost ten of eleven games in the major college Southland Conference. Gilstrap joked, "We were 6–4, lost six on the road and four at home."

The university is situated at the center of a "metroplex" which also includes Texas Christian in Forth Worth, and Southern Methodist at Dallas. Both are members of the more prestigious Southwest Conference. All three universities must compete with the Dallas Cowboys for fans and financial support. Not one university has been consistently successful.

Gilstrap said the University of Texas fears a $300,000 athletic deficit next year. He feels that Penn State, without exposure through the media, will experience a loss as well.

"I figured Penn State probably had $5 million ratholed somewhere," Gilstrap quipped. He conceded that powers such as Ohio State, Southern Cal, Penn State, Notre Dame, Alabama, Texas and Oklahoma could hold out longer than others, but not indefinitely.

"I think one of two things is going to happen," he continued. "Either we're going to have fewer colleges participating in intercollegiate athletics, or we're going to have to change our modus operandi . . . We may be fixing to find out just how many college football teams our society will support. It may be sixty. It may be one hundred. But under the present format, I predict the number will appreciably diminish in the near future." Gilstrap believes that football restricted to a small number of colleges will lose its overall appeal.

He concluded, "But if by some major restructuring, we can save the program that now exists, without really diminishing the quality, I say it's not only good for the schools, but good for the country. I'm not pessimistic . . . I believe college athletics has the capability of preserving itself by some means—maybe some that I've suggested here."

Quality Returns

Gilstrap feels that college-based athletic scholarships should be eliminated. "I truly believe that within five years the quality of competition would be back to as good as it is today," he said. The truly economically disadvantaged student now has greater access to more kinds of grants than at any other time in history. Without scholarships, students' motivation would simply be a desire to play. In Texas, he said, "We have a fine interscholastic program and the only reason I know of is because they want to play. I think this [the elimination of scholarships] would remove some of the feeling that's come into college athletics, that those guys knocking heads out there are not part of us, but a kind of group of paid gladiators representing our school . . . Maybe I'm too provincial, been a bush leaguer too long, but I can not conceive of the wise spending of $3 million on an intercollegiate athletic program. I think a lot of it has to be wasted. Of course, a lot of it is keeping up with the Joneses. Somewhere down the line we're going to have to put some restrictions on the Joneses."

Gilstrap admits having been asked, "If Penn State's having problems, how in the world do you people hope to survive?"

He answered, "If we can stay in business just a little while longer, we're going to meet a lot of the so-called biggies on their way back down. . . . Some people in higher places than mine in bigger schools . . . feel like I'm overdramatizing this thing, that their situation is not as critical as ours. . . But they may change their perspective in the next couple of years."

He believes that athletic programs are worth fighting for: "People just equate excellence in athletics and excellence in education. I simply come back to the premise that this has been a major part of the American scene for a good many decades. And I'm just prejudiced enough to believe there's some value that comes to society as a result of the unifying forces that are present."

On the same page of this newspaper, the following article appeared:[3]

GILSTRAP RESIGNS
AT UT-ARLINGTON
REEVES NAMED

ARLINGTON, TEX. (AP)

Chena Gilstrap stepped down as athletic director at the University of Texas-Arlington Tuesday and was succeeded by Dr. Bill Reeves.

UT-A President Wendell Nedderman made the announcement and said Gilstrap, 60, submitted his resignation a year ago but had stayed on at Nedderman's urging.

Gilstrap, a former football coach at UT-A and a renowned humorist and speaker, will keep his post as head of the physical education department.

Reeves, a three-year basketball letterman at UT-A, has served the university as an assistant coach, an assistant professor, and administrative assistant to Gilstrap, coordinator of physical education degree programs and athletic business manager.

PROFESSIONAL LEVEL

In another newspaper article the author made the following partial analysis:[4]

Hank Stram is an ex-coach in the National Football League for the first time in 15 years not because of Lamar Hunt's heart but his wallet.

The millionaire owner of the Kansas City Chiefs continued to believe in Stram as a coach even when he fired him.

To Hunt it was simple mathematics. Research indicated that fans were so turned off by what was happening to the over-the-hill Chiefs under Stram that season ticket sales in 1975 might drop as much as 30,-000 from this year's 60,000. At an average $56 per sale, that would take $1,680,000 out of the Chiefs' treasury next year.

The most optimistic projections were for a 15,000-ticket drop which is still $840,000.

Hunt can add. The $100,000 that Stram has coming for each of the remaining seven years of his contract is peanuts against what it might have stood Hunt to keep his coach.

Thus the man who engineered "The Offense of the 1970s" enters 1975 without an offense to coach. Stram can add, too, and Christmas is beginning to come out on the short side for him. It was Christmas Eve, 1958, that he as part of Terry Brennan's Notre Dame staff was swept aside. Then Stram's Chiefs lost the Longest Game, 27–24 to Miami in 82 minutes and 40 seconds, on Christmas Day of 1971.

Fans' tolerance turned to hostility as the Chiefs' slide began from there—the playoff loss to the Dolphins in 1971, after a 10–3 regular-season record, to 8–6 in 1972, to 7–5–2 in 1973, finally to the alltime low 5–9 this season.

Getting Old

The Chiefs were getting old. Customers could not understand why Stram would not rip out the deadwood and rebuild.

An old friend said, "Hank is a strong man. I call it courage. But others may see it as stubbornness."

That is exactly how KC fans saw it. That is why thousands stood and cheered at a hockey game in Kansas City when it was announced that Stram had lost his last game, 35–15, to Minnesota.

Screening Process

What of Stram? His hyperactive makeup hardly will permit him to sit back and draw on the $700,000 until he turns 57. He could take another pro job and collect from the Chiefs the difference between his new salary and the $100,000 annually for which Hunt is committed.

Meanwhile, the Chiefs without Stram will for a time seem like the Spirit of St. Louis without Lindbergh. Only Lindbergh, unlike Stram, did not fly his plane until it fell to pieces. Nor, unlike Hunt, did Lindbergh have to worry about selling season tickets.

QUESTIONS:

1. Why did the two athletic administrators—one, on a collegiate level; the other, on the professional level—lose their jobs?
2. Did they lose their jobs because of coaching ability?
3. What criteria are used to judge the success of an athletic program?
4. What functions have to be performed by an athletic administrator to make a successful program?

Case 1-3 THE VALUE OF THE ATHLETIC PROGRAM AT SSU*[5]

Dr. John Henry sat in his office pondering the results of two surveys he had made concerning the athletic program at Southwestern State University.

Dr. John Henry was recently appointed by the president to the University's Athletic Committee. He represented the faculty and student body in his decisions concerning the fate of competitive athletics as SSU. After attending meetings of the Athletic Committee, Dr. Henry realized that he did not know the faculty and student body's thoughts about the athletic program. How could he represent them in providing intelligent inputs into the decisions about the athletic program? Do the faculty and students support SSU's athletic program? What do they think about the value of various sports? If SSU had to cut back funding for athletic programs, which sport would be the first to go? If SSU had extra resources for athletics, which sport should be added to the roster? The answers he received prompted him to make a survey of the services provided for faculty and students by the athletic department.

Dr. Henry taught a class in communications theory. In his opinion, a semantic differential was the best research instrument he knew of which allowed a person to evaluate any concept. He decided to have his communications class use a semantic differential, to sample the faculty and students' evaluation of the athletic program.

The first study was conducted by class members in the spring semester. Each class member interviewed a random sample of faculty and students. Approximately 20% (about 148 members) of the total faculty in the col-

*Names have been disguised in this case.

leges of Education, Engineering, Business Administration, Agriculture, Law, and Arts and Sciences were interviewed. In addition, about 5% (415 students) of the student body from these colleges were polled.

Eighteen months later, Dr. Henry repeated the same class project in his summer school session. The class polled approximately 40 faculty members (15% of the faculty members on duty) and 260 students (8% of those attending summer school). A comparison of the two student body surveys is presented in Figure 1-1.

After comparing the two student body surveys, Dr. Henry then compared the two faculty surveys shown in Figure 1-2.

Dr. Henry noticed a striking similarity in the views of the students and faculty. Therefore, he made a four-way comparison of each sport, considering the responses of both sets of students and both sets of faculty members. The results are shown in Figures 1-3 and 1-4.

Dr. Henry then decided to rank each sport by the criteria "necessary," "productive," "exciting," and "good." These adjectives would assess the relative value of each sport. Figure 1-5 shows the final rank of each sport.

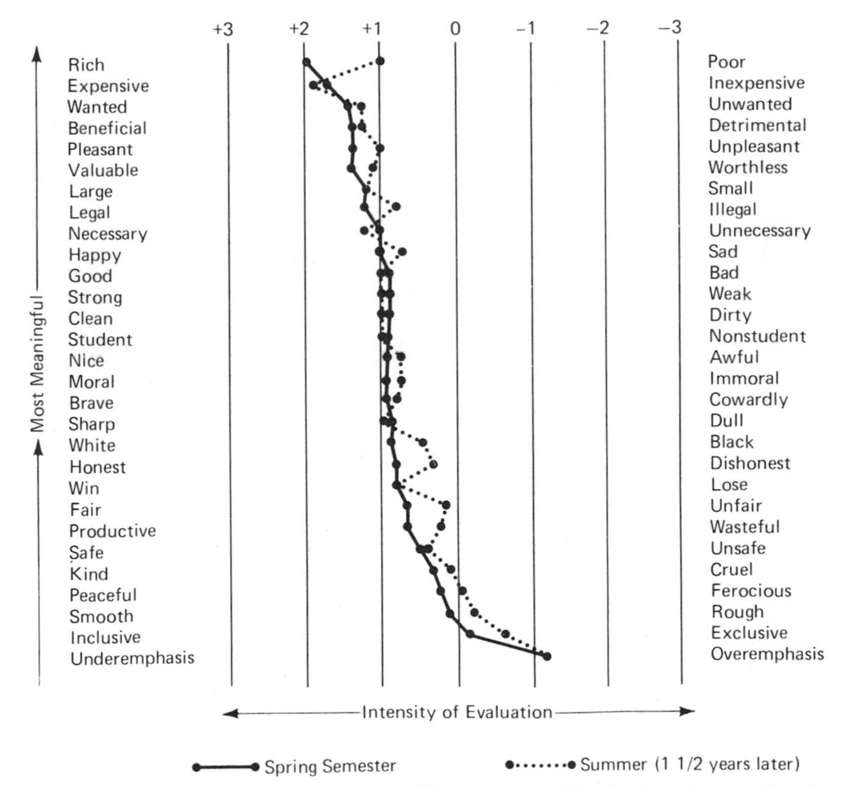

Figure 1–1 Overall Athletic Program (Comparative Evaluation by the Students)

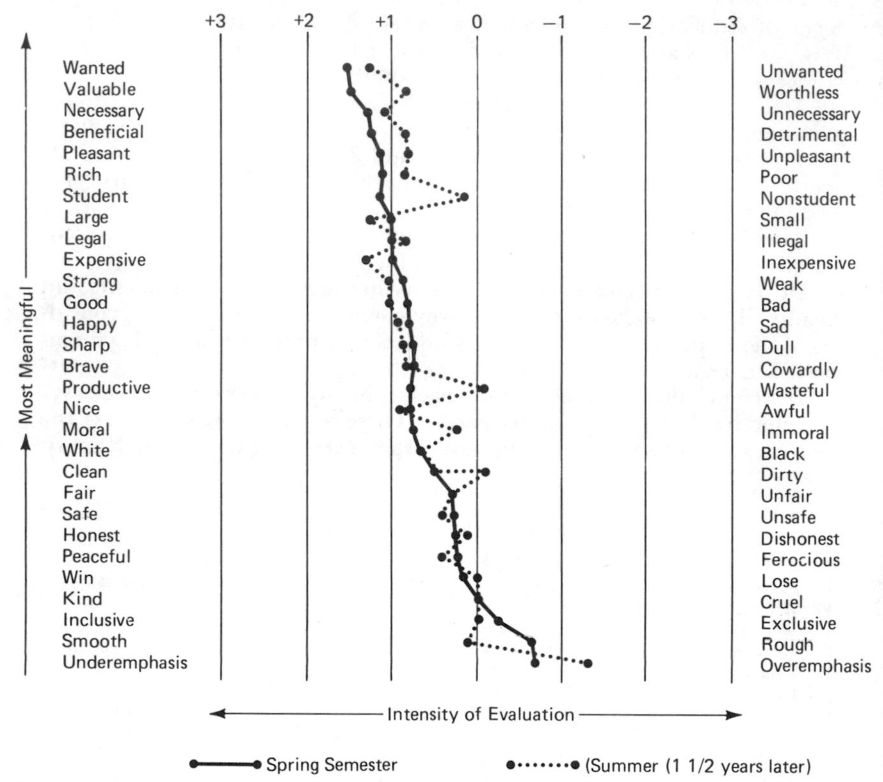

Figure 1–2 Overall Athletic Program (Comparative Evaluation by the Faculty)

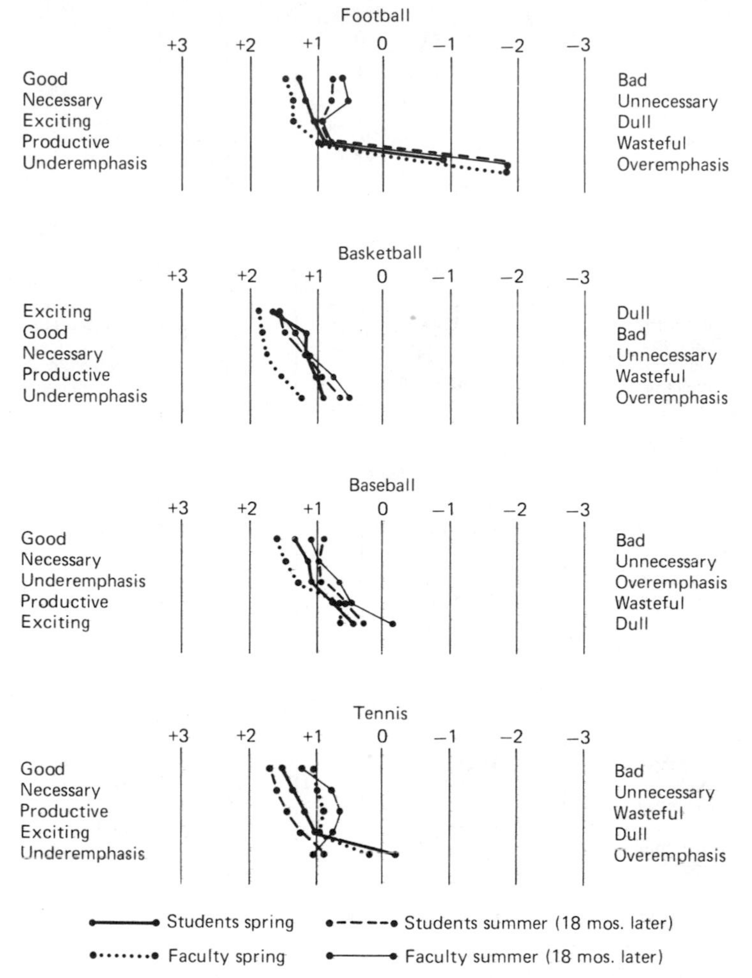

Figure 1–3 Comparative Evaluation by Students and Faculty during the Spring Semester versus the Summer Session

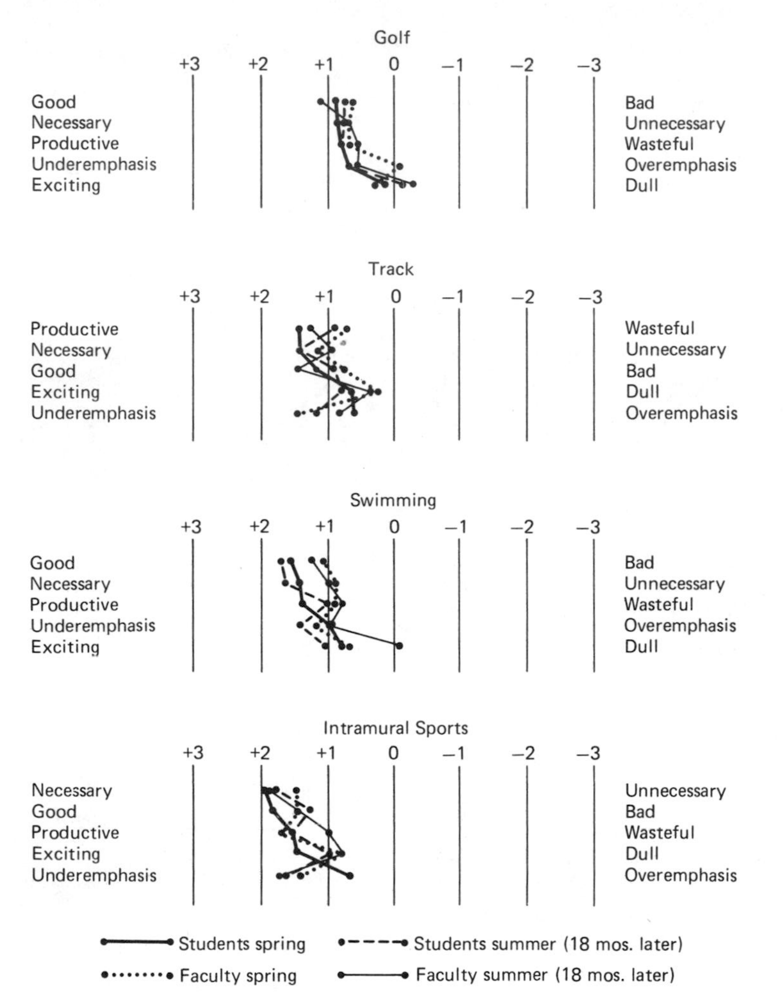

Figure 1–4 Comparative Evaluation by Students and Faculty during the Spring Semester versus the Summer Session

Figure 1-5 Ranking by Sports

Necessary		Productive	
Spring	*Summer*	*Spring*	*Summer*
Intramurals	Intramurals	Intramurals	Intramurals
Basketball	Track	Basketball	Tennis
Football	Swimming	Tennis	Swimming
Track	Tennis	Swimming	Basketball
Tennis	Basketball	Track	Track
Swimming	Baseball	Football	Football
Baseball	Football	Baseball	Baseball
Golf	Golf	Golf	Golf

Exciting		Good	
Spring	*Summer*	*Spring*	*Summer*
Basketball	Basketball	Intramurals	Swimming
Football	Tennis	Basketball	Tennis
Intramurals	Intramurals	Football	Basketball
Swimming	Track	Tennis	Track
Baseball	Swimming	Baseball	Baseball
Track	Baseball	Track	Golf
Golf	Golf	Golf	Football

Emphasis

Overemphasis		Underemphasis	
Spring	*Summer*	*Spring*	*Summer*
Football	Football	Swimming	Intramurals
Tennis (?)		Baseball	Swimming
		Track	Track
		Basketball	Golf
		Intramurals	Tennis
		Golf	Baseball
			Basketball

QUESTIONS:

1. What values do students place on the athletic program? What about the faculty? Any negative responses?
2. Do the students and faculty generally support the athletic program?
3. Are there any major differences between faculty and students about the athletic program or about each of the sports?
4. Are there any major differences between the evaluation periods, i.e., spring and summer (18 months later)?
5. Suppose a financial cutback had to be made in the athletic program. Which sport would be the most likely to be eliminated?
6. Suppose additional resources became available. Which sport should have increased financial support?
7. What do you think of the semantic differential as an evaluation instrument?

FOOTNOTES

[1] *Tulsa World*, 27 September 1975, in the Ann Landers column.

[2] Adapted from Mike Cochran, "Does College Athletics Need Complete Overhaul?," *Arkansas Gazette*, 23 April 1975.

[3] *Arkansas Gazette*, 23 April 1975.

[4] Adapted from an article written in the fall of 1975 by Edwin Pope, Knight News Service.

[5] This case was adapted from information in Robert D. Hay, "The Semantic Differential," *Athletic Administration*, NACDA, Summer, 1977.

Part II

Objectives of a Successful Athletic Program

An athletic program has several objectives. These objectives are oriented toward service, growth, survival, and image. Various strategies are designed to accomplish these objectives. The next three chapters discuss the various objectives and strategies of successful athletic programs. There are also summary analyses, in terms of strengths and weaknesses, of the strategies athletic administrators can use to evaluate their program's objectives.

2

OBJECTIVES AND STRATEGIES OF COMPETITIVE ATHLETIC PROGRAMS

The primary objective of a successful business organization is to produce a quality product and/or service to satisfy the needs of its customers; similarly, the main goal of a successful athletic program is to produce a winning team to satisfy some of the entertainment needs of its fans. By winning more than half of its competitive events, an athletic program establishes itself as a winner. Winning is the name of the game for athletic administrators. A winning tradition provides entertainment for customers; develops character in its athletes; improves the image of the athletic program; helps a program to grow, make a profit, and survive. Winning is probably the chief objective of any American athletic program—in high schools, in junior colleges, in colleges, and in professional sports.[1]

There are other objectives pursued by organized athletic programs, most related to winning. Athletic programs strive to develop character in their athletes. Called by various names, the objective is to satisfy some of the needs of the athletes who create the entertainment package so vital to the success of an athletic organization. The character development of athletes might very well be the first objective of some athletic programs, particularly at the high school, junior college, and lower division college level. At those schools where the athletic program is financially subsidized, that is, at those places where athletics is not a self-supporting entity, the development of character of its athletes could be the first objective of the athletic program. When the pressure of the market place, however, is brought to bear on the athletic program, development of athletes comes to be a collateral objective.

In some women's athletic programs, development of character may be the dominant objective. However, when women engage in competitive interscholastic athletic events, winning becomes the chief objective, although character development is also enhanced.

Another common organizational objective is to improve the image of the athletic program, particularly in the eyes of the fans, administrators, peer schools, and public. One might say that winning helps an athletic program to achieve recognition. In this light, organizational image improvement allows a program to gain stature in the eyes of the alumni, legislative authorities, or other influential people whose financial support can mean a lot to an athletic program.

Growth is an objective of most athletic programs. Increasing its size is an implicit objective of practically any athletic organization. Very few wish to remain small. Growth can be measured in several ways: attendance, dollars of revenue, dollar value of facilities, number of athletic scholarships, number of employees, and so forth.

Making a profit is a seldom-mentioned but very important goal of self-supporting athletic programs. An athletic administrator will privately admit that the athletic program has profit as an objective, maybe not the dominant one, but an objective which is constantly pursued, regardless of whether it is a high school, a college, or professional athletic organization.

Often those within an organization try to make their athletic program the best of its kind. To be a part of the most successful athletic team has a tremendous appeal for most athletes and fans. Many organizations strive for such recognition, although this type of prestige may be short-lived.

The one objective common to all athletic programs is the ability to survive through adversity. Particularly true in times of adversity, the survival objective becomes a very important one. Athletic programs do not like to die. Consequently, the maintenance of continuity is of importance to most athletic departments. This is especially true when a scholastic athletic program has been divorced from the physical education department, and it is forced to become a self-supporting, independent unit in a high school or college. Loss of status and of independence is damaging to athletic programs; survival and continuity are of the utmost importance.

A common objective is to improve the position of athletics in general. Improving the "industry position" may not be a primary objective of most athletic programs, but it is recognized as being of importance. Any strategies to improve the position of athletics in relation to other "industries" are supported by athletic administrators concerned with their personal and organizational livelihood.

In some athletic programs, to have a corner on the entertainment market is considered extremely important. The program with a monopoly position encounters fewer problems than other programs. This is especially true in large metropolitan areas where direct competition with other athletic programs is a fact of life. In large cities, athletics also faces indirect competition from other forms of entertainment. Consequently, acquiring and maintaining a share of the entertainment market becomes a very important objective.

A recently recognized objective of some athletic programs is to improve the quality of life for society. Athletics is considered to be an activity that flourishes during times of affluence. America is now affluent, and athletic programs are here to offer the American public a chance to improve their quality of life.

Although it is not always recognized by administrators, a major objective of athletic programs is to satisfy the needs of all those linked to organized sports. This group includes customers, athletes, employees, creditors, suppliers, owners, managers, government, community, athletic conferences, and society. Each group contributes something of value to athletic programs, and in exchange, a successful athletic program should contribute something of value to them.

The following is a summary of the various objectives of today's athletic programs.

ATHLETIC PROGRAM OBJECTIVES

1. Which of the following does the athletic director recognize as athletic program objectives?

		Yes	No	Degree of Emphasis
1.1	Producing a winning team to satisfy the entertainment needs of the customers (fans)?			
1.2	Developing character in athletes?			
1.3	Improving the image of the athletic program?			
1.4	Increasing its size (growth)?			
1.5	Making a profit?			
1.6	Being a leader in athletics?			
1.7	Maintaining survival of the athletic program?			
1.8	Improving the position of athletics in general?			
1.9	Obtaining a share of the entertainment market?			
1.10	Improving the quality of life for society?			
1.11	Satisfying some of the needs of			
	Customers?			
	Athletes?			
	Employees?			
	Creditors?			
	Owners?			
	Managers?			
	Suppliers?			

Government?			
Conference?			
Community?			
Society?			
Others?			
1.12 Others?			

PERSONAL OBJECTIVES OF ATHLETIC ADMINISTRATORS

The athletic program has organizational objectives; similarly, the athletic administrator has personal goals he/she hopes to achieve. There is a reciprocal relationship between organizational and personal objectives in this case: if the organization realizes its objectives, it is probable that the administrator will achieve his personal goals.

The personal objectives of an athletic administrator normally are to maintain or to improve his/her present salary and position. He/she also wants to achieve the organizational objectives. Normally, an athletic administrator will desire to either maximize or balance profits. He/she would like to achieve some degree of organizational efficiency—finding new and better ways to get things done. A common personal objective is to receive some type of recognition for his/her efforts in administering the affairs of an athletic program. In addition, some administrators wish to have an opportunity for advancement. He/she also desires information to make intelligent decisions. Sometimes they have a desire to avoid unionization of their operations. Many times they desire a chance to develop other administrators. Others desire to create a good atmosphere for accomplishing organizational objectives, including the development of effective policies and procedures for the accomplishment of organizational objectives. These are the typical personal objectives of athletic administrators. Administrators contribute their leadership skills to the athletic program; in return, they expect to achieve their personal objectives.

STRATEGIES USED TO ACHIEVE ORGANIZATIONAL OBJECTIVES

Once a set of objectives has been determined (and this is no easy task, particularly in light of the changing environment in which we live), an athletic administrator needs to ask, "What steps do we need to take to reach the objectives?" Selection of the right objectives and selection of the steps to accomplish them are the keys to the development of sound strategies. A master strategy for a particular objective should include: (1) recognition of the particular forms of athletic entertainment to produce and sell; (2) selection of the steps by which they will be created; (3) determination of the ways necessary to go from the present to the desired objective; (4) establishment of standards necessary to measure achievement. A strategy normally considers the external environment in which the athletic program operates and the internal environment of the athletic program in order to match the ways (means) of accomplishing athletic program objectives (ends).

Strategy considers resources, thrusts, priorities, and principles of accomplishing objectives. Since the environment changes, strategies may change. Strategies and plans are fairly similar terms. However, strategies usually follow the planning process, that is, once an environmental assessment is made (planning), strategies are usually developed to figure out ways to accomplish the objectives decided upon.

Producing a Winning Team to Satisfy The Entertainment Needs of the Fans

What product and service strategies have to be considered in producing a winning team to satisfy the fans? The first two are team quality and quantity, usually accomplished by acquiring an excellent staff of coaches and a quantity of talented athletes. There are no substitutes for a quality coach and a quality athlete, and having them in sufficient quantities to forestall unforeseen events.

The quality of the winning team may also have certain characteristics which are associated with a winner. The teams have to be durable (strong and in physical condition), adaptable (able to adapt to opponents' strengths and weaknesses), dependable (can they be counted on?), and quick (speed and quickness). In addition, there must be some degree of balance (offense and defense) necessary for a winner.

A winner also has a certain uniqueness (can do things an opponent cannot do). A certain amount of innovation is also necessary. In addition, a certain element of variety becomes necessary (can do many things). Obviously the product and service must be safe (protection against injuries for athletes and safe for the viewers). Scheduling of team events is also a part of a winning strategy.

Other strategies associated with a winning tradition are a well organized team, a clean environment in which to practice, first class accommodations at home and away, and top-notch equipment.

A winning team must market the entertainment it produces. This entertainment must be judiciously branded and competitively priced for the viewers. Athletic events should be available at the right place and time, and offer additional services (concessions, parking) to attract the fans. Sufficient information should be available to promote the entertainment. And normally the cost of the entertainment has to be less than the revenue it provides, unless it is subsidized in some way or another. Finally, the athletic event should offer something unique to its customers. It should appear more attractive than the competing entertainment. The structure of an athletic program is based on strategies designed to produce winning teams and to satisfy fans.

In summary form, an athletic administrator may wish to use the following chart to determine his/her athletic program's strengths and weaknesses. The administrator can evaluate his/her strategies for producing and marketing a winning team to satisfy the entertainment needs of the fans.

Objective: To Produce and Market a Winning Team to Satisfy the Entertainment Needs of Fans

Product Strategies for a Winning Team	**Evaluation** *Strength*	*Weakness*
Quality of Athletes		
Quality of Coaches		
Number of Athletes		
Number of Coaches		
Durability of the Team		
Adaptability		
Dependability		
Balance		
Quickness		
Uniqueness		
Innovation		
Variety		
Safety		
Scheduling		
Well-Organized Team		
Clean Practice Environment		
First Class Accommodations (Home & Away)		
Top-notch Equipment		

Market Strategies	**Evaluation** *Strength*	*Weakness*
Availability: Right Place and Facilities		
Availability: Right Time		
Availability: Information		
Concessions		
Parking		
Price		
Product Differentiation		
Overall Evaluation:		

A more detailed analysis of the strategies for producing and marketing a winning team are given in later pages. Suffice it to say that winning is the first objective to be accomplished, and various general product-market strategies are necessary to be performed in order to produce and market a winning team. In fact, the whole organization structure of an athletic program is usually built around the product and market strategies of an athletic program designed to produce winning teams to satisfy the entertainment needs of its fans.

Developing Character in Athletes

Should the primary objective of an athletic program be to produce a winning team or to develop the character of athletics? A tension exists between "the way it should be" and "the way it is." When pressed for an answer most athletic directors will admit that winning is of primary importance, and that character development is a peripheral goal closely linked to winning. If an athletic program has a losing season, a traditional explanation is that the season was devoted to character development.

There are a number of strategies used to promote character development. The most common is a group meeting between coaches and athletes. At these meetings, the coach and athletes discuss leadership and sportsmanship. The athlete—whose character is supposed to be developed—participates minimally in these discussions.

Another common strategy is a private conference between coach and athlete. Such a conversation is usually effective, particularly if a coach supports his statements with real-life examples of character building.

The athletic administrator might try to act as a role model for coaches and athletes. If he wants his coaching staff and athletes to develop integrity and honesty, he must keep his word, once given. He must tell the truth, even if it hurts. If he wants to maintain fairness and teach its value, he cannot play favorites without some repercussions. If he wants to teach humility, he must be humble in victory and gracious in defeat. Character can be developed effectively through emulation.

In athletics, individuals are forced to subordinate personal goals to team goals. Since by its nature competitive athletics stresses teamwork, it is natural for the athlete to stress team goals rather than individual goals. Teamwork is important for character development.

Athletic administrators must act as disciplinarians. Self-discipline is more effective than discipline imposed from the outside. However, when infractions of the rules do occur, some type of explanatory outerimposed disciplinary action has to be levied to instill in the athlete a respect for other individuals.

Athletes must learn the rules of fair play. Without set guidelines, it is difficult to enforce these rules. Therefore, a common policy among most athletic programs is to participate in and accept the standards of outside athletic associations in regard to fairness of athletes' eligibility, contest standards of fair play, and the fairness of rules. For example, most high schools join and participate in a state high school athletic association that regulates contest standards, rules of play, and athletes' eligibility. The state organizations, in turn, participate in a National Federation of State High School Associations.

Most collegiate athletic programs are members of the National Collegiate Athletic Association or National Association of Intercollegiate Athletics; professional athletic programs are members of various associations or leagues that determine the rules and regulations of a particular sport. Few regulatory agencies stress the educational values of athletic competition. However, these agencies do establish and enforce the fair play standards integral to the functioning of competitive athletic programs and the development of the athlete's character. Without these fair play standards, most competitive athletic programs would collapse and the values and corresponding objective of character development would not be accomplished. That is why it is a wise strategy for an athletic program to join the appropriate regulatory agency whose purposes, among others, are the development and preservation of fair play in the contests, officials, rules, and athletes.

According to the rules of fair play, all athletes at a particular level must abide by the same rules of eligibility. For example, at the high school and collegiate level, where amateurism is stressed, there are certain standards of eligibility. Among them are the following:

	High School	**College**	**Pro**
Upper age limit	19–20	None	None
Enrolled in school	Yes	Yes	None
Years of competition	4 limit	4 limit	None
Parental consent	Yes	Yes	No
Physical examination	Yes	Yes	Yes
Previous semester scholarship	15 hours	12 hours	None
Transfer rule limit	None, if parents move	1 year	Yes
Amateurism	Amateur	Semi-amateur	Pro
Special local rules	Yes	Yes	Yes

Uniform standards of fairness must be set and followed by competing athletic teams. The policies are normally made by the regulatory agencies for the purpose of promoting fair play. Included are the following policies:

	High School	**College**	**Pro**
Contracts for games	Yes	Yes	Yes
Eligibility list exchange	Yes	Yes	Yes
Registration of officials	Yes	Yes	Yes
Common rules of play	Yes	Yes	Yes
Faculty members present	Yes	No	No
Protests and forfeitures	Yes	Yes	Yes
No. of contests in a season	Yes	Yes	Yes

An athletic program may be evaluated on the basis of developing character by various levels. At the high school level more emphasis is usually placed on strategies which develop character than at the college level. At the college level some emphasis is placed on character development, but at the professional level very little emphasis is placed on accomplishing this objective.

In summary form, we may use a check list to determine the strategies and evaluate their strengths and weaknesses as follows:

Objective: To Develop Character in Athletes

Character Development Strategies	**Evaluation**	
	Strength	*Weakness*
1. Group Meetings		
2. One-on-one Discussions		
3. Setting an Example		
4. Subordination of Personal Goals to Team Goals		
5. Disciplinary Action		
6. Participate in Regulatory Agencies regarding Fairness in:		
a. Eligibility standards		
b. Athletic contests		
c. Rules		
7. Others		
Overall Evaluation:		

CHAPTER SUMMARY

This chapter has stated the most common goals of athletic programs—winning, character development, image, growth, profit, leader, survival, share of market, industry improvement, quality of life, and serving the needs of contributors. Strategies were discussed about the first objective—winning—and athlete character development, a related collateral objective. The chapter which follows discusses some additional organizational objectives and strategies used to accomplish them.

Case 2-1 FINLEY'S WINNING TEAMS

A recent newspaper article summarizes Charles O. Finley's strategies for his championship baseball team:[2]

Chicago. A few weeks from now, baseball's World Series will be upon us. And out in Oakland—borrowing an old saying from Paul Powell, the late Illinois politician—fans already can smell the meat a-cooking.

In the kitchen is master chef Charles Oscar Finley, a connoisseur of controversy and, more significantly, a championship cook.

Owner of and mastermind behind the Oakland Athletics, Finley again has his team headed for the playoffs, where they hope to bag a fourth straight Series crown.

I stopped him recently and attempted to pry loose his "secret" recipe for cooking up championship teams. At first, though, I had to get by the mule in him.

"My recipe?" he said. "Well, uh, I guess I do have some ideas on what I look for in players and in a team. But I don't care to toss them afloat. Anyway, I don't want it to seem like I know all the answers. I don't. I also don't want you to put me on a pedestal because, after all, whatever we do is done as a team. We've never been a one-man operation."

'A Humble Person'

"I'm a humble person as you already know," he said. "In spite of some of the criticism I get, you know, I'm not trying to show off or anything. We're just a bunch of guys out there trying to bust our (rumps) to do a job. People call me controversial, but just because I stand up for what's right."

Finley, however, has been the central catalyst in each trial and triumph. Managers and players and cities have come and gone. Even Oakland fans have been lukewarm in their support. Yet Finley and his A's have become today's winningest baseball enterprise. "They said we'd fall when (Manager Dick) Williams left," added Finley. "They said the same thing when Jim (Catfish) Hunter left—temporarily, if you will. Well, that was the biggest crock of (manure) that I've ever heard of. We're not only still standing tall. We're playing better baseball than we ever have in the 15 years I've owned the team."

For the next 20 minutes, Finley proceeded to reveal his secret recipe. And this is the gist of it.

Add one part speed: "We have more speed, especially in the outfield, than any teams's ever had in the history of the game. With players like Reggie Jackson, Claudell Washington, Bill South, and Joe Rudi, we have all kinds of speed."

Add one part versatility: "We strive to get players who do many things well—like play different positions. This way injuries don't hurt us as much as they do other teams. Our attack remains balanced. Rudi plays first base for us this year but makes the All-Star teams as an outfielder. Gene Tenace catches this year for us, but makes the All-Star team at first base. I also think we have the most versatile team ever."

Add youth, pride, strong competitiveness and luck: "We get 'em young, and they have to want to win and work hard. We've been lucky to get such players."

Next, marinate the ingredients in maturity and slowburn in experience on the farm: "We try to bring our players along slowly and surely. We try not to give them too much of anything (especially money) too quickly. Then, when they bloom, they flower for a long time."

Adds Controversy

Lastly, Finley stirs these ingredients with the spoon of controversy, brings them to an emotional boil and serves them piping hot to Series opposition. And for the last three years, no foe could stomach Finley's strong concoction.

Sure, he's made a few enemies with his canning of players and managers and his near-sacking of Commissioner Bowie Kuhn. But I've got to believe that America, for the most part, still loves him because he's a winner.

Indeed, many people hate him just because he IS a winner. But as long as Finley wins fairly and squarely and promotes the virtues of human respect and brotherly love, he deserves the prayers and applause of us all. He surely has mine. I believe in giving a man his flowers while he can smell them.

QUESTION

1. What product strategies does Charles Finley follow in developing a winning team to satisfy the entertainment needs of baseball fans?

Case 2-2 BARNHILL'S SCHEDULING STRATEGY FOR THE RAZORBACKS[3]

PART I

The late John Barnhill, Athletic Director for the University of Arkansas Razorbacks (1945–1968), had a philosophy that a "winning tradition" could overcome all obstacles. He did not believe in winning at all costs, but he did believe that a winning tradition would attract football players, aspiring coaches, fan support, alumni contribution, and security for coaches—all vital resources for a successful football program for the small University of Arkansas Southwest Conference school. "Winning is not everything but it surely beats second best," he used to say. "And a winning tradition is what we are shooting for. I don't like to be associated with a loser. What really counts for a football coach and his personnel is his win-loss record. Thirty days after a season is over, the win-loss record is what remains."

Barnie, as his associates called him, had another philosophy which became a part of his strategy of scheduling football games for the Razorbacks. Barnhill's thinking was expressed as, "Don't overschedule your potential." Or he would say, "Don't miss-match your resources." His conservative approach to scheduling of football games was seen in his scheduling strategy, particularly for the nonconference games. For conference games, however, he was confronted with all-Texas opponents.

The University of Arkansas was a member of the Southwest Conference. Other schools included the University of Texas Longhorns (traditionally the power of the conference), Texas A & M Aggies, Texas Tech Red Raiders, Southern Methodist Mustangs. Rice Owls, Baylor Bears, and

Texas Christian Horned Frogs. Scheduling for these teams was on a home and away-from-home basis each two years. Consequently, there was not much that John Barnhill could do about scheduling these games when they were played in Texas. However, Barnie did inherit a losing tradition when he came to the University of Arkansas in 1945. He had noticed that the Razorbacks had rarely won a football game on Texas soil during September and October. The reason was that the players from the Northwest Arkansas school were defeated by the heat. From 1948 on, Barnie scheduled all Texas games in September and October at night. From then on, his Razorbacks won many of those night games, primarily from T.C.U., Baylor, and Texas who were the first three SWC opponents each year.

John Barnhill's winning tradition and his scheduling strategy were made more specific in his scheduling of three nonconference games. Since his philosophy of not overscheduling your potential prevailed, he tried to make sure that the first two games, preceding the conference opener with T.C.U., were scheduled against teams where there was a reasonable chance to win. As it happened, those two teams were traditional rivals of the Razorbacks—the Oklahoma State Cowboys and the Tulsa Hurricanes. Both of these schools had great teams in the 1940s, but both had fallen upon hard times in attracting crowds for their football team in the 1950s and 1960s. Barnie prevailed upon both schools to play their games in Little Rock or Fayetteville for fifteen straight years because both O.S.U. and Tulsa could make more money playing away from home in Arkansas where football crowds on Saturdays in September would be anywhere from 20,000 to 40,000 people, many more than either school could attract at home.

John Barnhill figured that if the Razorbacks could win those first two games, the players would have a winning momentum when they played their first SWC opener with T.C.U., under the lights in Texas or in cooler weather in Arkansas when played at home. This strategy worked. The decade of 1959–1969 saw Arkansas beat Oklahoma State and Tulsa combined 19 times with only 2 losses. By "not overscheduling your potential" the Razorbacks started a winning tradition.

Another of Barnhill's scheduling strategies was to play a "breather" game half-way through the football schedule. Such a strategy allowed the Razorbacks a chance to regroup their forces, if necessary, to lick their wounds and allow the injured to heal, and to give the second stringers a chance to play to gain some experience down the home stretch of conference play with four strong SWC conference teams in Texas—Texas A & M, Rice, S.M.U., and Texas Tech—usually played in November. This breather game was always scheduled at home, playing against lesser known schools such as Hardin-Simmons, Wichita State, Kansas State, North Texas State, and others. The Razorbacks had never lost a breather game in the decade of the 1960s.

John Barnhill's scheduling philosophy and resulting strategies helped the Razorbacks gain football respectability with Frank Broyles as head football coach during the 1960s. The eleven-year period from 1959 through 1969 showed the Razorback's win-loss record as follows:

	Wins	*Losses*	*Ties*
1959	9	2	
1960	8	3	
1961	8	3	
1962	9	2	
1963	5	5	
1964	11	0 (National Champion)	
1965	10	1	
1966	8	2	
1967	4	5	1
1968	10	1	
1969	9	2	

When John Barnhill retired at age 65 as athletic director in 1968, he delegated the scheduling function with its corresponding responsibilities, authority, and accountability to Frank Broyles, his head football coach. George Cole became athletic director, but Frank Broyles was given the scheduling decisions.

In December 1969, the Razorbacks played the University of Texas (the Big Shootout I) before national television, with the U.S. President attending the game in Fayetteville. The AP poll showed Texas No. 1 and Arkansas No. 2. Both Texas' Darrell Royal and Arkansas' Frank Broyles had identical conference records (62–18–1). Texas won that game 15–14!

In January 1970, the NCAA surprised the nation with their decision to do away with the 10-game schedule, approving an 11-game schedule. Frank Broyles had to make a decision of whether to go to an 11-game schedule and if so, whom to schedule.

His teams of the 1960s had been very successful. His 1969 team had lost to Texas, but he still had the makings of an excellent team in 1970. He had recruited Joe Ferguson, a highly touted passer from Shreveport, who was to be the spark plug for the 1970 teams. Frank was confident that he would have a good team.

Criticism had arisen, however, of Barnhill's scheduling strategy. There were always those fans and sports writers who complained about the schedule of the Razorbacks—easy first two games and the breather game. Frank Broyles had received numerous letters which were critical of the Razorback's schedule. Those fans wanted Arkansas to enter big time football by playing national powers instead of Tulsa, Oklahoma State, and Wichita State. And Frank Broyles was not unmindful of the letters which he had always received and answered.

The financial resources of the Athletic Department were in the black. However, there was the constant pressure of other sports—basketball, golf, baseball, track, and others—to get more financial resources which the football team could and did generate for the Athletic Department. All sports were financially supported from football revenues, very little from State of Arkansas tax support.

Table 2-1 Financial Information of the Athletic Department

	Balance 7/1	*Income*	*Expenditures*	*Transfers*	*Balance 6/30*	*Cash*	*Deferred Income*
1955	$ 2,434	$ 747,835	$ 627,315	$ (29,934)	$ 94,200	$	$
1956	94,200	709,918	610,792	(94,200)	106,384		
1957	106,384	683,116	610,792	(112,839)	66,318		
1958		670,709	633,390	37,318		205,151	(205,151)
1959		501,068	558,666	(90,931)	33,333	258,078	(224,746)
1960	33,333	622,751	580,848	(7,502)	82,739	367,716	(284,977)
1961	82,739	662,237	664,890	(19,022)	99,107	424,705	(325,597)
1962	99,107	732,066	665,084	(13,176)	179,265	480,209	(300,944)
1963	179,265	720,912	722,176	(13,670)	191,670	726,053	(534,384)
1964	191,670	698,872	691,565	(3,575)	195,403	662,687	(467,284)
1965	195,403	920,839	917,238	41,585	240,589	1,006,638	(766,049)
1966	240,589	1,463,480	1,325,693	(118,817)	259,559	709,034	(449,475)
1967	259,559	1,151,112	1,092,739	6,841	324,772	768,793	(444,021)
1968	324,772	1,203,543	1,371,016	33,039	192,138	827,267	(635,129)
1969	192,138	1,203,679	1,665,126	13,330	234,021	1,099,366	(865,345)
1970	234,021	3,145,455	3,109,145	267,664	2,668	954,359	(951,691)

There was a need to pay for the astro-turf on the home field and in Little Rock, and for additional funds to fulfill a dream of improving the athletic facilities at the University. Although Frank did not consult his players, there seemed to be overwhelming support from the fans and alumni for an eleventh game.

Pacific Eight football teams had a certain glamour to Frank Broyles. Besides, he was sure that the coaches and players would enjoy a trip to California to play, let's say, Stanford, California, and Southern California. Those teams had good records—not outstanding—but they did have good images as national football powers. And national, rather than a regional, exposure was a significant factor in Frank's thinking.

However, there were other possible alternatives in the wings—Notre Dame, Oklahoma, Tennessee, Utah State, New Mexico State, and Colorado State.

Frank Broyles consulted John Barnhill about the eleventh game and about possible contenders. Barnie told Frank that he (Barnie) was against playing those West Coast teams. However, he said, "Frank, you have the scheduling authority. Do what you think is right."

PART II

Frank Broyles made the decision to go to an eleven game schedule. He further negotiated opening games with Stanford and California, both in Little Rock for 1970–71. He also arranged a home, away-from-home, and home game with Southern California for 1972, 1973, and 1974. In 1975 the first game was to be with the Air Force Academy. These opening games were scheduled in direct opposition to John Barnhill's scheduling strategy of playing opening games with teams where there was a reasonable chance to win and where some momentum could be gained in winning before the conference schedule began in October of each year.

In the fall of 1970, Frank arranged with ABC to televise a national TV opener with Stanford. To do so it was necessary to raise $500,000 for astroturf and lights for color TV, a feat performed by Little Rock supporters of the Razorbacks. The game matched two of several Heisman Trophy candidates, Jim Plunkett of Stanford and Bill Montgomery of Arkansas. The Razorbacks lost that game 34–28. However, they regrouped and finished the season with a 9–2 record, losing to Texas in the last game of the season (Big Shootout II).

In 1971 the Razorbacks won their opener against the California Golden Bears, followed by a victory against Oklahoma State, but then they were upset by Tulsa, 21–20. The season turned out to be an 8–3–1 with Joe Ferguson providing a passing attack for the Razorbacks.

In 1972 Frank Broyles knew that USC would be a national football power. Both Frank Broyles and John McKay, head coach of the Trojans, surmised that the winner of the Arkansas–USC game would probably be No. 1 in the polls. USC romped over the Razorbacks 31–10, and wound up No. 1 for the rest of the season. Arkansas' record was 6–5.

Barnie told Frank, "You ruined a good coaching job." Frank lamented, "We'll never know how much losing to USC took away from us. I'll bet we lost $50,000 in revenues in future games that year because of our loss to USC."

Table 2-2 Financial Information of the Athletic Department

	Balance 7/1	*Income*	*Expenditures*	*Transfers*	*Balance 6/30*	*Cash*	*Deferred Income*
1970	$234,021	$3,145,455	$3,109,145	$267,664	$ 2,668	$ 954,359	$ (951,691)
1971	2,667	2,435,275	2,462,531	30,500	4,812	1,055,956	(1,051,144)
1972	4,812	1,748,328	1,758,601	18,304	12,844	1,394,305	(1,381,461)

The opening game with USC in 1973 was another loss, 17–0, for the Razorbacks. It was followed by another loss to Oklahoma State. The momentum of winning the preconference games was lost. The season's record was 5–5–1.

During 1973, Frank Broyles was again faced with a scheduling problem. The University of Houston had been admitted to the Southwest Conference, and was to play Arkansas on a home, away-from-home basis on the date of the breather game in October. John Barnhill's scheduling philosophy again was being challenged. It was also during 1973 that Frank was deciding about his opening games for 1976–77 and 1978. He was considering New Mexico State, Utah State, and Colorado State along with Notre Dame, Tennessee, and Oklahoma.

Case 2-3 OBJECTIVES OF THE JACKSONVILLE HIGH SCHOOL ATHLETIC PROGRAM

The Jacksonville Public School System consists of one high school, two junior high schools, and eight elementary schools. It serves a town of 30,000 people. At a school board meeting, Dr. Harry Van Der Veer, Superintendent of the Jacksonville schools, was asked by a Jacksonville citizen to state the objectives of competitive athletics in the high school athletic program.

Dr. Van Der Veer, a former coach and athletic director for the school, replied: "Our athletic program is designed to provide students with the opportunity to participate in a variety of sports the year round. We are interested in those students who are willing to engage in extracurricular activities to represent our school system in competitive events. This privilege is granted to students to help them develop physically, emotionally, and socially in order for them to become better citizens in our society. Notice that I said 'participation in extracurricular activities' because I do not believe that competitive athletics is solely justified on the basis of curricular or academic values; athletics is extremely important outside the context of the classroom. We do think that competitive athletics is an integral part of our school program for both participants and those students who wish to witness the athletic events in which our athletes do participate. In addition to serving our students, our sports program acts as a cohesive force, unifying the school and the fans in our community. We stress competition, yet we must work within the limited resources provided by fans and the school system. Our program tries to serve the needs of the employees, suppliers, community, governmental units, and other groups that contribute to our athletic program."

On a separate occasion, the athletic director was asked to state his view of the high school athletic program. He replied: "The first objective of our athletic program is to satisfy our fans and other supporters. If we become a winning team, then we will consider other objectives—developing our athletes and building character. Without a winning tradition, it is difficult for me to see how character development of our athletes is enhanced. Athletic competition is good for our athletes. They will live in a highly competitive society when they graduate. They learn the values of fair play, competitive spirit, discipline, and decision making from sports. After a team becomes a winner, the other objectives can be realized. Criticize me if you will, but I am expressing views that are generally recognized by citizens of any community. My views may not be popular with those in academia, but I have to be realistic. In high schools, competitive athletic activities are not like physical education classes or intramurals. The athletic program objectives are different from those of academia. They are related, but different. A winning tradition that satisfies our student body and our nonstudent fans is really the primary objective along with developing character in our student-athletes."

Then the basketball coach was interviewed. He had been in the school system for 17 years as a teacher, an assistant coach, and finally as head basketball coach. Last year, his team had won the state championship. He stated: "Really, this sounds corny, but I never use the word *winning.* I tell my players to do their best, both on the floor and off the floor. If they give their best performance, I'm satisfied. If you had asked me to state the athletic program objectives five years ago, I would have told you that winning was the chief objective. However, now I find character development most important. I encourage my athletes to give their best performance at school, at church, at home, in the community, or wherever they are. Developing character means developing a winning team. Consequently other athletic program objectives—a good image, growth, profits, survival, improving athletics—may be realized.

QUESTIONS:

1. Discuss the philosophies and objectives of the three people interviewed.
   a. Does their role have any effect on their statements?
   b. Do their personal objectives have any influence?
2. What is the effect of different philosophies on the athletic program?

FOOTNOTES

[1] Much of the information in this chapter has been adapted from "Objectives of High School Athletic Programs," J. Frank Broyles and Robert D. Hay, Interscholastic Athletic Administration, Spring, 1977 issue.

[2] *The Arkansas Gazette*, September 17, 1975.

[3] This case problem was prepared by Robert D. Hay and Frank Broyles, University of Arkansas. It was presented at the Southern Case Research Association Workshop in Atlanta, November 11-13, 1974, held in cooperation with Intercollegiate Case Clearing House, Harvard.

3

OTHER STRATEGIES AND OBJECTIVES OF ATHLETIC PROGRAMS

Growth is an important objective of most athletic programs. Growth can be measured by increases in attendance, total revenue, assets, or personnel. Most high schools, colleges, and professional athletic organizations consider growth a legitimate objective.

STRATEGIES TO ACCOMPLISH A GROWTH OBJECTIVE

An athletic program can expand by using four strategies. The first, horizontal growth strategy, involves selling the same products and services in greater quantities. An athletic program could either "sell" more athletic events to its present fans, or increase the number of customers who attend the traditional number of events. However, it is difficult for most athletic programs to expand by finding different markets. A second growth strategy, sometimes called vertical growth, involves adding a new product and service that would improve the original product. A third strategy, circular growth, entails adding a different but related product/service to the existing line of products. Lateral growth, the fourth strategy, consists of adding different but unrelated product/services to the existing line.

The horizontal growth strategy may be illustrated in several ways. For example, if a consistently losing team starts to win, several potential fans who have not been attending games may appear at the gates. The best supported teams are the teams that win. To expand its market, an athletic program might extend its appeal to women customers who are not traditionally devotees of athletic programs. A third example of a horizontal strategy is a consequence of Title IX of the Civil Rights Act. Since women, by right, are able to engage in competitive athletics, an athletic program may expand by adding women's sports to its roster. The athletic team could augment its number of customers by playing some home games in areas larger than the home market. Using a horizontal growth strategy, the University of Indiana plays some of its home basketball games in the relatively large city of Indianapolis, rather than in the college town of Bloomington. To increase their revenue, athletic programs could add more games to their schedules. In 1970, the NCAA allowed colleges to increase their football schedule from ten to eleven games, and the professional league increased its schedule from ten to twelve to fourteen games each season. Both actions were attempts to expand through an increase in attendance. To increase revenue, leagues might also add preseason or postseason games to their schedules, add home franchises in different cities, or schedule games at night or on weekends when fans can attend. These examples show how the horizontal growth strategy may be used to increase revenue, assets, and personnel. When this strategy proves successful, the growth objective is accomplished.

A second growth strategy, sometimes called vertical growth, involves adding a new activity that enhances the activity already produced and marketed. For example, Branch Rickey is generally credited with the creation of a farm system to develop seasoned baseball players who are ready for the professional league. Rickey was expanding by means of a backward vertical growth strategy. Similarly, high school athletic programs could develop better athletes by establishing a working agreement with junior high school programs. Colleges could develop relationships with certain high schools, and professional teams could become interested in certain colleges, to improve the overall development of athletes. Other examples would be to add a tutorial and counseling system or housing facilities for college athletes. This would help produce a better sports program by providing the athlete with needed comforts. These are examples of vertical growth—adding services necessary to improve the existing line of sports.

A third growth strategy, circular growth, involves the addition of related services or sports to the existing line. For example, some collegiate conferences only accept teams from colleges that are involved in eight different sports. If a college engaged in five sports wants to enter a conference, it must add three related sports to its schedule. Often, atheltic programs provide their customers with concessions as a related service. Perhaps another example is to have radio and/or television coverage of an athletic event. These examples increase the revenue of an existing program by adding related services or sports to the original line of activities.

A fourth strategy, adding unrelated activities to the original line of sports, is used infrequently. This is sometimes called the lateral growth strategy. When CBS bought the New York Yankees, it was adding a rather unrelated activity to its original activity of broadcasting for radio and television, although perhaps a good case could be made that the Yankees are a related activity to broadcasting.

In summary form, growth strategies for an athletic program may be evaluated by considering their strengths and weaknesses in particular situations facing any athletic program which desires to grow:

Objective: To Increase the Program's Size (*Growth*)

Strategies	**Strength**	**Weakness**
1. Horizontal—adding more of the same		
a. Win		
b. Appeal to women		
c. Add women's sports		
d. Play home games in larger markets		
e. Increase scheduled number of games		
f. Add preseason exhibition or postseason games		
g. Schedule games at night or weekends		
h. Others		
2. Circular—add related activities		
a. Add related sports		
b. Add concessions		
c. Add radio and TV		
d. Others		
3. Vertical—add activities necessary for production		
a. Add informal "farm" system		
b. Add housing for athletes		
c. Add tutorial and counseling systems for athletes		
d. Others		
4. Lateral—adding unrelated activities		
a. Others		
Overall evaluation:		

STRATEGIES TO IMPROVE THE IMAGE OF THE ATHLETIC PROGRAM

Most athletic programs hope to improve their image. Athletic administrators realize that winning is essential if they hope to be recognized by outsiders and other athletic programs. In fact, improving its image may be a higher objective than winning although most athletic administrators recognize that winning to satisfy the entertainment needs of its fans is the chief strategy to follow if an organization wants to improve its image.

It is necessary to instill a positive attitude toward the athletic program in the minds of the coaches, players, and employees. Hopefully, this positive attitude is transmitted to all those associated with the athletic staff: the local faculty and student body; the press; officials at the community, state, and national level.

A team is more likely to be recognized if its games are televised or on the radio. Television is the best way to improve a team's image, provided that the team wins those games that are broadcast.

A team hoping to improve its image must have good press relations. It is wise for a program to treat the press as an ally, not an enemy. Bad relations with the press could prove detrimental to the team's image.

Most athletic programs are evaluated by radio, TV, and newspapers. To be ranked with the top twenty teams is another strategy that could improve a program's image. Although the athletic administrator may not think the polls are fair, he must realize that the top twenty teams are recognized and emulated.

If a program participates in the end-of-season play offs, it will enjoy an improved image, increasing revenues, and other benefits. A play-off team will attract more talented players than other teams.

The athletic administrator should occasionally survey the public to determine what type of image his athletic program projects. After defining the strengths and weaknesses of his program, the administrator can build on the strengths and correct the weaknesses to improve his program's overall image.

When appearing before the general public, an athlete should be well dressed. This is particularly true when a group of athletes are traveling to and from an athletic event. The athlete's appearance as well as the team's overall image influences the amount of support fans are willing to give an athletic program.

The athletic program's image is likely to improve if its employees hold offices in professional and community organizations. The members of professional organizations recognize this participation. Often they transfer their support to the athletic program represented by the civic-minded employees and athletes.

To improve its image, an athletic program might support community projects. If an athletic program participates in a desirable community building project, the Community Chest, the Heart Fund, or any other worthy cause, the program's image could improve and gain citizen support.

Another strategy is to stress beauty in the location of the athletic program. A beautiful setting could inspire goodwill toward an athletic program.

In summary, the following strategies may be evaluated by an athletic administrator:

Objective: To Improve the Program's Image

Strategies	Strength	Weakness
1. Winning		
2. Positive attitude of coaches, players, and athletic personnel		
3. Television and radio coverage		
4. Press relations		
5. End of season play offs		
6. Getting into top twenty		
7. Image surveys		
8. Well-groomed employees and athletes		
9. Holding offices in professional organizations		
10. Support for community projects		
11. Stress beauty in surroundings		
12. Others		
Overall evaluation:		

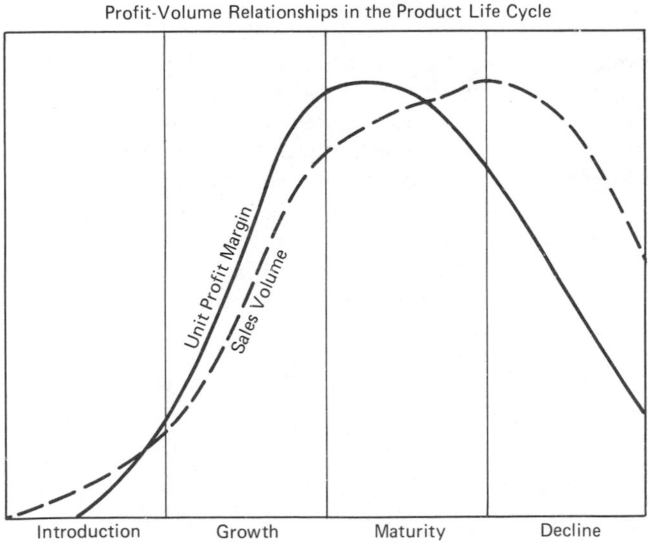

Figure 3–1 Concept of the Product Life Cicle.
Source: Hay, Robert D., Introduction to Business, *N.Y., Holt, Rinehard and Winston, 1968, p. 285.*

KEY QUESTIONS FOR AN ATHLETIC ADMINISTRATOR TO ASK:

1. For each sport, how and to what extent can the shape and duration of the sport life cycle be predicted?
2. For each sport, how can I determine what stage it is in?
3. Given those answers, what strategies do I use to get a share of the entertainment market?

OBTAINING A SHARE OF THE ENTERTAINMENT MARKET

Athletic programs located in large cities must contend with direct competition from other sports and with indirect competition from different forms of entertainment. A major objective of athletic programs is to obtain a share of the entertainment market especially for those athletic programs that are not in a monopoly position with regard to competition.

There are a number of strategies designed to assure the athletic program a spot in the entertainment market. The administrator can analyze these strategies by examining the product life cycle (Figure 3-1). Most products and services have a distinct life cycle that forms the basis for different strategies such as product differentiation, price, promotion, personnel, financial, and place strategy. There are four stages in the life of a product: (1) development, (2) growth, (3) maturity, and (4) decline.

The development stage is characterized by high financial risk, lack of demand, high costs, fatalities, a long development period, and gradually rising attendance and revenue. Professional tennis leagues and women's athletics are examples of athletic programs in the development stage. The various strategies to be used might be summarized as follows:

Stage I. Development Stage of an Athletic Program

A. *Sport Strategy* Take the initiative to create the sport, or follow the leader and avoid the risks of failure. Use a noncompetitive sport strategy, that is, be sure there is no direct competition with another sport.

B. *Price Strategy* Usually high prices prevail unless one wishes to enter the market quickly. In this case, a below the market price strategy might prevail.

C. *Promotion Strategy* Use a pioneering "try the product" advertising theme, as opposed to pushing a specific team.

D. *Place Strategy* Promote the new sport in places where there is no competition and where there is a fairly high concentration of people.

E. *Personnel Strategy* Use creative salesmen backed up by missionary salesmen.

F. *Pecuniary Strategy* Be willing and able to lose money during the development stage. Have high profit margins.
G. *Target Market* Usually the target market is defined during this stage to determine who the fans are, how many exist, when they attend, where they are, and what characteristics they exhibit.

The next stage in the life cycle is the growth stage. It is characterized by a rapid increase in attendance and revenue. Now, the athletic administrator tests prices and determines where to hold events. The athletic program operates at full capacity, and often more facilities are needed. At this point, other competitors and copiers enter the market. The various strategies employed are summarized below.

Stage II. The Growth Stage

A. *Sport Strategy* Be innovative to make the event distinctive. For example, use animated scoreboards, bat girls, colored basketballs, or new rules.
B. *Price Strategy* Use lower prices than original high price.
C. *Promotion Strategy* Use competitive promotion without involving price. Some degree of brand differentiation should be used in advertising and promotion plans.
D. *Place Strategy* Open new places to play and new channels for distribution of tickets.
E. *Personnel Strategy* Use creative salesmen, backed by supporting salesmen.
F. *Pecuniary Strategy* Make a large profit with lower profit margins.
G. *Market Targets* Customer characteristics should now be identified to properly promote, price, sell, and finance the product.

College and professional football, bowling, and golf are athletic programs that have grown tremendously. The athletic administrator must undertake the difficult task of identifying the product life cycle stage of each sport under his/her jurisdiction.

The maturity stage is characterized by market saturation, a steady per capita decline (although there may be a small increase in attendance), the start of over-capacity in facilities, and difficulty in determining whether the maturing process is short term or long term. The strategies which may be used are:

Stage III. Maturity stage

A. *Sport Strategy* Make a finer distinction between your sport and others by providing customer services, packaging, advertising, and special deals. Determine special market segments for the sport.

B. *Price Strategy* Use prices that are competitive at the marketplace.

C. *Promotion Strategy* Use prices when promoting the sport. Communicate directly with customers. Stress brand preference. Use special promotion techniques.

D. *Place Strategy* Hold the sales outlets. Use intensive distribution channels.

E. *Personnel Strategy* Use order takers as much as possible rather than order getters and missionary salesmen.

F. *Pecuniary Strategy* Be prepared for occasional financial losses. Use break-even analyses and ratio analyses.

G. *Market Target* Look for special markets.

It is likely that most sports under the jurisdiction of an athletic administrator are in the maturity stage. He/she may find that the local, conference, and national trends indicate a maturity stage strategy for football, basketball, baseball, bowling, and golf.

The decline stage is usually indicated by dwindling attendance and revenue. There is the constant plague of over-capacity in facilities. There are many failures. The most common strategies are:

Stage IV. Decline stage

A. *Sport Strategy* Could use mergers. Use sport life extensions such as (1) more frequent usage, (2) varied usage, (3) finding new users, (4) finding new uses.

B. *Price Strategy* Sell below the market price. Use discounts.

C. *Promotion Strategy* Use special sales and promotion techniques such as contests, trading stamps, incentive travel.

D. *Place Strategy* Cut back on distribution outlets.

E. *Personnel Strategy* Use order takers.

F. *Pecuniary Strategy* Take the financial losses as tax write-offs.

G. *Market Target* Find hard-core fans by name.

In the decline stage, one must try to extend the sport life by using the strategies suggested: more frequency, varied use, new users, and new uses.

In summary form, an athletic administrator may wish to evaluate each sport against the following strategies used to obtain a share of the entertainment market:

Objective: To Obtain a Share of the Entertainment Market

Strategies	Strength	Weakness
1. *Market target identification*		
a. Developmental stage—find out:		
(1) Who the fans are		
(2) How many there are		
(3) Where they are		
(4) When they attend		
(5) What characteristics		
b. Growth stage—market segmented		
c. Maturity stage—special market segmentation		
d. Decline—find out names		
2. *Sport strategy*		
a. Developmental stage		
(1) Leader		
(2) Follower		
(3) Noncompetitive		
b. Growth stage—sport differentiation		
c. Maturity stage—finer sport differentiation		
d. Decline stage		
(1) Mergers		
(2) Sport life extensions		
3. *Price strategy*		
a. Developmental—high price		
b. Growth—lower price		
c. Maturity—competitive		
d. Decline—below market		
4. *Promotion strategy*		
a. Developmental stage—"pioneering" advertising		
b. Growth stage		
(1) Promotion without mentioning price		
(2) Brand differentiation		
c. Maturity stage		
(1) Price promotion		
(2) Direct communication		
(3) Brand preference		
(4) Special promotions		
d. Decline stage		
(1) Special sales		
(2) Specialized techniques		
5. *Place strategy*		
a. Developmental stage		
(1) No competition in place		
(2) High concentration of fans		
b. Growth stage—open new places and channels		
c. Maturity stage		

Objective: To Obtain a Share of the Entertainment Market (continued)

Strategies	Strength	Weakness
(1) Hold outlets		
(2) Intensive distribution		
d. Decline stage—cut back on outlets		
6. *Personnel strategy*		
a. Developmental stage		
(1) Creative salesmen		
(2) Missionary salesmen		
b. Growth—creative and supportive		
c. Maturity—order takers		
d. Decline—order takers		
7. *Pecuniary strategy*		
a. Developmental stage		
(1) Willing to lose money		
(2) High profit margins		
b. Growth stage		
(1) Large profit		
(2) Lower margins		
c. Maturity stage		
(1) Occasional losses		
(2) Break-even analyses		
(3) Ratio analyses		
d. Decline—tax write-offs		
Overall evaluation:		

MAKING A PROFIT FROM ATHLETIC OPERATIONS

Profits serve to finance growth, maintain continuity, and measure efficiency of athletic programs. Perhaps the major role of profit to an athletic program is that of serving as an internal means of financing growth. Expanding physical facilities and adding personnel may be financed by external sources such as borrowing or donations. However, it is easier for athletic programs with substantial profits to finance expansion using profits from operations. Athletic profits may be reserved for a period of years to finance growth rather than going to outside sources where it is more difficult to raise money by borrowing or from donations.

Athletic profits, rather than funds from outside sources, are also used to maintain continuity of the program. As profits increase, the program becomes more capable of maintaining continuity rather than having to rely on institutional funds. Profits act as a cushion against unexpected losses (perhaps due to bad decisions or game losses) and the threat of inflation. Without profits, the high costs of equipment, salaries, and travel due to rapid inflation would erode the financial position of an athletic program.

If the athletic program is a professional team rather than an amateur one, profits serve as a measure of efficiency. One measure is the rate of return on total assets. This type of return is computed by dividing the profits by the total assets and using this rate as a device to compare similar athletic programs. Another measure of efficiency is the rate of return on revenue (dividing profit by total revenue). A further measure is the rate of return on owner's equity (dividing profit by owner's equity). These measures of efficiency are made possible by profits. The administrator can compare return rates of one particular program over a specific length of time; also, one can compare the rates of a number of similar athletic programs.

Athletic administrators have used a variety of strategies in their quest for organizational profits. The most common, particularly among high schools and colleges, is that of breaking even. Normally, high schools are subsidized by local tax revenues if their athletic programs do not break even. Rather than rely on subsidies, many administrators would prefer that the athletic program's expenses equal their revenue.

Another profit strategy is to increase the revenue of the athletic program, allowing expenses to remain the same. Increased attendance, increased ticket prices, or increased revenue from concessions are ways to increase revenues to make a profit.

A fairly common strategy is to reduce expenses, maintaining a constant revenue. The thought here would be to cut spending wherever appropriate by, for example, not buying equipment as often, going tourist rate when traveling, cutting back on personnel, and the like. Profits can be made by reducing expenses, assuming that revenues would remain the same.

A balancing of profits strategy is also used. If an administrator knows that the revenue will exceed expenses, he may "balance" the expected profits against an increase in pay raises for personnel, or an increase in funds spent on quality equipment. If expenses are greater than revenue, a cut in expenses is in order. Many administrators know that their superiors do not like to see an athletic program make too much money. Therefore, profits will be balanced against greater expenses. Administrators also know that their superiors do not like to see red ink in the account books. Therefore, they will make sure that some profit is made by balancing revenues against expenses to make sure that some profit is shown in the financial operating statements.

One type of profit strategy is to shoot for a target profit. For example, if an owner of a professional team expects a 10% return on his investment of $5,000,000, an athletic administrator might shoot for a target profit of $500,000 for the year.

A maximizing revenue strategy may sometimes be used, keeping expenses about the same. For example, some administrators will sell all the tickets they can so that a stadium capacity will be filled for every game. If they sense that demand is still there among fans, next season they will raise the price of the tickets and hope that the stadium will be filled to capacity again.

Another common profit strategy is to minimize the expenses, keeping

Assume: Owners made $1,000,000 from nonathletic activities; also team owner had $200,000 loss from team

	Team Owner	Nonteam Owner
Taxable income from activities other than from the team	$1,000,000	$1,000,000
Deduct team loss	200,000	-0-
	$ 800,000	$1,000,000
Less income tax (70%)	531,000	671,000
Cash after taxes	$ 269,000	$ 329,000
Plus $100,000 cash flow before depreciation	$ 100,000	-0-
Plus $200,000 allowed for tax deduction	200,000	-0-
Actual cash after taxes	$ 569,000	$ 329,000

Difference between team owner and nonteam owner of $240,000.

revenues the same. Paying a minimum wage to employees, not paying a fair stadium rental, and buying the most inexpensive equipment are ways to minimize expenses.

Maximizing profits means getting the most profits possible under the situations facing an athletic administrator. Such a strategy is very difficult to achieve because administrators may not know how much fans will pay for tickets, how much employees will work for, what kind of bargain they could get in stadium rentals, and so forth. They may not know what competitors are doing in the marketplace. Although it is a temptation for athletic administrators, a maximizing profit strategy is virtually impossible to use.

Another profit strategy, fairly common to owners of professional teams, is the use of athletic teams' losses to offset profits from other activities for tax purposes. For example, consider an existing team that is sold to new owners for $2 million. For this price, the owners acquire the old team's franchise, player contracts, and other equipment. The owners of the new team allocate $1,500,000 to player contracts, $400,000 to the franchise, and $100,000 to the equipment. The reason for the $1,500,000 allocation of the price to player contracts is that these contracts may be depreciated over their estimated useful lives in computing taxable income. Therefore, the $1,500,000 is depreciated, let's say over five years, resulting in an annual depreciation expense of $300,000 (a straight line depreciation on intangible assets). Further, let us assume that the net income of the team before depreciation is $100,000. The depreciation deduction will result in a net loss of $200,000 ($100,000 profit less $300,000 depreciation). This loss is allocated among the owners and is reported by them for income tax purposes. If the owners are, let's say, in the 70% tax bracket, every dollar of this loss will reduce their personal tax liability by 70 cents, meaning that the $200,000 net loss reduces the owners' taxes for which they would be liable by $140,000. Thus, the owners would have $100,000 cash profits and $140,000 in personal tax savings, for a total of $240,000 cash flow while the team reports a $200,000 net loss.

This illustration is shown in the opposite table comparing a team owner to a nonteam owner. It exhibits the financial effect of the profit strategy on both.

The tax-loss profit strategy affords the owner the prestige of being a team owner while he/she improves his financial position.

In summary form an athletic administrator may evaluate the profit strategies used in the situations facing the administrator:

Objective: Making a Profit

Strategy	Strength	Weakness
1. Break even		
2. Increase revenues, OTE		
3. Reduce expenses, OTE		
4. Balancing profits		
5. Target profit		
6. Maximizing revenue, OTE		
7. Minimizing expenses, OTE		
8. Maximizing profits		
9. Tax write-off		
10. Others		

Overall evaluation:

CHAPTER SUMMARY

In this chapter, the strategies that help a program to grow, to improve its image, to obtain a share of the entertainment market, and to make a profit have been considered. Various strategies are suggested to accomplish each of these organizational objectives. Further, each objective may be analyzed as to the strengths and weaknesses of the strategies which might be used by an athletic administrator to accomplish each objective.

Case 3-1 STRATEGIES TO ACHIEVE GROWTH OBJECTIVES FOR A COLLEGIATE BASKETBALL PROGRAM

Frank Broyles, Athletic Director at the University of Arkansas, sat in his office one summer day, contemplating some strategies for the growth of the university's basketball program. He had just had a conference with Eddie Sutton, the head basketball coach, and Wilson Matthews, assistant athletic director, regarding the Razorback basketball program.

Frank remembered that a little over a year ago Lanny Van Eman, former basketball coach for the Razorbacks, had resigned. Although Van Eman had compiled an unimpressive 39–65 win-loss record during his reign, he had made basketball an exciting sport for the fans with his "runnin' Razorback" offensive displays. However, the University of Arkansas' basketball program had merely existed. It had never been really promoted like the football program. Its budget was limited. The facilities for playing were below par. Fans were never really interested in the team. As a result, the U of A's basketball team had won only one Southwest Conference Championship (tied with SMU in 1958) in the past 25 years.

Frank met with the Athletic Committee of the University Board of Trustees the day after Lanny Van Eman's resignation. They discussed the future of the basketball program. The Board of Trustees was committed to putting the basketball program in full gear. The program was to increase its fan attendance, facilities, and budget. Finding talented coaches and players was a primary concern. The Arkansas team was to compete not only in the SWC but also on a national scale.

Frank recognized that the university needed a winning basketball team as well as a fine football team in order to grow. His first step was to hire a basketball coach with a winning tradition. After lengthy interviews with several prospects, Frank finally hired Eddie Sutton, basketball coach at Creighton, an independent school in Omaha.

Eddie Sutton's win-loss record as a college coach was a respectable 73%. The previous five-year record at Arkansas was a 35% win-loss. Sutton pledged to reverse Arkansas' record. Only a few fans believed a reversal was possible. Still, Frank maintained that hiring a quality coach would be instrumental in the growth of a basketball program.

Eddie Sutton believed in the Henry Iba school of defensive basketball. However, Sutton also developed a strategy called patient offense. Using this strategy, Creighton had won 23 games. Creighton had a chance to win the NCAA playoff the year before Sutton was hired by Arkansas as the highest paid coach in the Southwest Conference. He pledged to Frank Broyles that he would turn the basketball program around. Most of the fans scoffed, some forgot about it, while a few believed that he could do it.

Sutton hired Gene Keady, head coach of Hutchinson Junior College with an 80% win-loss record, to be one of his assistant coaches. The other was Pat Foster, assistant coach under Van Eman. The three of them, with a graduate assistant named Tom Skipper, began recruiting efforts.

Sutton taught defensive basketball with the hard-nosed discipline U of A had lacked in the past. The first year's team had a 3–4 win-loss record by Christmas. Then the Sutton philosophy began to take shape. The Razorbacks filled Barnhill Fieldhouse (capacity 5200) for their opening game against Texas Tech, the traditional powerhouse of the SWC. The house was packed when Arkansas played Texas A & M on regional television. U of A won in overtime. During his first year, Sutton's team generated a great deal of fan interest. Their 17–9 record represented the most wins by an Arkansas team in 17 years. Their 11–3 record in conference play gave them a second-place tie. They had won more conference games than any Arkansas team since 1943. Eddie Sutton was named SWC basketball coach of the year.

After the first basketball season ended, additional plans had to be made to reach the growth objectives determined by Frank Broyles and the Board of Trustees. Therefore, an informal three-man strategy committee was formed to discuss and formulate the growth strategies for the basketball program.

The old strategy was summarized by Orville Henry, sports writer for the *Arkansas Gazette*: You cannot make any money in basketball. Therefore, just budget so much money, turn your head, and hope that losses can be held to a minimum. The new philosophy was to be: You can have a first-rate basketball program anywhere in the collegiate field if (1) you hire a man who knows what to do, and (2) you provide him with the facilities and support required to win. If you are going to spend money, why not go first class, get the people involved, and make money.

One of the first strategies considered by the three men (Broyles, Sutton, and Matthews) was directed toward new basketball facilities. Barnhill Fieldhouse had a seating capacity of 5200. The court sat on a mounting in a dirt-filled facility used for football, baseball, and track during inclement weather. The 20-year-old building was losing its attractiveness. A facility was needed to hold bigger crowds. How much seating capacity should it have? How much would it cost? How would it be financed? Should it be a multi-purpose building? Should Barnhill be renovated or should a new building be proposed? What is the relationship between winning and attendance and seating capacity?

The information in Table 3–1 was gathered from other schools regarding their win-loss percentage and attendance figures.

An estimate was received from local architects and building construction companies. It suggested that renovation of Barnhill Fieldhouse would cost about $400 a seat. Further information, shown in Table 3–2, was obtained regarding facilities at other schools.

For financing new facilities, the three men devised a tentative strategy to obtain capital: (1) raise money from the Razorback Fund, a private source from supporters of the U of A athletic program; (2) get a "grant" from the state legislature; (3) float a bond issue; (4) if any deficit exists, use money from the football program.

The three planners discussed ticket policies. Should prices be competitive with other schools? Should we price at the market or below the market? What about prices for faculty and students?

What should we do about selling season tickets?

The information in Table 3–3 was gathered from different schools concerning ticket policies and prices.

Financial data for the various schools were difficult to obtain. Only two schools made a yearly profit from basketball—Texas Tech and Hutchinson Junior College. The financial data estimates are listed in Table 3-4.

Table 3-1

University	*Five-year average percentage of games won*	*Five-year average yearly attendance*
Oral Roberts	84	102,000
Texas Tech	65	97,000
Hutchinson Jr.	81	85,000
Creighton	64	77,000
Baylor	61	74,000
Texas	50	63,000
Texas A&M	55	55,000
Southern Methodist	48	48,000
Texas Christian	48	44,000
Tulane	40	39,000
Rice	37	39,000
Arkansas	34	39,000
Mac Murray	24	5,000
Okla. City Univ.	65	22,000
Univ. Nebraska-Omaha	57	13,000

The planners wondered if they could increase attendance at games without expanding the market area. The U of A's basketball crowds averaged around 3000 people—two-thirds students and one-third nonstudents. For 13 home games the average yearly attendance was about 39,000 for the past five years. Few people attended who lived more than 10 miles from the University. However, if the drawing power could be extended to a

Table 3-2

University	*Yearly attendance*	*Gymnasium seating capacity*	*Gymnasium quality*	*Parking facilities*
ORU	102,000	10,750	Good[a]	Good
Texas Tech	97,000	10,000	Good	Good
Hutch Jr.	85,000	7,500	Good	Good
Creighton	77,000	9,800	Good	Good
Baylor	74,000	10,000	Good	Good
Texas	63,000	7,800	Poor[b]	Poor
Texas A&M	55,000	7,500	Fair	Poor
SMU	48,000	9,000	Good	Good
TCU	44,000	7,200	Good	Good
Tulane	39,000	5,000	Poor	Poor
Rice	39,000	5,000	Fair	Good
Arkansas	39,000	5,200	Poor	Poor
Mac Murray	5,000	1,100	Poor	Fair
OCU	22,000	3,400	Good	Poor
UNO	13,000	4,000	Good	Fair

[a] *From judgments made by those interviewed*
[b] *A new facility is being built*

Table 3-3

University	*Yearly attendance*	*General admission*	*Reserve seats*	*Number of season tickets sold*	*Faculty and students*	
ORU	102,000	$1.50	$2.00–3.00	4500	F 17.50;	S 1.25–1.50
Texas Tech	97,000	2.00	3.50	3500	F 1.00;	S 1.00
Hutch Jr.	85,000	1.50	2.00	2500	F free;	S free
Creighton	77,000	2.00	3.50	2000	F ½;	S .50
Baylor	74,000	2.00	3.50	1400	F free;	S free
Texas	63,000	2.00	3.00	00	F free;	S free
Texas A&M	55,000	2.00	3.00	750	F free;	S free
SMU	48,000	3.00	3.00	1000	F free;	S free
TCU	44,000	2.00	3.00	500	F free;	S free
Tulane	39,000	2.50	4.00	200	F 1.00;	S free
Rice	39,000	2.00	2.50	100	F Nom.;	S free
Arkansas	39,000	1.50	3.00	300	F ½;	S free
Mac Murray	5,000	1.00	1.00	25	F free;	S free
OCU	22,000	2.00	2.50	400	F free;	S free
UNO	13,000	2.50	2.50	160	F free;	S free

50-mile radius (a four-county rural area), a potential population of 200,000 could be estimated. The additional information in Table 3–5 was also revealed.

The University of Arkansas had no major competition from college teams. The closest team was Tulsa, 125 miles away. However, the University is located in Fayetteville with a population of 35,000

Promotion of basketball in Razorback country was handled by nine radio stations connected to a U of A sponsored sports network. The Razorbacks had been on regional TV about ten times during the last five years. Although approximately 300 season tickets were sold each year to interested fans, the tickets were not actually promoted. The State of Arkansas is really known as a football state. As a result not much coverage was given to basketball through the newspapers. Further information is provided in Table 3-6.

Table 3-4

University	*Net profit (net loss)*	*University*	*Net profit (net loss)*
Texas Tech	$25,000	Arkansas	(100,000)
Hutch Jr.	14,000	OCU	(105,000)
SMU	Break even	Tulane	(150,000)
Mac Murray	(21,000)	TCU	(loss)
UNO	(26,000)	Rice	(loss)
Creighton	(30,000)	Texas	??
Baylor	(50,000)	ORU	??
Texas A&M	(60,000)		

Table 3-5

University	Yearly attendance	Population market area	Percent customers Stud.	Percent customers Nonstud.	Radius draw. power	No. comp. teams
ORU	102,000	350,000	20	80	40 mi	1
Texas Tech	97,000	250,000	50	50	50	0
Hutch Jr.	85,000	100,000	20	80	25	0
Creighton	77,000	500,000	20	80	25	3
Baylor	74,000	160,000	60	40	25	0
Texas	63,000	400,000	75	25	30	5
Texas A&M	55,000	75,000	66	34	10	0
SMU	48,000	1,500,000	50	50	30	5
TCU	44,000	1,500,000	34	66	50	6
Tulane	39,000	1,200,000	60	40	50	3
Rice	39,000	1,200,000	60	40	15	4
Arkansas	39,000	200,000	66	34	50	0
Mac Murray	5,000	35,000	90	10	20	1
OCU	22,000	500,000	25	75	15	8
UNO	13,000	500,000	80	20	20	3

There was constant discussion among the three as to whether the Razorbacks should play two or three basketball games in Little Rock, 200 miles away. The meetings usually centered around the question of whether the University should try to get the support of central, eastern, and southern Arkansas fans for their basketball program, as well as their football program (at least four games of football were played in Little Rock each

Table 3-6

University	Yearly average attendance	Number of radio outlets	Number of times on TV (five years)	Number of stars on team (five years)
ORU	102,000	1	7	2
Texas Tech	97,000	6	10	6
Hutch Jr.	85,000	2	0	20
Creighton	77,000	2	10	1
Baylor	74,000	2	10	6
Texas	63,000	1	13	2
Texas A&M	55,000	3	12	3
SMU	48,000	1	10	1
TCU	44,000	2	11	2
Tulane	39,000	0	1	0
Arkansas	39,000	9	10	1
Rice	39,000	1	10	1
Mac Murray	5,000	0	0	0
OCU	22,000	0	1	2
UNO	13,000	1	0	0

year and three games in Fayetteville). Two years ago, the Razorbacks played in two games in Little Rock. The crowds were sparse and the project was a financial failure. Last year another attempt was made to play basketball in Little Rock. The results were the same—small crowds and financial losses.

Frank Broyles wondered what strategies to follow to achieve the growth objectives he had presented to the Board of Trustees.

Case 3-2 SOCCER STRATEGY

The athletic director of a state university is thinking about adding soccer to the present line of sports sponsored by the athletic department. As a result, he gathered some statistics and information about soccer. He studied the information before formulating his strategy.

The "Great Pele," a noted soccer player, has been quoted as saying that on recent trips to the U.S. he has seen more and more youngsters playing soccer. In 1964, the American Youth Soccer Organization started in Torrance, California, with 9 teams comprised of 100 boys. Today, the association has 4100 teams in 14 states. The teams include 15,000 girls and 45,000 boys. The U.S. Soccer Federation estimates that more than 500,000 youngsters play organized soccer; three million youngsters should be playing by 1980.

One should expect the U.S. professional leagues to enjoy sustained growth. Talented American youngsters who are already playing soccer promise a bright future for the professional leagues. In addition, young women may play professionally someday. According to one Atlanta coach, "Girls have a better sense of position on the field and don't bunch up as the boys do."

The United States is now importing talented foreign players to promote soccer in North America. The best example is Pele from Brazil. In 1975, the

U.S. Soccer Attendance (1967–77)*

Year	*Attendance*	*Percent increase from previous year*
1967	3,969,745	NA
1968	4,049,139	1.999
1969	4,076,639	.68
1970	4,280,470	4.999
1971	4,794,070	11.998
1972	4,930,000	2.835
1973	5,028,600	2.0
1974	5,631,460	11.988
1975	6,476,179	15.0
1976	6,605,701	1.9
1977	6,935,986	4.9

* *Source: Yearly attendance figures compiled by Triangle Publications, Inc. Hightstown, N.J. 08520.*

New York Cosmos of the North American Soccer League lured Pele out of retirement with $4.5 million. Wherever Pele plays, stadiums are filled and attendance records set (Washington, Los Angeles, Seattle, and Vancouver, B.C.). In addition, the English are now more willing to share their stars. Scheduled to take effect in the 1977–78 season is a ruling similar to the American Rozelle Rule. It allows English players to fulfill their present contract, then sign with another team—even an N.A.S.L. team. America's more stable economy, coupled with lucrative offers from American teams could lure many English stars across the Atlantic to compete in the North American Soccer League.

Case 3-3 SOUTHWESTERN CITY GOLF

The director of athletics and recreation for a southwestern city, population 40,000, was contemplating building a municipal golf course for the local residents. Present competition consisted of a private club of 400 members, with monthly dues of $50; a small 9-hole daily fee course with prices at $2.50; and an excellent 18-hole daily fee course, with prices at $4, that was to become a private club when its membership reached 300.

If the city were to build the planned municipal course, he was wondering what kind of administrative strategies should be followed? What advice would you give in light of the statistics in Tables 3-7, 3-8, 3-9, and 3-10?

Case 3-4 PROFIT STRATEGIES OF FORT SMITH'S ATHLETIC PROGRAMS*

Six years ago Bill Stancil, head football coach at Fort Smith's Northside High, was hired to be the first athletic director of the combined school system. In addition to Northside High, he would now be working with Southside High School and four junior high schools (Ramsey, Darby, Kimmons, and Chaffin). Among other objectives, he was asked to improve the financial situations of all six schools.

After the football season at Northside, Bill Stancil viewed his 13-year coaching career with pride (110 wins, 28 losses, and 3 ties; 3 undefeated seasons). Bill was now dedicated to producing a program that would make the school board proud. He hoped to make a profit for the school's athletic program.

Bill did not want to rely on taxpayers' funds to finance his program. He hoped to increase revenue from game operations and other sources. He concluded: "If we generate our own funds, I will be doing a good job as an administrator. Coaches will appreciate my efforts. If I'm concerned about income and if my coaches are concerned about income, we'll both be more concerned about how the funds are used. We'll be more efficient than if we

* This case was prepared by Robert D. Hay, University of Arkansas, a member of the Southern Case Research Association. This case is to be used as a teaching tool and is not intended to portray correct or incorrect administrative practices.

Table 3-7 Estimated Number of Golfers in the United States

Growth since 1947

YEAR	NUMBER OF GOLFERS
1947	2,516,506
1948	2,742,234
1949	3,112,000
1950	3,215,160
1951	3,237,000
1952	3,265,000
1953	3,335,632
1954	3,400,000
1955	3,500,000
1956	3,680,000
1957	3,812,000
1958	3,970,000
1959	4,125,000
1960	4,400,000
1961	5,000,000
1962	5,500,000
1963	6,250,000
1964	7,000,000
1965	7,750,000
1966	8,525,000
1967	9,100,000
1968	9,300,000
1969	9,500,000
1970	9,700,000
1971	10,000,000
1972	10,400,000
1973	11,000,000
1974	11,660,000
1975	12,036,000
1976	12,328,000
1977*	12,451,000

Comparative study: private, daily fee, municipal

	1974	1975	1976	1977
At Private Clubs:				
Men	1,100,700	1,122,000	1,133,000	1,144,000
Women	494,400	534,000	571,000	577,000
Juniors	270,500	284,000	287,000	290,000
TOTAL	1,865,600	1,940,000	1,991,000	2,011,000
At Daily Fee Courses:				
Men	3,368,600	3,403,000	3,437,000	3,471,000
Women	1,107,100	1,195,000	1,279,000	1,292,000
Juniors	771,300	810,000	818,000	826,000
TOTAL	5,247,000	5,408,000	5,534,000	5,589,000
At Municipal Courses:				
Men	2,955,800	2,985,000	3,015,000	3,045,000
Women	1,045,900	1,130,000	1,209,000	1,221,000
Juniors	545,700	573,000	579,000	585,000
TOTAL	4,547,400	4,688,000	4,803,000	4,851,000
At All Courses:				
Men	7,425,100	7,510,000	7,585,000	7,666,000
Women	2,647,400	2,859,000	3,059,000	3,090,000
Juniors	1,587,500	1,667,000	1,684,000	1,701,000
TOTAL Golfers in U.S.	11,660,060	12,036,000	12,328,000	12,451,000

* *For 1977, add an additional 3,200,000 casual players. Source: National Golf Foundation*

Table 3-8 Relative Growth of Types of Golf Facilities

Year	*Total*	*Private*	*Daily fee*	*Municipal*
*1931	5,691	4,448	700	543
1934	5,727	4,155	1,006	556
1937	5,196	3,439	1,070	637
1939	5,303	3,405	1,199	699
1941	5,209	3,288	1,210	711
†1945	4,808	—	—	—
1946	4,817	3,018	1,076	723
1947	4,870	3,073	1,051	736
1948	4,901	3,090	1,076	735
1949	4,926	3,068	1,108	750
1950	4,931	3,049	1,141	741
1951	4,970	2,996	1,214	760
1952	5,026	3,029	1,246	751
1953	5,056	2,970	1,321	765
1954	5,076	2,878	1,392	806
1955	5,218	2,807	1,534	877
1956	5,358	2,801	1,692	865
1957	5,553	2,887	1,832	834
1958	5,745	2,986	1,904	855
1959	5,991	3,097	2,023	871
1960	6,385	3,236	2,254	895
1961	6,623	3,348	2,363	912
1962	7,070	3,503	2,636	931
1963	7,477	3,615	2,868	994
1964	7,893	3,764	3,114	1,015
1965	8,323	3,887	3,368	1,068
1966	8,672	4,016	3,483	1,173
1967	9,336	4,166	3,960	1,210
1968	9,615	4,269	4,110	1,236
1969	9,926	4,459	4,192	1,275
1970	10,188	4,619	4,248	1,321
1971	10,494	4,719	4,404	1,370
1972	10,665	4,787	4,484	1,394
1973	10,896	4,720	4,710	1,466
1974	11,134	4,715	4,878	1,541
1975	11,370	4,770	5,014	1,586
1976	11,562	4,791	5,121	1,650
1977	11,745	4,847	5,203	1,695

Figures include Regulation, Executive and Par-3 facilities.

** 1931 is the earliest year for which golf facility statistics are available.*

† Breakdowns for 1945 are not available.

Source: National Golf Foundation

Table 3-9 Per Capita Income and Product for Selected Items in Current and Constant (1958) Dollars: 1950 to 1974

Item	*1950*	*1955*	*1960*	*1965*	*1969*	*1970*	*1971*	*1972*	*1973*	*1974 (prel.)*
Current Dollars										
Gross national product	1,877	2,408	2,788	3,525	4,590	4,769	5,095	5,545	6,155	6,594
Personal income	1,501	1,881	2,219	2,773	3,705	3,945	4,173	4,521	5,015	5,429
Disposable personal income	1,364	1,666	1,937	2,436	3,130	3,376	3,605	3,813	4,295	4,623
Personal consumption expenditures	1,259	1,539	1,800	2,228	2,859	3,015	3,222	3,491	3,827	4,137
Durable goods	201	240	251	341	448	446	502	567	619	602
Nondurable goods	647	746	837	983	1,213	1,288	1,315	1,435	1,606	1,794
Services	412	553	712	903	1,198	1,282	1,376	1,489	1,601	1,741
Constant (1958) Dollars										
Gross National Product	2,342	2,650	2,699	3,180	3,580	3,526	3,605	3,795	3,989	3,875
Personal income	1,810	2,027	2,157	2,549	2,999	3,050	3,105	3,273	3,438	3,311
Disposable personal income	1,646	1,795	1,883	2,239	2,534	2,610	2,683	2,779	2,915	2,815
Personal consumption expenditures	1,520	1,659	1,749	2,047	2,315	2,331	2,398	2,525	2,621	2,546
Durable goods	229	261	248	343	422	409	447	502	540	487
Nondurable goods	752	797	828	919	993	1,008	1,020	1,055	1,087	1,056
Services	539	601	673	785	899	914	930	968	998	1,003

Source: Survey of Current Business

Table 3-10 Personal Consumption Expenditures, by Product: 1950 to 1973

Type of Product	*1950*	*1955*	*1960*	*1965*	*1969*	*1970*	*1971*	*1972*	*1973*
Percent	100.0	100.0	100.0	100.0	100.0	100.0	100.0	100.0	100.0
Food, beverages, and tobacco	30.4	28.4	26.9	24.8	22.6	22.9	22.1	21.5	22.2
Clothing, accessories, and jewelry	12.4	11.0	10.2	10.0	10.3	10.2	10.1	10.1	10.1
Personal care	1.3	1.4	1.6	1.8	1.7	1.7	1.6	1.6	1.5
Housing	11.1	13.3	14.2	14.7	14.5	14.7	11.9	14.8	14.5
Household operations	15.4	14.7	14.4	14.3	14.2	14.2	11.1	14.4	14.6
Medical care expenses	4.6	5.0	5.9	6.5	7.4	7.7	7.8	7.8	7.8
Personal business	3.6	3.9	4.6	5.1	5.7	5.7	5.7	5.7	5.6
Transportation	12.9	14.0	13.3	13.5	13.4	12.6	13.6	13.7	13.6
Recreation	5.8	5.5	5.6	6.1	6.4	6.6	6.4	6.6	6.5
Other	2.4	2.8	3.3	3.5	3.8	3.9	3.7	3.8	3.6

Source: Survey of Current Business

were to rely exclusively on tax revenues. Chances are good that if we must rely on taxpayers' money, we'll spend it more extravagantly than if we rely on revenues we make ourselves."

Bill continued: "If we make a yearly profit, we won't have to worry about our win-loss records. If we have a bad season, we should have adequate retained profits to serve as a financial cushion. If the weather turns bad, or if inflation hits too hard, or if there is an unexpected event, like Title IX of the Education Act, we'll have profits to help us out. In addition, if we want to buy some capital assets like special equipment, we can.

"I really don't expect our athletic program to be fully self-supporting, but I'd like to make a profit from game operations—enough to build a fund to handle unforeseen events. The school board must pay coaches' salaries and supply funds to maintain athletic facilities. Yet, I intend to make a profit to get our schools in the black."

Early in his administration, Stancil learned that Southside's athletic program (in the red by $1,890.89) needed about $5,000 worth of equipment. Jim Rowland, Bill's assistant football coach at Northside, went to Southside as head coach. Together, Bill Stancil and Jim Rowland went to various community people to ask them to contribute $100 each for Southside's athletic program. They eventually raised $4,800.

The soft drink machine at Northside High's stadium produced a profit of about $1,200 each year. Why not place a soft drink machine at Southside High? Bill did, and it netted about $125 each month, or approximately $1,500 a year.

Before Bill became athletic director, there were two concession stands for athletic events at Northside. One was run by the band members and the other was run by members of student clubs. Neither made a profit. In addition, the State Health Department did not like the way they were managed. Bill turned them over to an outside vendor, and split the profits 60-40 (60% for athletics, 40% to the vendor). Yearly profits since then have averaged $700–$800 for the athletic program. He did the same at Southside, and profits averaged about $600 a year.

Bill was constantly looking for ways to make a profit, particularly from activities related to the major athletic contests.

Using another profit strategy, Bill began to take bids on athletic equipment. Prior to this, each school bought equipment by telephoning the local

Athletic Fund

School	*Debit*	*Credit*
Northside High		$1,971.04
Southside High	$1,890.89**	
Darby	778.60**	
Darby Concessions		$1,426.68
Kimmons	$2,331.99**	
Ramsey		$1,967.13
Sub totals	$5,001.48**	$5,364.85
Total Balance in Athletic Fund		$ 363.37

** *Indicates financial losses.*

sporting goods retail store. Bill Stancil felt that by combining the athletic equipment needs of all six schools, he could have four stores bid on the list. This way he could take advantage of quantity discounts and still buy quality equipment. He had the coaches specify the equipment they desired. Bill then asked the stores to bid. As a result several hundreds of dollars were saved. Bill deliberately overbought certain items that would be used frequently. His policy was to have the coaches and players use all the old equipment first, then use the new equipment. This is the first in-first out (FIFO) method of issuing the equipment from a central warehouse.

Another profit strategy was to increase ticket sale revenues by selling season tickets in advance of actual games. No other high school in the area sold season tickets. Bill started this program. The football season tickets were sold between 40-yard lines. Basketball season tickets, never sold in advance before Bill's arrival, were soon promoted to local citizens. If a season ticket holder could not attend a game, the athletic program would already have the revenue from his ticket. As a result the season ticket sales did increase, and each year Bill tried to beat last year's sales record.

Bill instituted a booster club at each of the six schools. He promoted them by planning watermelon feasts, chili suppers, candy sales, and by auctioning TV sets. The idea was to get each person to join for a yearly fee of $2.00. This revenue was administered in a separate fund, controlled by the coaches. Although most people did contribute the usual $2.00, Bill reported that one person contributed $1,000. The funds were used to buy specialized equipment such as a universal weight machine and to carpet the dressing room floor. It was a considerable saving for individual schools when their booster clubs bought athletic equipment. Bill found that each club usually had a 200-person membership, but that four or five people did most of the membership and promotional work.

At the end of Bill's first year of administration the financial position of the athletic fund was as follows:

Athletic Fund
Bill's First Year

Northside Grizzlies		$ 7,974.57
Southside Rebels	$ 892.42**	
Ramsey		3,398.82
Chaffin		1,512.84
Kimmons		77.39
Darby	344.96**	
Darby Concessions		857.40
Sub-total	$1,240.38**	$13,821.02
Total Balance in Athletic Fund		$12,580.64

** Indicates financial losses

It was to Bill's advantage that Northside's football season's record was 9–2, and that Northside was the conference champion in basketball with a 20–4 record. Southside had a 5–5 record in football and a 20–4 record in basketball.

During the second year of Bill Stancil's administration he concentrated on improving the concessions, the purchasing, the season ticket sales, and the booster clubs—the accomplishments of his first year. In addition, he started a scheduling system for football games at the two stadiums—Mayo Thompson Field at Northside, where Southside also played, and at Buck Wells Field at Ramsey Junior High. Mayo Thompson was built by Works Progress Administration funds. Bill estimated its current replacement cost at $1,000,000. Buck Wells could be replaced for $500,000.

Before Jim's tenure, Mayo Thompson Field was the home field for the Northside Grizzlies. Occasionally, the Southside Rebels would also play there. But there were many times when both teams played away from home and Mayo Thompson was empty. Consequently, Bill conscientiously planned the schedules of the two high school teams so that one would play at Mayo Thompson while the other was away. As a result on every Friday night there was a "home" football game, for either Northside or for Southside.

On Thursday nights there would be two junior high games—one at Mayo Thompson and one at Buck Wells. On Tuesday afternoons, the seventh and eighth grade teams would play in the two stadiums. On Monday afternoons, there would also be seventh and eighth grade teams playing. On Monday evening the junior varsity played their games. As a result of Bill's scheduling, there was full utilization of the two fields every week on Monday afternoons and nights, Tuesday afternoon, and Thursday and Friday evenings.

During the junior high games, voluntary collections were taken, normally amounting to 25¢ or 50¢ from each person attending. In addition, the booster clubs started to sell parking tickets at all the games.

Bill was particularly proud of the athletic equipment warehouse started during his second year. The idea came from Lindy Callahan, a friend of Bill's who was athletic director at Gulfport. Bill met Lindy at several coaches' clinics where they exchanged ideas.

Bill gradually started to stock everything needed for athletes except actual game equipment, such as jerseys, pants, and gear. Other coaches, who saw Bill's successful practice of bidding, started to take bids on game equipment. Bill encouraged this practice. He, therefore, took bids on everything except game equipment and awards. He suggested that coaches do this. Coaches began to save small amounts of money here and there. Bill had instilled in the coaches the desire to economize.

Bill developed a system for buying athletic supplies. Each coach gave him orders. Then Bill, after considering the bids from four or five stores, would buy the equipment. The various bids and the amount of money saved were available for anyone to examine. Both the athletic director and the school board's business office kept an inventory at cost plus sales tax as a double check. The business office recorded each coach's requisition and charged the cost to each school and to each sport.

Bill started making income and expense statements for each school and each sport to evaluate what was going on at each school.

On September 30, in the early months of his third year, the financial position of the athletic programs appeared as follows:

Athletic Funds During Bill's Third Year

	Balance on hand August 31	*September collections*	*September disbursements*	*Balance on hand September 30*
Northside				
Administrative	$19,808.93	$ 47.63	$ 178.30	$19,678.26
Basketball	845.37	116.71	69.95	798.61
Football	67.33	9,718.15	8,763.82	887.00
Programs	–0–	175.34	–0–	175.34
Track	389.11	–0–	273.21	662.32
Golf	20.28	–0–	–0–	20.28
Total	$18,486.84	$10,057.83	$ 9,285.28	$19,259.39
Southside				
Administrative	$ 3,997.33	–0–	217.81	3,779.52
Basketball	–0–	–0–	163.77	163.77
Concessions	120.70	43.10	–0–	163.89
Football	1,316.39	8,929.44	2,224.05	5,389.00
Programs	–0–	219.89	–0–	219.89
Track	17.00		282.84	299.84
Golf	–0–	–0–	18.23	18.23
Total	$ 2,784.64	$ 9,192.52	$ 2,906.70	$ 9,070.46
Kimmons	$ 112.73	$ 1,733.81	$ 742.72	$ 878.36
Darby	$ 79.16	$ 950.35	$ 112.00	$ 917.51
Ramsey	$ 3,252.14	$ 3,080.25	$ 1,058.65	$ 5,273.74
Chaffin	$ 901.99	$ 1,479.31	$ 429.21	$ 1,952.09
Grand Total	$25,392.04	$26,494.07	$14,534.56	$37,351.55

During the next three years Bill Stancil concentrated on building the athletic funds. He emphasized the profit strategies started during his first two years on the job as athletic director. Retained profits at various times for the high schools were as follows:

Athletic Fund Balances
Northside High School

Year 1, June 30	$ 1,971.04
2, June 30	8,074.57
3, June 30	20,015.49
4, June 30	26,340.98
5, June 30	25,922.74
6, June 30	30,591.98
7, June 30	27,963.30
8, Dec. 31	33,214.57

Southside High School	
Year 1, June 30	1,890.89**
2, June 30	695.42
3, June 30	4,513.55
4, June 30	5,868.75
5, June 30	816.45
6, June 30	8,201.35
7, June 30	4,340.22
8, Dec. 31	9,569.77

The junior high schools were also in the black on June 30 of this year:

Athletic Funds	
Kimmons Junior High	$1,131.15
Darby Junior High	4,630.88
Ramsey Junior High	2,517.80
Chaffin Junior High	469.35

The total retained profits for all the schools for the past few years were as follows:

Total Athletic Fund Balances June 30, 19xx	
Year 1 of Bill's Administration	363.37
Year 2	12,880.64
Year 3	29,237.53
Year 4	46,447.96
Year 5	36,273.34
Year 6	47,052.51
Year 7	41,052.70
Year 8, Dec. 31	56,828.50

**Indicates financial losses.

After Bill's third year, the school board took away his soft drink machines' profits and gave them to the cafeteria.

This year Bill was confronted with the school board's decision to start a girls' athletic program for the Fort Smith School system. One of the problems facing the athletic program was how to finance the initial investment in equipment and supplies. Once that was done, how would the yearly operations of girls' athletics be financed?

Bill estimated that it would take $40,000 to initially finance the girls' programs. Should the girls use the retained profits of the boys' programs? Should the school board initially finance the girls with local tax funds? Should the board use operating funds to finance the extracurricular activity of girls' athletics each year? Should booster clubs be expected to support the girls' program? Bill pondered these alternatives before deciding what to recommend to the school superintendent and the athletic committee of the school board.

4

STRATEGIES TO ACCOMPLISH OBJECTIVES OF ATHLETIC PROGRAMS (continued)

Somewhat less important but still significant objectives of most athletic programs include maintaining the continuity of the program, of being a leader in athletics, improving the position of athletics in general, and improving the quality of life for society. The strategies that can be used to accomplish these athletic program objectives in high school, college, and professional levels will be discussed in this chapter.

MAINTAINING CONTINUITY OF THE ATHLETIC PROGRAM

Those athletic programs in trouble of losing their continuity are usually in that position because they are not making a profit. Consequently a major strategy for maintaining survival is to have sufficient revenues to offset the expenses of managing a program. If those revenues are not sufficient, the program should be subsidized in some way. High school and college programs have a better chance of getting subsidies than the professional programs have because professional programs depend exclusively on ticket, television and radio, and concession revenues to offset their expenses. But making a profit is fundamental to the continuity of an athletic program.

Another strategy is to keep substantial funds in reserve to cover emergencies due to financial losses. Because most athletic programs do not prosper every year, such reserves would insure survival of the program during bad years. It is advisable to distribute reserve funds among several financial institutions to insure against losing the entire account should one institution suffer a reverse.

Another strategy is to have several sources of the raw materials necessary for the management of an athletic program, such as player talent, money, equipment, space, and information. If one source dries up, then another is available—again, avoid "putting all your eggs in one basket."

Likewise, it is advisable to have a variety of product lines. For a high school or college program, this strategy is translated into carrying several sports in a total athletic program. If one sport does not succeed, perhaps another sport could be used to carry the total program. This would insure survival of the program because if a certain sport has several bad years, another can carry on during slack periods.

Providing for such backup should be the aim of an executive development program. Reliance on only one coach jeopardizes the continuity of the athletic program. Consequently, a well-managed program will use a variety of tactics to develop its coach-executives, such as switching coaches around so they can learn several skills. Another strategy is to devise a training program to develop assistant coaches into head coaches or to develop coaches into athletic directors. One mark of a successful athletic program is the number of assistant coaches who later became head coaches at other institutions.

Obeying the rules of the regulatory agencies is another way to insure continuity. If the program violates the rules of the regulatory agencies, they may put it on probation or eventually force it out of business. Likewise, ethical behavior is one way to insure some degree of continuity; if people cannot trust an athletic program to act fairly, honestly, and with integrity, there is no reason to have dealings with the program.

The athletic program must adapt to changes in the environment to maintain continuity. The reason is obvious: The only sure thing is constant change. If a program does not adapt to changes, the changing environment will leave it behind to die. If there are no forward-looking plans for an athletic program, it is likely that the program will survive only by chance. Programs that do not adapt to the participation of black athletes or the popularity of women's sports will be left behind.

To survive, athletic programs must have insurance programs for their major assets. A major fire or other disasters could wipe out an athletic program. It is a wise strategy to maintain a substantial insurance policy.

Having a preferred market position insures continuity of the athletic program. A market share large enough to receive sufficient revenues is necessary for survival. An athletic program has a preferred market position when it is part of a large market, or after it has secured a monopoly position with regard to competitors. If an athletic program has no direct competitors for customer revenue or player talent, chances are excellent for the program's continuity. The franchising system of professional teams is an example of preferred market position strategy. The franchise is an attempt to insure a team's preferred market position in relation to a market territory.

Finally, engaging in some sort of research and development program is a way to assure some degree of continuity. The R & D strategy can be used in relation to various sports, players, markets, and coaching techniques. The athletic programs experimenting with a research and development program are usually assured of some organizational continuity.

The following is a list of the strategies used to maintain continuity. They might be evaluated by an athletic administrator for his/her program:

Objective: To Maintain Continuity of the Program

Strategies to Be Used	Strength	Weakness
1. Making a profit		
2. Keeping large financial reserves for emergencies		
3. Insurance program for major assets		
4. Several sources of supply for important resources		
5. Large variety of sports programs		
6. Executive development program		
7. Obey rules of regulatory agencies		
8. Adapting to environmental changes		
9. Preferred market position		
10. Research and development program		
11. Others		
Overall Evaluation:		

BEING A LEADER IN ATHLETICS

Often an athletic program will attempt to be a leader in its field. To be a leader, the program should be an innovator, developing new ideas other programs will follow. Being "first" in developing new ideas is a sign of being a leader which other programs will emulate.

Carving out fields for possible leadership is a necessary strategy. It is probably better to select those fields in which a program has strength rather than those in which an athletic program is weak. Building upon strengths rather than weaknesses makes sense if a program is to lead a certain field.

Once a field is decided upon, some sort of research and development program must be initiated to innovate successful techniques such as new techniques in coaching or in athletics. For example, development of the T formation was new when the single wing was popular. It was followed by the split T and then the wishbone. The run and gun in basketball was new when the two-handed set shot was in vogue. The backroll in high jumping is a new technique. Likewise, the bamboo pole in the pole vault was made obsolete. The use of aluminum baseball bats is a result of a research and development program. Innovative thinking is fundamental to the R & D effort which is so vital to athletic programs aspiring to leadership in athletics.

If the athletic program wishes to be a leader, it might use the following summary to evaluate its strengths and weaknesses:

Objective: To Be a Leader in Athletics

Strategies to Be Used	**Strength**	**Weakness**
1. Being first in athletic activities		
2. Carving out fields in which to be a leader		
3. Research and development of athletic innovations		
4. Others		
Overall Evaluation:		

IMPROVING THE POSITION OF ATHLETICS IN GENERAL

Most athletic administrators recognize that their programs will prosper if the position of athletics is improved. Various strategies are used to improve athletics in general.

Joining professional organizations that promote athletics is probably the favorite strategy of most athletic administrators. The most typical are state high school athletic associations, the National Association of Intercollegiate Athletics, the National Collegiate Athletic Association, the National Association of Collegiate Directors of Athletics, and other organizations that promote athletics. Often administrators will sponsor athletic clinics, special athletic events, Fellowship of Christian Athletes activities, seminars, or similar activities to promote athletics. In addition, they might participate in athletic promotions of all kinds, such as bowl games, athletic events for handicapped children, intramurals, school events, community athletic events, and others with the idea of promoting athletics in general.

The following strategies can be evaluated for their strengths and weaknesses:

Objective: To Improve the Position of Athletics in General

Strategies	Strength	Weakness
1. Joining professional organizations that promote athletics		
2. Sponsoring athletic events		
3. Participating in athletic promotional events		
Overall Evaluation:		

IMPROVING THE QUALITY OF LIFE FOR SOCIETY

Currently, the country is demanding that organizations try to improve the quality of life for society. Such an objective suggests that organizations be concerned with strategies dealing with pollution, minority groups, consumerism, urban problems, public recreation, and cooperation with government. An athletic organization can do its part, just like any other business or public organization, to improve the quality of life.

A pollution strategy involves cleaning up the grounds after an athletic event. Cooperation with local governmental units regarding solid waste disposal is fundamental to a successful athletic program. It is imperative that an athletic program not harm the physical environment in any way, either by solid waste or noise pollution.

Support for public recreation is a natural strategy used by athletic programs. One member of the athletic staff could serve on public recreation commissions or assist in a bond drive to raise money for public recreation; perhaps the athletic program could allow the public to use its facilities for special purposes. Since public recreation is normally associated with an improved quality of life, it is wise to support this strategy.

Athletic programs have supported minority groups' wants and needs for a number of years. Athletics provides a natural avenue for excellence for all races. However, the issue of women in athletics has not been resolved by athletic programs in general. Support for minority groups, though, should continue to receive the attention of an athletic program if it wants to do its part in improving the quality of life for society.

A strategy to cope with urban problems is fundamental for the athletic programs located in big cities. Athletic programs could help to raise money for urban renewal projects, assist in youth programs during the summer months, help to transport people to and from athletic events, and provide security for fans and employees who work in big cities where urban crime exists.

It is wise for those involved in athletic programs to cooperate with the government, thereby helping to improve the quality of life. Since government is supposed to represent the citizens of society, it is a wise strategy to work with, rather than against, those people who are in governmental service. For example, working with HEW officials will help resolve the problem of sex discrimination. It is wise to work with governmental officials on issues concerning taxes, rules and regulations regarding employment, contracts, land, and a host of other legal problems. Together, athletic administrators and government personnel can work toward their common goal—to improve the quality of life.

The consumerism movement is also designed to improve the quality of life. In support of this movement, athletic programs must practice good ethics when dealing with ticket-paying customers. This includes using honest advertising practices, handling customer complaints objectively, and holding athletic events in safe places with adequate safety precautions. Since customers provide much of the revenue for an athletic program, they should be treated in a manner that the athletic administrator would like to be treated.

In summary, then, an athletic administrator may wish to evaluate the strengths and weaknesses of the strategies that improve the quality of life for society.

Objective: To Improve the Quality of Life for Society

Strategies	Strength	Weakness
1. Not polluting the environment either by solid waste, or noise pollution.		
2. Support for public recreation		
3. Support for minority groups		
4. Support for urban problems		
5. Deliberate cooperation with government		
6. Support of consumerism in truthful advertising, customer complaints, and customer safety		
Overall Evaluation:		

CHAPTER SUMMARY

The less important objectives of most athletic programs are (1) to maintain continuity of the athletic program, (2) to be a leader in athletic activities, (3) to improve the position of athletics in general, and (4) to improve the quality of life for society. Various strategies have been suggested to achieve these objectives. A checklist has been provided for the athletic administrator to evaluate the strengths and weaknesses of his/her program in light of the objectives and strategies suggested in this chapter.

Case 4-1 THE WORLD FOOTBALL LEAGUE*

Chris Hemmeter, recently elected President of the World Football League, sat in his office contemplating the WFL's next strategic move. It was about a year ago when his responsibilities and authority were thrust upon him, accountable to the owners of the then twelve teams making up the WFL. As he sat there he wondered how the owners' unrestrained optimism toward the WFL of approximately two years ago had turned to an atmosphere of pessimism and gloom after two seasons of professional football. He recalled the enthusiasm of Gary Davidson, former President of the WFL, in promoting twelve franchises to form the World Football League—the newest independent professional football league since the old American Football League was formed and eventually merged into the National Football League.

Formation of the WFL

It began in October two years ago when Gary Davidson announced the formation of a new professional football league, claiming the Southern California franchise as his own. Traveling 200,000 miles around the United States and some foreign countries, Davidson found 12 owners. He opened the WFL office in Newport Beach, California.

Gary Davidson had created the American Basketball Association, the World Hockey Association, and professional track. His experience in professional sports organization suggested that a new football league could be created, and the time was ripe. Football's popularity was at an all-time high and had a constant growth pattern (see Table 1). There were several owner-promoters who were willing to risk their money on a new league, buying and selling franchises. The NFL was being threatened with a player strike next year. There were plenty of football players around who did not make the cut for the NFL teams. The supply of resources necessary for a new league seemed to be plentiful.

Assistants to Gary Davidson were announced—Don Regan, sports counsel; Max Muhleman, sports marketer; and Don Andersen, former sports information director at USC. These men formed the nucleus of the WFL office with the twelve franchises sold as shown in Table 2, showing

* This case was prepared by Robert D. Hay, University of Arkansas, as a teaching tool. Much of the data was gathered from Associated Press newspaper reports. The case is not intended to portray correct or incorrect administrative practices.

Presented at a Case Workshop and distributed by the Intercollegiate Case Clearing House, Soldiers Field, Boston, Mass. 02163.

Table 4-1 Attendance at National Football Regular League Games, Yearly Figures

Season	*Total attendance*	*Games played*	*Average per game*	*Average per club*
1958	3,006,124	72	41,752	250,510
1959	3,140,409	72	43,617	261,700
1960	4,047,452	134	30,204	192,735
1961	4,985,756	154	32,375	226,625
1962	5,150,722	154	33,446	234,124
1963	5,405,384	154	35,100	245,699
1964	6,010,924	154	39,032	273,224
1965	6,571,156	154	42,670	253,234
1966	7,497,413	168	44,627	312,392
1967	8,304,784	175	47,456	332,191
1968	8,516,817	182	46,796	327,569
1969	8,939,577	182	49,119	343,829
1970	9,533,333	182	52,381	366,666
1971	10,076,035	182	55,363	383,693
1972	10,445,827	182	57,395	401,762
1973	10,730,933	182	58,961	413,728

the franchise locations, principal owners, stadium capacity, franchise evaluation, and reported season ticket sales/capacity.

Davidson's modus operandi was simple: offering franchises for bargain prices and then upping the league ante by $100,000 each time the franchise was sold. He signed up the TVS independent TV network to do one game a week on Thursday nights. Since the TV networks were saturated with football on weekends, Davidson decided to play games on Wednesday nights, starting in July.

Five original organizers of the WFL received their franchises free. Others were sold at varying prices from $250,000 to $550,000. The original organizers were Ben Hatskin, Steve Arnold, Robert Schmertz, Nick Mileti, and John Bassett. The Chicago Fire Franchise was sold by Mileti to Tom Origer for a price reported at between $250,000 to $400,000. Three men (Arnold, Schmertz, and Bassett) kept their franchises.

Immediately after Davidson sold his Southern California franchise for $250,000, multimillionaire Lamar Hunt, one of the founders of the AFL and present owner of the Kansas City Chiefs of the NFL, stated, "It seems to me that the World Football League, World Hockey Association, and American Basketball Association are operating on a hit-or-miss basis. They pick up franchises, squeeze all the money out of the venture and sell for a quick profit, then they move on. Hardly a day passes that you don't see one of these franchises being shifted to another city. New franchises always are up for grabs. The backers of the WFL are franchise hucksters playing a loose and easy game of high finance."

Hunt was also quoted as saying, "Organizers of some of these new leagues stake out cities. They grab franchises for nothing. Then they sell them to prospective buyers for $250,000 to $500,000. They retain certain

Location	Owners	Stadium capacity	Franchise evaluation	Reported season tickets sold and capacity
EASTERN DIVISION				
1. New York Stars	Bob Schmertz, Owner Boston Celtics	Downing Stadium 27,000		10,000/27,000
2. Philadelphia Bell	Jack Kelly, Past President AAU	JFK Stadium 90,000	Franchise nearly shifted to Mexico City	6,200/90,000
3. Florida Blazers	E. J. Wheeler, Marine Engineer	Tangerine Bowl 27,000	Franchise shifted from Washington, Norfolk, Orlando (possibly Annapolis and Baltimore)	1,500/27,000
4. Jacksonville Sharks	Fran Monaco, Medical Labs	Gator Bowl 70,000	Weak	18,000/70,000
CENTRAL DIVISION				
5. Detroit Wheels	34 partners	Rynearson Stadium 24,000	Weak	5,000/24,000
6. Chicago Fire	Tom Origer, Construction	Soldier Field 56,000	Financial strength	18,000/56,000
7. Birmingham Americans	Bill Putnam, Past Pres. Atlanta Hawks and Flames	Legion Field 72,000	Strong franchise	20,000/72,000
8. Memphis Southmen	John Bassett, Television	Memphis Stadium 50,000	Formerly Toronto	5,000/50,000
9. Houston Texans	R. S. Arnold, Attorney	Astrodome 47,000		4,000/7,000
10. Portland Storm	Bruce Gelker, Hotels	Civic Stadium 33,000	Weak	4,000/33,000
11. Southern California Sun	Larry Hatfield, Trucking	Anaheim Stadium 47,000		1,800/47,000
12. Honolulu Hawaiians	Sam Battisone, Sambo's Restaurants	Honolulu Stadium 27,000		10,000/27,000

override privileges. The franchises may flounder or shift from one place to another, but the original operators get their money out of it."

Hunt further stated, "The success of the NFL could be traced to Commissioner Pete Rozelle, who is a terrific administrator. He has kept the league financially stable. Other sports are not as fortunate. For example, I think the New York Knicks, Los Angeles Lakers, and Milwaukee Bucks are the only teams in the NBA operating in the black. I am disturbed by the trend of some of the new leagues to throw tremendous amounts of money into their operations without knowing where the money will come from. They spend without the income to offset the huge outlays. The operation becomes top heavy. It is financially unstable."[1]

Chris Hemmeter remembered Hunt's words well because now the WFL's survival was being threatened because of the lack of profits and financial reserves of the teams. However, at the time there seemed to be a tremendous optimism about a new football league. Even Lamar Hunt was quoted, "I am in favor of free enterprise. I am not alarmed about what people call the sports explosion. There is room in sports for more leagues and more teams in all sports. After all, we have 210 million people in the country compared with 140 million before World War II. That means 50 percent more people with $9 and $10 to spend for a ticket. Sports have become a tremendous theater. I don't think there is an end in sight to the recreation dollar or recreation time. There is opportunity for new franchises to succeed, but not without stability of operation."[2]

Hemmeter recalled very well that last day in March before the first game was played in July when the WFL signed up Larry Csonka, Jim Kiick, and Paul Warfield of the NFL champion Miami Dolphins to play for Toronto after having one more year of playing with the Dolphins. That signing, which cost the WFL $1 million outright plus a $2.4 million package for the three players, made believers out of those people who pooh-poohed the formation of the WFL. All 12 teams pooled their resources to build the $3.4 million pot. Gary Davidson explained that it was based on the precedent of the Bobby Hull signing in the World Hockey League. In that league there was a combined effort to sign Hull. However, Davidson made it clear that there would be no more cooperative efforts to sign other players. He had to use some political muscle to get each franchise to pool the money necessary to sign the trio of Dolphin players.

The pooling of resources created a rush of other NFL players to sign with the WFL. Ken Stabler, Craig Morton, Calvin Hill, Darrell Lamonica, Jim Nance, Jim Seymour, and Mike Taliaferro signed. But they would not be able to play the first season because each had to play out his option for one year before they could switch from the NFL to the WFL. Immediately the Cincinnati Bengals brought a court suit against the WFL for the signing of Bill Bergey. The Dallas Cowboys also sued the WFL for signing Calvin Hill.

The WFL attorneys maintained in the court that the new league gives players a freedom of choice and allows them to improve their financial position in the NFL because of the competition. They attacked the Rozelle rule under which players are prevented from playing with the teams of their own choice or from getting bigger salaries. Under the Rozelle rule a player plays a year beyond his signed contract and then his option runs out. However, Commissioner Rozelle can determine compensation due the team the player leaves to join another. During the trial William F. Byrne, an official of the Chicago Fire (WFL), stated that the Fire had signed 300 players, including 10 rookies. He stated that the group was a lot of quantity, not quality. For this reason, the Fire was seeking NFL players.

Byrne was correct. The WFL had signed no superstars to play during the first season. Perhaps during the second season, the Dolphin trio and other big names could play, but until then the WFL could actually play only some disaffected Canadians, ex-minor leaguers, some NFL jumpers, and a host of college rookies. The quality of players was in doubt.

The WFL eventually won the Cincinnati court suit. The U.S. District Judge ruled that granting the injunction of the Cincinnati Bengals against allowing Bill Bergey to sign with the WFL would harm the public interest in fostering free competition in the marketplace for the sports dollar. The Bengals' argument, that Bergey would have divided loyalties between the Bengals and the Virginia Ambassadors, was evidently not sufficient to win their case. Bergey's contract called for him to play for three years for $525,-000, plus a $100,000 signing bonus, with the WFL guaranteeing full payment even if Bergey were never able to play.

Several other NFL players, after the court suit, signed to play with the various teams of the WFL. Commissioner Pete Rozelle suggested that he was not worried about the divided loyalties, but he did suggest that the signings had been a factor in escalating professional football salaries. He mentioned, in an Associated Press interview, that the success of the WFL would be related to the amount of money the WFL would be willing to spend. He also wondered about a possible saturation on the TV for football, pointing out that football would be on TV every day except for Tuesday and Friday.

Gary Davidson was elated about the Cincinnati ruling. He also commented about Lamar Hunt's earlier criticism. He suggested that Hunt had inherited his money and that he was working for his. He admitted to the repeated shifts in franchises, but stated that any new league has frequent shifts before it becomes stabilized. He also stated that the WFL had no desire to merge with the NFL. He had divested himself of all basketball, hockey, and tennis associations to concentrate on football. (It was later reported that he had sold the Philadelphia franchise for $700,000.)

Davidson had designed twelve different football rules under which the WFL teams would play in order to make pro ball more lively and offensive minded:

1. The ball will be kicked from the 35-yard line to ensure more runbacks.
2. The goal posts will be moved to the rear of the end zone.
3. Missed field goals will be returned to the line of scrimmage except when attempted inside the twenty.
4. Eliminate the bump-and-run defense. Receivers may not be hit after they are three yards beyond the line of scrimmage.
5. Receivers need just one foot in bounds for a completion.
6. There will be a fifth quarter, split into two 7½ minute periods, in case of a tie.
7. Fair catches will not be permitted on punts. Returners are allowed a five-yard clearance zone to catch the ball.

8. An offensive back will be allowed to go in motion toward the line of scrimmage before the ball is snapped, providing he is at least 10 yards away from the ball.
9. The hash marks will be moved to the center of the field.
10. Any incomplete pass on fourth down will be returned to the line of scrimmage rather than to the 20, if attempted inside the 20.
11. Touchdowns are worth seven points.
12. Action point conversions are worth one point. The ball will be placed on the 2½ yard line, from which it must be run or passed into the end zone.

Davidson's product differentiation strategy had immediate effects on the NFL. It immediately adopted almost verbatim the WFL's rule changes. The hope of the NFL was to make the games similar. The more similar, the more easily detected would be the quality of the game. Thus the differentiation strategy of Davidson did not work, Hemmeter recalled.

But, as Chris Hemmeter remembered, there was another favorable factor. The NFL players were planning a strike. If that strike were to continue, and it did, throughout the summer, the WFL's chances of attracting fans to its games would increase. The NFL player strike took a terrible toll on the NFL owners because no exhibition games were played during the summer. And those exhibition games provided that extra margin of revenue that made teams financially profitable. So the WFL benefited.

As Chris Hemmeter remembered when the first season approached, the supply of resources seemed to be in place. All the WFL wanted were customers. But had any franchise owner made any market research to determine how many potential fans there were in the franchise cities? Did the owners know, other than advance ticket sales, who the fans would be? When they preferred to see games? What prices they preferred for tickets? How far they would travel to see the games?

Jimmy (the Greek) Synder had said, "The WFL is even money to fold during the first year. I'm not quoting odds on their games. After all, it's nothing but minor league football."

But the mood of optimism was there among the WFL owners as July 10, the first date of the opening games, approached.

The Opening First Season of the WFL

The opening night arrived with five games being played and a nationally televised game between New York and Jacksonville the following evening. The differentiation of the 12 rules prevailed.

TVS, an independent national TV company, broadcast the Thursday evening game. The fan attendance was high, with the stadium practically filled. The first week's attendance for the five Wednesday games was 188,978.

The second week's attendance at the five Wednesday night games was 116,197. The top game was at Anaheim with a crowd of 32,038.

Ten thousand fans appeared at Rynearson Stadium to watch Detroit play Florida. New York attracted 18,000, including 1200 complimentary ticket holders. A nickel beer night brought 26,000 fans to Houston's game.

Chicago attracted 29,000 while playing Jacksonville. During this part of the season the NFL strike of players was in full progress, with no preseason exhibition games being played.

During this time, the WFL office reported that 105,000 season tickets had been sold by the 12 teams. However, it became known that Birmingham's reported 20,000 season tickets had really been only 7200 for the 72,000 seat stadium. In addition, complimentary tickets had been issued, made to appear that they had been sold, for the televised game. Furthermore, huge discounts had been given to companies for their "purchase" of tickets.

Tom Origer, owner of the Chicago Fire, stated that he estimated that if the Fire attracted an average of 30,000 fans at 10 home games, his season losses would range between $250,000 and $500,000.

With the season ticket sales exaggerated, the WFL's credibility was damaged. By Labor Day weekend, the fan attendance had reached a new low. The ninth week of the five Wednesday night games showed an average of just 19,412 spectators. Gary Wright, a WFL employee, said that the teams were expecting to average 30,000 a game for the entire season. He mentioned that 1,280,182 fans had attended so far during the season.

The New York Stars drew 6,000 fans, a record low WFL home crowd. Even fewer fans, 5,100, attended a game in London, Ontario. The game attendance was discouraging.

By the end of the first season, several teams had financial problems.

In October, with just a few games remaining, the WFL owners, with Tom Origer threatening withdrawal of the Chicago Fire from the League, forced the resignation of Gary Davidson as President of the WFL. Two franchises had already collapsed, leaving just 10 teams. An executive committee of six members actually started to run the League, with Donald J. Regan, chief counsel, as Executive Director. Davidson became a member of the six-man executive committee. John Bassett announced that the League office would be switched from Newport Beach, California, to New York. Davidson mentioned that he would prefer to be in the selling end of the game rather than in the administrative end.

Chris Hemmeter Elected President of the WFL

About a month later, Christopher B. Hemmeter recalled, he was named President of the WFL. Chris had been a passive investor in the Hawaiians' franchise. He recalled that he had very little knowledge of the "inner workings" of the League other than that received from attending a few league meetings in Los Angeles. He was not too well aware of all the events of the first year of operation of the WFL. However, he felt that a prudent business approach could be applied to professional football by devising strategy which would recognize the wild fluctuation of income of professional sports. He thought that if the teams could maximize variable expenses by minimizing fixed overhead, such overhead to include player salaries, perhaps the League's financial problems could be alleviated.

When he was elected president, Chris divested himself of his financial holdings in the Honolulu franchise to avoid any conflict of interest. John Bassett, his friend at Memphis, stated that a professional management approach would give the WFL credibility in the financial community.

Chris felt that the bottom had dropped out when most teams squandered their season ticket money and within weeks found themselves without any revenue source. He said, "The prime reason for the failures was unfounded optimism that we could launch a new league and survive on the proceeds. Even our Hawaiians lost about $3.5 million this first year. It was poor economic planning. The collective judgments made by this League should be questioned since they obviously didn't work."

Chris could cite many problems:

1. Only two teams met every payroll and five teams were behind in paying their players.
2. Two franchises dropped, one quit, and four were taken over by the League. Chris thought that only three were strong enough to play next season.
3. One team could not buy tape, another was begging meals from local citizens, and two had their uniforms seized by sheriff's deputies.
4. Losses totaled at least $20 million.
5. Promises to pay back salaries were broken most of the time.
6. Several NFL players who had signed with the WFL threatened to stay in the NFL.
7. Three large television markets were vacated—New York, Detroit, and Houston—and moved to Shreveport, Orlando and the like where the market is too small.
8. The World Bowl almost did not happen because of a player boycott.
9. No television contract was available for next season.

Stability and continuity were his goals for the league. He instituted a series of by-laws giving the league dictatorial powers over how owners could spend their money. He required owners to place $750,000 in escrow to cover all operating expenses. Personal backgrounds of any potential owner were investigated. He needed two or three months to restructure the league for next season. If he failed, he said he would have no part of another season like the first one.

Hemmeter instituted a new financial formula for paying players. Most players were guaranteed a contract that promised each player, for each game, a percentage of his team's gross revenue or a guaranteed amount, whichever was higher. The percentage for each player varied, depending on his negotiating ability, but the average was 1% of revenue or $500. For example, let's say a game had 12,000 fans at $7.50 a ticket. The $90,000 was split 60–40. The home team got $54,000, the visitor, $36,000. One percent of the $54,000 was $540. The player would get $540; but the opposing team player would get $500, the minimum, rather than the $360. Some players, however, had contracts originally signed. For example, a quarterback made $220,000 a year. His life style was a marked contrast to the 1% player.

In addition, a bankruptcy petition was filed for the first season's version of the WFL. It stated in part that the League "agrees to pay a sum equal to one-half percent of the net revenues received by its members presently located in Southern California, Memphis, Hawaii, and Philadelphia, and one and a half percent of the net revenues received by all members" in order to meet the creditors' payments. The first season of the WFL was renamed the Football Creditors Payment Plan, Inc. From this group, the "new" WFL purchased for $10,000 the name, initials, service mark, and goodwill of the WFL and incorporated as the New League, Inc., doing business as the WFL.

Under the New Plan, the second season's WFL was not legally responsible for the first season's WFL's debts. But the New League wanted to make good on the first season's debts. To pay them, the New League proposed an initial payment of $200,000 to the Payment Plan with the remaining $6 to $8 million in debts to come from the 1½% payments of gross revenues. Priorities would be given to back wages, and then to governmental taxes, and then to general creditors. The WFL's bankruptcy petition did not include debts of individual teams, which were estimated at $20 million.

Second Season of the WFL Opened Under the Hemmeter Plan

Ten teams started the second season. A new marketing plan was instituted, using better promotion techniques, and the rules differentiated a little more. The financially strong teams—Memphis, Birmingham, Philadelphia, and Southern California—were accompanied by San Antonio, Hawaii, Jacksonville, Shreveport, Virginia, and Portland. There was no television contract, amounting to $1.2 million last year, compared to the $50–60 million contract of the NFL. Chris stated that in the NFL paid attendance was about 60% of total revues. But in the WFL, paid attendance was 100%. It had no TV package, no marketing contract, and had to depend solely on big gates.

The big gates did not materialize. Chris called a meeting of the owners in October of the second season. He felt that the WFL had three choices: disband, eliminate weak teams and continue, or prop up weak teams and continue. After a 15-hour meeting, Chris made a statement to the press that he would not entertain any questions about the future of the League because they implied that the WFL was weak. Furthermore, no more questions about the financial condition of the League because these were internal matters.

A new marketing plan evolved to help prop up the dropping weekly attendance. Chris was very disappointed that the WFL had been unable to penetrate the market. Revenues were far less than anticipated. However, the League was meeting its current financial obligations.

John Bassett was quoted as saying, "You're damned right it's critical. I can't say that anything will happen. I don't have any grand design."

Chris Hemmeter wondered what to do.

Case 4-2 THE BILL VEECK STORY

The following script appeared on TV on January 11, 1976, for the NBC Nightly News. It is reproduced as it was given by Bob Jamison.

O'Hare Arrival	1. OPENS WITH SOF, COMBO PLAYS "HAPPY DAYS ARE HERE AGAIN" 2. VOICE OVER: For Bill Veeck, it's just what the song says, "Happy days are here again," because he is back in baseball . . . his first and deepest love.
Greeting fans	His return to Chicago, after a 15-year absence was triumphant. He was again owner of the White Sox and the team's fans . . . who are also Veeck's fans . . . believe that will mean happy days for them, too. Veeck, who is 61, says his return to baseball is like a politician's last hurrah. It is important to him, he says, because he wants to prove that he can still do it.
Veeck walking	He is not slowed by his peg leg . . . the result of a World War Two wound while he was a marine in the South Pacific. His hearing aid enables him to hear all that he wants to hear . . . his thick glasses to see what he needs to see. With a laugh, he asks, "What's an old man who can't walk, hear, or see want to run a ball club for?" It is because baseball is in his blood.
Shot of Veeck as child	As a boy, Veeck sold peanuts at Wrigley Field where his father was general manager of the Cubs.
Shot of Veeck with fans	Veeck says he learned a lot from his father, but that he learned from the fans, as well. He enjoys mingling with them during the game . . . and believes, after all, that's who baseball is played for.
Cleveland Stadium	His first chance to try and please major league fans was in 1946, when he bought the Cleveland Indians.
Victory celebration	Two years later, they won the American League pennant . . . and the World Series.
Various shots of fans	His promotional ideas, often grating to the baseball establishment, worked. In

1948, Cleveland drew 2.6 million fans to its games in Municipal Stadium. It was an American League record . . . one that still stands, 27 years later.

Veeck in stands

Veeck believed in having special days to give fans bats, balls, caps, hats and jackets. One time his door prizes were greased pigs.

His ideas, then frowned upon by the other owners, are commonplace in baseball today:

Veeck on camera

3. SOF, VEECK:

"I really can't say that I feel I have made any great contributions. I think that maybe the only thing that I can take particular personal pride in is the fact that I wasn't formed into the mold of conformation. And that at least I tried to entertain fans along with giving them a good ball game."

Veeck at desk

4. MORE VOICE OVER:

Veeck with babies

Veeck bought the St. Louis Browns in 1951. The Browns were so awful that for the future, Veeck signed babies to contracts. That way, he said, he'd have first crack at them when they became old enough to play.

Shot of midget

But the stunt that became his most famous was the secret signing of midget Eddie Gaedal and then putting him into the Browns' lineup as a pinch hitter. He was three feet, seven inches, in his spikes, and Veeck said his strike zone was an inch and half in a crouch. Gaedal got a walk on four pitches.

Veeck got criticism from baseball purists who said he was making a travesty of the game. The league outlawed midgets.

Veeck in Sox jacket

In 1959, Veeck bought the Chicago White Sox, . . . declared opening day an illegal holiday, complete with certificates, and preceded the game with a parade. That team went on to win the American League pennant legally.

Walkers with sign
Team on field
Helicopter landing

During his two and one-half year ownership of the Sox, Veeck didn't change his way of promoting the team. He flew in Martians to capture his short to second double-play combination.

Martians
Explosion and zoom to board

But the most explosive idea he had in Chicago was his scoreboard.

Exploding scoreboard

5. SOF, SCOREBOARD:

6. MORE VOICE OVER:

Shot toward plate

It did that when White Sox players hit a home run. Opposing teams got so mad that one player threw a ball at it . . . some teams even wanted it outlawed.

Scoreboard

7. SOF, VEECK:

Veeck on camera

"Oh, yes. That again was making a travesty of the game and it gave an advantage to the home team which, of course, it was meant to do. Why should we help the visitors. That's a funny kind of sportsmanship. I've never been accused of being a sportsman. I believe you should adhere exactly to the rules. Also, you should also test their elasticity from time to time."

Film of Veeck in office

8. MORE VOICE OVER:

In 1961, Veeck's love affair with baseball was interrupted. Doctors thought he had a brain tumor and told him to sell the White Sox. He sold the team but tests later showed he didn't have a tumor at all. (He eventually recovered from his illness, but it took years.)

Walks in to home

His forced retirement took him to Easton, Maryland. Doctors advised him to live in an area that had a seasonal change but was remote enough to discourage visitors.

Veeck walking

The 17 acres of wooded land with a hundred-year-old home was perfect for his recuperation.

9. SOF, VEECK:

Veeck walking around property

"I fooled around with a greenhouse. I like to grow flowers and propagate plants a little bit. I had a couple of years in which I worked with driftwood. I think that wood is beautiful and the youngsters would pick up the pieces that washed up on the shore and I would play with them and fool with them and see imaginary things in them and ultimately sell them."

10. MORE VOICE OVER:

Veeck in home

During his retirement, Veeck, who smokes five packs of cigarettes a day, wrote three books, a syndicated column, devoured hundreds of books, collaborated on a teevee talk show with his wife, Mary Frances, gave a lot of speeches . . . but perhaps most important to Veeck, he spent time with his children, the youngest 13.

Flashback to children

11. SOF, VEECK:

Children

"In our family, we have a great deal of mutual respect and liking for each other and I think it comes from the opportunity to spend a lot of time and not to come home at six o'clock and say, 'Hello, and sorry I have to go out to dinner.' "

12. MORE VOICE OVER:

Veeck at table

He has three other children by a previous marriage. There hadn't been much time for baseball and children. And, said Veeck, he enjoyed being busy.

Veeck at card file

But always, there were thoughts of baseball promoting. Efforts to buy the Washington Senators failed. But finally, the major league owners agreed that, yes, Bill Veeck could come back to baseball.

More card file

The other owners might not like the news, but Bill Veeck says he has maintained a card catalog, with 1500 ideas, which he hopes to use with the White Sox, ideas of how to make baseball more entertaining . . . more fun. Because, Veeck says, that's what baseball should be:

Veeck walking along road

13. "Once in a while, I believe, you have to illustrate that it is entertainment, that it is fun and isn't grim and serious. It's a game."

14. MORE VOICE OVER:

Bill Veeck is back in baseball . . . at a time when professional sports in the United States is on a decline, economically . . . at a time when baseball may need Bill Veeck.

QUESTIONS:

1. What innovations is Bill Veeck noted for?
2. Discuss personal characteristics that show that Veeck is an innovator.
3. What does Veeck consider baseball to be for?

FOOTNOTES

[1] Quotes were taken from an Associated Press interview by Will Grimsley with Lamar Hunt and reported in various newspapers throughout the U.S.

[2] *Ibid.*

Part III

Producing Successful Athletic Programs

5

PRODUCING ATHLETIC PROGRAMS

The coach is the executive in charge of producing athletic teams necessary to accomplish the athletic program objectives. A coach, however, also has certain program objectives which he/she wishes to accomplish. The most common objectives of coaching are to improve the win-loss record, to develop athletes, to improve the quality of athletics, to reduce athletic costs, to improve coaching methods and processes, and to help to accomplish other program objectives.

STRATEGIES TO IMPROVE THE WIN-LOSS RECORD

Most winning coaches have learned, by trial and error, the strategies necessary to produce a winning team. Their wisdom can be passed on to others.

The first strategy is to have quality athletes. The professional teams draft and trade players and purchase player contracts. Colleges must recruit quality athletes. Youngsters whose skills—strength, speed, agility—are recognized in physical education classes will develop into quality athletes for high school teams. The best players are easily distinguishable. Some players need coaching, but are still easily developed. Those with little aptitude in athletics are difficult to develop; they will find their place with other dependable but not outstanding athletes. Determination can make up for a lack of aptitude.

The second strategy is to have quality coaches. Good coaches with skill and experience are highly sought after, especially if their win-loss records are above average and they have been coaching for a long time. Most quality coaches spend twelve months a year coaching. During a season they coach all day, seven days a week, sacrificing time they would normally spend with their families. One becomes a quality coach through hard work. Several seasons will pass before an outstanding coach is recognized.

A winning team must have a sufficient number of athletes available for athletic events. If the population of athletes is large, the chances of winning are greater. If a team must rely on only one athlete in each position, the team will not win if a key player is injured or tired. Maintaining adequate reserve strength is a strategy fundamental to a winning team.

Hiring a number of coaches so each can work on a specialized aspect of the sport will help to produce a winning team. Efficiency will be increased; offensive and defensive coaching staffs could be developed as teams are created. To increase the number of coaches is one strategy that could produce a winning team.

Another strategy is to create a physical conditioning program that will keep the team durable both off and during season. Good practice habits, repeating drills, and recruiting durable players are tactics to develop team durability. The hard physical conditioning takes place before scrimmages begin. During the playing season, scrimmages are not too severe, and they taper off as the season progresses. Teams generally grow stale during a season. Consequently a Go-Go team may play occasionally to give the regulars a chance to rest. This helps to boost the morale of the Go-Go team as well. To increase their durability, team members are encouraged to follow a balanced diet that includes breakfast.

Winning teams must be adaptable. Winning teams adapt to their players' talents and vice versa. Drills are used to adapt to competitors' strengths and weaknesses. Players are taught to adapt to various situations all the time. As a result it takes time for players to develop their learning curves. Another tactic is for players to be cross-trained to fill in where needed.

Members of a team must be dependable. Players who do not show do not play. Players late for practice will be penalized. Disciplinary action must be taken for any laxity. Another tactic is to let players group together to form their own teams. The members of each team must keep track of each other. Therefore, most players will not select undependable peers. Through constant practice, team members become more dependable.

Team balance is another winning strategy. There must be balance between defense and offense. There must be balance within the offense as well as within the defense. If team balance cannot exist, most winning coaches would prefer team defensive strength. If team balance does not exist, the other team will attack the weakness.

In order to win, a team must be quick. Weights, running, and agility drills help to develop quickness. Speed and quickness work together, but quickness is more important for winning.

An athletic team should be unique. A team should not use gimmicks. Rather, the team should develop its uniqueness over time. A *difference* makes a difference—in player talent, coaching, recruiting, or style of play—and usually, successful teams develop a unique character.

A team should be an innovator. Team innovation is another winning strategy. A team should study, analyze abilities, and develop innovative schemes if winning is its goal. New procedures develop from creative thinking, experimentation, and by accident.

Athletic teams should try a variety of different line ups, multiple offensive and defensive schemes, flexible practice sessions, and a number of team members in various positions. The reason for variety is to prevent competitors from capitalizing on the team's standard pattern.

All teams should practice safety measures. Unsafe practices cause accidents and injuries that threaten a team's chance of winning. If a player holding a key position is injured, the team becomes ineffective. In high school it might be wise to invite parents to a scrimmage and explain the safety practices and methods of play. Buying of safe equipment makes sense. Having a team doctor available is a precautionary measure. A trainer with experience in first aid is necessary.

Games should be scheduled strategically. Successful coaches know that a team will not achieve peak performance at every game. A tight schedule increases the possibility of injury. Therefore a "breather" game placed in the middle of a schedule is a wise tactic. It is better to start a season with games that the team might win. If a team wins, good morale and team spirit will result.

It is a useful strategy for teams to be well organized. Coaching handbooks should outline procedures as well as the function of each team member. There should be no confusion about anyone's responsibilities on game nights. Players and coaches should review game films to determine specific actions for each position. If older, experienced coaches are in charge, it is often a sign of a well-organized team.

Team leadership is another strategy to be followed. Team leaders should be elected and identified within the informal group structure. Team leaders should set team goals. The leaders chosen should have positive feelings toward the team.

Team dedication and pride are fundamental to winning. One develops these feelings by making sacrifices for the team. Emulation of coaches is another tactic to develop dedication and pride. Cases of trophies and pictures may be used.

Successful teams always spend money to improve their practice facilities. Cleanliness in practice areas, locker rooms, and showers creates conditions necessary for safety, pride, and good morale.

Top-notch equipment is fundamental to a winning team. Physical conditioning programs demand first-class equipment. Good team morale depends upon it.

First-class accommodations at home and away uplift team spirit. It is depressing to use third- and fourth-class hotels, eat poor meals, and use tourist-class transportation. Going first class is a symbol of success.

The various strategies and tactics to develop a winning team may be evaluated using the chart below.

Coaching Objective: To Improve the Win-Loss Record

Strategies and Tactics	Strength	Weakness
1. Quality Athletes		
1.1 Identifying them		
1.2 Finding them		
1.3 Having blue chippers		
1.4 Players with extraordinary determination		
1.5 Others		
2. Quality Coaches		
2.1 Having quality coaches		
2.2 Working long and hard hours		
2.3 Others		
3. Sufficient Quantity of Athletes		
3.1 Two-man depth for each position		
3.2 Others		
4. Sufficient Quantity of Coaches		
4.1 Specialized coaches		
4.2 Others		
5. Team Durability		
5.1 Agility drills		
5.2 Strength drills		
5.3 Balanced diets		
5.4 Off-season conditioning		
5.5 Go-Go team		
6. Team Adaptability		
6.1 Build around players' strength		
6.2 Cross-training		
6.3 Practice against competitors' strengths		
7. Team Dependability		
7.1 Strong discipline		
7.2 Peer selection		
8. Team Balance		
8.1 Defensive and offensive		
8.2 On defense		
8.3 On offense		
9. Team Quickness		
9.1 Weights		
9.2 Running		
9.3 Agility drills		
10. Team Uniqueness		
10.1 What is it?		
11. Team Innovation		
11.1 What is it?		
12. Team Variety		
12.1 Multiple schemes		
13. Team Safety		
13.1 Safe equipment		

Strategies and Tactics	Strength	Weakness
13.2 Team doctor		
13.3 Trainer		
14. Scheduling		
14.1 Several home games		
14.2 Some "easy" teams		
15. Well-organized Team		
15.1 Coaches' handbooks		
15.2 Players' handbooks		
15.3 Specific responsibilities		
15.4 Experienced coaches		
15.5 Delegated authority		
15.6 Review of game films		
17. Clean Practice Environment		
17.1 Clean practice area		
17.2 Clean locker rooms		
17.3 First-class facilities		
18. Top-notch Equipment		
18.1 High quality		
18.2 New equipment		
19. First-class Accommodations		
19.1 First-class lodging		
19.2 First-class meals		
19.3 First-class travel		
Overall Evaluation:		

STRATEGIES TO DEVELOP BENEFITS FOR ATHLETES

In some high school and college programs, the major objective is to benefit the athlete-student. Winning is a by-product of the strategies that produce benefits for athletes, or vice versa, depending on the philosophy of the coaches.

A healthy body is a result of physical training, weight drills, agility drills, running, and other types of physical conditioning. A healthy, balanced diet, and superior medical attention also contribute to a healthy body.

Constant repetition of the skills involved in athletics develops the physical skills and stamina useful in daily life.

Through participation in sports, an athlete becomes self-disciplined. Athletic skills, such as getting off on the snap count, running specific pass routes, and getting the timing down, demand constant discipline imposed from the outside. This develops into the self-discipline and dependability necessary for a successful life.

Athletics also promotes moral values. Athletes must respect others and deal with them fairly, be good sports, and work hard. They develop this set of values from following game rules, losing games, emulating the coach, and joining the Fellowship of Christian Athletes, for example.

Athletes grow emotionally as they respond to the various pressures of an

Coaching Objective: To Develop Benefits for Athletes

Benefits for Athletes	**Strength**	**Weakness**
1. Healthy body		
2. Physical skills and stamina		
3. Discipline		
4. Moral values		
5. Emotional maturity		
6. Social competence		
7. Competitiveness		
8. Cooperation		
9. Goal achievement		
10. Others		
Overall Evaluation:		

athletic program. Athletes must keep their cool during stress situations; they must learn from their mistakes. From these experiences, athletes mature emotionally.

Through sports programs, athletes gain social competence. Working, living, and playing together—giving and taking orders—helps to socialize individuals. Those who participate in athletic programs are taught to use proper manners and maintain a proper appearance.

Athletics inspires competitiveness. Athletes develop the aggressiveness necessary to succeed in today's competitive world.

Through team sports, athletes learn to cooperate. Participants learn to work with others while carrying out individual responsibility. Coaches are more likely to praise teamwork than to single out individuals, particularly when speaking to the press.

Through sports, athletes learn to set personal goals. Achieving these goals on the athletic field is similar to accomplishing objectives throughout life.

A coach must recognize how athletics benefits athletes; he/she should then develop strategies to accomplish the objective of improving the athlete—emotionally and physically—through sports. The coach can determine whether his/her program benefits athletes from the chart above.

STRATEGIES TO IMPROVE THE ENTERTAINMENT VALUE OF ATHLETICS

Those involved in a successful coaching program might hope to improve the entertainment value of athletics. Various strategies can be employed to achieve this objective.

One strategy is to develop new ideas and techniques to make athletic events more appealing. It is necessary to determine how receptive the fans are toward each innovation. In football, a number of alterations have made the sport more entertaining. These include the system of two points after touchdown, the two-platoon system, spring practices, the use of astroturf, and an interracial mix of players. In basketball there have been innovations such as the 30-second clock, colored balls, pom-pom girls, and towel girls. In baseball, flashing scoreboards, the designated hitter rule, bat girls, helmets, aluminum bats, and new colored uniforms have been tried. The elimination of long sets in tennis, so the game will not seem monotonous, has been a recent innovation. In golf, the aluminum and graphite clubs; in pole vaulting, the fiber glass pole; in bowling, the automatic pinsetters have been developed to increase the entertainment value of athletics.

Should an athletic team become a leader or a follower in research and development? A leader is one who practices an offensive policy in developing innovations. A follower practices a defensive policy; he tries to improve on an already successful innovation.

Usually the professionals develop a new practice by an offensive R & D policy. It is then copied by colleges and high schools that practice a defensive policy. The highly competitive professionals are forced to develop new techniques and practices in order to survive. The pros are often—but not always—the leaders. A benefit of the free enterprise system, R & D turns new ideas into accepted practices, improving products and services for the customer.

Coaching Objective: To Improve the Entertainment Value of Athletics

Strategies	Strength	Weakness
1. Research and development		
1.1 For the sport itself		
1.2 For fan entertainment		
2. Offensive R & D policy		
3. Defensive R & D policy		
Overall evaluation:		

STRATEGIES TO REDUCE THE COST OF ATHLETICS

Any good coach knows that it is expensive to build a good team, and expenses cut into an athletic program's profits. Often coaches feel that it takes money to make money. However, there are some strategies to reduce the cost of athletics.

The coach can control the flow of money if he helps to prepare the expense budget. In this case, the coach must see that the budget is followed.

Since he is held accountable, it is difficult for the coach to spend money without justification.

Money may be saved by centralized purchasing of equipment and supplies. There are discounts when quantity purchases are made and paid for with cash, thus reducing the costs of equipment and supplies. Also the actual purchasing costs of submitting orders, checking in orders, and filing can be reduced by a centralized purchasing strategy.

Efficient use of facilities is another strategy to reduce costs. If a basketball court can be used twice a week rather than once a week, the overhead costs per game will be reduced. If a football stadium has revenue coming in each time it is used, the overhead costs of maintaining the stadium can be reduced on a per game basis.

A coach can reduce the travel budget by using less expensive modes of transportation, lower priced lodging, more economical meals, reduced tips, and fewer telephone calls.

If necessary, there may be other ways to reduce expenses. The chief reductions are in recruiting costs, training table costs, travel costs, maintenance costs, and purchasing costs.

In summary, the various strategies to reduce the cost of athletics may be evaluated.

Coaching Objective: To Reduce the Costs of Athletics

Strategies	**Strength**	**Weakness**
1. Use of an expense budget		
2. Centralized purchasing		
3. Efficient use of facilities		
4. Reduction in travel costs		
5. Others		
Overall Evaluation:		

STRATEGIES TO IMPROVE COACHING METHODS AND PROCESSES

Since competition is usually keen among athletic organizations, most successful coaches look for ways to improve their coaching techniques. Development of new coaching methods is usually accomplished by several strategies familiar to most coaches. Some coaches attend coaching clinics held by high schools and colleges; these clinics usually feature outstanding coaches who discuss their new coaching techniques. Another strategy is to read the articles, books, monographs, and newspapers that suggest new coaching techniques. Another is to experiment with new techniques. All of these methods will improve coaching methods and process.

Coaching Objective: To Improve Coaching Methods

Strategies	Strength	Weakness
1. Attending coaching clinics		
2. Reading extensively		
3. Experimentation		
4. Others		
Overall Evaluation:		

CHAPTER SUMMARY

Chapter Five considers the objectives and strategies of coaching. An important objective is to improve the team's win-loss record. Discussed were strategies such as securing a number of quality athletes and coaches; working to produce the characteristics of a winning team: durability, adaptability, dependability, balance, quickness, uniqueness, variety, organization, and motivation; playing in safe, well-equipped facilities.

Coaches also try to help athletes develop. Strategies include developing a healthy body, physical skills, and stamina in the athlete; encouraging self-discipline, moral, and emotional growth; increasing social competence, competitiveness, and cooperation; helping athletes to define their goals and achieve them.

Improving the entertainment value of athletics is a coaching objective. The major strategy discussed was the research and development (R & D) strategy. The choice between an offensive or defensive R & D strategy was considered.

Another objective is to reduce the cost of an athletic program. This can be accomplished by a strict expense budget, centralized purchasing, efficient use of facilities, or reduction in travel costs.

The final strategy considered is to improve coaching methods by attending coaching clinics, reading extensively, and experimenting with new techniques.

Case 5-1 BELLEVUE HIGH*

Jerry Vanwaart was assistant football coach at the suburban Bellevue High School, located near Omaha, Nebraska. He was proud of his football team. During the past eleven years in the Metro Conference, the varsity

* This case was prepared by Robert D. Hay, University of Arkansas, as a basis for classroom discussion. It is not intended to present a correct or incorrect handling of an administrative situation.

Bellevue Chieftans had won 80 football games, lost 19, and tied 3. As Jerry reviewed those years, he thought about the two other teams that contributed to a winning tradition. The sophomore teams had a 74-6-4 record and the junior varsity had a 64-14-2 record. Combined, the three Bellevue teams compiled a 218-39-9 win-loss-tie record. This was a respectable record for a high school that had grown from 1000 to 2400 students in eleven years. Bellevue was indeed proud of its 82% win record.

Bellevue High's teams had been state champs for three out of eleven years. Their football players were in great demand by college teams; each year, about ten players received football scholarships. The football program always made a profit, totally supporting other Bellevue sports (including basketball and 17 different sports for boys and girls).

Jerry was one of six coaches, under Bill James, the head coach. The turnover of coaches was minimal; in the past five years, perhaps two had left to improve their salary and position. A spirit of closeness and camaraderie existed among the seven coaches as they welded together the strategies necessary to become one of the top football high schools in the state of Nebraska and a supplier of many football players to a Big Eight power, the University of Nebraska.

The quality of their players was of paramount importance. Jerry stated, "We start with youngsters and develop their speed, agility, and strength as we spot them during practice, especially on the sophomore team. Our philosophy is built on the theory that the cream of the players will rise to the top during their sophomore, junior, and senior years, playing those three levels of football. About 80 to 100 sophomores will come out for football. Our strength is in those numbers; with those numbers will come blue chippers. Including the head coach, we need seven coaches, usually two for the sophomore team, and four for the juniors and varsity who usually practice together. We do specialize, but we all have to be generalists in both offense and defense. If we had an extra coach, we could put out two teams of sophomores," he mused to himself.

"The coaches spend lots of time with students and other coaches. Football is a twelve-month job, even though we get paid for only nine months. During the season we work seven days a week. Our wives have to understand this. We become very close to each other as coaches and as human beings," Jerry thought.

Bellevue High has a physical conditioning program, both off-season and during season. "The first of August to the sixteenth, we have formal conditioning. But we could scrimmage on the first day of practice because of our off-season conditioning program of weights, running, and drills. We're ready and we're unique in this respect," he recalled.

"We build our team around our players' strengths. Of course, we have a system, but it is secondary to the strategy of adaptability to our players. We never have to worry about dependability. It's built in. If a player doesn't show, he doesn't play. We also find out about player dependability by our method of letting two different team members select ten other members. We do this constantly. The same names keep coming up. Acceptability is important to team members and they will not select players who are not dependable. This idea came from a football clinic where spring games are played at colleges.

"Team balance is important. We stress both offense and defense, and in the offense we push both running and passing. If we cannot pass, we concentrate on running. If you've got the ball, the other team cannot score very well. And when you pass, three things can happen and two of them are bad. To us defense is very important. Our strength generally has been our offensive line, averaging 220 pounds.

"Quickness is very important. We develop it by weights, running, and agility drills. We repeat the 'forty' times, using the challenge of improved times.

"The *wear you down* philosophy is taught in practice. I guess we are unique in this regard because we keep running the same thing at the opponent until we wear him down and he changes his defense; and then, pop, we try something different, like a pass or option play.

"We innovate from week to week, depending on our opponent. We try to take advantage of our opponent weaknesses, depending on what we spot in films and scouting reports.

"We'll use a little variety, especially changing practices to give more variety. We'll also use a variety of players.

"Our players' parents are invited to a 'soap' scrimmage before the season starts. We explain to them our methods of safety, about helmets, equipment, doctors, trainers, and the like. Admission to the soap scrimmage is two bars of soap, supplying us with enough for the whole season.

"I guess we are best in team organization. Our coaches' handbook is as heavy as our players' handbook. I have certain responsibilities that I perform, and I don't worry about what the other coaches do because they know their duties and perform them. We know who does what on game nights, on Saturdays, and the like. All of our coaches are old timers and they know what they're doing!"

Jerry considered other strategies developed by Bellevue. He made sure that the practice environment was always clean. He had lines laid before practice to give the players some perspective of the space measured by five yards.

He remembered that top-notch equipment was always purchased on a bid basis. Cheap equipment was often replaced. Good equipment lasted and could be passed down from the varsity to the juniors and sophomores.

"Team leadership was elected by the team members. We have to rely on team leaders to help us motivate our players. These leaders help to influence our other players with the attitudes we want—team dedication and team pride. We want players to set immediate and long-term goals and then accomplish them.

"We always try to end our practices on a positive note. Of course, we chew out players on the practice field. We assistant coaches do most of that—not our head coach."

As Jerry recalled the various team strategies that had made Bellevue successful, he could not help wondering about next year. The administrative staff had recommended that two high schools be created in Bellevue—East High and West High. Their rationale was that 1200 students made a reasonably sized high school, at least from an administrative point of view.

A community election was held in an off-year for the approval of a bond issue to finance the proposed split. The local citizens voted to create two high schools.

Various reasons were given to justify building a new school. Major considerations were the large size of the existing school and its extended class schedule—classes were held daily from 7:15 A.M. to 5:00 P.M. The growth of the community was also cited—the flight of people from urban Omaha to suburban Bellevue. All of these reasons were sufficient for the voters to approve the bond issue.

Jerry wondered how the creation of a new school would affect him and the athletic program.

Case 5-2 KANSAS STATE BASKETBALL

"I was very fortunate to play for such a great 'basketball school' as Kansas State. Several times I told myself that I could not wait to get away from that place because I worked so long and hard to play. However, now I vividly remember only the pleasant experiences," stated Bob Noland, reflecting on his former days as college basketball player at Kansas State.

"During my stay there we won an average of twenty games a season. Our overall record was 60 wins and 30 losses, participating in three postseason tournaments. We were even ranked fourteenth in the country one year. How did we do it?"

Jack Hartman was the basketball coach at Kansas State. "We had an excellent head coach as well as quality assistant coaches. They worked long and hard hours, taking a personal interest in us as players as well as persons. I found that we players worked harder when the head coach was at the practice sessions, which he was most of the time.

"We had plenty of quality athletes. K-State could identify them in high school ranks and junior colleges. The school found them and recruited some blue chippers, but most of them were players with extraordinary determination to win. We played together as a team on the court as well as off the court. We had a team unity. Our depth chart usually had three players per position. One reason for our excellent practices was that we had at least 40 walk-ons try out for the team each year.

"We stressed team durability by means of agility drills and strength drills. We had plenty of rest and sleep. Our diet was balanced and excellent. Of course, we had off-season conditioning. We were strong and durable. Just ask our opponents!

"Our team could adapt to most situations. We were almost always ready to play because we worked hard in practice as well as in our games. Our team was built around Coach Hartman's system, but he also built our team around individual strengths of our players. Each player tried to learn two positions so that we could adapt, if necessary. Of course, we would try to practice against our competitors' strengths before each game, but our major strength was that we were ready to play.

"We had strong discipline imposed by the coach and by ourselves. We players trusted each other on and off the court. We became friends. We developed a team spirit which always pays off.

"Our teams had balance, overall, and both offense and defense. We particularly had a strong defensive team, which is a trademark of Coach Hartman's teams.

"We built a certain degree of quickness into our team by use of weights, running, agility drills, reaction drills—all of which were designed to give us quickness and speed.

"I suspect that K-State teams had a certain uniqueness in them that others did not have. We had a winning tradition, fan support, good coaching, and Ahearn Fieldhouse, which was often called our sixth man.

"During my stay we innovated a new offense to 'go to' our guards. Such an innovation complemented our other offensive and defensive play.

"We had a variety of schemes that we knew by heart. But among our players we found each one to be unique and tried to capitalize on those multiple schemes made possible by a player's skill.

"Team safety was made possible by the use of safe equipment and good facilities. We had a team doctor and good trainers.

"We tried to schedule several home games to take advantage of Ahearn Fieldhouse. But we also tried to schedule some tough teams as well as a couple of weaker teams.

"Organization was fundamental. There were coaches' handbooks but no players' handbooks. You had to know it in your head. Coach Hartman had long tenure so things were very well organized. We reviewed game films and we would even film our practice sessions to assess the team. We were well organized.

"Spirited practices helped to get us motivated. The coaches used various tactics to motivate us. We players used positive reinforcement on each other. We elected our team leaders; we tried to emulate our coaches; we were proud seeing all the trophies of former teams.

"We had excellent facilities—cleanliness prevailed in the practice area, in locker rooms, everywhere. We used only top-notch equipment, especially good shoes. We travelled in first-class accommodations.

"What else does it take to produce a winning basketball team? I don't know, but I do know that our fans enjoyed our basketball games, and so did I."

Case 5-3 THE WINNING TRADITION OF THE MINNESOTA VIKINGS

The Minnesota Vikings have a winning tradition. In 1976, they established themselves as a winner, maintaining a record of 84–28 since 1968 when Bud Grant took over as head coach. They had an overall record of 116–87–7 since 1961 when they first entered the NFL. They had won one NFL championship, two NFC championships, and seven central division championships in eight years.

Jim Lindsey was a former captain of the special team for the Vikings. During his eight-year tenure as running back, he considered why the Vikings had produced winning teams during Bud Grant's stewardship.

"In the first place, we had quality players. We had a system of identifying them and we did find them. Our strength was that most of our players considered intelligence just as important as running fast.

"We also had quality coaching. If there was any one factor that accounted for our success, it was Bud Grant, the head coach. He and the other coaches worked long and hard hours. That pays off in winning.

"We had a sufficient quantity of players—usually a two-man depth for each position. We had to have depth in case of injury or other reasons for not being able to play. Of course, we had our 'taxi' squad available if we needed them.

"We also had a sufficient quantity of coaches—a head coach, three offensive coaches (line, backs, receivers) and three defensive coaches (line, linebackers, and secondary).

"Our team was durable. We used agility drills and strength drills. We emphasized eating balanced diets and even had an off-season conditioning plan.

"We practiced specialization to the nth degree. We did not have cross training, but we did use cross training with our special utility players. We built our team around the players' strengths. Of course, we practiced against our competitors' strengths each week.

"Team dependability? Man, we had very strong discipline, and we stressed consistency! These two factors allowed our team to become dependable.

"I sometimes wondered about our team balance. We had a good defensive and offensive balance. We were strong defensively, but sometimes we lacked offensive strength. Our 'on the field' strategy was a strong point of our team.

"Team quickness was stressed by our constant running and agility drills. However, we did not stress weights.

"We had some degree of team uniqueness, and that was the discipline imposed by Bud Grant that I suspect other teams lacked.

"But Grant also built an innovation in the Vikings from the previously coached teams. He developed a consistency in our team that we never had. We were not an 'up and down' team. He innovated schemes that made us consistent as opposed to inconsistency of other teams.

"We did not have a multiplicity of schemes. We kept it simple. Variety on our team was not one of our strengths.

"We had safe equipment, a team doctor, and a trainer. Team safety was always stressed.

"We had very little control over our team schedule. The year-to-year schedule was very unpredictable. I'm not sure that our schedule was as tough as other teams' in the other conference, but who knows?

"We were a well-organized team. Our front office was well organized as well. Everyone knew his exact assignments. We had coaches' handbooks and players' handbooks. Our coaching staff had long tenure. They were delegated authority, accountability, and responsibility to win; and they did! We reviewed game films and practiced according to a game plan.

"Our team was well motivated and we had pride. Our players emulated the coaches, we elected team leaders, we had a positive working atmosphere, a dedicated staff, and team sacrifice. I'd say that Bud Grant's motivation of players was excellent.

"Our working conditions were excellent. We had a clean practice environment, clean locker rooms, and first-class facilities.

"Our equipment was top-notch. It was excellent and always maintained.

"When we travelled on the road, we always went first class. We stayed at the best lodging, ate the best food, and travelled in first-class accommodations.

"If you put all these factors together, I'd say that the Vikings have done a great job producing winning teams, year after year, and I am proud to have been a part of their success."

Case 5-4 SPORTSMANSHIP: AREAS OF RESPONSIBILITY

Statements of philosophy on good sportsmanship and outlines of the responsibilities of the various parties involved are not new; many have been prepared and distributed by any number of organizations during the past several years. A report developed by a committee some years ago at Ohio State University contains a basic presentation of the concern, an appropriate statement of the general fundamentals of good sportsmanship and an excellent outline of the specific responsibilities of the coach, the players, the students, the cheerleaders, the officials, the athletic director, and the chief school administrator. The report has been revised on two occasions, most recently in 1968 by Delbert Oberteuffer, Don R. Bethe and Joe D. Willis, also of Ohio State.[1]

Introduction

In our society the ideal of sportsmanship permeates virtually every aspect of our culture. This ethic of "fair play" can be seen in every facet of modern life—business, commerce, law, education—in all human interaction. It seems to be a code of expected behavior originating in sport which requires that its definition be explicit for the high ideal which it demands and implicit for the breadth and magnitude of its scope. Therefore sportsmanship is defined as that quality of responsible behavior characterized by a spirit of generosity and a genuine concern for an opponent.

Because the responsibility for the development of sportsmanship involves many persons, the contribution of educational athletics is of great importance. Within the framework of the school athletic program, the responsibility for good sportsmanship is vested in all of those who are in any way associated with the program. Coaches, players, administrators, officials, and spectators—each has a share of the responsibility.

In recent years the ideal of sportsmanship in schoolboy, community, and professional sport has been severely challenged by increasingly numerous examples of unsportsmanlike behavior. Incidents involving coaches, players, and spectators have occurred in ever-increasing numbers. The gravity of the situation has been pointed up by wide press, television, and magazine coverage. Writings in professional journals have discussed the seriousness of flagrant breaches of the code. It appears that many of the educational objectives of competitive athletics, including sportsmanship, are not being optimally met. These unfortunate examples of poor sportsmanship have done much to spoil this once great tradition.

What has led to the deterioration of values and the decline of morality in contemporary sports? Numerous explanations could be offered but probably the most plausible is simply that sports are reflecting the values of the larger, unsettled and heterogeneous society. Through the years there has been developed in this country a mania for success both social and monetary. Winning has become so important that frequently players and spectators care little of the manner in which victory is attained. There is, therefore, an immediate need to restore balance and proper perspective to educational athletics. The "ends justify the means" philosophy, a common example of misplaced values, has no place in the school athletic program. The continued obsession with winning is a flirtation with disaster.

The great questions with which we are now confronted are not can we, but will we accept the challenge of preserving the high moral and ethical qualities which are intrinsic to the ideals of sportsmanship; and will we educate sport-oriented individuals to revitalize the integrity of competitive athletics? The answers to these questions must of necessity be in the affirmative. For without the ethic of sportsmanship operating realistically in the control of player and spectator behavior, sport will not only lose its integrity as an educational instrument but may degenerate into a device actually subversive to the best interests of our schools and communities.

It has been suggested that sports competition may be one of the last bastions of decency in our society. With the decline in the influence of the home and the church, sports may be called upon to assume more of the responsibility for the teaching of basic humanistic values. To make such an important contribution to the development of the individual, positive programs must be initiated. The efficiency of these programs will be dependent upon a solid foundation which is well conceptualized and clearly defined. The behavior expected of a sportsman must be spelled out and to that end the following fundamentals, applicable to all competitive situations, are presented.

The Fundamentals of Sportsmanship

1. Show respect for the opponent at all times. The opponent should be treated as a guest, greeted cordially on arriving, given the best accommodations, and accorded the tolerance, honesty and generosity which all human beings deserve. Good sportsmanship is the Golden Rule in action.
2. Show respect for the officials. The officials should be recognized as impartial arbitrators who are trained to do their job and who can be expected to do it to the best of their ability. Good sportsmanship implies the willingness to accept and abide by the decisions of the officials.
3. Know, understand, and appreciate the rules of the contest. A familiarity with the current rules of the game and the recognition of their necessity for a fair contest is essential. Good sportsmanship suggests the importance of conforming to the spirit as well as the letter of the rules.
4. Maintain self-control at all times. A prerequisite of good sportsmanship requires one to understand his own bias or prejudice and the ability to prevent the desire to win from overcoming rational behavior. A proper perspective must be maintained if the potential educational values of athletic competition are to be realized. Good sportsmanship is concerned with the behavior of all involved in the game.
5. Recognize and appreciate skill in performance regardless of affiliation. Applause for an opponent's good performance is a demonstration of generosity and goodwill that should not be looked upon as treason. The ability to recognize quality in performance and the willingness to acknowledge it without regard to team membership is one of the most highly commendable gestures of good sportsmanship.

With the fundamentals of sportsmanship as the point of departure, specific responsibilities and expected modes of behavior can be defined.

The Responsibilities of the Coach

The coach bears the greatest burden of responsibility for sportsmanship. His influence upon the attitudes and behavior of the players, the student body, and the community are unequalled. In order for good sportsmanship to become a reality, it is essential that the coach subscribe to the values of sportsmanship and teach its principles through word and deed.

Specifically, it is recommended that the coach:

1. Always set a good example for others to follow.
2. Teach the values of honest effort in conforming to the spirit as well as the letter of the rules.
3. Instruct the players in their sportsmanship responsibilities.
4. Discipline those students who display unsportsmanlike behavior; if necessary, forfeit their privilege of representing the school.
5. Be a perfect host to opponents; treat them as guests.
6. At every opportunity remind the student body that the opposing team is their guest and that as host they should be polite and courteous.
7. Provide opportunities for social interaction among coaches and players of both teams before and after the contest.
8. Select only officials who have demonstrated the highest ethical standards.
9. Respect the officials' judgment and interpretation of the rules. Public protests can only lead to similar behavior by the players and spectators.
10. Publicly shake hands with the officials and opposing coach before and after the contest.

The Responsibilities of the Players

The responsibility of the players for sportsmanship is second in importance only to the coach. Because players are admired and respected, they exert a great deal of influence over the actions and behavior of the spectators.

Desirable for players would be to:

1. Treat opponents with the respect that is due them as guests and fellow human beings.
2. Shake hands with opponents and wish them good luck before the contest.
3. Exercise self-control at all times, accepting decisions and abiding by them.
4. Respect the officials' judgment and interpretations of the rules. Never argue or make gestures indicating a dislike for a decision.
5. Only the captain should communicate with the officials regarding the clarification of a ruling.
6. Accept both victory and defeat with pride and compassion, never being boastful or bitter.
7. Congratulate the opponents in a sincere manner following either victory or defeat.
8. Cooperate with the coach and fellow players in trying to promote good sportsmanship.

9. Welcome the opportunity to discuss the rules and strategies of the contest with parents and friends so they can better understand and appreciate the finer points of the game.
10. Accept seriously the responsibility and privilege of representing the school and community.

The Responsibilities of the Students

The students' frequent role as spectators and their tremendous enthusiasm for sports are indicative of their vital responsibility for good sportsmanship. Their habits and reactions determine the quality of sportsmanship which reflects upon the reputation of their school. It is recommended that students:

1. Know and demonstrate the fundamentals of sportsmanship.
2. Respect, cooperate, and respond enthusiastically to cheerleaders.
3. Censure fellow students whose behavior is unbecoming.
4. Respect the property of the school and the authority of school officials.
5. Show respect for an injured player when he is removed from the contest.
6. Do not applaud errors by opponents or penalties inflicted upon them.
7. Do not heckle, jeer, or distract members of the opposing team.
8. Never criticize the players or coaches for the loss of a game.
9. Respect the judgment and strategy of the coach. Refrain from being a second guesser.
10. Avoid profane language and obnoxious behavior which are antithetical to good sportsmanship .

The Responsibilities of the Cheerleaders

Since the cheerleaders are the chosen representatives of the student body they have an unusual opportunity and a significant responsibility for promoting good sportsmanship. Cheerleaders should be chosen who are respected by fellow students. The most aggressive and vocal individual does not necessarily make the best cheerleader. By setting a good example the cheerleaders can influence and help control the reactions of student spectators.

Cheerleaders should:

1. Establish standards of desirable behavior for the cheerleaders and pep club.
2. Select positive cheers which praise their own team without antagonizing their opponents.
3. Use discretion in selecting when to cheer. Give the opposing team equal opportunity to execute their cheers.
4. Give encouragement to injured players and recognition to outstanding performances for either team.

5. Serve as hosts to the visiting cheerleaders. Meet them upon arrival and if time permits introduce them to friends and show them the school. Visit at half-time.
6. Hold a series of well-planned pep meetings in which students are reminded that the reputation of the school depends largely upon the behavior of its students at athletic contests. It should be emphasized that no derogatory remarks or booing should be made at any time.
7. For desired spectator response cheers should be executed with precision and ease.
8. Develop a large repertoire of desirable and timely cheers which may be called upon at appropriate moments.
9. Always maintain enthusiasm and composure especially in trying circumstances, remembering your responsibilities for leadership.

The Responsibilities of the Officials

Competent officials are essential for a smoothly functioning and fair contest. They determine to a great extent the behavior of the spectators. A competent official will:

1. Place the welfare of the players above all other considerations.
2. Accept his position in an unassuming manner. Showboating and over-officiating are never acceptable.
3. Know the rules thoroughly and give intelligent interpretations to the players and coaches whenever necessary.
4. Maintain confidence and poise, controlling the game from start to finish. "Rabbit ears" detract from an official's efficiency.
5. Publicly shake hands with the coaches of both teams before the contest.
6. Work cooperatively with fellow officials, scorers, and timers for an efficient contest.
7. Withdraw from the playing area without delay at half-time and at the end of the contest.
8. Never attempt to "even-up" or compensate for a previous mistake.
9. Never exhibit emotions or argue with a player or coach when enforcing the rules.
10. Be swift and decisive when reacting to a violation and be explicit in communicating the nature of the foul.

The Responsibilities of the Athletic Director

Less visible than the coaching staff but nevertheless of great importance to the overall program of sportsmanship is the Athletic Director. The numerous details which are essential for a smoothly functioning educational contest require the efforts of an individual dedicated to the true purpose of school activities. The philosophy which this person holds is reflected in the policies and procedures which he initiates, the behavior of the coaches and players, and in the conduct of all athletic contests. This person must subscribe to and promote the ideal of sportsmanship.

A responsible athletic director will:

1. Secure competent officials who will be completely satisfactory to both teams. Provide adequate compensation to assure quality of officiating.
2. Provide sufficient faculty and police supervision for spectator control.
3. Provide opportunities for informing student and adult spectators of the rules, strategies, and penalties of various athletic contests.
4. Schedule only opponents who have similar standards and who are equal in ability.
5. Avoid scheduling opponents when rivalry has reached the point that unruly behavior has become an accepted matter of course.
6. Enlist the support of student leaders in the development of sportsmanship programs.
7. Work closely with the cheerleaders in the techniques of spectator management.
8. Secure competent public address announcers who promote the fundamentals of sportsmanship and who do not elicit undesirable spectator reactions.
9. Maintain a good relationship with the press; keep them well-informed of the activities and the objectives of the program.
10. Provide opportunities for pregame social interaction among the players and coaches of both teams.

The Responsibilities of the Administrator

The administrator must establish the importance of the fundamentals of good sportsmanship in the minds of the entire school family and all those who associate with any of the school's activities. The quality of sportsmanship displayed at athletic contests reflects the leadership provided by the administration.

A responsible administrator would:

1. Never allow any activity to supersede or interfere with the educational objectives of the school. Victory celebrations, game rallies, and unscheduled bursts of mass enthusiasm should not be permitted to interfere with the school program.
2. Establish definite eligibility policies and procedures and be sure that they are thoroughly understood.
3. Prevent outside influences from exerting undue pressure upon the athletic program.
4. Promote good relationships with civic organizations and acquaint them with their responsibilities for good sportsmanship.
5. Be sure the parents thoroughly understand what the school expects of its players.
6. Take an active role in the development of athletic policies.

7. Be sure that all students have a definite understanding of the kinds of behavior expected of them.
8. Support and encourage school programs designed to deepen an understanding of sportsmanship.
9. Recommend to the Board of Education the employment of athletic coaches who are concerned primarily with educational objectives and the well-being of the students.
10. Establish good rapport with press, radio, and television relative to their obligation for promoting good sportsmanship.

Communications

Press, radio, and television personnel have a considerable influence in molding public opinion and behavior concerning interscholastic athletics. Writers and commentators frequently have opportunities to point out favorable and unfavorable behavior and make it a topic of public discussion. The cooperation of these individuals could do a great deal to foster good sportsmanship in the community.

It is essential that representatives of the communication media:

1. Promote the ideals and fundamentals of good sportsmanship.
2. Report acts of sportsmanlike behavior without giving undue publicity to unsportsmanlike conduct.
3. Report the facts without demonstrating partiality to the other team.
4. Give recognition to the efforts of all who participate in the contest.
5. Refrain from riding or making a "goat" of a player who has had misfortune in the contest.
6. Know the rules and help communicate this knowledge to the public.
7. Sponsor sportsmanship awards for players and spectators.
8. Refrain from any criticism of game officials, including statements or implications of blame for nature of contest.

Conclusion

Far-reaching efforts are currently being made to improve the quality of sportsmanship in school athletic programs. Several state high school athletic associations have designated sportsmanship days. Schools are encouraged to give special emphasis to sportsmanship on these occasions. Athletic conferences have developed special sportsmanship rating systems for which schools compete. Many high schools in all parts of the country have developed codes which students themselves have authored. Other attempts to "sell" the ideal of good sportsmanship include assembly programs, clinics, essay contests, forensic topics, editorials in the school newspaper, rating forms, sportsmanship handbooks, and promotional programs sponsored by clubs and student councils.

In developing sportsmanship behavior, the most meaningful growth occurs when an individual experiences acts of good sportsmanship. To acquire such behavior patterns one must be exposed to numerous situations in which he can accumulate first-hand experiences. Probably one of the best methods of promoting sportsmanship is the "critical incident" technique. This technique involves the use of specific instances as they arise in a school's athletic program. When an act of unsportsmanlike behavior occurs, creative leaders should reconstruct the incident providing students with the opportunity to discuss and evaluate the occurrence in terms of good sportsmanship. Sports in America are significant. Sports in schools and colleges set the pattern for the entire structure of sports in our communities. Without appropriate behavior on the part of all personnel involved in playing, administering, and patronizing athletic contests, the opportunity to create and maintain a favorable atmosphere for the preservation of democratic values through this facet will be lost.

Case 5-5 THE LONGHORNS OF TEXAS' WINNING TRADITION

"What does it take to produce a winning collegiate football team?" Larry Kottoff, former University of Texas tight end, thought about that question before he answered.

"I played for the University of Texas, under the coaching genius of Darrell Royal, for three years on the varsity. Actually, during my sophomore year, I did not play too much, but during my junior and senior years on the varsity at Texas we won nineteen games, lost three, and tied one. After graduation I played part of a season for the Dallas Cowboys. But the University of Texas' winning tradition has been built in large part by Coach Royal. Perhaps I can illustrate the various strategies, at least from the perspective of a player for the Longhorns who played in the Big Shootout of 1969, beating Arkansas 15–14 to become number one in the nation.

"Quality athletes were developed by good recruiting and by stress on fundamentals. Each player developed a knowledge of the position to be played and then concentrated on the fundamentals of that position.

"Quality coaches had something to do with our Texas tradition. They were recruited by Darrell Royal and taught his basics—stress on fundamentals, teamwork, building desire, coaching on and off the field, identification of player talent or lack thereof, and hard work.

"We had a quantity of excellent athletes. I suppose that the winning tradition at Texas had something to do with getting a large number of athletes, plus good facilities, and good coaches. Our depth charts always had two excellent athletes, sometimes three.

"Our teams were durable. We developed that by physical fitness programs, weight training, diets (protein, calcium, and carbohydrates), agility drills, good trainers and excellent facilities.

"If we did not have a quantity of athletes, we would adapt. Adaptability becomes necessary when depth is lacking. But that was not too difficult, for most talented athletes are capable of playing more than one position. Normally, each athlete was taught fundamentals of two similar positions.

"We tried to have team balance—good offense and good defense. On offense, though, we stressed running much more than passing. Darrell

Royal has been quoted many times saying that three things can happen to a pass, and two of them are bad.

"Team dependability was developed by having strong discipline—having a good set of rules with a set of penalties. The team as a whole was penalized and not just an individual who broke the rules. Good scholastics also developed team dependability.

"Our teams were quick. We developed this quickness by weight training, agility drills, running (long distance and sprints), and by general physical fitness programs.

"Our uniqueness, I guess, was the belief that fundamentals can and will win. We proved that many times.

"When I was at Texas, we did not innovate too much. However, the chief innovation for which we were known throughout the country was the wishbone. We ran it to perfection.

"Scheduling helped us to win. We tried to schedule as many home games as possible. That helps!

"Knowing that team safety was consciously planned also helped us to win. Having the equipment checked, good diets, good trainers, medical facilities, weight training, and required physical exams all helped promote team safety.

"Our teams were well organized. Everyone knew his responsibilities. We practiced specialization. Objectives were clear, we had game books, rules, and standard practice schedules. Everything was coordinated. Athletes knew who was boss.

"Team leadership was important. We had team spirit—a desire instilled in us to win. We were motivated. We had cohesiveness. We had a positive approach by the coaches.

"We practiced in a clean environment. Everything was spic and span. We had closed practices, if necessary, without outside distractions.

"Our equipment was top-notch—the best available. Money was not a problem. There was a daily check and good maintenance. Each athlete took good care of his gear.

"We always traveled first class. Travel plans were prearranged as a group. We stayed at well-known hotels or motels—always the best. We were first class on the field and we were first class off the field.

"I still maintain that good scholastics makes a winning team. A person needs to be well rounded and have a sharp mind on the field and off the field. We had group study sessions, maintained a respectable team scholastic average. If we goofed scholastically, we were suspended from the team and did no traveling. Sometimes we had extra running.

"From my perspective as an athlete, there were four or five key reasons for our winning tradition: good recruiting of quality athletes, good coaches, good facilities, and a weak conference. It's hard to pin winning down to any one strategy. All of them have to be practiced."

FOOTNOTE

[1] *Interscholastic Athletic Administration,* Vol. 2, No. 4, Fall, 1976.

6

THE ATHLETIC ADMINISTRATOR'S RELATIONSHIP WITH THE COACHING STAFF

Coaches who produce the winning teams create entertainment that fans will pay for and enjoy. These coaches contribute to the general athletic program objectives. They help the team to be productive, the first objective of a successful athletic program. They contribute time, effort, knowledge, skills, and loyalty during competitions. They try to develop athletes' character, and they work to produce a winning team.

The coaches also contribute their competitive skills to accomplish other program objectives—to improve the image of the program, to make a profit, to grow, to survive, to maintain a share of the market, to become a leader, and to improve the quality of life for society.

What do coaches expect in return for their contributions? Most of them have personal objectives. A fundamental personal objective is adequate salary. Another is some form of job security. Most coaches want fringe benefits in exchange for their skills. They also like to have two-way communications with their superiors and subordinates. A certain degree of recognition, both from their peers and the general public, is fundamental to their thinking. Opportunity for advancement is also a personal objective of most coaches. There must be a mutual exchange of benefits between the coach and the athletic program so that objectives—both organizational and personal—can be accomplished. This basic concept must be understood by the successful athletic administrator.

Objective: To Have an Equitable Exchange of Contributions between Coaches and the Program

Factors	Strength	Weakness
A. Do the coaches contribute the following to the athletic program?		
1. Competitiveness to win		
2. Effort		
3. Time		
4. Knowledge		
5. Skills		
6. Loyalty		
7. Others		
Overall Evaluation:		
B. Does the athletic program contribute the following to the coaches?		
1. Adequate salary		
2. Job security		
3. Fringe benefits		
4. Two-way communication		
5. Recognition		
6. Opportunity for advancement		
7. Others?		
Overall Evaluation:		
C. Is there a mutual exchange of contributions?		
1. For the coaches		
2. For the program		
Overall Evaluation:		
D. Evaluate the coaches' contributions to the following program objectives:		
1. Acceptable win-loss record for fan entertainment		
2. Develop character in the athletes		
3. To improve the program's image		
4. To grow		
5. To make a profit		
6. To maintain continuity		
7. To maintain market share		
8. To become a leader		
9. To improve the quality of life for society		
10. Others		
Overall Evaluation:		

SELECTION OF COACHES

One of the foremost tasks of any athletic administrator is the selection of a coach. This process involves at least five steps:

1. Assess the coaching position requirements and the situation.
2. Once the position requirements and situation are known, list the coach's specifications in a matrix.
3. Weigh the requirements and specifications to show their relative importance for the position.
4. Once candidates are known, evaluate each candidate's qualifications against the position requirements and position specifications.
5. Make the decision.

The first step is accomplished by making a position analysis and description, usually consisting of clearly defined position objectives, functions (duties), with their corresponding responsibilities, authority, and accountability relationships. This position description should include some notion of the situation facing the athletic administrator concerning task structure, position power, and group relations.

After studying the position description and situation for a coach, the administrator is ready to list the position specification factors. The position specifications are usually the human factors; the position descriptions are the job factors. Such specifications might include the following:

1. Abilities and skills
   - 1.1 Intellectual ability
   - 1.2 Communications ability
   - 1.3 Human relations ability
   - 1.4 Technical competence
2. Experience and education
3. Personality characteristics
   - 3.1 Drive
   - 3.2 Self-confidence
   - 3.3 Ethical standards
   - 3.4 Courage and decisiveness
   - 3.5 Accepts responsibilities
   - 3.6 Adaptiveness
   - 3.7 Task-oriented leader
4. Physical characteristics
   - 4.1 Good health
   - 4.2 Personal appearance
5. Others

The third step is to integrate the descriptions and the specifications into a matrix that will help to evaluate the candidates. These factors are weighed against each other to determine their relative importance. The matrix technique aids in the selection of a coach, allowing the athletic administrator to quantify the variables involved in making the decision.

Once several candidates have expressed an interest in the coaching position and have been interviewed and screened, the administrator may evaluate each candidate's qualifications against the weighted factors in the matrix. This step is usually performed by assigning points to the qualifications of each candidate, to indicate the degree to which he/she satisfies the factors on the matrix.

Finally, the points are totaled for each candidate and the administrator can make a decision. The matrix method provides an excellent means of justifying the selection decision. By comparing the total points received by each candidate, it is easy to see which candidate is best qualified for the position.

An example of a decision matrix is shown.

Coach's Requirements (Factors)	Weighted Values	Various Candidates I	II	III
1. Have 8 years experience as a coach	10	6	3	10
2. Hold a M.S. degree	10	10	10	10
3. Be between ages of 30–40	5	5	5	5
4. Have good personal appearance	5	5	3	2
5. Possess high degree of human relations ability	10	7	10	10
6. Have outstanding communications ability	10	7	10	10
7. Have demonstrated courage and decisiveness in dealing with players	10	10	10	10
8. Possess high ethical standards	5	5	5	4
9. Must have a great deal of self-confidence	10	7	10	10
10. Be in good health	5	5	4	4
11. Be task oriented	15	13	10	15
12. Willing to accept responsibility	5	5	5	5
13. Have a high level of self-motivation	10	10	10	10
14. Be adaptive	5	5	5	5
15. Be a winner	15	10	15	15
Totals	130	110	116	125

Conclusion: Candidate III is most qualified

The preceding analysis shows the importance of weighing each candidate's qualifications against the job requirements. This process can be effectively used by several persons in joint decision making, or by one person in a unilateral decision.

Decision: Selection of a Coach

Factors	Strength	Weakness
1. Analysis of the situation		
2. Position description available		
3. Position specifications		
4. Weighing of factors in a matrix		
5. Evaluation of each candidate		
6. Objective decision		
Overall Evaluation:		

ATHLETIC LEADERSHIP THEORY

How does a successful athletic administrator help coaches to achieve organizational and personal goals? The administrator must know and understand effective leadership theory.

A number of leadership theories have evolved during recent years. They investigate the conditions under which one particular type of leader will effectively achieve organizational goals. Two types of leaders—task-oriented and relationship-oriented—have been analyzed by many researchers. The contingency model developed by Fred Fiedler is perhaps the most researched leadership theory.[1] It suggests that the most effective leadership, whether task-oriented or relationship-oriented, depends on or is contingent on at least three situational variables: (1) the relationship between the leader and followers, (2) the structure of the tasks to be performed, and (3) the position power of the leader.

Fiedler began his research in 1951, and even now he continues to work with interacting groups in which members coordinate their thoughts and actions to reach group goals. Examples of these groups are a basketball team, a policy-making group, and a B-29 air crew. Fiedler used *hard* performance criteria to measure the goals of at least 800 different groups. As a result, Fiedler has developed a contingency model of the variables which affect the type of leadership which is most effective in reaching its goals.

The contingency model is based on the *situational* approach to leadership; when the situation changes, the type of leadership that proves most effective also changes. Let us take the role of an athletic administrator and consider the three situational variables. We should be able to predict which types of coaching behavior and administrative behavior will be most effective under various situations.

The first and most important situational variable is leader-member relations. A coach has authority only if he is accepted by the players. If the players are willing to follow him, the coach has good leader-member relations. On the other hand, if the players distrust the coach, he/she will have poor leader-member relations. A group atmosphere must be measured to determine whether the leader-member relations are good or poor. This variable is the most important of the three.

A second variable of a situation is the task-structure dimension. The highly structured task of coaching emphasizes detailed operating procedures, a step by step approach, a clearly defined goal, and a means to make the right decision. It would be very difficult for a player to challenge a coach's authority if the coach has adhered to his manual—the gospel of the athletic program. Yet, highly unstructured and vague tasks often confront a coach. For example, often there are a number of solutions to a problem. Whether a decision is correct may be difficult to verify. The task-structure variable is less important than the leader-member relations variable.

A third variable, position power, involves a leader's right to plan, organize, direct, coordinate, and evaluate his team. In most situations, the players know that the coach has authority to reward or punish, to promote or demote, and to evaluate performance. Most coaches have strong position power—unlike committee chairmen, for example, who have weak position power. This is the least important of the three variables.

The three situation variables of an interacting group determine the most effective form of leadership. The administrator must decide whether the leader-member relations are good or poor, whether the task is structured or unstructured, and whether the position power is strong or weak. A particular group can be classified according to eight different situations (I through VIII) as follows:

	I	II	III	IV	V	VI	VII	VIII
Leader-member relations	Good	Good	Good	Good	Poor	Poor	Poor	Poor
Task structure	Structured		Unstructured		Structured		Unstructured	
Position power	Strong	Weak	Strong	Weak	Strong	Weak	Strong	Weak

Determining the leadership personality is the next step. The administrator must decide whether the coach is a task-motivated or a relationship-motivated leader by issuing him a least preferred co-worker test. Once that has been established, we can see what type of coach is most effective for

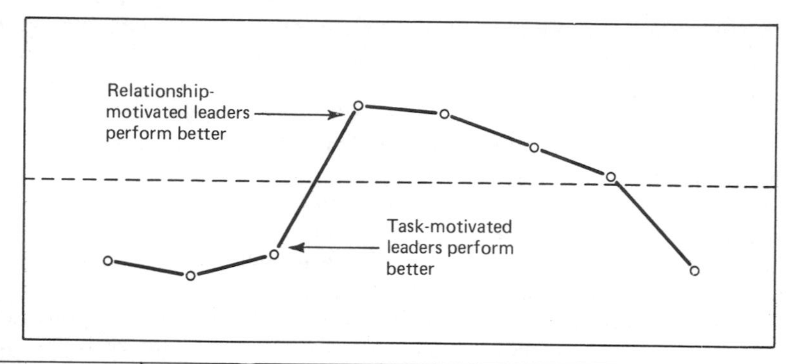

	I	II	III	IV	V	VI	VII	VIII
Leader-member relations	Good	Good	Good	Good	Poor	Poor	Poor	Poor
Task structure	Structured		Unstructured		Structured		Unstructured	
Leader position power	Strong	Weak	Strong	Weak	Strong	Weak	Strong	Weak

Figure 6–1 How the Style of Effective Leadership Varies with the Situation. Source: Modified from Fiedler, 1965, with the permission of the *Harvard Business Review.*

each of the eight situations in the contingency model (see Figure 6-1).

By carefully analyzing the chart, an athletic administrator can see that in situation I (where the leader-member relations are good, the task is structured, and the position power is strong) a task-motivated leader will be most effective. A successful coach often is in this type of situation.

Suppose situation V (the leader-member relations are poor, the task is structured, and position power is strong) prevails. In this situation a relationship-motivated coach will perform better. Suppose the situation facing a coach is number VIII (the leader-member relations are poor, the task is unstructured, and the position power is weak). In situation VIII, the task-motivated leader performs better.

The task-motivated coaches perform better in the favorable situations (I, II, and III) and in VIII, an unfavorable situation. Relationship-motivated coaches are more effective in moderate situations such as IV, V, VI, and VII. The contingency or situation model suggests that coaching effectiveness depends on the coach's relationship with the players, the task structure, and the position power. Both types of leaders—task-motivated and relationship-motivated—perform well, depending on the situation.

Using the Fiedler theory, an athletic administrator can evaluate the

Decision: Determining Effective Leadership of Coaches, Supervisors and Administrators.

1. Leadership Situation of Coach-Players	Leadership Theory	Compared with Actual Situation	Evaluate *Strength*	*Weakness*
1.1 Situation I	Task			
1.2 Situation II	Task			
1.3 Situation III	Task			
1.4 Situation IV	Relations			
1.5 Situation V	Relations			
1.6 Situation VI	Relations			
1.7 Situation VII	Relations			
1.8 Situation VIII	Task			
2. Leadership Situation of Head Coach-Coaches				
2.1 Same analysis				
3. Leadership Situation of Supervisor-Employees				
3.1 Same analysis				
4. Leadership Situation of Administrator-Coaches				
4.1 Same analysis				

Overall Evaluation:

leadership of coaches, noncoaching supervisors, and administrators. He/she can then compare the actual to the theory to determine strengths or weaknesses of the theory.

Suggested Leadership Strategies

Suppose that a coach's leadership style (personality) matches a highly favorable control situation. For example, a successful, task-oriented coach might face a situation characterized by good leader-member relations, a rigid task structure, and a high degree of leader position power. This is a favorable match of a coach's personality and the three situational vari-

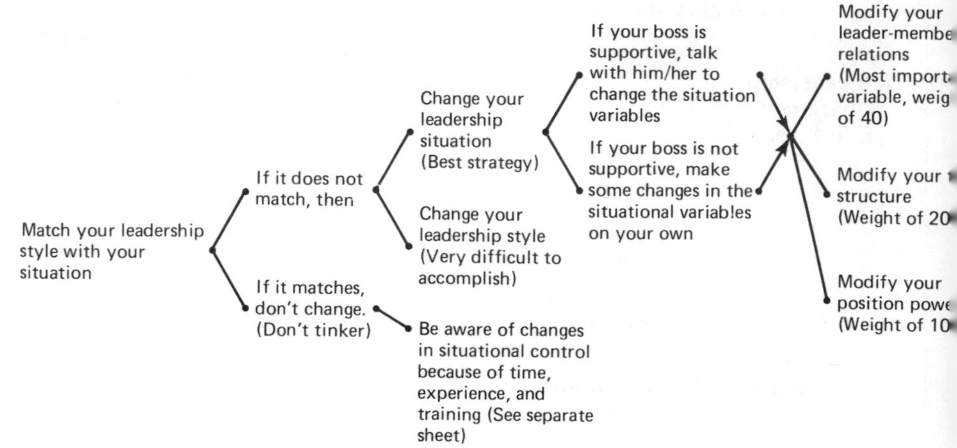

Figure 6–2 Suggested Leadership Strategies*

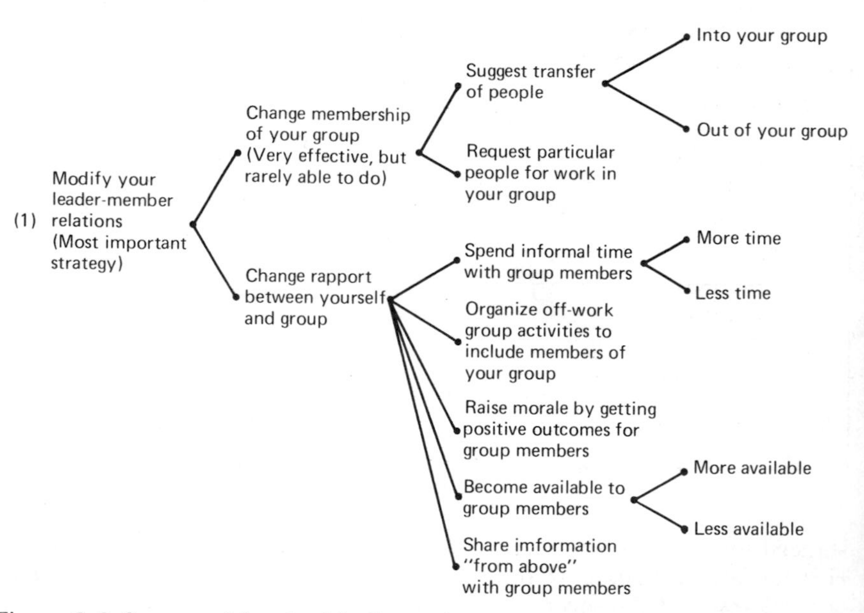

Figure 6–3 Suggested Leadership Strategies

* All figures based on Fiedler's Leadership Studies and Contingency Model. See in particular Fiedler, Chemers, and Mahar, *Improving Leadership Effectiveness* (New York: Wiley and Sons, 1976).

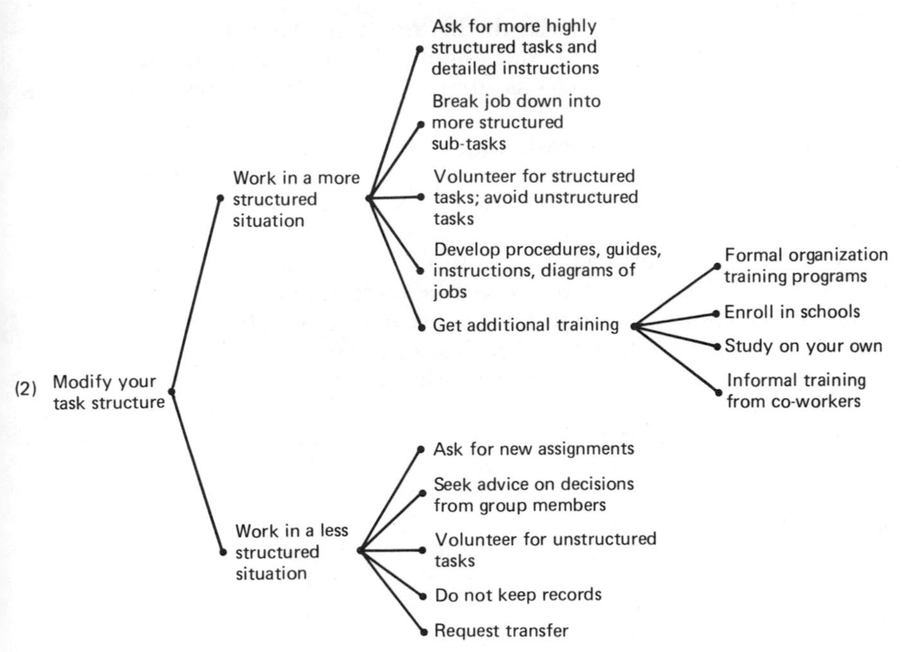

Figure 6–4 Suggested Leadership Strategies

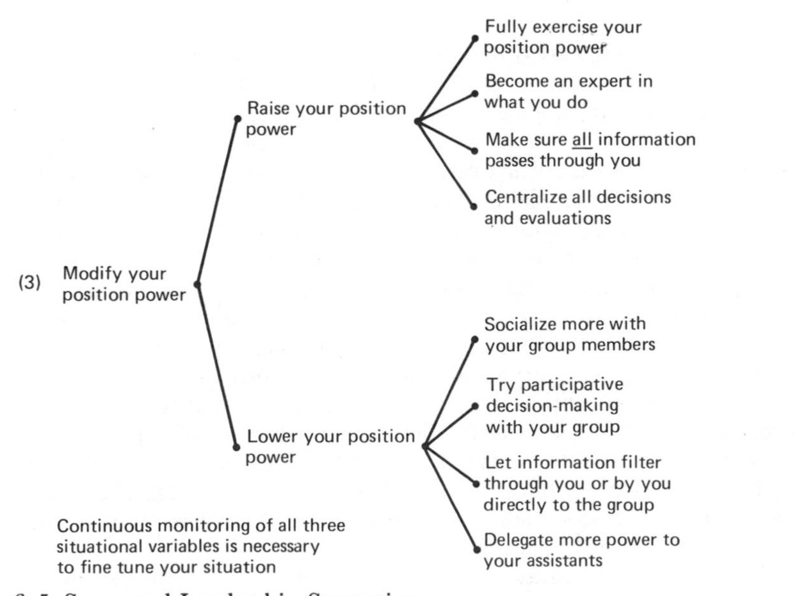

Figure 6–5 Suggested Leadership Strategies

ables; it is best not to tinker with this situation. However, when dealing with high control situations, one should be aware of factors that could change the situation, such as time, experience, or training of the coach/supervisor.

Suppose that a coach's leadership style does not match the situational variables. There are two strategies open: (1) change the leadership situation, or (2) change the coach's leadership style. It is much easier to change the leadership situation to fit the coach's leadership style than to change the coach's personality. There are three ways to alter the situation: (1) modify the leader-member relations (the most important variable, given a weight of 40 points); (2) modify the task structure (weight of 20); (3) modify the position power (weight of 10). Various ways to change the situation variables are presented in Figures 6-2 through 6-5.

If an administrator wishes to change the leader-member relations, he/she could change the membership of the group (possible, but not too probable). He/she might suggest ways for the coach to either relax or limit relations between the coach and the group.

The administrator can change the task structure by suggesting ways to make the program either more or less flexible, depending on the match between the coach's leadership style and the three situational variables.

If the administrator decides to change the position, he could suggest that the coach raise or lower the position power by various means.

SETTING SALARIES

When coaches and other personnel are hired, the administrator must determine their salaries. There are three alternatives normally involved in setting a salary: to pay above the market price, to pay at the market price, and to pay below the market price. Once the market price has been determined, the administrator must choose one of the three alternatives.

If the desire to get the best coach for the position is important to an administrator, theory would suggest that an above-the-market salary should be offered. A higher salary could also be offered to compensate for an athletic program's unfavorable location or for poor working conditions. If the administrator is pressured by fans to hire an eminent coach, or by unions to pay a high wage, then an above-the-market salary should be considered.

Suppose that the situation which an athletic program faces has very poor working conditions. If the administrator wants to offset the poor working conditions, an above-the-market salary would have to prevail.

If the administrator is faced with terrific pressure from the fans to give them a distinctive program and to hire a coach who has the reputation of being able to do so, then good theory would suggest that an above-the-market salary would prevail.

If the athletic program (such as in the case of professional sports) is subject to industry-wide union pressure, then good theory would suggest that an above-the-market salary would prevail. All of the preceding factors (a

Objective: To Determine Proper Salary Strategy

Factors	**Theory** *compared to* *Above Market*	*At Market*	*Below Market*	**Actual Situation**	**⟶Evaluation** *Strength*	*Weakness*
1. Desire to get the best	X					
2. Offset unfavorable location	X					
3. Offset poor working conditions	X					
4. Desire to give fans distinctive program	X					
5. Subject to industry-wide union pressure	X					
6. Desire to neutralize salary as a competitive factor—rely on others		X				
7. Need only mediocre coaches and personnel			X			
8. Large supply of coaches available			X			
9. Personnel are "locked in" for personal reasons		X	X			
10. Others?						
Overall Evaluation:						

desire to get the best, to offset unfavorable location, to offset poor working conditions, to give the fans a distinctive program, and to respond to industry-wide union pressure) would suggest an above-the-market salary.

However, if the administrator does not want salary to be the main factor in attracting coaches and other personnel, and wants to rely on other factors, then good theory would suggest paying an at-the-market salary.

If only mediocre coaches and personnel are needed in the athletic program, good theory suggests that a below-the-market salary would be appropriate.

If there is a large supply of coaches available, theory would suggest a below-the-market salary. Likewise, if a coach is locked into a situation for personal reasons, an administrator might want to pay a below-the-market salary or at-the-market salary. There may be other factors affecting the decision of what to pay coaches and other personnel.

If the athletic administrators wish to evaluate their salary strategies, they can compare their situations with theory and determine the strengths and weaknesses by using the analysis on page 129.

CHAPTER SUMMARY

There has to be a mutual exchange of personal contributions of coaches and the organizational contributions of the athletic program if it is to be successfully administered. Coaches contribute competitiveness, effort, time, knowledge, skills, and loyalty to the program; in return, they expect to receive salary, security, fringe benefits, two-way communication, recognition, and the opportunity for advancement from the athletic program.

The selection of coaches is an important decision if the program is to be a winner. The selection decision involves a series of steps: (1) assessing the coaching position requirements and the situation variables; (2) listing the coach's specifications in a matrix, showing the alternative choices; (3) weighing the factors to determine relative importance; (4) evaluating each candidate against the position and personal factors; (5) making the decision.

The effective administrator should be aware of Fiedler's theory, since the style of leadership practiced by a coach, a supervisor, or an administrator is important to an athletic program's success. This situational leadership theory suggests that effective leadership depends on two variables; (1) leader's style (personality), and (2) the leader's control over three situational variables. The three variables are: (a) leader-member relations, (b) task structure, and (c) position power.

Both task-motivated and relationship-motivated coaches, supervisors, and administrators can be effective, depending on the situation variables. Task-motivated leaders are most effective in high control situations and in low control situations (situations I, II, III, and VIII in Fiedler's model). Relationship-motivated leaders are effective in moderate control situations (situations IV, V, VI, and VII).

If there is good match between leadership styles and the three situational variables, then it is not wise to change any of the variables. If, on the other hand, there is not a good match, then an administrator should change the situation variables to match the leader's style by employing various strategies.

In addition, the administrator must determine the proper salary strategy for paying personnel. Three alternatives are normally available—to pay above the market, to pay at the market, and to pay below the market. The administrator must consider several factors. A desire to employ the best coach, to offset an unfavorable location, to offset poor working conditions, to give fans a distinctive program, and to respond to industry-wide union pressure would all suggest paying above the market. Other factors would suggest paying at or below the market salary—the desire to neutralize pay as a competitive factor, the need to employ only mediocre personnel, or the ability to choose from a large supply of available coaches. Often a coach will accept a low salary for personal reasons.

Case 6-1 THE HUMPIN' HOGS BASKETBALL COACH SELECTION*

This spring the Southwestern State University Humpin' Hogs basketball team had again fallen short of a hoped-for future. When Larry Eagan was hired as head basketball coach four years ago, there were high hopes that he could bring basketball to a place of status in the conference. However, his record of 5 wins and 21 losses in the first season was followed by a 8–18 record the next year, then a 16–10 record. The Humpin' Hogs had a 10–16 record this year. The hoped-for winning tradition had failed.

Fred Baker, the athletic director for Southwestern State University and also head football coach, was about to make one of his major decisions regarding the status of basketball in a football-dominated athletic program. He conferred with Larry Eagan two weeks before the latest basketball season ended and asked Eagan for an early decision regarding his future as the University's basketball coach. Eagan's contract originally ran for three years and was renewed last year for one year on the basis of his 16–10 record. On a Thursday, Eagan announced his resignation to the press. The next day, Friday, the University's Board of Directors happened to be in town for a routine meeting. Fred Baker immediately asked for the Board's Athletic Committee to meet with him regarding the future direction of basketball at Southwestern State.

There was immediate speculation regarding the future of the basketball program. Most people were saying that basketball would remain a stepchild of the Athletic Department since basketball had never paid for itself with its own revenues. Their hypothesis was that the basketball program would remain the same since financial resources and the physical facilities of the athletic program were being diverted to the new football program, not toward basketball facilities.

A minority felt that Fred Baker did not like to be associated with a losing tradition, and that he should try to influence the Board of Directors to go "big time" and make the University a two sports University—football *and* basketball.

The following week Fred Baker called for a meeting of the Faculty Athletic Committee of the University to present his plans to them. Fred made a lengthy presentation to the Committee stating that he had asked the Board of Directors' Athletic Committee to give him some guidance on the direction of finances and facilities for the basketball program. He stated that he wanted this guidance so that he could relay it to the new basketball coach. Fred reported that the Board did not really commit itself to him, but he felt that they wanted to go "first class" and become competitive in

* Names have been disguised.

basketball. Still under consideration by the Board was the latest student petition to build a student recreation center. It was felt that new basketball facilities could be incorporated into the student recreation center.

The Faculty Athletic Committee asked for Fred's recommendation regarding the basketball program. Fred Baker emphatically and persuasively stated that he wanted the University to get competitive in both basketball and football. In other words, he was willing to commit himself and his Athletic Department to becoming a two major sports department.

Fred stated that he had done some research on schools with two major sports programs—Notre Dame, Alabama, and Kansas, for example. He further had made a financial projection of the additional revenue and expenses it would take to get competitive. He had conferred with basketball coaches—Hank Iba, Tex Winter, and Jack Hartman—to get their advice on the direction of the basketball program. He even called several successful basketball coaches to get their views on the salary and other costs it would take to get competitive. He concluded by asking for the support of the Faculty Athletic Committee. The potential was there to make money from the basketball program.

Questions were then asked by members of the committee. "What is the salary picture?" Fred responded by stating that he called one highly successful coach who reported that his yearly salary was $31,000 plus $20,000 from TV shows and basketball camp programs. The present salary (competitive with other conference schools) of the coach at Southwestern State was $17,000 with two assistants at $12,000 and $9,000. After talking with several basketball coaches around the country, Fred stated that he thought $24,000–$26,000, perhaps up to $26,000 would be the salary he had in mind. Two assistant coaches' salaries would be raised to $17,000 and $12,-000. With the additional head coach's salary of $8,000 plus $8,000 additional for the two assistant coaches' salaries, plus an additional $7,000 for other expenses, Fred estimated that it would cost approximately $25,000 more to get competitive. That meant selling approximately 750 to 1000 more season tickets at $36 each. He was willing to try. Fred was willing to give the fans a first-class program.

"What is the present financial position of the basketball program?" A schedule was given to the Faculty Committee members, summarized as follows:

Revenue	**3 Years Ago**	**2 Years Ago**	**Last Year**	**This Year**
Season books	$ 8,183	$16,212	$17,122	$24,330
Single tickets	13,526	12,980	18,794	11,194
Guarantees	7,000	9,121	2,450	4,500
Other	7,960	4,813	13,078	3,427
Total	$36,069	$43,126	$51,423	$43,450
Less Guarantees Paid	4,600	7,750	17,954	INC
Net Revenue	$32,069	$35,376	$33,469	INC
Expenditures				
Total	$125,579	$143,404	$135,097	INC
Net Loss	($93,510)	(108,028)	(101,618)	INC

The major issue of financing the new basketball program via ticket sales or by some form of underwriting was still undecided by the Board of Trustees, according to Fred. However, he stated that the field house, the present basketball facility, had a seating capacity of 5600 seats, and that 550 season tickets were sold this year. However, the present field house was in poor condition compared to other conference schools.

"We have some additional revenue coming in from investments that the Athletic Department has made which could be used to put in some new 'arm type seats' for next year. The new coach could have his say regarding the design."

"What about the competition? And what about recruiting the state's basketball players?" Fred answered, "As you know, our conference has been a rather weak basketball conference. We could conceivably become a conference winner in two years. However, I view a winning tradition in the conference to take from four to eight years. As you know, we are in an unfavorable location to attract large numbers of players."

"Our high schools (only about 400) have talented players. But as you know, the better players come from big cities, particularly in Kansas, Illinois, and Indiana. If we could recruit half of our players each year from the state and the other half outside the state, we'd be in good shape."

"According to the press reports, our school is a diamond in the rough for a basketball coach." Fred stated, "If we could find the right man with a gleam in his eye who really has waited a long time to come to Southwestern State, that's the man I'd like to find." One member asked, "Do you mean another fellow like you, Fred?" And Fred responded, "Yes."

"If a new coach does come, what about the present assistant coaches?" "Well, the new coach will probably make that decision," Fred replied.

After further discussion, the Faculty Committee on Athletics voted to endorse Fred Baker's plans.

Fred had inquiries from 200 applicants who were interested in the head basketball coaching position. After preparing a mental description of the position and the specifications required for the job, he sought the advice of several head basketball coaches from all over the country. Eventually, Fred interviewed and narrowed down his choice to three candidates.

Norman Grigsby was a young, thirty-year-old assistant basketball coach at UCLA who had a dynamic personality. He could communicate well and seemed very sharp. Fred did notice, though, that his "demands" for the position were very fixed and not subject to negotiation. Grigsby had six years of assistant coaching experience under the tutelage of one of the most successful college coaches in the country. In addition, he had a bachelor's degree. Grigsby had a lot of drive and self-confidence; however, there was some doubt about his ability to adapt to a small university which had a dominant football tradition. Fred sensed that Grigsby was a task-motivated person who was used to winning. He made a good appearance, was in excellent health, but did not know much about Midwest geography in recruiting. He believed in Fellowship of Christian Athletes, and was willing to work hard to develop a winning tradition. Although married, he had no children.

Robert Sauls was a second candidate. He had been a head basketball coach and athletic director at Omaha State, a small independent university in the Midwest, where he had compiled a 63% win-loss record during the past five years. Prior to that he was head basketball coach at a junior college where his record was .856 and before that he was head basketball coach at a high school where his record was .700. His career total was 286–114 for .715. Sauls played for Hank Iba and received his master's degree while serving as Iba's graduate assistant, fifteen years ago. He had good rapport with the press and TV and was highly thought of as being a strong disciplinarian and task-motivated personality. He wanted to take charge of the entire basketball program, but was willing to adapt to the local situation. He was in good health and made a good appearance. His technical competence and ability to recruit players made a good impression on Frank Baker. Robert Sauls was married and had two small sons.

Johnny Modisette was the third candidate. Born on the East Coast, Modisette was a product of Dean Smith, noted basketball coach, who recommended Johnny very highly. At age 29, Johnny had been an assistant coach at Smith's school for five years and was ready to become a head coach after receiving his MBA degree. Johnny had a pleasing and jovial personality and was eager to help his players in any way he could. Although he considered winning important, he preferred to develop the character of his athletes as a primary objective. Johnny Modisette had plenty of drive and self-confidence. His father was a Baptist minister whom he respected very much. He was ready and eager to give the head coaching position his best shot. A very handsome man and in good health, Johnny planned on marrying his college sweetheart next month. He made no demands on Frank Baker, who considered him a very able coach.

Whom should Fred recommend to the athletic committee? What salary should he offer? Fred took off for a day to collect his thoughts before he approached the athletic committee.

Case 6-2 NEW COACHES FOR BELLA VISTA HIGH

Bella Vista High School was located in a Midwestern suburban community of 30,000 people, about ten miles from a metropolitan area of 1,-500,000. In fact, Bellevue was a member of the "metro" conference and had competed very successfully with other teams, especially in football and track during the past 10–15 years. Its record in basketball, however, was not as good as its football and track records. Also offered were wrestling, swimming, and golf.

More specifically, the Bella Vista varsity football win-loss record, under head coach Bill Jones* for the past 12 years, was 86–21–3. The junior varsity, under the direction of Coach Jerry Vawter, had compiled a 72–14–2 record; the sophomore team had compiled a record of 81–7–4 during the same time frame. Bella Vista's grand total was 239–43–9.

The track coach, Don Pearson, was proud of his excellent record. For example, during the last six years his track and field teams had won four state championships. He had a 60–7 win-loss record in the last ten years; his teams had won 21 major meets, seven division championships, two metro championships, five district championships, and four state champi-

* Names and places have been disguised.

onships. His athletes had won 15 individual championship awards in track and field events.

In cross country events, Don's teams had a 210–18 win-loss record. He was particularly proud of the fact that during the spring season 142 youngsters were out for the track team and 55 were competing for the cross country team.

John Long was the assistant basketball coach at Bella Vista. During the four seasons he had been there, he was instrumental in helping the head coach compile a 43–42 win-loss record. However, John had charge of the sophomore basketball teams whose record for the past four years was 42–7.

The next year, Bella Vista was going to create a new high school across town. As a result, Jerry Vawter was selected to be the head football coach at the new school (West High) and John Long was to remain as the new head basketball coach at Bella Vista (East High). The present coach, Mike Lassiter, was transferred to the position of head basketball at the new high school (West High). Bill Jones was to remain as head football coach at East High.

Bill Jones, the present head football coach, had a considerate and supportive behavior pattern with his associates. However, he considered himself to be a task-motivated coach. He had excellent relations with his associates, having very little difficulty getting along with his subordinates. Bill found the job of head football coach to be highly structured since the goals were clearly known, there was a step-by-step procedure to accomplish the tasks involved, a correct solution was easily seen, and it was easy to check whether the job was done right. He had power in his position and was confident that the team's record indicated his effectiveness.

Jerry Vawter, his chief assistant, was of the same personality as Bill Jones, his mentor. Jerry mentioned that he was mainly concerned with getting the job done, that is, winning. He was pleased with his record as the Junior Varsity Coach for the past seven seasons of 47–5–1. He was task-motivated. He also had good personal relations with the athletes, coaches, and others. He did not view coaching as a highly structured occupation. He thought it was half-way structured and half-way unstructured. The coach held a position of power, in his opinion. He was eagerly looking forward to next season to see how he would perform as the new head football coach at West High.

Don Pearson, the track coach, faced a different situation at Bella Vista High. He had the personality of a relationship-motivated coach. He had a very high regard for people and the athletes he coached. His behavior was considerate, open, and participative. He had a good relationship with his associates, except sometimes he viewed his subordinates as unreliable and not always cooperative. He did not find his job as track coach to be highly structured. He had no clear-cut goals; there were many ways to coach his track athletes. However, he had absolute power over his athletes and subordinates. He was happy in his job, and was looking forward to many more years as head track coach in his moderately favorable situation.

John Long, the present assistant basketball coach, was a fairly young coach who did not have any experience as a head coach. He considered himself a relationship-motivated personality. His present relations with his peers, players, and coaches were good. He viewed the new head coaching position as being highly structured. He felt he would have a lot of power as the new head coach. He, too, was looking forward to the next season when he could try his prowess at his first real head coaching job. Jerry mentioned that he (John) would have a tough row to hoe following in Mike Lassiter's footsteps as head basketball coach.

QUESTIONS:

1. How would you evaluate the match between the leadership personality and present leadership situation of
   a. Bill Jones, present head football coach?
   b. Don Pearson, present head track coach?
2. What would you predict to be the success of the next year's program in light of the leadership situation facing
   a. Jerry Vawter, newly selected football coach?
   b. John Long, newly selected basketball coach?

FOOTNOTE

[1] Fred E. Fiedler and Martin M. Chemers, *Leadership and Effective Management* (Glenview, Illinois: Scott, Foresman, and Co., 1974).

7

THE ATHLETIC ADMINISTRATOR'S RELATIONSHIP WITH THE COACHING STAFF (continued)

It is important for an athletic program to survive and to maintain continuity. To do this, the coaching staff and other executives must be flexible enough to meet the changing situations facing an athletic program. An executive development program that will help to accomplish two objectives—maintaining continuity and developing flexibility to endure the pressures of competition—is particularly helpful. Such a program can achieve its goals in two ways: (1) it can improve coaching effectiveness and coaching efficiency, and (2) it provides the athletic program with an adequate supply of effective managers to produce, market, and finance the sports program successfully.

ON-THE-JOB TRAINING

There are two major types of training in an executive development program—on-the-job and off-the-job. If the program sends its coaches to classes at a nearby university, it is practicing off-the-job training; if the coaches are instructed, then rotated in their daily work, they are practicing on-the-job training. On-the-job training often produces winning teams and accomplishes other athletic program objectives. In an on-the-job training program, coaches learn by doing. They can easily try out new ideas; they do not lose productive time away from work; and they can put into practice what is being learned. These are the advantages of on-the-job training.

There are at least three methods of employing on-the-job training: (1) actual coaching, (2) multiple management, (3) job rotation. When a coach gives instructions, criticizes, comments, suggests, cajoles (all in a positive attitude), it is an example of coaching at its best. Another method, sometimes called multiple management or group management, gives coaches experience in group decision making and teamwork. If the head coach must make a decision, his coaching staff will analyze the problem and offer suggestions. This form of on-the-job training is fundamental to winning. A third method is job rotation. When the coach switches from a defensive backfield to an offensive backfield, or from a defensive line to an offensive line position, he/she is getting valuable experience that will be useful in the future. It hurts to get burned on the playing field when the opponents try something new or even the tried and true, especially when prior experience, gained through job rotation, suggests what to do or what not to do.

OFF-THE-JOB TRAINING

When training is not an integral part of the daily schedule, it is called off-the-job training. Although it might not be as effective as on-the-job training, there are several ways to acquire off-the-job training. Some of the common methods are (1) sensitivity training—helps trainee to develop an awareness of one's self and one's impact on others; (2) case method—helps trainee to develop analytical skills and to apply principles and concepts through study of different situations; (3) role playing—trainee acts out different situations to gain new perspectives; (4) programmed instruction—a trainee learns in small units at his/her own pace with immediate knowledge of results; (5) university clinics—trainees engage in programs centered around athletic problems in a university atmosphere. These off-the-job methods are excellent for gaining new knowledge and reaffirming old information.

STRATEGIES AND TRAINING AND EXPERIENCE

Various studies have been made to determine the effectiveness of executive training. Most studies conclude that it is difficult to assess the value of training, expecially off-the-job training. The methods of evaluation do not measure on-the-job performance. For example, one common method of evaluation is to have the trainees comment on changes in their behavior as a result of training. Another is to measure attitudes of trainees toward the subject matter before the training and then after the sessions. However, neither method measures an actual change in behavior on the job.

It is Fiedler's theory that experience and training on the job do affect the amount of control a coach has over the situation he/she faces. For example, if a situation for an experienced leader is highly favorable (high control), for an inexperienced leader the same situation would be moderately favor-

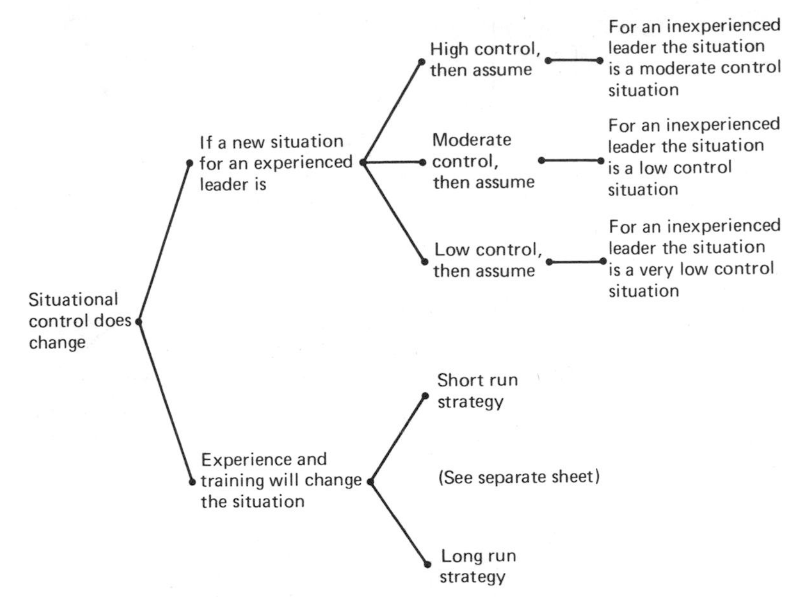

Figure 7–1 Strategies and Training Experience

able (moderate control). If the situation is moderately favorable for an experienced leader, then that same situation is low control for an inexperienced leader. A low control situation for an experienced leader would be a very low control situation for an inexperienced leader. Different kinds of leadership are required depending on the length of time a coach stays with his team (see Figure 7-1).

A situation at the time of selection of a leader would not be the same after a year or two of on-the-job training and experience. In a moderate control situation, an inexperienced leader should be relationship-motivated to be effective in the short run. However, after being on the job, the leader would probably find more structured goals, more power, and better group relations. The result would be a high control situation. In the long run, as the situation changes from moderate to high control, a task-motivated leader would be much more effective than a relationship-motivated leader (see Figure 7-2).

Likewise, a low control situation becomes a moderate control situation after the leader acquires training and experience. Consequently, a relationship-motivated leader would perform poorly in the short run, but would be effective in the long run because the situation would change to a moderate control one. At first, a task-motivated leader would perform very well in a low control situation. After experience and training, the coach's effectiveness would deteriorate as the situation changed from a low control to a moderate control one, as seen in Figure 7-2.

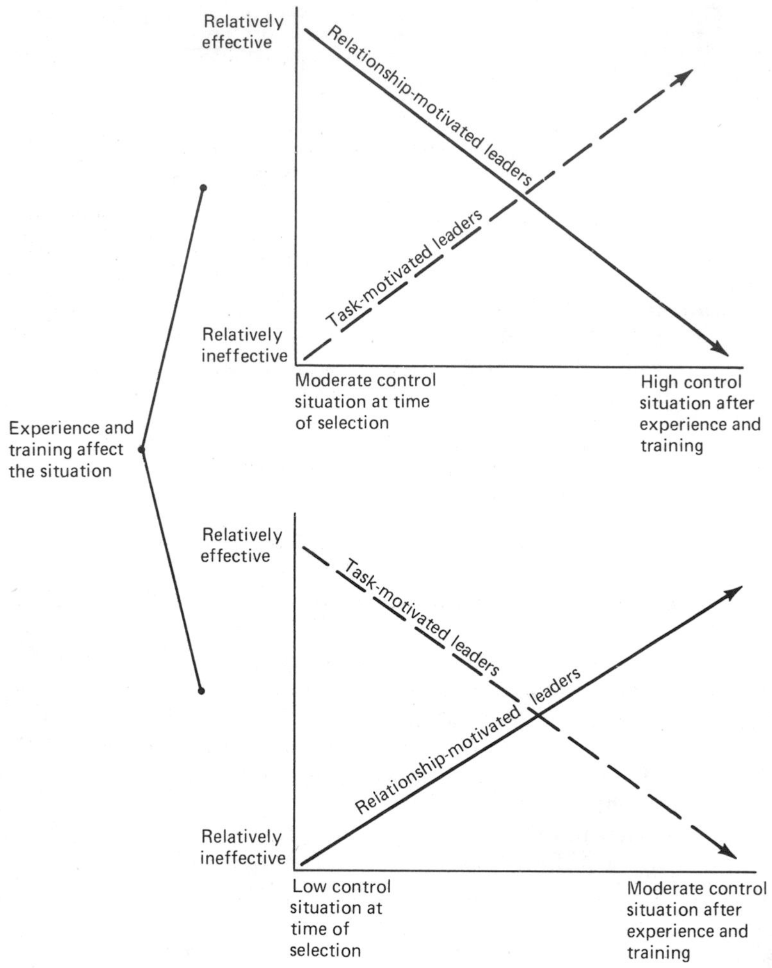

Figure 7–2 Strategies and Training Experience

SELECTION AND PLACEMENT STRATEGIES

If an administrator follows the implications of the Fiedler studies, he/she could implement several placement and selection strategies. For example, if the situation for a new, inexperienced person is a moderate control situation and the person is a task-motivated leader, the best strategy for the short run is not to select the person. If selected, however, it is wise to train the leader, to structure the task, and provide more power in the position (change to a high control situation). The best long-run strategy is to change the situation to a high control situation to fit the task-motivated leader's personality.

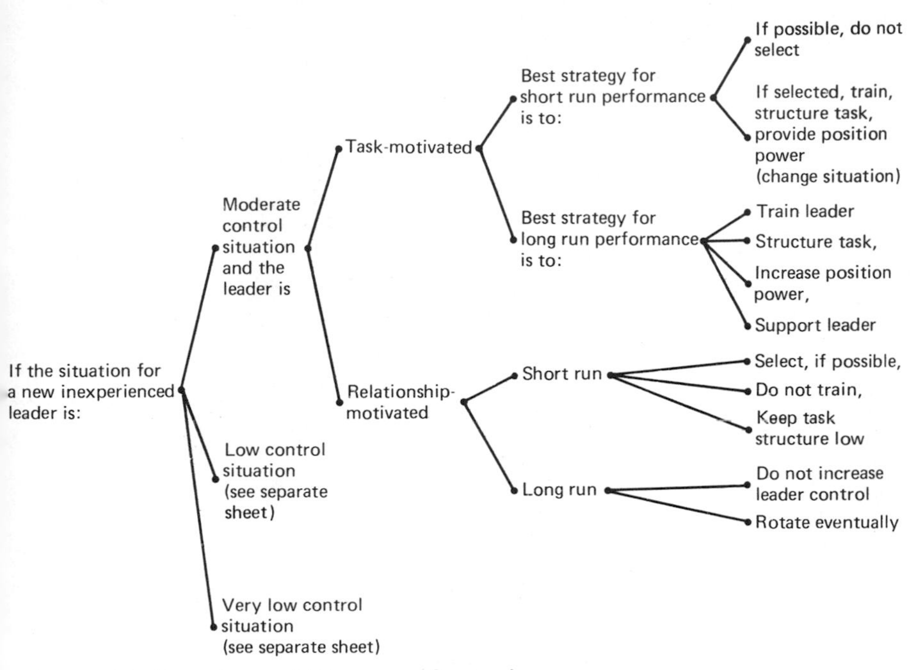

Figure 7–3 Selection and Placement Strategies

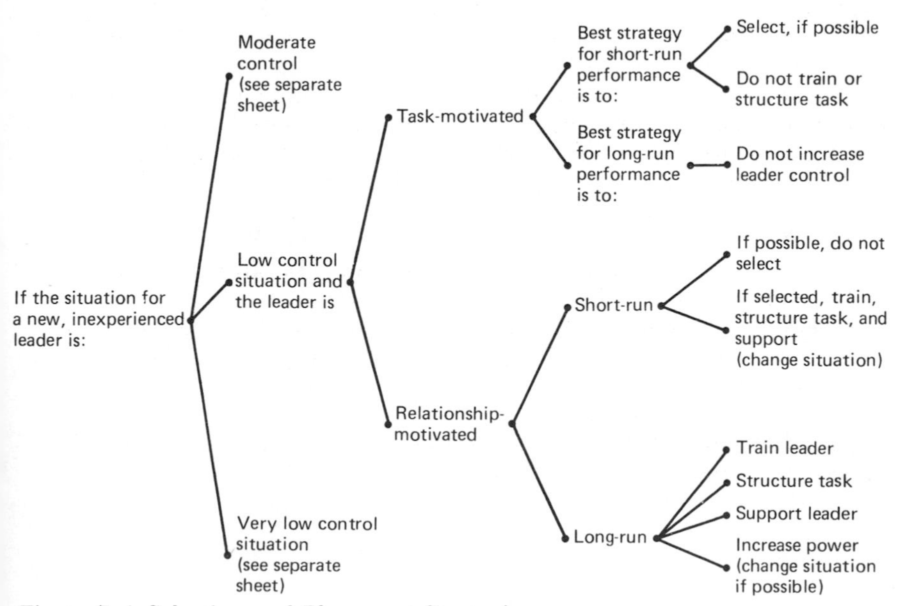

Figure 7–4 Selection and Placement Strategies

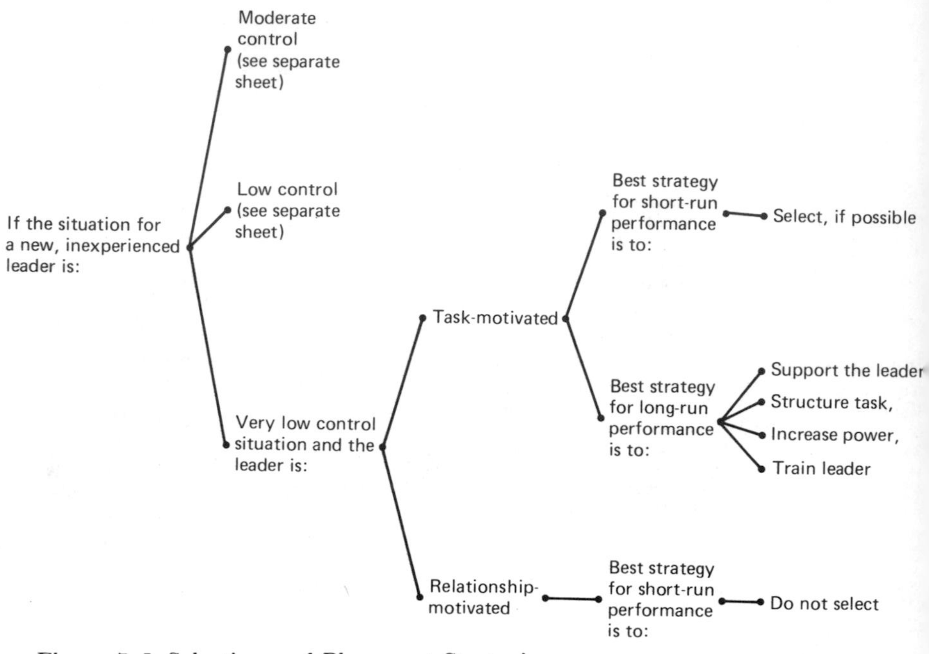

Figure 7–5 Selection and Placement Strategies

If the new person is relationship-motivated and the situation is one of moderate control, then the short-run strategy is to select but not train the new coach and to keep the task structure low. The long-run strategy is not to increase leader control and to rotate the person eventually because he/she will not fit the changing situation. After some experience is gained by the relationship-motivated person, the situation will change from a moderate control one (suitable at first) to a high control one (unsuitable for a relationship-motivated person), as seen in Figure 7-3.

Suggested strategies for placing inexperienced leaders in low control situations, both short run and long run, are presented in Figure 7-4. Basically, in a low control situation, a task-motivated leader performs very well; a relationship-motivated leader should not be selected.

Suggested placement and selection strategies for a new, inexperienced leader faced with a very low control situation are shown in Figure 7-5. A task-motivated leader performs better than a relationship-motivated leader in a very low control situation.

An athletic administrator can evaluate the strengths and weaknesses of his training program by the following analysis:

Objective: Coaching and Supervisory Training Program to Maintain Continuity and Flexibility, to Improve Coaching, and to Assure Supervisory Effectiveness

Strategy	**Strengths**	**Weaknesses**
1. Does the athletic program have on-the-job training as follows:		
1.1 Actual coaching OJT		
1.2 Multiple management OJT		
1.3 Job rotation OJT		
1.4 Other OJT methods		
2. Does the program have off-the-job training in:		
2.1 Sensitivity training		
2.2 Case method		
2.3 Role playing		
2.4 Programmed instruction		
2.5 University clinics		
2.6 Others		
Overall Evaluation:		
3. Does the athletic program recognize and practice effective strategies of training and experience for		
3.1 Proper selection and placement of coaches and supervisory personnel for the following situations:		
3.11 High control		
3.12 Moderate control		
3.13 Low control		
3.2 For experienced leaders		
3.3 For inexperienced leaders		
3.4 For the short run		
3.5 For the long run		
3.6 For task-motivated leaders		
3.7 For relationship-motivated leaders		
(See analysis for proper strategies)		
Overall Evaluation:		

MOTIVATION OF COACHES AND SUPERVISORY STAFF

What motivates coaches and other supervisory personnel of an athletic program? Motivation theory has been researched by several psychologists and behavioral scientists, most of whom have based their research on Maslow's hierarchy of needs.[1] Frederick Herzberg and his associates[2] have advanced the theory that people are affected by two types of motivating forces. The *satisfiers* are the positive motivators that satisfy people's needs. The hygiene factors or *dissatisfiers* are necessary for the health of a person, but do not serve as positive motivators for producing results.

The satisfiers are those that motivate coaches and other supervisory personnel to be productive and satisfy their needs. For example, recognition received from an athletic director or from a head coach is a positive satisfier for his/her subordinates. If a coach or supervisor were to make the following comments, he/she would be highly motivated.

I have been praised for my efforts by the athletic director, head coach, or supervisor.
I received praise and a reward for my efforts.
My idea was accepted by the team.
I received an unexpected promotion.
I received an expected promotion.

Another satisfier is the completion of tasks. If the coach or supervisor were to make the following comments, he/she would be expressing a high degree of motivation.

I successfully completed a task or some aspect of it.
I solved a difficult problem.
I see the results of my efforts.

Another satisfier is the work itself. The coach might comment:

My tasks are interesting.
My tasks are challenging.

Accepting responsibility is another positive motivator. This is expressed in the following phrases:

I am responsible for my own efforts.
I am given responsibility for the efforts of others.
I am allowed to perform tasks without supervision.

Opportunity to advance and to gain experience is another positive satisfier. The coach might state:

I have an opportunity to complete a whole task (all phases).
This experience will help me to become better and to advance.

To be accepted by the team and to be able to work with other people is a positive motivator. It satisfies the needs of coaches and other athletic supervisors, and may be expressed by the following comments:

I like the people I work with.
The people I work with cooperate
I am part of a cohesive group.

The higher level of needs according to Maslow—self-realization, self-esteem, recognition from others, and acceptance from other people—are all related to the job of coaching and to other aspects of supervision. When they are fulfilled, these needs become the motivators and satisfiers.

However, the necessary hygiene factors or dissatisfiers do not inspire coaches or supervisory personnel to high levels of productivity.

Working conditions, although necessary, are hygiene factors, which may be expressed as follows:

Working conditions are poor.
The work load is too heavy.

Other hygiene factors are concerned with administrative policies. They are commonly expressed as follows:

The administration and organization of the group are very poor.
The personnel policies and practices are poor.
I disagree with group policies and goals.
Group policies are poorly communicated.

Poor relationships with supervisors, head coaches, or athletic administrative personnel are often the dissatisfiers. They may be expressed as follows:

I have unfriendly relations with the head coach/athletic administrator.
My head coach/administrator does not give me support when I have problems.
My head coach/administrator is not willing to listen to my suggestions.
My administrator was dishonest.
My administrator/head coach does not give credit for work done.

Another hygiene factor concerns interpersonal relationships. For example:

I have poor working relationships with my subordinates.
I have poor personal relationships with my subordinates.
I do not like my peers.
The people I work with will not cooperate.
I am socially isolated from my peers.

Salary is another dissatisfier, usually expressed in these terms:

I did not receive an expected pay increase.
I received a pay increase that was less or later than expected.
My salary compares unfavorably with my peers' salaries.
My salary is very poor.

Poor supervision is a hygiene factor that serves as a dissatisfier. It can be expressed in the following ways:

I have an incompetent coach/administrator.
My supervisor shows favoritism.
My superior is consistently critical.
My coach/administrator tries to do everything by himself.

The hygiene factors or dissatisfiers are the lower level needs in Maslow's hierarchy. They are associated with physiological and security needs, and to some degree with social acceptance. The lesson is fairly clear: If an athletic administrator hopes to motivate his coaching and supervisory personnel to win, to satisfy fans, to make money, to improve the program's image, or to achieve other program objectives, he/she must motivate his subordinates with satisfiers. Once the lower level needs of people are satisfied (physiological and security), they do not serve as motivators like the acceptance, esteem and recognition, and self-actualizing needs.

Generally, coaches and supervisors seek satisfaction of hygiene factors only when motivators or satisfiers are not satisfied. The decision to join an athletic program and to remain with it is influenced mainly by hygiene factors, but the decision to become productive is influenced by satisfiers. Strategies to improve morale are associated with hygiene factors while strategies to increase productivity are associated with satisfiers.

EVALUATION OF COACHES: A SYSTEM OF MANAGEMENT BY OBJECTIVES

As stated previously, the most common organizational objectives of coaching are (1) to improve the win-loss record, (2) to develop athletes' character, (3) to improve the quality of athletics, (4) to reduce athletic costs, (5) to improve coaching methods and processes, (6) to improve the

Objective: To Motivate Coaches and Other Supervisors

Strategies	Strengths	Weaknesses
Are the following satisfiers used to motivate coaches and supervisors to high degrees of productivity?		
1. Achievement		
2. Recognition		
3. Work itself		
4. Responsibility		
5. Advancement		
Are the following hygiene factors used to motivate coaches and supervisors to high degree of productivity?		
1. Administrative policies		
2. Supervision		
3. Salary		
4. Personal relationships		
5. Working conditions		
If "yes" to any of the hygiene factors, consider it as a weakness.		
Overall Evaluation:		

image of the athletic program, and (7) others. How does an athletic administrator evaluate the coaching staff to determine whether these objectives are being accomplished? One way is to install a system of Management by Objectives (MBO).

Effective management has been defined as the art and science of reaching objectives through people and other resources. According to the MBO system, the superior and subordinate of an organizational unit jointly identify the unit's objectives, define each individual's major areas of responsibility in terms of results expected of him/her, and then use these measures as guides for operating the unit and evaluating each member's contribution. An athletic program is a unique organization which can apply this concept for its own effectiveness.

There are two preconditions necessary to make an MBO system work: (1) the support and equitable treatment of the top administration, and (2) the various levels in the organization must have a well-coordinated and identified hierarchy of objectives which fit together from the bottom to the top. If one unit in the organization is not rewarded in the same manner as another, a problem of fairness will crop up. Thus, a principle of equity will be violated if the MBO system is allowed to operate in only one unit and not in another. Further, the objectives must be known and accepted if an MBO system is to work.

The first step in an MBO system is to identify the objectives of each sport for the coming year, preferably in quantifiable terms such as measures of performance. The results to be achieved can be expressed in terms of quantity, quality, time, expense, and others. For example, one sport may agree to have a 60% win-loss record this year (a 15% improvement over last year). Another might be to research and develop one major innovation during the coming year. Perhaps another would be to reduce expenses by 5% over last year. Or another would be to attend three coaching clinics this next year. Another might be to cut disciplinary actions by 10% next year, or it might be appropriate to visit personally five new faculty members next year.

The second step in an MBO system is to clarify the responsibilities of each individual so that everyone will have a clear understanding of what is expected of him/her. This step may be accomplished by preparing a position description or modifying the present one.

The third step is a most crucial one—the setting of objectives for the next budget year with each person individually by means of joint agreement between superior and subordinate. For example, the superior sets down the objectives for each of his subordinates; each subordinate proposes the objectives as he/she perceives them; together they reach agreement on a set for the next year. Individual participation in defining the objectives is very much encouraged because a personal commitment to an objective makes it more probable that the objective will be achieved.

Checking the results of the promised milestones during the budget year is the fourth step in an MBO system. To find out whether a coach is meeting his/her targets, the administrator must have some prompt feedback on performance. This feedback is necessary for two reasons: (1) to eliminate inappropriate objectives, and (2) to introduce new inputs that could help the coach reach his/her objectives.

Setting a date to review each coach's performance is the fifth step. During this evaluation of actual versus promised performance, the coach can give reasons for any variance between actual and planned.

The sixth step is to set up a meeting to discuss any problems that a coach may have. This is the time to discuss uncontrollable events that could hinder the coach's plans.

The seventh step is to review the performance of the individual sport and determine objectives for the coming year. The purpose is to set more realistic objectives for the next period and to start a new cycle of MBO.

Advantages and Disadvantages of MBO

Probably the major advantage of MBO is that it measures the coach's or supervisor's contribution to the program. This contribution can be evaluated for promotion or other rewards. The MBO system measures actual results not activities. As such its emphasis is on the accomplishment of ob-

Objective: To Evaluate Coaching Performance by an MBO System

Factors	Theory Compared to Actual Situation	Evaluation: Strength	Evaluation: Weakness
Does the athletic program use an MBO system to evaluate coaching performance?			
1. Preconditions			
a. Support and equitable treatment of top administration			
b. Hierarchy of objectives			
2. Steps involved			
a. Identify objectives of each sport, in quantifiable terms			
b. Clarify responsibilities			
c. Joint setting of objectives			
d. Checking results			
e. Review performance			
f. Discuss results			
g. Recycle			
Overall Evaluation:			

jectives, not processes by which objectives are accomplished. Another advantage is that the MBO stresses teamwork and coordinated effort through a common definition of objectives. When the objectives are mutually agreed upon, a greater degree of coordinated effort can be expected. Another advantage is that the responsibilities for various positions are defined—no one can pass the buck. The individual is responsible for his own performance. When results are emphasized, rather than processes, favoritism is reduced. Evaluation can be based on objective measures rather than subjective ones subject to favoritism. Promotable coaches may be identified through the MBO method, since evaluation is based on performance rather than on personality. Through the MBO method, communications are improved between sender and receiver: messages are simplified since they are directed to the individual responsible for certain results. The MBO system is integral to the effective administration of athletic programs.

However, there are some limitations. If the system cannot produce measurable results, it has limited value. Win-loss records, profit figures, and attendance are subject to an MBO system. However, character development, image, and quality of life are very difficult to measure. Another limitation is that some organizational goals cannot be subdivided into a hierarchy of objectives. Sometimes administrators will put a halo over the head of one coach whose impressive performance in one area proves beneficial to other areas. When the administrator disregards the bad results and overemphasizes the good, he is practicing the halo effect. The opposite of the halo effect is the hypercritical effect, the tendency of an administrator to stress a coach's poor performance in one area and to ignore any strengths the coach may later exhibit.

A fifth limitation of MBO is the assumption that the administrator and coach will set fair objectives and accurate standards. If an administrator sets unreasonably high objectives, chances are they will not be achieved. A sixth limitation is that the MBO is built on results alone. It does not provide a measure for methods of achieving the results. If unethical practices of a coach are being used to win, is it right to consider only the successful results? Finally, it must be taken into account that luck—good or bad—can affect the success of an athletic program.

An administrator can evaluate the strengths and weaknesses of an athletic program's MBO system from the chart on the preceding page.

CHAPTER SUMMARY

Both on-the-job and off-the-job training are used to improve coaching effectiveness. When an administrator decides on strategies for the selection and placement of coaches or supervisors, on-the-job training and experience are an important consideration. Other considerations are whether the situations are high control, moderate control, or low control; whether the coaches are experienced or inexperienced; whether the opening is a long-run or short-run position; and whether the coach is a task-motivated or relationship-motivated leader. The figures in this chapter illustrate various strategies.

Head coaches can use satisfiers to motivate their staff. The satisfiers are achievement, recognition, work, responsibility, and advancement; they are used to increase workers' productivity and satisfaction. The dissatisfiers or hygiene factors—administrative policies, supervision, salary, personal relationships, working conditions—may not be used to attain high degrees of satisfaction and productivity.

Evaluation of coaches can be accomplished by a system of Management by Objectives (MBO). The MBO system depends on two preconditions: (1) support and equitable treatment of the top administration and (2) the availability of an internal hierarchy of objectives. There are seven steps in an MBO system: (1) identify objectives of each sport in measurable terms, (2) clarify responsibilities, (3) jointly set the objectives, (4) check results, (5) review performance, (6) discuss results, and (7) recycle. The MBO system may be used effectively to evaluate coaching performance.

Case 7-1 TRAINING FOR HEAD COACHES

Dr. Lon Farrell, assistant athletic director at the University of Arkansas, responded cheerfully to a series of questions concerning Frank Broyles's coaching philosophy about training of assistant coaches.

"I'll say this. When Frank Broyles resigned as head football coach, he left a legacy that no major school in the country can match. Sixteen men who have either played or coached under Frank's direction have become head coaches at university division schools in the NCAA. At least sixty have become assistant coaches at university division schools. In fact, I made a list of coaches who have been influenced by Frank's philosophy of training coaches [see list].

"As you may know, Frank Broyles was an assistant coach himself and never received any encouragement to become a head coach. When he became a head coach nineteen years ago, he vowed that he would encourage his assistants to become head coaches and provide training opportunities for them. Compare that philosophy with several coaches I know personally who will not train their assistants to become head coaches. They do not want to spend extra time training coaches in the summer because it's too much work. They do not want their assistants to leave. Many highly successful football programs have kept their football coaching staffs in tact. But Frank's unselfish philosophy has been to actively help his assistants to better their positions, if possible.

"Why did he follow this philosophy? He found that training for head coaching positions made his coaches more effective. When they become effective, our program becomes effective. We have flexibility in our coaching staff, allowing us to move them around if necessary. If one coach leaves, it's easy to move one of our present coaches into his slot.

"I've been here for sixteen years and during that time I know that it's easier to move a coach from defense to offense than to go outside and hire a new offensive coach. Our old defensive secondary coach, for example, knows our offensive philosophy and the peculiarities of our situation much better than a new coach. Not too much time is spent moving him from secondary defense to offensive backfield because he already knows about it. I've seen this movement in the case of Johnny Majors, Doug Dickey, Bill Pace, and most recently Bill Lewis, all of whom appreciated the move.

Frank Broyles' Coaches

UNIVERSITY DIVISION HEAD COACHES

*Freddie Akers—Texas
*Jim Carlen—South Carolina
*Jerry Claiborne—Maryland
Charlie Coffey—Virginia Tech
*Doug Dickey—Florida
*Hayden Fry—North Texas
Bill Fulcher—Georgia Tech
Hootie Ingram—Clemson
*Bill Lewis—Wyoming
*Jim MacKenzie—Oklahoma
*John Majors—Pittsburgh
*Bo Rein—N.C. State
*Pepper Rogers—Georgia Tech
*Jackie Sherrill—Washington St.

*Present coaching position of men who have played or coached under Frank Broyles.

*Barry Switzer—Oklahoma
Richard Williamson—Memphis St.

UNIVERSITY DIVISION ASSISTANTS

*Richard Bell—South Carolina
*Buddy Bennett—Virginia Tech
*Don Boyce—Arkansas
*Jessie Branch—Arkansas
*Tommy Brasher—Northeast La.
*Don Breaux—Texas
*Louis Campbell—Alabama
Billy Clay—Virginia Tech
*Jim Crowson—Arkansas
*Jim Collier—L.S.U.
*Clay Cooper—Missouri
Gunther Cunningham—Stanford
Jack Davis—Mississippi State
*Frank Falks—Arkansas
*Bobby Fields—Mississippi State
Bob Ford—Arkansas
*Bob Gatling—Arkansas
Ken Hatfield—Florida
*Harold Horton—Arkansas
*Jim Johnson—Arkansas
*Mervin Johnson—Notre Dame
*Harry Jones—Pittsburgh
*Pat Jones—SMU
Billy Laird—Tulane
*Bill Lewis—Arkansas
*Don Lindsey—USC
Borys Malczycki—Arkansas
Wilson Matthews—Arkansas
Billy Michaels—Oklahoma
George McKinney—Virginia Tech
*Leroy Montgomery—Arkansas
*Larry New—South Carolina
Bobby Nix—Arkansas
Gordon Nix—Arkansas
*Lanny Norris—East Carolina
*Gordon Norwood—Rice
*Bill Pace—Georgia
*Mike Parker—Wyoming
*Terry Phillips—Virginia Tech
*Tom Reed—Arkansas
*Bo Rein—Arkansas
*Bruce Shaw—Arkansas
*Bobby Roper—Pittsburgh
Gordon Smith—Iowa State
*Steve Sprayberry—Mississippi St.
Ron Toman—Tulane
*Ray Trail—Tennessee
*Richard Trail—Vanderbilt
Don Trull—Arkansas
*Ken Turner—Arkansas
*Fred Von Appen—Oregon
*Steve Walters—Morehead State
Steed White—Arkansas
*Joe Fred Young—Arkansas

COLLEGE DIVISION HEAD COACHES

Glen Gossett—Northwest La.
Floyd Huggins—Hardin-Simmons
*Bud Mercer—Missouri Mines
*Russ Sloan—Northeast Missouri State
*Ken Stephens—University of Central Arkansas

COLLEGE DIVISION ASSISTANT COACHES

Gary Howard—Central Oklahoma
*Jerry Welch—Emporia State
*Joe Kinnan—Eastern Kentucky

PROFESSIONAL ASSISTANTS

*Raymond Berry—Cleveland Browns
*Wally English—Detroit Lions
*Joe Gibbs—St. Louis Cardinals
*Billy Kinard—Green Bay Packers
*Hank Kuhlmann—Green Bay Packers
*Paul Lanham—Washington Redskins
*Dixie White—New Orleans Saints

HIGH SCHOOL HEAD COACHES

*Mike Bender—El Dorado
Jackie Brasuell—Van Buren
*Harry Burnham—Memphis Overton
Danny Geoghagen—Marshall
*Merrill Green—Bryan, Texas
Don Horton—El Dorado
Charlie Moore—Marianna

*Gary Parsons—Marvell
*Ernest Ruple—Conway
*Rickey Sayle—Memphis White Station
*Jerry White—Star City
Darrell Williams—Graham, Texas
*Jarrell Williams—Springdale

ASSISTANT HIGH SCHOOL COACHES

Martine Bercher—Little Rock
Rodney Brand—Little Rock
Jim Brawner—Little Rock Pulaski
*Wesley Bryant—Texarkana, Texas
Dick Bumpas—Van Buren
Roger Callahan—Jonesboro
Roy Fears—Springdale
*Gerald Gardner—Nacogdoches, Texas
*Lynn Garner—Houston, Texas
*Melvin Gibbs—San Antonio, Texas
*Larry Gosney—Blanchard, Okla.
Lynn Greenwell—Trumann
*Ronnie Hammers—Marshall, Texas
Mike Hedges—Bentonville
Alvin Jones—Searcy
*Bob Lee—Columbia, Missouri
*Jim Long—Green Forest
Danny Loundsbury—Morris Plains, N. J.
Mickey Maroney—Fort Worth, Texas
*Pat May—Florida
Jack Moran—Jacksonville
*Ron Myers—St. Louis, Missouri
*Mickey McShane—Garland, Texas
*Jim Pullen—Lake Jackson, Texas
*Ken Ramey—Fayetteville
*Billy Redell—Paris, Texas
Doug Scheel—West Fork
*Bob Stankovitch—Texarkana
*Gary Starr—Joplin, Missouri
*Champ Thomas—Fort Smith Northside
*Lyndell Thomas—Elkins
*Tommy Trantham—Hot Springs

ATHLETIC ADMINISTRATORS

*Wilson Matthews—Arkansas
*Dr. Lon Farrell—Arkansas
*David Cawood—NCAA
*Butch Henry—Arkansas
*Hootie Ingram—Southeast Conference

"Most of our training occurs on the job. For example, it's routine to have group staff meetings every morning to discuss problems and tactics. As a result everyone is encouraged to participate and to learn from others. In fact, our eager beaver coaches take copious notes during these meetings. What better way is there to pass along knowledge, experience, and savvy for a head coaching position?

"I've already mentioned the job rotation plan, if and when it becomes apparent to use it. And after Frank calls the shots before the game plan is formulated, he then delegates the responsibility, authority, and accountability to his assistants to carry out the plan. If anything goes wrong (and it always does!) Frank takes the blame from the fans.

"We also use off-the-job methods. For example, we have our coaches attend pro camps where knowledge is shared with all the coaches. It's fantastic! Ours is the only profession I know of where there is a constant sharing of ideas among all coaches with no strings attached. No lawyers, doctors, engineers, or business managers I know will share their professional information like football coaches will.

"We do not attend clinics . . . in fact, we put them on for high school coaches. However, occasionally we'll bring in outside speakers to talk about offensive philosophy, motivation, and other topics. We also travel to other schools during spring practices to see what we can learn, and we reciprocate with any coach who wants to see what we are doing. We read all the time. We borrow film and watch it by the hour. Films are perhaps the best teachers we have.

"These philosophies, strategies, and methods have allowed us to become well-known in the coaching profession."

Case 7-2 HUTCHINSON JUNIOR COLLEGE BASKETBALL

Gene Keady, basketball coach at Hutchinson Junior College, pondered his future plans. Nine years ago he became an assistant coach at Hutchinson Junior College, under Samuel Butterfield. That year Hutch Juco went 22–7 and was third in the nationals. Then Gene Keady was promoted to head basketball coach after only one year as an assistant.

During the next eight years Keady's teams had compiled an enviable record:

1st year as head coach (won Kansas Jayhawk Conference; 12th in Nationals)	18– 6
2nd year as head coach (12th in Nationals)	25– 3
3rd year	22–11
4th year	16– 8
5th year (6th in Nationals)	28– 6
6th year (8th in Nationals)	22– 4
7th year (2nd in Nationals)	29– 4
8th year	25– 4
Overall	185–46

Gene Keady was quite proud of his 80% win-loss record at Hutchinson. He recalled the strategies he used to accomplish that record.

His experience told him that quality players were a must. He had to have a great center, a great quarterback, and two or three great shooters and rebounders. However, he had to recruit these types of players with a handicap—it was a rule in the Jayhawk Conference that a school could only give an athletic scholarship consisting of books, tuition, and a job, no room and board. He could find the prospective athletes, but he had some difficulties in getting them to sign with Hutch Juco.

He had one assistant coach who had to be enthusiastic, aggressive, and knowledgeable about junior college basketball. This person had to have a sound philosophy, work hard and long hours, be well organized, and be prepared to sacrifice in order to win.

A quantity of athletes was important for good practice sessions and for depth in games. Seven to eight quality players were enough players, if they could really play. He liked to have from two to two and one-half players for each position, with about half freshmen and half sophomores.

His great trainers made his teams durable. Of course, he used weights, agility drills, and the like. Off-season conditioning was a must. The only real weakness was the lack of control over the players' diets since they did not live in an athletic dorm.

Gene Keady believed that a good team had to adapt to his system, but he also adapted his system to the players' strengths. Both players' talent and a system were necessary, but his players must believe in the coach's philosophy. Constant practice against opponents' strengths was stressed, as well as practice for special situations.

It was very important to have discipline on the team, particularly in regard to promptness. If a player promised to be at a particular place and time, he had better be there! Keady had to depend on the players and they had to depend on him.

Both offense and defense were necessary for team balance, but hard-nosed defense was fundamental. His experience taught him that defense won more games than offense.

His teams were drilled in quickness, particularly on defense. Agility drills were constantly stressed. Weight training was important. He constantly yelled at his players to be quick in order to play great defense.

His teams were unique in that they had a great fieldhouse and facilities. Of course, a winning tradition also helped. Because of the fieldhouse, the National Junior College Tournaments were played at Hutchinson. When players and potential players viewed the facilities, they were impressed with the 10,000-seat capacity. Attendance was at least 85,000 each year. The nice profit made on basketball supported other types of athletics at Hutch Juco.

Keady always looked for innovations. He attended coaching clinics and read books, articles, and newspapers. He used his own intuition in trying to innovate. However, he stressed fundamentals in coaching, trying to stay simple.

Multiple offensive and defensive schemes were used. He had to have a variety of schemes to counter any competitor's strengths and to prevent any competitor from ganging up on his team's strengths.

He always worried about keeping the team healthy. He had a trainer, a medical doctor, and a dentist available. Equipment was inspected for safety. Some of his key players sometimes played while in pain, but always with team and player safety in mind, since an injured player made the team less effective.

Scheduling was very important to Gene Keady. Experience told him not to overschedule, and if possible, to play the majority of games at home.

His teams were well organized. Coaches' and players' manuals were used. He would videotape his practice sessions to show proper assignments and "busted" plays. The videotaping's initial cost was high, but he used it many times. He was the boss and everyone knew it. He practiced an authoritarian leadership style, perhaps too much so, he readily admitted.

A clean practice environment was very important for team morale and team spirit. And he used first-class travel accommodations. He maintained that he could not recruit the best players without a clean practice environment or without going first class in lodging, meals, and travel.

Top-notch equipment was always used. Only the best was good enough. It was very important to be first class all around!

He used motivational films to promote leadership on his teams. He used to say that a team cannot win without leadership. As a result he had to have top character players. As a coach he was concerned with being a leader. One of his pet peeves was weak officials who could be intimidated by a coach. He tried to get rid of them after the season was over.

The three main strategies he considered important if he were going to have a winning season were (1) a good schedule, (2) quality of athletes, and (3) coaching ability.

Gene Keady was suddenly offered the position of assistant coach at the University of Arkansas. He was asked to become Eddie Sutton's assistant. Keady had to decide whether to leave his winning tradition, strategies, and resources and become an assistant coach at a major institution. The basketball tradition at Arkansas was very weak. Their quality of players was questionable. Sutton, a new coach, was being hired, with Keady as one of two assistant coaches. The past twenty years of basketball at Arkansas had been dim, with a 36–65% win-loss record the past five years. The teams were stronger offensively than defensively. The practice facilities were marginal. All of these negative factors weighed on his mind. Could he, as an assistant coach, help reverse Arkansas' tradition?

Case 7-3 THE EVALUATION OF COACHES

Southwestern State University's head football coach was particularly proud of his system of evaluating coaches. It was based on a self-rating and superior rating scheme. The following coaching objectives were highlighted:

1. Coaching effectiveness
2. Recruiting effectiveness
3. Disciplinary effectiveness
4. Academic relationships
5. Players and staff relationships
6. Improving professional knowledge and staff efficiency
7. Department business
8. Personal image regarding school, community, and state

A copy of the evaluation shows the individual activities required of each coach.

The evaluation system is used primarily for salary purposes, once a year. Three people are involved—the coach himself, the head coach, and the athletic director. All three have an input into the final evaluation.

The athletic director recently attended a seminar on Management by Objectives and was wondering what types of modifications would have to be made to switch to an MBO system. What would you advise?

DATE: ____________________
PRESENT SALARY ____________
RECOMMENDED SALARY ________
APPROVED SALARY __________

SELF-EVALUATION AND HEAD COACH EVALUATION

PROCEDURE: Please read each statement carefully, and then rate yourself 5 4 3 2 1. Circle the number that most accurately describes your efficiency or status. A five rating means you evaluate yourself very highly, a three indicates that you consider yourself to be average. Less than three means below average.

EMPLOYEE'S SIGNATURE ____________________
HEAD COACH'S SIGNATURE: ____________________
DIRECTOR OF ATHLETICS' SIGNATURE: ____________________

( ) Head Coach's Evaluation
( ) Asst. Coach's Own Evaluation

A. COACHING

1. I make an effort to coach all players, not just the top ones. Example: Working with B Team and freshmen personnel during scrimmages and after practices.

   5 4 3 2 1

2. I make a point of trying to praise players for good things done, rather than just constantly harping about their mistakes. In simple terms trying to motivate daily with positive psychology to instill confidence in the player. Players tend to dislike coaches who constantly criticize and never throw a rose.

   5 4 3 2 1

3. My drills, etc. are varied to the extent that they do not become boring.

   5 4 3 2 1

4. I take full advantage of getting written material in the hands of my players, holding meetings, giving tests, and watching films in an effort to promote learning and understanding.

   5 4 3 2 1

5. My meetings and practices are run in such a manner that I tolerate nothing that detracts from learning. I am strict with players and demand mental discipline.

   5 4 3 2 1

6. I spend as much time as necessary on the job (office or meetings).

   5 4 3 2 1

B. RECRUITING

1. I personally make an effort to visit each prospect who comes to campus, not just shake his hand.

   5 4 3 2 1

2. I have a large working list of prospects at the conclusion of their junior year of high school, or very early in their senior year. I contact each of the prospects personally several times before their season has ended.

   5 4 3 2 1

3. I personally contact parents as well as the prospect to share with them my interest in their son.

   5 4 3 2 1

4. I try to get each prospect interested in college. I help him to understand that it is not merely a question of "what he can do for us" but rather "what we can do for each other."

   5 4 3 2 1

5. I spend my time wisely on Thursday and Friday of each week during the season, recruiting and corresponding with prospects.

   5 4 3 2 1

6. I do a good job of organizing alumni in my area before the recruiting season so they can assist me.

   5 4 3 2 1

7. I personally give follow-up consideration to each prospect I evaluate by film or observation. In other words, I reject him in a prudent manner to insure a good working relationship with his school, coach, and community.

   5 4 3 2 1

8. I personally acknowledge faculty and supporters for their help with our recruiting weekends.

5 4 3 2 1

9. When I go into a home to visit with parents I have a ritual worked out so I can tell our story effectively. In other words, I have film, pictures, charts, and literature to sell our program. I am informed and I have a plan.

5 4 3 2 1

10. When I sell our program I try to sell myself also. In other words I can make the prospect feel I have an interest in him that will continue for four years and beyond, and that his happiness and welfare will be of great concern to me for at least the duration of his stay.

5 4 3 2 1

11. I invite prospects to visit with players I have recruited and to ask them questions. I encourage them to ask questions about my role as a recruiter and coach, and about me as an individual.

5 4 3 2 1

12. I always take advantage of opportunities to promote public relations with all coaches in my area and not just with prospects.

5 4 3 2 1

13. I make an effort to make all high school coaches who visit our department feel at home.

5 4 3 2 1

14. I make an attempt to constantly keep myself advised regarding the structure of our university, our strengths and weaknesses, what our colleges are, and what proposed major fields are available.

5 4 3 2 1

C. DISCIPLINE

1. I do my part to enforce rules or guidelines we have set up, and I do not rely on other coaches to avoid involvement.

5 4 3 2 1

2. I fulfill assigned discipline chores to the fullest extent. I am involved

with help sessions, and I counsel the individual disciplinary problems assigned to me.

5 4 3 2 1

3. I make sure that my players are at practice and on time. I do this for all varsity players and T-Teamers who play the position I coach.

5 4 3 2 1

4. I help with team travel. I make sure that our players dress properly, conduct themselves properly, promote a good public image, and maintain a team frame of mind.

5 4 3 2 1

5. I notify parents if I must discipline a boy I have recruited or coached. A well written letter will suffice; only drastic problems merit a phone call.

5 4 3 2 1

6. I try to anticipate the disciplinary problems my players may be involved in before they actually surface.

5 4 3 2 1

D. ACADEMICS

1. I know the courses my players are enrolled in and their status from an academic and eligibility standpoint.

5 4 3 2 1

2. I follow up and get on top of class cutting problems when one of my players is reported to me.

5 4 3 2 1

3. I am constantly trying to promote good public relations with the faculty and the administration in an effort to get their help in recruiting. Also, I encourage the faculty to report players not doing well in their classes.

5 4 3 2 1

4. I visit each player I have recruited on a regular basis to discuss his academic and personal problems.

5 4 3 2 1

5. I keep in touch with parents of my players who are academic risks and solicit their help in motivating their son.

5 4 3 2 1

E. RELATIONSHIP WITH PLAYERS AND STAFF

1. I do not make unfounded statements when judging players; such statements might affect our staff's evaluation of a player.

5 4 3 2 1

2. I am courteous to all players at all times.

5 4 3 2 1

3. I regularly visit each floor of our dormitory to promote a feeling of good player-coach relationship.

5 4 3 2 1

4. I am courteous to members of our staff as well as to coaches. An atmosphere of common courtesy often increases the staff's productivity.

5 4 3 2 1

F. IMPROVING PROFESSIONAL KNOWLEDGE AND STAFF EFFICIENCY

1. I read all literature sent out by professional organizations.

5 4 3 2 1

2. I attempt to seek out new literature and knowledge.

5 4 3 2 1

3. At staff meetings, I suggest new trends and ideas I have learned. I do not just sit back and let one or two set the pattern for our offense, defense, or program.

5 4 3 2 1

4. I use good judgment by not discussing internal staff problems with people outside our department.

5 4 3 2 1

5. In conversation with friends, I always speak highly of our staff members even if I do not agree with their teaching, philosophy, or effort.

5 4 3 2 1

G. DEPARTMENT BUSINESS

1. I do a good job of filling out travel reports accurately so that they don't take additional time.

5 4 3 2 1

2. I am prudent when spending department funds. I do not make false claims of expenses in travel. I do not feed and entertain people who are not important to our program.

5 4 3 2 1

3. I plan recruiting trips wisely. I plan so I can see the maximum number of prospects in one trip. I do not just hop here and there without careful planning.

5 4 3 2 1

4. I am punctual in turning in travel reports after I return from a trip, or on a weekly basis.

5 4 3 2 1

5. I fulfill my obligations when returning my loan car to the dealer. I replace tires, repair dents, give regular oil and lubricant service, and return the car in tiptop shape.

5 4 3 2 1

6. I do a good job of showing my appreciation to car dealers for their contribution.

5 4 3 2 1

7. I do not use National Watts, Credit Cards, and Station Calls for personal use unrelated to business.

5 4 3 2 1

8. I do not use the phone when a well planned letter in advance would suffice.

5 4 3 2 1

9. I thoroughly understand what travel expenses are allowed and

how much for each (example: laundry money is not included). I understand how much is allowed for meals and hotels.

5 4 3 2 1

10. I make an effort to avoid staying in the most expensive hotels. Also, I make an effort to stay where we can get special rates.

    5 4 3 2 1

11. I investigate the possibility of getting courtesy cars in areas where they are available.

    5 4 3 2 1

12. I am prompt in settling travel accounts with our own departmental business office.

    5 4 3 2 1

H. PERSONAL IMAGE IN REGARD TO SCHOOL, COMMUNITY, AND STATE

1. I do not use alcoholic beverages in excess. I present a good image of myself at gatherings that reflect our program.

   5 4 3 2 1

2. If I am a married man, I uphold marital responsibilities that are expected of me as a teacher and a coach.

   5 4 3 2 1

3. I keep my business and financial affairs in a state not embarrassing to me, my family, or the athletic department.

   5 4 3 2 1

4. I present a satisfactory image to the public regarding grooming and dress, particularly when recruiting and representing our department at public functions.

   5 4 3 2 1

FOOTNOTES

[1] Abraham Maslow, *Motivation and Personality* (New York: Harper Brothers, 1954).

[2] Frederick Herzberg, *Work and the Nature of Man* (Cleveland: World Publishing Co., 1966).

8

THE ATHLETIC ADMINISTRATOR'S RELATIONSHIP WITH THE ATHLETES

Although the coaching staff has more direct contact with athletes than any administrator, there are certain areas in which an administrator plays a significant role in dealing with athletes. There has to be an equitable exchange of athletes' personal objectives for those of the athletic program, and the athletic administrator plays a key role in providing that exchange. Normally, an athlete expects to accomplish certain personal objectives by participating in athletics. Most athletes expect personal recognition and esteem from others. They hope to feel a sense of accomplishment; most would accept the responsibility of performing a task as a starter or a team member. Athletes often seek an opportunity to advance and to gain experience for the first team or other, more lucrative positions. Athletes look for security, good working conditions, and acceptance by teammates and supervisors. In the case of a pro, more money is another objective to be accomplished. These are a few of the athlete's many goals. Likewise some degree of security is another objective which most athletes would prefer to have. And there are others.

In exchange for these personal objectives the athlete is expected to contribute, among other things, talent, time, effort, and loyalty to the program. The athlete helps to produce a winning team to satisfy the fans. Consequently, profits are made, attendance grows, the team's image improves, and other related organizational objectives are achieved.

The exchange of the athletes' personal objectives and the program's objectives has to be understood and practiced by any successful athletic administrator.

Objective: To Maintain an Equitable Exchange of Contributions by the Athletes to the Program and Vice Versa

Factors	Strength	Weakness
A. Do the athletes contribute the following to the program:		
1. Skills and talent		
2. Effort		
3. Time		
4. Knowledge		
5. Loyalty		
6. Competitiveness		
7. Others		
Overall evaluation:		
B. Does the program contribute the following to the athlete:		
1. Recognition		
2. Sense of accomplishment		
3. Responsibility to perform		
4. Opportunity to advance		
5. Opportunity to gain experience		
6. Acceptance by peers		
7. Acceptance by supervisors		
8. Salary (professional)		
9. Good working conditions		
10. Fringe benefits		
11. Degree of security		
12. Others		
Overall evaluation:		
C. Is there a mutual exchange:		
1. For the athletes		
2. For the program		
Overall evaluation:		
D. Evaluate the athletes' contributions to the following program objectives:		
1. To provide an acceptable win-loss record for fan entertainment		
2. To develop character in athletes		
3. To improve the program's image		
4. To grow		
5. To make a profit		
6. To maintain continuity		
7. To maintain market share		
8. To become a leader		
9. To improve the quality of life for society		
10. Others		
Overall evaluation:		

RECRUITING ATHLETES

A winning team's key resource is having a number of quality athletes. It is vital for professionals, colleges, and to a lesser degree for high schools and junior highs to recruit athletes who will produce a team or event that attracts fans. A recruiting system is necessary to produce a successful program.

Usually several steps are involved in a recruiting system jointly directed by an administrator and the coaches. First, the coach must determine what types of athletes are needed. Normally the coaching staff will make this decision jointly, but sometimes the administrator is also involved. A list of the types of athletes needed is usually compiled and saved.

The second step is to prepare a position description and a position specification for those desired. This is a fairly easy step since most coaches know the functions involved in a particular position. Such criteria as speed, weight, height, age, marital status, injuries, and academics are fairly easy to discern. However, the intangibles—attitude, competitiveness, desire, willingness to sacrifice, prejudices, ethics—are difficult to determine but integral to the personality of a winning athlete.

The next step is to find the athletes. Fortunately, most teams can rely on two sources—internal and external. The internal sources are athletes on the team, their friends and acquaintances. Most athletic programs consciously try to develop a number of external sources for recruiting athletes. Colleges maintain a relationship with junior high and high school coaches; pros contact college coaches, alumni, and parents, as well as former players and fans, to provide suggestions about upcoming athletes. Development of good public relations is an absolute necessity when dealing with sources for recruiting athletes.

Normally, an athletic program will keep a list of potential athletes found through internal and external sources. The next step is to contact, usually by mail, those potentials to see if they are interested in the athletic program. Each one is usually asked to fill out a questionnaire or application if he/she is interested. This application allows the coach to begin his screening process.

Next comes intensive screening. If the coach is interested in a prospect, he requests that the athlete's present coach appraise the athlete's strengths and weaknesses. Films are also requested for a detailed analysis of the athlete's skills. These films are carefully scrutinized by other coaches who give their appraisals. Sometimes outside scouting reports are requested from professional scouting services or from former players who can spot talent. After examining the appraisals, the coach must decide whether to pursue the athlete further.

If the athlete is considered worthwhile, an intensive selling campaign is initiated. At this stage, competition for the athlete's services is keen. A marginal advantage might determine which program an athlete will select. In an effort to persuade the athlete to select a particular program, he/she receives literature about the program, letters written by the school and by

Objective: Maintain an Effective Recruiting System

Factors	Strength	Weakness
1. Does the recruiting system practice the following:		
1.1 Determine types of athletes needed		
1.2 Prepare specifications		
1.3 Locate sources		
1.31 Internal		
1.32 External		
1.4 Have athlete fill out application		
1.5 Intensive screening of athletes		
1.6 Selling campaign		
1.7 Visit the athlete		
1.8 Athlete visits program		
1.9 Testing (professionals)		
1.10 Final decision		
Overall evaluation:		

"friends" of the school, postcards, telephone calls, and other types of communication.

Finally, a trip is arranged so the program's representative can interview the athlete. The professionals might even ask for demonstrations by the athlete. After the interview, the athletic program's representative must decide whether the athlete is worthy of pursuit.

If the athlete passes this test, then he/she is usually asked to visit the athletic program. Here he/she visits coaches, athletes, faculty, friends, and other interested persons. The athlete has an opportunity to see the facilities, the practice areas, the training rooms, showers and locker rooms, eating and lodging facilities, the physical, social, and cultural environment of the area.

In the professional ranks, the athlete must be tested. Many times a player is tested, both physically and mentally, before being invited to try out for the team. In college ranks, testing is not permitted. As a result many colleges mistakenly recruit athletes who cannot make the team, physically or mentally.

Finally, a decision is made to have the athlete join the athletic program. If the team is fortunate, and if the recruiting system has worked well, chances are good, other factors equal, that the athlete will make a contribution to a successful program.

There are many problems in recruiting caused by the amateurism rule, particularly in colleges. Such things as automobiles, money, clothing, and stereos are offered as illegal inducements by "interested parties" to attract athletes to attend a particular school. Alumni and friends of the school are the biggest violators, and they cannot be controlled by athletic programs. Current recruiting rules do not punish the athlete; unfortunately, illegal practices will not stop until the athlete is punished or amateurism is abolished.

In any event, recruiting is an important part of athletic administration, particularly in the pros, in colleges, and in private high schools (Catholic high schools, for example). An administrator can use the analysis on the preceding page to determine the strengths and weaknesses of his recruiting system.

POLICIES AFFECTING ATHLETES

A policy is a general guide to thought and action, based on a set of principles, and instituted to accomplish objectives in recurring situations. In that definition there are four concepts: (1) a recurring situation, (2) an objective, (3) a principle, and (4) a guide to thought and action. When several policies are brought together in a policy manual, they generally reflect a philosophy of administration that sets the tone for an athletic program.

Most effective athletic programs are based on a written and unwritten administrative philosophy; this philosophy is often reflected in a policy and procedure manual. Consequently, when a situation recurs, there is a set of guidelines to follow that will help accomplish personal and organizational objectives. If the reason for the policy is stated or implied, that reason is usually the principle behind the policy. When there are certain steps to be followed in administering a policy, these steps usually form a procedure, or a series of sequential actions which have to be followed. Athletic programs, to be effectively administered, should have a written policy and procedure manual.

The contents of a policy manual for an effective athletic program will usually be organized around the following topics:

1. Organization structure
2. Athletes' policies
3. Coaches' policies
4. Financial policies
5. Others

For this discussion, a set of general policies is suggested for administering athletic programs.

1. Admissions, especially for colleges
   - 1.1 Transcripts and records
   - 1.2 Standards for admission
   - 1.3 Scholarships

   1.4 Physical exams
   1.5 Fees and books
2. Academics, both high schools and colleges
   2.1 Standards
   2.2 Tutors
   2.3 Postseason games
   2.4 Study hall
3. Benefits, for colleges and schools
   3.1 Complimentary tickets
   3.2 Insurance
   3.3 Hospitalization
   3.4 Outside and summer jobs
   3.5 Courtesy cars
   3.6 Alumni relations
   3.7 Trips
   3.8 Advertising by athletes
   3.9 Entertainment
4. Living arrangements, colleges
   4.1 Lodging rules
   4.2 Meal rules
   4.3 Personal cars
   4.4 Fraternities/sororities
5. Participation in contests, high schools and colleges
   5.1 Eligibility
   5.2 Transfers
   5.3 Lockers
   5.4 Training room
   5.5 Travel uniforms
   5.6 Participation in other sports
6. Recruiting, colleges
   6.1 Tryouts
   6.2 Trips and travel
7. Sportsmanship, all programs
   7.1 Awards
   7.2 Visiting team courtesies
8. Others

For a professional team, the policy and procedures manual might include the following topics (pertaining only to athletes):

1. Recruiting players
   1.1 Screening
   1.2 Draft
   1.3 Tryouts

    1.4 Hiring
    1.5 Firing
2. Salaries and wages
    2.1 Merit ratings
    2.2 Job evaluation
3. Fringe Benefits
    3.1 Insurance
    3.2 Pensions
    3.3 Tickets
    3.4 Others
4. Training
    4.1 Orientation
    4.2 Practices
    4.3 Conditions
    4.4 Safety
    4.5 Others
5. Union relations
    5.1 Contracts
    5.2 Negotiations
6. Others

To evaluate the strengths and weaknesses of policies affecting athletes, the administrator can use the analysis on the next page.

Disciplinary Action

Normally, disciplinary action involves the athlete and the coach. However, many times an athletic administrator is involved in important disciplinary actions.

Self-discipline means self-control. It is necessary for the athlete to have self-control and to adhere to standards of conduct if he is to be part of a successful athletic team. Disciplinary action, an administrative process, conditions individual and group behavior to accomplish organizational and personal goals. Self-discipline implies a degree of personal restraint and calls for subordination of personal objectives to an athletic program's objectives. Disciplinary action, on the other hand, motivates the athlete toward restraint through rewards and punishment. The objective is to maximize desired behavior and minimize undesired behavior to assure correct behavior in the future when program goals must be accomplished.

Unfortunately, disciplinary action is considered to be negative reinforcement. Yet, an administrator must recognize and practice sound disciplinary procedures. The administrator must be just, but sufficiently severe to maintain a high standard of conduct.

Decisions governing penalties or rewards should be based on thoroughly investigated facts; those punished must be aware of the facts and under-

Objective: To Administer Policies Regarding Athletes

	Strength	Weakness
1. Does the program have a written policy manual regarding athletes? yes/no		
2. If yes, does it include the following policies? (for colleges and schools)		
2.1 Admissions and related policies		
2.2 Academics and related policies		
2.3 Benefits		
2.4 Living arrangements		
2.5 Participation in athletic contests		
2.6 Recruiting		
2.7 Sportsmanship		
2.8 Others		
3. If yes, does it include the following policies? (for professional teams)		
3.1 Recruiting and related policies		
3.2 Salaries and wages		
3.3 Fringe benefits		
3.4 Training		
3.5 Union relations		
3.6 Others		
Overall evaluation:		

stand what they have done wrong. The nature and degree of disciplinary action should be carefully determined, based on findings from an investigation. The investigation should try to determine why the person acted as he/she did.

It is fair that similar disciplinary actions be taken for similar situations. Negative disciplinary action should be administered privately whenever possible so the person will not lose face with peers, subordinates, or superiors. The person's immediate superior should impose all punishment. Such action strengthens the leadership position of the superior. After the disciplinary action has been taken, the immediate superior should resume a normal attitude toward the offender. The offender should not feel permanently shamed. Finally, disciplinary action should not be taken unless there is a real need for it. If punishments are handed out freely and often, there will be continued undesired behavior.

If the administrator does not adhere to these principles, he/she can expect the following ill effects: loss of personal morale, weakened standards of conduct, little understanding of disciplinary action, undesirable personal behavior, no integration of personal and organizational goals, a weakened leadership role, a feeling of unfairness, possible "loss of face," and little assurance of desired behavior in the future. The ultimate result is a losing team that cannot accomplish its program objectives.

An administrator can evaluate disciplinary actions by using the following analysis.

Objective: To Administer Disciplinary Actions

	Strength	**Weakness**
1. Does the administrator practice the following principles in administering negative disciplinary actions when required?		
1.1 Just but sufficiently severe action		
1.2 Based on facts		
1.3 Individual intent considered		
1.4 Reasons made clear		
1.5 Consistent for identical situations		
1.6 Administered privately		
1.7 Imposed by immediate superior		
1.8 Resume normal attitude after penalty has been paid		
1.9 Real necessity prevails		
Overall evaluation:		

Legal Questions Concerning Athletes

Recently legal questions concerning athletes have arisen. Legal problems will play a role in the affairs of athletic programs as long as athletics continues to approach the status of American business. Some of the more recent court decisions may be of interest to athletic administrators.

One case involved the issue of a suspended athlete who wanted to participate in a high school football game. At the trial it was ruled that participation in athletic events is a privilege, not a constitutionally protected right. This same concept has been reinforced by two other decisions—one involving the Kentucky High School Athletic Association, and another involving the Iowa High School Athletic Association. The Indiana Supreme Court has stated, "that a student has no constitutional right to participate in interscholastic athletics."[1]

Another common legal question involves athlete-students who state that they are being denied economic opportunities if they are ruled ineligible to participate in sports. They ask for an injunction against the athletic association. The Behagen case[2] stated the criteria for granting a request. However, most athletes only want enough time to complete the season. By the time the case comes to court, the issue is usually resolved.

Procedural due process must be observed before athletes or schools are denied their right to compete. For example, in the Kelley case[3] the court found a lack of procedural due process because there were no standards and regulations for disciplinary action. Granting an injunction, the Tennessee court said that an athletic association was subject to the Fourteenth Amendment and the "due process" clause.

In another case, a transfer student was denied the right to play football for a year due to a state association rule. Since the refusal was not motivated by racial prejudice, the case was dismissed. The rule was instituted to prevent raids on athletic teams. The rule also prevents athletes from transferring to other schools if they dislike a coach.

One case involved discrimination on the basis of sex in Minnesota, where a high school association prohibited girls from participating in boys' athletics. The trial court in Brenden[4] concluded that the girls were discriminated against solely on the basis of sex and held that the rule was an arbitrary and unreasonable violation of the Fourteenth Amendment.

The recent enactment of Title IX of the Education Amendments Act of 1972 has made it mandatory to provide equal athletic opportunities for boys and girls. Title IX allows the Federal Government to withdraw funds, debar schools from future funds, and bring suits against schools that discriminate against students on the basis of sex. One argument for equalizing funds spent on boys' and girls' athletics is that parents pay taxes on an equal basis; therefore tax money should be distributed equally to boys' and girls' athletic programs.

Members of an athletic program should be aware of the first amendment to the Constitution of the United States, which guarantees every citizen freedom of speech and association. Although these freedoms are not absolute, they are usually given the highest judicial protection. Since athletes can express their freedom of speech in various ways, such as wearing armbands, or changing hairstyles, any undue restraint imposed on them may be protested freely.

In the 1969 case *Tinker* v. *Des Moines Independent School District*[5] the U.S. Supreme Court ruled on a freedom of speech issue. The Supreme Court ruled that it was legal for the public school students to wear black armbands during school hours to protest the Viet Nam War. The students actions were "a silent, passive expression of opinion, unaccompanied by a disorder or disturbance." They were exercising "free speech" involving "direct primary first amendment rights." The Court stated that free speech is legal if (1) a student exercises his rights without "materially and substantially interfering with the requirement of appropriate discipline in the operation of the school," and (2) a student expresses himself "without colliding with the rights of others."

It would seem that the Tinker case would not allow athletic programs to restrict speech rights or assembly rights of student-athletes because of vague or unsubstantiated arguments as a need for strong, authoritarian rule in athletics, morale of team might be impaired, or concentration of team member would be hampered. These may be valid reasons for strong discipline but they probably would not suffice as arguments to overrule a freedom of speech argument. However, if freedom of speech causes injury or harm to others, then disciplinary action regarding this freedom might be appropriate.

If an athlete is injured, most athletic programs provide for the medical costs. However, in some situations the athlete may prefer to go to sue the institution not only for the medical expenses, but also for the pain and loss of future earning power. Or, more realistically, the athlete may decide to rely on workmen's compensation laws.

Workmen's compensation allows employees to receive money for accidental injuries they have sustained at work. The employer-employee relationship must be proved. In the case of a student-athlete who receives a scholarship, it is not difficult to make a case that the athlete received "pay for play," thereby forming an employer-employee relationship. The athletic administrator should make sure that the athletic scholarship is a true scholarship; otherwise, the court might construe the business relationship to be one of an employer-employee. The institution should be prepared to consider total compensation—medical costs, loss of salary, disability pay—for an athlete. Such an action is ethically sound for the institution to discharge its obligation to remunerate athletes for accidental injuries incurred on behalf of their participation for the benefit of the institution.

Perhaps the biggest legal action in professional sports involved a recent decision regarding the National Football League's ruling that prevents players from becoming free agents who sell their services to the highest bidder. The court ruled that antitrust laws were violated by a portion of the college draft, the Rozelle Rule, the tampering rule, and portions of a standard player contract. All of these are part of the NFL's reserve system of binding a player to one team. Under the Rozelle Rule, the NFL commissioner decides what compensation must be made to the club of a free agent after the player has switched to another club. The Rozelle Rule is put into effect if the two teams are unable to agree on a fair compensation. The court declared this rule illegal, stating that it perpetually restrains a player from pursuing his occupation among the clubs of the league that holds a virtual monopoly on professional football in the United States.

The court stated that the college draft was unreasonable since it permitted other NFL teams to boycott a draft prospect even when the club drafting him refused or failed within a reasonable time to reach a contract agreement.

The court also declared the NFL's tampering rule and standard player contract rule illegal because they were used to prevent free employment choice. Under NFL rules it was illegal for a club to talk contract with a player under contract or playing out his option with another team.

These and other court decisions affect the administration of athletic programs.

Objective: To Administer Rules Legally

	Strength	Weakness
1. Does the program provide for the following in order to obey recent court decisions:		
1.1 Make it clear that athletics is a privilege, not a right		
1.2 Have an instituted due process procedure for infractions of rules		
1.3 Forbid transfer students from playing for one year		
1.4 Prevent discrimination on the basis of sex		
1.5 Guarantee the right of freedom of expression to athletes		
1.6 Have a true scholarship (not a pay for play)		
1.7 Have an insurance program for injuries		
1.8 Others		
2. Do professional teams allow the following practices?		
2.1 Practice the Rozelle Rule		
2.2 Prevent draftees from negotiation with other teams		
2.3 Boycott players who play out their options		
2.4 Bind a player to only one team		
2.5 Others		
Overall Evaluation:		

CHAPTER SUMMARY

There must be a mutual fulfillment of the athlete's personal objectives and the objectives of the athletic program if the program is administered effectively. In addition, there must be a recruiting system for quality athletes if the program is to be a winner. A written policy manual should exist to serve as a guide to thought and action for the administrator. Adherence to a set of principles for proper disciplinary action of athletes is necessary. Finally, some recognition must be given to legal questions concerning athletes.

Case 8-1 UNIVERSITY OF WYOMING AND FREEDOM OF SPEECH FOR STUDENT-ATHLETES[6]

In 1971, fourteen football players at the University of Wyoming wanted to wear black armbands during their game with Brigham Young University. They hoped to demonstrate against BYU's ties with the Mormon Church, which had a policy of restricting black participation in the church to the lower official ranks.

The head football coach, Floyd Eaton, upon hearing of the athletes' proposed action dismissed them from the team claiming they had violated a football coaching rule prohibiting all demonstrations and protests. The players appealed Eaton's decision through the President, who referred it to the Board of Trustees. A meeting was held with all parties concerned. The Board, after the athletes refused to refrain from their intention to wear black armbands at the BYU game, dismissed all fourteen from the squad. Their scholarships, however, were not revoked.

The athletes relied upon the Tinker case for their freedom of speech claims. Since their actions constituted speech, they argued that their activity would not affect the orderly process of the educational system or interfere with the rights of others.

State officials, however, argued that the student-athletes' protest was action by the State and subject to the first amendment establishment-of-religion clause. Since this clause requires actions by the State to be neutral in religious matters, the activities of the athletes showing disfavor toward the Mormon Church would be a violation of the neutrality concept. Therefore, the State officials were justified in their dismissal actions to prevent acts that were improper in light of their State constitution obligations.

QUESTIONS:

1. Does wearing of black armbands constitute freedom of speech?
2. Does the wearing of armbands appear to others as a hostile expression of religious thought?
3. Does the wearing of black armbands constitute any interference with the educational process? With discipline necessary for the operation of the team?
4. Does the wearing of armbands by the team constitute action by the State?

Case 8-2 SCHEMBECHLER: HOW TO TREAT ATHLETES*

"Oh, hello, John. What's going on?" said Bo Schembechler, answering a telephone call that interrupted the Michigan football coach during a recent interview in his office.

"Oh, don't worry about that, John," he said, after listening about 20

* An Associated Press article appearing in *The Arkansas Gazette*, February 22, 1976, p. 83.

seconds. "We'll graduate you. You just do what you have to do and we'll get you through. Don't worry about it."

He was talking to junior John Ceddia, a reserve quarterback who has played very little in his varsity career.

"He just had a shoulder operation and is going to have to drop some classes while he's recuperating," Schembechler said. "He was worried that dropping the classes would prevent him from graduating, but since it is a football injury, I told him not to worry, that we'd just extend his grant."

Perhaps that little conversation best illustrates the recruiting philosophy of Schembechler and his staff: "Take care of the ones you have before you worry about the ones you don't."

"The three things that attract players to Michigan," Schembechler said, "are academics, our winning tradition, and the excellent facilities we have here. Those are what get a recruit interested. The crucial point comes when the prospect visits the campus—does he like the players and coaches he meets?"

Recruiting has a bad name now, expecially in the wake of the National Collegiate Athletic Association sanctions against Michigan State for alleged violations.

But, despite the belief by some critics that every school is guilty of at least minor recruiting violations, Schembechler insists Michigan is clean of such wrongdoings.

"I talk to everyone who is going to do any recruiting for me to make sure there are no slipups," Schembechler said. "They all know what we can say to a recruit and how often we can say it."

"We can phone all we want to, and if we accidentally bump into a prospect, we're allowed to say hello—the NCAA calls it the 'Rule of Civility'—but we can't mention Michigan."

"Coaches at Michigan are picked first on their ability to coach and teach," said Schembechler, whose teams have a 66–9–3 record in his seven years with the Wolverines.

"I turned down a lot of coaching offers coming out of Miami (Ohio) before I accepted the Michigan job." Schembechler said.

QUESTION:

1. Comment on the recruiting philosophy at Michigan.

Case 8-3 ATHLETIC AWARDS*

Under the leadership of Athletic Director Ben Jones, Susquehanna Township Senior High School in Harrisburg, Pennsylvania, has developed six categories of awards:

1. Letter Awards

To earn a letter award, an athlete must participate in a sport for the complete season. The athlete must attend all practice sessions unless the

* From an article in *Interscholastic Athletic Administration.*

absence is caused by injury or illness, or unless the athlete is excused by the coach. The athlete must display a proper attitude toward teammates, the game and opponents, and have a record of good conduct in school. A letter is awarded only after the first year of competition in the sport. Certificates are awarded after fulfilling the requirements in subsequent years. The requirements for each sport are as follows:

Baseball—Participation in 50% of the innings
Basketball—Participation in 50% of the quarters
Cross Country—Finish in top ten in half the dual meets
Football—Participation in 50% of the quarters
Golf—Participation in 50% of the matches
Gymnastics—Finish in the top three places in half the meets
Hockey—Participation in 50% of the quarters
Softball—Participation in 50% of the innings
Swimming—Earn 25 points
Tennis—Participation in 50% of the matches
Track and Field—Earn points equivalent to the number of meets, times five, divided by three—except in the two mile run where the individual must earn points equivalent to the number of meets (10 meets, 10 points). Each person on a relay team earns the total points scored by the relay team. In addition, an individual receives a two point bonus for breaking a school record.

Managers receive letters and certificates if they fulfill the duties assigned by the coach. Athletes who are injured or move during the season may be recommended for letters or certificates by their coach. Cheerleaders receive letters and certificates for fulfilling their obligations. If an athlete participates three consecutive years in the same sport and does not meet the specific requirements for a letter, the coach may recommend the individual for a letter.

2. School Board Awards

The school board sponsors an all sports dinner at the close of each school year as a means of rewarding athletes for performance in the athletic program. Cheerleaders, managers, coaches, and players are invited to the dinner, whether or not they earned a letter for their sport.

The board presents to each senior cheerleader, manager, and player a participation wall plaque. It lists the athlete's name, the sports in which the individual played, and the years of participation as a varsity letter winner.

The school board also makes awards to teams and individuals which are undefeated and/or win league, district, regional, and state championships.

3. Coach's Awards

Each year at the all sports dinner, coaches are given an opportunity to make special awards as they see fit to outstanding team members.

4. Community Awards

The community has developed special awards for outstanding student-athletes. There is a scholastic football trophy which goes to the senior boy who earns a varsity letter and has the highest scholastic average for the senior year. An award is given to the outstanding tenth grade boy or girl athlete. Another award is given to the senior athlete who has shown the most improvement in wrestling during the previous season. There is a sportsmanship award and also an award of $1,000 scholarship which goes to the outstanding scholar-athlete.

5. Award Jackets

Athletes are eligible to wear a varsity award jacket after they have earned a varsity letter. A jacket is not given by the athletic department. They are paid for by the athlete or through letter club projects. The jackets may be worn only with the permission of club advisors.

6. Lobby Award Picture

If an athlete or team finishes a season with an undefeated record, a large framed picture is placed in the senior high school lobby. Teams which finished the season as league champions are also shown in a picture which is placed in the lobby. Teams or athletes which go on to greater levels of accomplishment, such as district, regional, and state championships, are identified with a description plate beneath the picture.

QUESTION:

1. Comment on the article.

Case 8-4 STUDY REVEALS GRID HAZARDS*

Football causes an estimated 20 deaths and 300,000 injuries each year, making it the most hazardous sport to play in America. This information was disclosed by the Consumer Product Safety Commission.

Nearly 40% of the injuries occur among boys ages 15 to 19, the commission added.

A commission-sponsored study of North Carolina High School football players revealed that nearly a quarter of all injuries were caused by a player's receiving a blow from the helmet, shoulder pad, or shoes of another player.

As a result, the commission recommended that "consumers, coaches and others responsible for athletic activities demand safer equipment from manufacturers."

The commission also recommended that manufacturers design equipment with added external padding to limit injuries to opponents.

The report cited the inadequacy of some protective equipment as another safety problem area. "While only a small percentage of injuries were directly attributable to defective, ill-fitting or broken equipment," the report said, "injuries did occur beneath the equipment indicating that it may not be providing adequate protection."

The commission also cautioned players to wear all protective equipment available. The report cited one man who suffered a cracked vertebra in his neck because he failed to wear a neck collar as well as his helmet.

Use of soccer shoes instead of cleated football shoes would reduce ankle and knee injuries, the commission said. Soccer shoes also cause fewer injuries to opposing players, researchers said.

Of injuries studied by the commission 30% were sprains and strains. Se-

* An Associated Press newspaper article apearing in *Arkansas Gazette* in 1974.

vere bruises and scrapes represented another 30%. Broken bones occurred in 22% of injuries reported, and serious cuts amounted to 10%.

Concussions, which the commission called a small but serious threat, resulted in 1% of injuries.

The most serious threat to life, according to one researcher, is posed by repeated injuries, especially to the head.

QUESTION:

1. Comment on the article.
2. What suggestions could you offer to reduce hazards?

Case 8-5 CLOSING THE LOOPHOLES*

Wait a minute. That was NOT a do-nothing National Collegiate Athletic Association convention they just finished in Washington. The fine print has arrived. And college presidents, faculty representatives, athletic directors, and head coaches had better alert their recruiters and alumni. In a hurry.

What the NCAA did, and in this context the NCAA should be viewed as several hundred voting colleges and universities and not the administrative office in Kansas City, was to declare all-out war on recruiting cheaters. Or cheaters at anything. They voted in penalties so severe, an entire new phase of the legal profession may come into being.

Slaps on the wrist are out.

Fines amounting to hundreds of thousands of dollars are in. And forfeitures. And perjury traps. Items:

* Before a player can be eligible in any sport in any season, he must sign a statement that he has not been the recipient of any illegal aid nor has he been involved in any violation of the rules. Athletic directors and coaches must sign a similar statement. This affidavit-type statement is supposed to act as a deterrent. Could one of them turn up in a court of law? Interesting question.

* Should a team be guilty of using an ineligible player, the penalty would not end with forfeiture of the game. (No one really counts Oklahoma's eight forfeitures of 1972 as losses.) The presidents, faculty reps, and athletic directors who voted at the NCAA convention this week decreed that the guilty team in the future would not only have to forfeit the game, but also forfeit its share of the gate receipts to its conference (if an independent, to the NCAA office in Kansas City). That is strong. Shares of gate receipts can run from $5,000 or less for a Division Three team to around $200,000 for a Division One team playing in a 70,000-seat stadium with tickets scaled to $7 and $8.

* If a school or a bowl violates the rule against ANY contact before the end of the third Saturday in November, shrugs are out. If premature con-

* An article by Orville Henry in the *Arkansas Gazette*, December, 1974.

tact is proved, the bowl will be fined half of its revenue and could lose its NCAA sanction, without which it could not exist. A bowl keeps 25% of its game's revenue. Tough stuff. Real teeth.

* Except for the Rose Bowl, which is closed at both ends, Big Ten vs. Pac-8, neutral officials (not affiliated with the conference of either team) must be used in bowl games.

* Anyone who practices with the football team and is on scholarship must be counted against the maximum number of grants allowed. This closes a loophole (coaches are masters at locating loopholes) in which an athlete could be classified as, say, wrestler, for two years and then, when he's ready to play, be listed as the holder of a football scholarship. If he's brought in as a "wrestler" on scholarship, he can't practice football.

* Complimentary tickets issued to athletes in all sports can only be picked up at a ticket window the day of the game. The recipient must identify himself as a member of the family, or whatever he is, and attest that he has not paid more than the face value for the ticket. This might be called the Texas A & M rule. Bear Bryant taught the Aggies how to take care of their football players—by buying up their comps at $25, $50, $100 each. It is widely believed that A & M exes never forgot this. Until now, the practice has been unstoppable. "The down-town ticket broker, the big booster who has handled this sort of thing, is now out of business," a man said in Washington Friday. "And a lot of players' cars are going to be for sale." The point is, what moneyed, respectable booster is going to risk signing such a paper falsely and perjuring himself? (Has someone already found a loophole?)

* No representative of a school can make contact with a high school athlete until after his junior year. This isn't best—but it's better.

* The NCAA office, which used to hire a couple of private detectives to follow up on complaints, now will employ eight full-time investigators, one for each NCAA district. Each man will circulate in his district, listening and inquiring.

* If a coach is guilty of illegal activities and then leaves the school for another, he could be punished at the next school. Jerry Tarkanian left Long Beach State's basketball program in the throes of problems with the NCAA, then turned up fresh and pure with a fat contract at Nevada-Las Vegas. No more, maybe.

* * *

What's the reason for this sudden series of punitive bombshells?

One coach explained it a year ago: "If they think Watergate is a mess, they ought to get into college recruiting. And recruiting is the name of the game."

The extreme nature of the latest legislation is calculated to get the attention of college presidents. So they'll hire people who won't cheat.

QUESTION:

1. Comment on the article.

Case 8-6 SWC ADOPTS 'POLYGRAPH TEST' POLICY*

In a landmark decision for intercollegiate athletics, the Southwest Conference announced Saturday that lie detector tests will be part of any investigations of illegal practices by coaches, athletes, or friends of a league school.

"This is the first effort in the collegiate area in this respect with teeth in it," said J. Neils Thompson of the University of Texas, president of the SWC. "To accomplish it at the winter meeting amazes me. Without exception, we had support from all the conference coaches."

Legal Bugs Remain

On the historic conference legislation, Thompson said, "It has some legal bugs in it, but it's a start—a milestone. It's new across the country because no other conference has done it. I think the Big Eight has it under consideration."

The SWC faculty representatives voted in favor of the polygraph tests in investigations to become effective immediately.

The new legislation read: "In the investigation of alleged SWC and NCAA violations, the results of polygraph tests shall be considered by the SWC to be part of the fact-finding process.

"As a provision in the written or oral contract of employment of all coaches, the institution shall require the coach to give full cooperation in any investigation by the SWC or the NCAA in which information is sought from the coach, and if asked to do so by a conference representative submit to a polygraph test.

"A representative of athletic interest shall be required to cooperate in any SWC or NCAA investigation in which information is sought from such person, and if asked to do so by a conference representative, shall submit to a polygraph test.

Refusal or failure to comply renders him ineligible to serve in such capacity thereafter.

"A student-athlete shall be required to cooperate in any SWC or NCAA investigation and, if asked by a conference representative, shall submit to a polygraph test."

Thompson said any student athlete failing to do so would probably not lose his scholarship but the "right to participate."

Thompson said the precedent-setting move would have a "tremendous psychological effect" on any coaches who might want to stray from the straight and narrow while recruiting high school athletes.

QUESTION:

1. Comment on the article.

* An article by the Associated Press appearing in *Arkansas Gazette,* December 15, 1974.

FOOTNOTES

[1] Hass V., *South Bend Community School Corporation,* 289 N.E. 2d 495 (Cir. Ct. Ind., 1972). See also *The Bulletin,* Arkansas High School Activities Association.

[2] Behagen V., *Intercollegiate Conference of Faculty Representatives,* 346 F. Supp. 602 (DC Minn., 1972).

[3] Kelley V., *Metropolitan Board of Education of Nashville,* 293 F. Supp. 485 (DC MD Tenn. 1968).

[4] Brenden V., *Independent School District* 742, 342 F. Supp. 1224 (DC Minn. 1972).

[5] 393 U.S. 502 (1969).

[6] The material for this case problem was adapted from the Appendix in Carlos Alvarez, *The Report on the American Council on Education on a Need for a National Study of Intercollegiate Athletics.* See also 468 F. 2d 1079 (1972).

Part IV

Marketing the Athletic Program

A successful athletic program should provide various economic utilities to satisfy the needs of paying fans. The marketing function of an athletic program is to provide the primary customer utilities: place, time, services, and possession of tickets. These utilities are the concern of the marketers; coaches provide the form utility that the fans desire.

9

MARKETING THE ATHLETIC PROGRAM TO ITS FANS

There must be an equitable exchange of contributions between the fans and the athletic program if the administration of the program is to be effective. The athletic program must provide various utilities that will satisfy the needs of the paying customers. The chief objective of those who market an athletic program is to provide the primary customer utilities: place, time, service, and possession of tickets. The coach creates a winning team, providing the form utility desired by fans. In exchange, the fans buy tickets, support the program, and sometimes donate money to maintain the program.

MARKETING STRATEGIES TO ACCOMPLISH PROGRAM OBJECTIVES

As mentioned previously, the first objective of a program is to provide entertainment for its fans. The chief marketing strategies to accomplish this are twofold. The first is to schedule the right place and time for an athletic event. The second is to create supporting services—concessions, half-time entertainment, cheerleaders, and pom-pom girls.

Effective promotional tactics can enhance the image of an athletic program. Of course, promotion is easier if there is a winning tradition to promote. Athletic administrators have often said that winning takes care of everything, but if a team cannot win, then promotion takes on added significance. It is important to push individual performances, stars, records, and statistics to take the fans' minds off losing.

Marketing helps to provide revenue through ticket sales, television and radio, concessions, and donations from booster clubs, thus satisfying the program's profit objective. To provide revenues to offset expenses is a chief strategy of effective marketing.

Marketing strategies help an athletic program to grow through increased attendance. And horizontal growth is accomplished in two ways—by expanding the present market area attendance or by expanding into a new market area to create new attendance. Various marketing strategies may be used to increase attendance. Adapting a pricing strategy for regular and season tickets is one way to grow. Another is to differentiate the products and services of an athletic program to make them different from competitors. To select the right types of sales personnel to market the program is extremely important. A fourth strategy is to advertise and promote the program, hoping to attract more people to become fans. A fifth is to secure the right place and time for the athletic event to occur. Obviously, producing a winning team is the most effective way to improve attendance and corresponding growth.

Maintaining a share of the entertainment market is another objective often accomplished through a marketing strategy. The product life cycle, discussed in a previous chapter, serves as a basis for determining the appropriate marketing strategies to achieve this objective. The introductory stage, the growth stage, the maturity stage, and the decline stage of each major sport will usually dictate the types of marketing strategies to be used—product, price, place, promotion, personnel, and pecuniary. Again, though, a winning team usually can be counted on to maintain a share of the entertainment market.

The marketing strategies are also instrumental in accomplishing other program objectives such as continuity, industry position, being a leader in the field, and improving the quality of life for society.

The athletic administrator can evaluate the strengths and weaknesses of the marketing strategies by using the following analysis:

Objective: To Have General Marketing Strategies Accomplish Program Objectives

Strategies	Strength	Weakness
1. Is there an equitable exchange of contributions between the fans and the athletic program?		
1.1 Do the fans contribute		
1.11 Ticket revenue		
1.12 Fan loyalty		
1.13 Financial donations		
1.14 Other		

Strategies	Strength	Weakness
1.2 Does the program contribute 1.21 Adequate place utility 1.22 Adequate time utility 1.23 Adequate services 1.24 Ticket utility 1.25 Others Overall Evaluation: 2. Do the marketing strategies contribute to the following program objectives? 2.1 Providing fan entertainment 2.11 Right time 2.12 Right place 2.13 Services 2.31 Concessions 2.32 Pom-poms 2.33 Cheerleaders 2.34 Half-time 2.35 Others 2.2 Image objective 2.21 Promotion 2.22 Others 2.3 Profit objective 2.31 Ticket revenue 2.32 Radio and TV revenue 2.33 Concessions revenue 2.34 Booster club revenue 2.35 Other revenues 2.4 Growth in attendance 2.41 Market target 2.42 Pricing 2.43 Differentiation 2.44 Right sales personnel 2.45 Promotion 2.46 Time and place 2.47 Others 2.5 Share of market 2.51 Adapt to product life cycle 2.52 Others 2.6 Program continuity 2.7 Leader in the field 2.8 Industry position 2.9 Quality of life 2.10 Others Overall Evaluation:		

Segmentation Strategies for Market Targets

The athletic administrator should be aware of various strategies that he/she may use to market a successful athletic program. The first is to determine the market target for the services and products to be provided. One strategy, segmentation of the market, suggests that an administrator separate customers into classes according to their common characteristics. Once these segments are established, various strategies may be developed to appeal directly to the different groups of fans. Resources can be wasted by not knowing the people who make up a market. It is logical to shoot for a target market rather than to devise strategies at random.

Normally, one determines the target market through research. It is practical to determine who the fans are (including an analysis of names, if possible), their locations (by specific addresses), their numbers, their buying habits, and other statistical information (age, occupation, income status). Why people become fans is also important. The preceding information will help to determine the known target market. Also, the administrator will become familiar with the characteristics of those who are not fans. Determining the target market and utilizing the market segmentation strategy are fundamental to the development of a sophisticated set of administrative strategies.

Objective: To Segment the Marketing and Define Target Markets

Strategy	Strength	Weakness
1. Has the program defined its target market?		
2. Has the market been segmented according to the following characteristics:		
2.1 Who		
2.2 Where		
2.3 When		
2.4 Why		
2.5 How much		
2.6 What prices		
2.7 How many		
2.8 Kinds of customers		
2.9 Other information		
Overall Evaluation:		

Differentiation Strategy

Another strategy that is usually followed is the differentiation of tickets. It is wise to distinguish between preseason, regular season, and postseason tickets; one should differentiate between tickets for reserve seats, regular seats, and end-zone or bleacher seats. A price differentiation strategy logically follows. For example, people will pay a high price for good seats at a regular season game and a low price for end-zone seats during a preseason game; they recognize that seating and the time a game is played make a difference in viewing pleasure.

A product and service differentiation strategy is particularly appropriate where competition is keen. For example, place differentiation is a very wise strategy to follow. People are attracted to athletic events if the location of the event provides special facilities for fan convenience. Customers differentiate between teams; often, they choose to attend the games of a winner. If a team modifies the rules somewhat (to make its game different from the rest), fans might choose to attend its games over others. Playing at different times could also make a difference in fan attendance.

Product and service differentiation strategy may be evaluated by using the following analysis:

Objective: To Differentiate Various Products and Services

Strategy	Strength	Weakness
1. Are tickets differentiated by		
1.1 Location of seats		
1.2 Postseason, preseason		
1.3 Prices		
2. Is place differentiated?		
3. Are other products/services differentiated?		
Overall Evaluation:		

Pricing Strategy for Products and Services

Another key strategy in marketing the services of an athletic program involves a pricing decision. The three pricing alternatives are to price above the market, to price at the market, or to price below the market. What are the key factors to be considered in determining a pricing strategy?

The first is the competition facing an athletic program. If the athletic program is in a monopoly position regarding direct competition for its services and products, then an above-the-market price can be charged. If the program is in an oligopoly market position, then an at-the-market price is reasonable. If the program is in a highly competitive market position, then an at-the-market price is also reasonable. Indirect competition for services is another market factor to be considered when determining the market price. Other forms of entertainment, sometimes called substitute goods and services, will usually have a bearing on the market price to be charged.

Objective: To Determine Proper Pricing Strategy

Factors	**Theory →**			**Compared to →**	**Actual Situation →**			**Evaluation**	
	Above the Market	*At the Market*	*Below the Market*		*Above the Market*	*At the Market*	*Below the Market*	*Strength*	*Weakness*
1. Competitive situation facing the program									
1.1 Monopoly	X								
1.2 Oligopoly		X							
1.3 Highly competitive		X							
2. High quality product and service	X								
3. High quality personnel	X								
4. High quality promotional activities	X								
5. High degree of fan loyalty	X								
6. Life cycle stages									
6.1 Introductory	X								
6.2 Growth	X								
6.3 Maturity		X							
6.4 Decline			X						
7. Rapid penetration of market desired			X						
8. Others									
Overall Evaluation:									

The quality of the product and service is another factor that influences pricing. If the team is a consistent winner, the high quality of the team usually suggests an above-the-market pricing strategy. Likewise, high quality products in the concession booths suggest an above-the-market pricing strategy. Superior locations and times for an athletic event also suggest a high price.

High quality promotion of the athletic event also suggests an above-the-market pricing strategy. National television, glossy programs, and good press releases all suggest high quality promotion and an above-the-market pricing strategy.

High quality sales personnel also would suggest an above-the-market pricing strategy. Superstars, well-known announcers, winning coaches, and superior athletes are all high quality sales personnel; people will gladly pay an above-the-market price to see and hear them.

A high degree of fan loyalty and support also would suggest an above-the-market pricing strategy. True fans will pay a higher than market price to support their team.

The life cycle of the sport will also dictate the necessary pricing strategy. If a sport is in the introductory stage, a high price or skimming of the market price strategy should be used. If it is in the growth stage, a high price (but lower than in the introductory stage) should also be considered. In the maturity stage, an at-the-market price strategy should be used. If it is in the decline stage, a below-the-market pricing strategy should be used, perhaps with discount pricing.

If the program is designed to penetrate the market fast, then a below-the-market price should be considered. There may also be other factors to be considered, such as conference-related prices.

The administrator can evaluate the pricing strategy of each product and service of his athletic program as shown on the opposite page.

The price strategy model can be compared to the actual situation, and an appraisal of the program's strengths and weaknesses can be made. It can be used on each sport, on concession items, on any other product/service which is offered to the consuming public.

Channels of Distribution for Tickets and Other Services

Should an athletic administrator use a short, direct channel of distribution to sell tickets and other products and services? Should an indirect, longer channel be used? A short, direct channel implies few middlemen. The tickets pass directly into the hands of the customers. A longer, indirect channel involves a number of middlemen before tickets are distributed to the public. What factors govern the number of middlemen in a channel of distribution?

The first factor is the nature of the customers. If the customers are scattered throughout a large area, a number of middlemen are needed to cover the market target. However, if the market target is highly concentrated, then a direct channel with few middlemen is used. If there are a few cus-

Objective: To Determine the Number of Middlemen in the Channel Distribution for a Product of Service

Factors	Theory → *No. of Middlemen in Channel*	Compared →	Actual Situation →	Evaluation *Strength*	Evaluation *Weakness*
1. Nature of Customers					
1.1 Geographically dispersed	More				
1.2 Geographically concentrated	Fewer				
1.3 Few large volume customers	Fewer				
1.4 Small volume customers	More				
2. Market Structure					
2.1 Monopsony	Few				
2.2 Oligopsony	Few				
2.3 Several buyers	More				
3. Nature of Products and Services					
3.1 Able to be stored	More				
3.2 Perishable	Few				
3.3 Technical	Few				
3.4 High value	Few				
3.5 Bulk	More				
3.6 Others					
4. Market Exposure Desired					
4.1 Intensive	More				
4.2 Selective	Fewer				
4.3 Exclusive	Few				
5. Personnel					
5.1 Available	More				
5.2 Not experienced	More				
6. Money					
6.1 Not available	More				
7. Other Factors					
Overall Evaluation:					

tomers who buy tickets in large volumes, fewer middlemen are needed than if there were a number of small-volume buyers.

Another factor is the market structure. If the program is in a monopsony (one buyer) situation, a direct channel is used. If the program is in an oligopsony situation (a few buyers), a direct channel, or very few middlemen, is appropriate. If there are several buyers, then more middlemen are used.

The nature of the product and service is another governing factor. If the product and service can be stored and serviced, a longer channel is required. On the other hand, a product or service that cannot be stored usually requires a short, direct channel with few middlemen. If the product and service is perishable, a more direct channel is required. If the product/service is technical, a more direct channel is normally used. If the product/service is of high value, a more direct channel is used. A low value one requires more middlemen in the channel. A bulk product/service requires more middlemen in the channel.

The degree of market exposure desired must be considered when deciding the number of middlemen in the channel of distribution. If a high degree or intensive market exposure of the product and service is contemplated, then more middlemen will be required. A selective degree of market exposure of products and services implies a multifranchised channel of distribution with fewer middlemen. An exclusive degree of market exposure suggests an exclusive franchise for a market area, requiring even fewer middlemen in the channel.

Another key factor in selecting a channel is the number of available sales personnel. If no qualified sales personnel are available, then more middlemen will be needed to sell the products and services.

Money is another important factor. If a program has insufficient funds, middlemen must do the selling for the program. More middlemen are needed in the channel.

An analysis of the factors affecting the number of middlemen in the channels of distribution of the various products/services of an athletic program can be made by comparing the actual situation to theory, then evaluating the overall strengths and weaknesses.

This decision model can be used to compare theory to an actual situation regarding tickets, concessions, radio and TV, booster clubs, and other products and services offered to the general public.

Place Strategy—Where to Play

A decision of considerable importance in generating sales revenue and in minimizing costs is where to play the games. High schools, colleges, and pro teams usually play in the cities where they are located. However, that decision may not be the best in terms of sales revenue. Consequently, it is necessary to look into the factors determining the general location strategy (not specific site selection).

Since sales revenue for tickets and concessions depends on fan attendance, one must first determine where the target market is located. Proxim-

Objective: To Determine Proper Place Strategy to Play the Games

Factors	Strength	Weakness
1. Proximity of densely populated area		
2. Number of direct competitors		
3. Sufficient seating capacity		
4. Adequate availability of motel and hotel space		
4.1 Food services		
4.2 Drinking services		
5. Availability of part-time employees		
6. Availability of adequate		
6.1 Parking		
6.2 Security		
7. Others		
Overall Evolution:		

ity to huge blocks of people, other factors equal, makes the game readily available when and where the fans want to attend. The administrator whose primary objective is to satisfy the fans' entertainment needs will determine the location of an athletic event by population density. If people are not available, it is difficult to attract them from long distances, even if the team has an excellent win-loss record.

Another factor in location strategy is the number of direct competitors in the market area. If the number is large, the competition is severe. To offset severe competition, the product and service must be highly differentiated. Athletic programs in a competitive market are at a distinct disadvantage when generating ticket revenue. This is why professional leagues usually limit teams to one franchise in a market area—to reduce competition so sufficient ticket revenue can be generated to financially support the team's operations.

An administrator must be sure that sufficient motel and hotel space is available for those fans who travel to games, especially for overnight trips. If it becomes a hassle for prospective fans to travel, eat, drink, and sleep to attend a game, chances are that they will stop attending games.

Another factor to be considered is the availability of part time employees, and the salary they should be paid to provide services necessary to put on a game. It is difficult to find volunteers to administer game operations and to work as security guards, ticket takers, and ushers.

The availability of adequate parking facilities for all fans who drive to the games is extremely important. Adequate security is necessary to protect the cars and to provide security for the fans.

The administrator should find a facility with the capacity for large crowds. However, it is better to have a standing-room-only crowd in a small facility than a minimal number of fans in a large facility. If there is little competition for tickets (the situation in a stadium too large for the audience), chances are good that preseason ticket sales will drop. On the other hand, when the fans perceive a scarcity of tickets (the situation in a crowded facility), chances are good that preseason ticket sales will increase.

Some of the many location factors have been discussed in this chapter. They may be evaluated by an athletic administrator, using the analysis on the opposite page.

Team Travel

Since it is imperative for team members to be fresh before playing an out-of-town game, a travel and lodging strategy must be implemented. Sometimes the coach takes care of team travel, but often this task is delegated to a member of the administrative staff. Most successful teams try to have their members ready to play, both physically and mentally, before each game. Administrators insist on traveling first class. Not only is travel planned, but also first class meals and lodging are usually arranged for

Objective: To Determine Team Travel Policy

Factors	Strength	Weakness
1. Does the team travel policy reflect first-class treatment on:		
1.1 Airplane		
1.2 Bus		
1.3 Auto		
1.4 Other		
2. Do team members get first-class treatment regarding:		
2.1 Lodging		
2.2 Food and drink		
2.3 Other		
3. Is travel arranged for so that sufficient time is available for rest?		
4. Others		
Overall Evaluation:		

team members. Anything less than first-class travel is usually considered a negative factor in determining a team's ability to win. Therefore, a team's travel policy is to go first class with plenty of time to spare.

CHAPTER SUMMARY

A mutual exchange of contributions between fans and the athletic program must exist if the program is to be effective. In addition, various marketing strategies are discussed in this chapter. These strategies provide the customer utilities that fans will pay for—entertainment at the right time and place, and extra entertainment. This chapter considers how customers are provided with tickets, and how the market segmentation strategy and product and service differentiation strategy are used.

A pricing strategy depends on several factors: the competitive situation, the quality of product and service, the quality of promotion, the quality of sales personnel, fan loyalty, and the product life cycle.

The use of a short or a long channel of distribution to sell tickets is a marketing decision to be made by the administrator. This strategy depends on a number of factors—the customers, the product and service, the degree of market exposure desired, the availability of sales personnel, and the availability of financial resources.

Place strategy—where to play the games—is influenced by the proximity and density of population; the number of direct competitors; the availability of food, lodging, and drinks for out-of-town fans; the number of part-time employees; the accessibility of adequate parking and security; and the capacity of the facility.

Team travel must be arranged to insure team freshness. Consequently, first-class arrangements are usually made.

This chapter summarizes general marketing strategies, price strategies, and place strategies. The next chapter discusses the promotion, personnel, and pecuniary strategies that affect the marketing of athletic programs.

CASE 9-1 BILL STANCIL'S HIGH SCHOOL ATHLETIC TICKET-PRICING STRATEGY*[1]

Bill Stancil, Athletic Director for the Fort Smith School System (two high schools and four junior highs) sat in his office contemplating a problem facing the athletic program. A new growth program in girls' athletics was being considered by the Fort Smith school system. One of the questions being considered was how to finance the new girls' program. One alternative Bill was considering was to raise ticket prices to football games. Such additional revenue from a possible price increase should help absorb some

* This case was prepared by Robert D. Hay, University of Arkansas. This case is designed to be used as a basis for class discussion rather than to illustrate either effective or ineffective handling of an administrative situation.

of the expenses of a fledgling girls' program, estimated to cost at least $45,000 initially.

Football ticket prices for both Northside High School and Southside High School were presently $1.50 for general admission, $1.00 for students, and $2.00 for reserve seats between the 40-yard lines. These prices had been in effect for approximately ten years, inflation notwithstanding. Prices for football tickets at the four junior highs was 50¢ for students and $1.00 for adults.

Competing prices for AAAA conference schools of which Fort Smith Northside was a member and for the AAA Western conference of which Southside was a member, were $2.00 for general admission and $1.00 for students. These prices had been in force for the schools in the AAAA and AAA conferences in which the two Fort Smith high schools compete.

Bill had not raised the football ticket prices at Fort Smith because there were sufficient athletic funds available to support the existing programs. In fact he was proud of his record. When he assumed the role of the first and only athletic director of all the schools seven years ago, there was $360 in the athletic fund. Today there was approximately $50,000 in the athletic fund. During those seven years there had been no increase in ticket prices.

Direct competition for high school football and other forms of athletics in the Fort Smith area were the two high schools and Westark Community College, a two-year junior college. Bill had worked out an agreement with the athletic director at Westark whereby Northside and Southside would not play games on the nights when Westark would play and Westark would not play games on those nights when Northside and Southside played. This agreement had worked very well for both the high schools and the community college, according to Bill Stancil.

The win-loss records of the two high schools for the past several years were as follows:

	Northside Grizzlies		*Southside Rebels*	
YEAR	RECORD	HEAD COACH	RECORD	HEAD COACH
1958	9–2	Stancil		
1959	7–3–1	Stancil		
1960	9–2	Stancil		
1961	10–0	Stancil		
1962	7–3	Stancil	(1963—First Year in Being)	
1963	9–1	Stancil	4–5–1	McGibbony
1964	7–4	Stancil	6–3–1	McGibbony
1965	8–3	Stancil	4–3–2	McGibbony
1966	9–2	Stancil	10–2	McGibbony
1967	12–0	Stancil	5–5	McGibbony
1968	10–0–1	Stancil	5–5	McGibbony
1969	9–2	Stancil	5–5	McGibbony
1970	8–3	Presley	6–5	Rowland
1971	11–1	Presley	5–7	Rowland
1972	5–5–1	Crovella	7–4–1	Rowland
1973	6–4	Crovella	7–4–1	Rowland
1974	3–9	Crovella	5–5	Rowland
1975	5–6	Thone	7–3–1	Rowland

Promotion for sales of season tickets was handled mainly by the booster clubs of each school. The boosters held chili suppers, candy sales, and other events to promote ticket sales. The individual club members would personally telephone potential ticket buyers to invite them to join and to promote the sale of tickets. Bill Stancil thought the quality of promotion was very high.

The personnel of the Booster Clubs were well known people in the community. The membership changed somewhat with the influx of new athletes and new students into the high school from the junior high schools. However, Bill was proud of the quality of personnel who devoted much time and effort to promoting the athletic programs at the six schools.

Bill was concerned with the attitude of some of the coaches in the school system who did not want to promote athletics to the general public. For example, one of the coaches did not make appearances and talks to the local civic clubs. Such an attitude, according to Bill, was not in the best interest of the Fort Smith athletic program.

Bill did not know whether the price of tickets would affect attendance at the ball games. However, he felt intuitively that price was a sensitive factor. Although price might be important, he often stated, "Where can you get entertainment for $1.00 or $1.50 equivalent to junior high or high school football or basketball? It costs $2.00 to $2.50 to go to a movie, and that form of entertainment has diminished in quality."

The Fort Smith athletic program was the only high school in the area that promoted the sale of season tickets. As a result, Bill thought there was a fairly high degree of fan loyalty to the athletic program. He pulled out of the drawer of his desk the following tabulation of season ticket sales for the last few years.

Bill estimated that at least 600 of the same fans bought season tickets each year. He felt that the fans in Fort Smith were good supporters of the athletic program.

He also estimated that yearly attendance at Northside football games was 17,500 fans, with about 65% being students and 35% nonstudents. The same estimates applied at Southside.

As Bill Stancil pondered the factors affecting his pricing recommendations to the superintendent to whom he reported, he wondered what pricing strategy he should follow. He knew that his initial recommendation would proceed from the superintendent to the athletic committee to the

Season Ticket Sales—Football

Year	*No. Sold by Northside*	*No. Sold by Southside*	*Total*
1969–70	264	None	264
1970–71	338	239	577
1971–72	290	281	571
1972–73	294	299	593
1973–74	337	325	662
1974–75	376	428	804
1975–76	354	458	812

school board. They obviously would like to have a sound rationale for any pricing decision.

Case 9-2 FOOTBALL TICKET PRICES*

Recent newspaper accounts indicate that due to inflation and possibly other factors, 90% of the nation's college athletic departments are now operating at a loss. For example, the University of Oklahoma had a deficit of $218,000 last year and as a result had to make cuts in some programs. There have been reports in the press about colleges that have dropped some of their athletic programs entirely. These developments, together with increases and changes in athletic programs that may be required in order to comply with Title IX of the 1972 Higher Education Act (women's athletics), demonstrate a need for increased revenues for college athletic departments. One alternative strategy for generating more revenues is to increase football ticket prices.

Since football is the major revenue producer at the University of Arkansas and at most other schools, it was decided to study experimentally the U of A's football program to determine if revenue from it could be increased by changing the price of football tickets.

Personal interviews were held at random with people attending football games in Fayetteville. Interviews were conducted just prior to the games. Individuals were asked about the number of tickets that they were purchasing at the current price and the number that they would buy at progressively higher prices.

First Sample: U of A–Tulsa Game

The first sample was taken before the U of A–Tulsa game on the morning of September 28. Forty-eight individuals were interviewed representing yearly ticket sales of 517. The individuals questioned were asked the number of tickets that they had purchased in the current year and in preceding years to Razorback football games. They were then asked how many tickets they would purchase at increasing price levels up to $20 each. Personal information such as income level, distance traveled to game, and others was also obtained in an effort to find what variable, if any, affected the buying behavior of individuals.

Price information obtained from the first sample was shown as indicated in Table 9–1.

Second Sample: U of A–Baylor Game

Our second sample was taken before the U of A–Baylor game on the morning of October 12. Fifty-nine individuals were interviewed representing total yearly ticket sales of 1174. Our questionnaire was slightly

* The information in this case was adapted from the article, "An Exploratory Study of Pricing Razorback Football Tickets," Robert D. Hay and Michael Dardin, *Athletic Administration,* NACDA, Winter 1978.

Table 9-1 Revenue at Varied Prices for Razorback Football Tickets (Random Sample of 58 Individuals at the U of A–Tulsa Game)

Price	Tickets that would be purchased	Revenue
$ 7*	517	$3619*
8	467	3736
9	416	3744
10	291	2910
11	188	2068
12	168	2016
13	140	1820
14	140	1960
15	140	2100
16	136	2176
17	136	2312
18	136	2448
19	136	2584
20	136	2720

* *Current Prices and Revenues*

Table 9-2 Revenue at Varied Prices for Razorback Football Tickets (Random Sample of 59 Individuals at the U of A–Baylor Game)

Price	Tickets that would be purchased	Revenue
$ 3	1265	$ 3795
4	1263	5052
5	1218	6090
6	1214	7284
7* Current Price	1174	8218
8	1103	8824
9	1097	9873
10	1029	10290
11	902	9922
12	846	10152
13	802	10426
14	784	10976
15	762	11430
16	699	11184
17	635	10795
18	557	10026
19	557	10583
20	547	10940

Table 9-3 Revenue at Varied Prices for Razorback Football Tickets (Random Sample of 31 Individuals at the U of A–Rice Game)

Price	*Tickets that would be purchased*	*Revenue*
$ 3	355	$1065
4	355	1420
5	331	1655
6	329	1974
7*	320	2240*
8	284	2272
9	272	2448
10	256	2560
11	217	2387
12	203	2436
13	154	2002
14	149	2086
15	128	1920
16	101	1616
17	90	1530
18	90	1620
19	90	1710
20	90	1800

* *Current Price*

modified on the basis of our experience with the first sample. The people interviewed were also asked the number of tickets that they would buy at prices lower than the current price of $7.00.

Third Sample: U of A–Rice Game

Our third sample was taken before the U of A–Rice game on the morning of November 9. Thirty-one individuals were interviewed representing total ticket sales of 320. We again modified our instrument used on the basis of our experience with the previous samples. In this sample an effort was made to pinpoint the counties where the fans lived. They were also asked the section of the stadium where their seats were located.

In the third sample, for the first time the interviewers experienced difficulty in obtaining answers from the people they approached. A number of people refused to be interviewed and some of the people who were interviewed seemed reluctant in their answers. The first two samples had received rather ordinary comments about the weather, the team's record, traffic, and so forth, but in third sample many people commented specifically on inflation. People interviewed resisted any discussion of price increases and this attitude may be reflected in the price information obtained.

Table 9-4 Number of Tickets, Prices, Revenues by Seat Location U of A–Rice Game (31 Ticket Holders Selected at Random)

THE 14 TICKET HOLDERS IN END ZONE–20 YD.			THE 9 TICKET HOLDERS IN THE 20–40 YD. SEATS			THE 8 TICKET HOLDERS IN THE 40–40 YD. SEATS		
Price	*Tickets*	*Revenue*	*Price*	*Tickets*	*Revenue*	*Price*	*Tickets*	*Revenue*
$ 7	107	749	$ 7	72	514	$ 7	141	987
8	85	680	8	70	560	8	129	1032
9	85	765	9	70	630	9	117	1053
10	77	770	10	70	700	10	109	1090
11	57	627	11	62	682	11	98	1078
12	43	516	12	62	744	12	98	1176
13	29	377	13	40	520	13	85	1095
14	29	406	14	40	560	14	80	1120
15	13	195	15	40	600	15	75	1125
16	13	208	16	40	640	16	48	768
17	13	221	17	29	493	17	48	816
18	13	234	18	29	522	18	48	864
19	13	247	19	29	551	19	48	912
20	13	260	20	29	580	20	48	960

Table 9-5 Optimum Revenue Through Suggested Differential Price Increases by Seat Location (Based on Third Sample Only)

	End Zone–20 Yd. Suggested Price $10	*20–20 Yd. Suggested Price $12*	*40–40 Yd. Suggested Price $12*	
Present No. tickets	107 × $7 =	72 × $7 =	141 × $7 =	
Present Revenue	$749	$504	$987	Total—$2240
No. Tickets w/price increase	77 × 10 ($)	62 × 12 ($)	98 × 12 ($)	
Revenue	$770	$774	$1176	Total—$2690
				Difference $ 450

Total Present Revenue—$2240
Total Revenue w/price increase $2690 (21% increase)

In the third sample, for the first time a variable was found that seemed to affect the price that individuals were willing to pay for tickets. The location of seats in the stadium apparently does affect the fans' attitudes toward price.

QUESTION:

1. What recommendations could be made, based on the data gathered?

Case 9-3 PRICING RAZORBACK BASKETBALL TICKETS*

Eddie Sutton, head basketball coach at the University of Arkansas, after his first year at the U of A was selected Southwest Conference Coach of the Year, guiding the Razorbacks to a second place finish in the conference. His overall team record of 17–9 was the best performance for the Razorbacks in twenty years. Since he had established the Razorbacks as a strong competitor in the SWC, he had received excellent support from dormant basketball devotees from years past. Now he had to determine some scheduling strategy for next year.

One of the strategies was whether to play basketball in Little Rock, 200 miles from the campus in Fayetteville where his team had played 15 home games this past year, winning 13 and losing 2.

Frank Broyles, Athletic Director at the U of A, had suggested to Sutton the advisability of playing some basketball games in Little Rock next year. This past year none of the games were played in the state capitol, but two years ago, a game was played at Christmas time at which attendance was very small and turned out to be a financial disaster for the Razorbacks. A similar experience occurred three years ago in which a Christmas Holiday tournament was sponsored by the University of Arkansas. Attendance was sparse and money was lost on the venture. Why should the Razorback basketball team try again?

Frank Broyles had a football scheduling policy of playing three or four football games in Little Rock each year and three games at Fayetteville. His rationale for this schedule was that he wanted and received fan support from the whole state of Arkansas. The Razorbacks got support from more people if they played some of their games in Little Rock. Besides, he wanted the University of Arkansas to be a truly state university rather than a Northwest Arkansas regional university. Such fan support had several positive features—financial contributions to the Razorback Scholarship Fund were easier to get from more people, recruiting of state athletes was easier to accomplish, financial assistance was available to build athletic facilities, and other objectives of the athletic program were easier to accomplish if fan support came from the whole state, not just a geographic portion of it. If the football market were larger, then the athletic program objectives would be more easily obtained. Why should not the same policy be applied to basketball?

Frank thought to himself that the present market for Razorback basketball included a four-county rural population area of approximately 200,000 people. If the team played some games in Little Rock, the market area would be extended perhaps to an additional 300,000 people. If the basketball program were to catch on, the whole state's population of 2,000,000 might support the basketball team as they have done for football for the past twenty years. Was the time right for expansion into the Little Rock area since the U of A now had a quality team, could effectively promote that team, and had a high quality coaching staff and athletes?

Eddie Sutton, aware of local student and faculty discontent with the

* This case was prepared by Robert D. Hay and Eddie Sutton, University of Arkansas. It is meant to be a teaching tool and not to illustrate correct or incorrect administrative practices.

Little Rock policy, decided to schedule three games in Little Rock for the upcoming basketball season. He further decided to play three big name schools—Tulane, Oklahoma, and Texas. His rationale was if the U of A could play and defeat those teams with good athletic reputations, chances would be better for additional fan support from the whole state of Arkansas. The University of Texas game expecially would attract basketball fans since Texas was an arch rival of the Razorbacks in all athletic endeavors.

The next big strategy decision was what price to charge for the upcoming season's games, both in Fayetteville and in Little Rock. Sutton conferred with Wilson Matthews, Assistant Athletic Director, about pricing strategy.

Last year the Razorbacks' ticket prices were $3.00 for reserved seats at home. Students were allowed "free" admission upon presentation of their I.D. card. Faculty members paid half price. General admission at home games was $1.50.

The present ticket policies allowed about 2,500 students to sit in bleachers on one side of the court. The other side was reserved for season ticket holders and for general admission buyers. Both Eddie Sutton and Wilson Matthews wanted to differentiate the seats for the coming year on a price basis. Students would sit in the bleachers. However, only one-half of the total seats available (5,200 capacity) would be sold to students. The other half would be allocated to season ticket holders and general admission buyers. Students would have first priority for half the tickets. Long time season ticket holders, both faculty and Razorback Fund donors, would have second priority. Then would come "new" Razorback Club members who had not purchased tickets before. Finally, the general public (both faculty and part-time fans) could purchase any remaining tickets.

For the past five years (not including last year), an average of 3,000 fans attended each game—approximately 2,000 students and 1,000 nonstudents. Only 300 season tickets were purchased on the average for the past five years. Wilson Matthews, "sold" on Eddie Sutton as head coach and "sold" on the new winning success of Razorback basketball, estimated that 2,600 season tickets could be sold to Razorback Club members and present season ticket holders. His optimism was based on the fact that there were 6,400 members of the Razorback Scholarship Fund who could be counted on to purchase season tickets if those season tickets were promoted in the right way. (The U of A had never really promoted basketball season tickets before this time. However, very elaborate promotion plans had been used to sell 20–30,000 football season tickets each year for the past several years.) Matthews suggested that efforts could be made to promote season ticket sales so that all seats would be sold out before the basketball season began. He thought that 2,600 season tickets could be sold in Fayetteville to Razorback Club members and about 7,000 seats could be sold at Barton Coliseum in Little Rock if the proper promotion were made to the Razorback Club members and to the general public. Matthews was of the opinion that if a scarcity of tickets existed in the general public's mind, then sales could be made at practically any price.

Additional information regarding ticket prices and policies was obtained from several colleges:

Table 9-6

UNIVERSITY	YEARLY ATTENDANCE	GENERAL ADMISSION	RESERVE SEATS	NUMBER OF SEASON TICKETS SOLD	FACULTY AND STUDENTS	
ORU	102,000	$1.50	$2.00–3.00	4500	F 17.50;	S 1.25–1.50
Texas Tech	97,000	2.00	$3.50	3500	F 1.00;	S 1.00
Hutch Juco	85,000	1.50	2.00	2500	F free;	S free
Creighton	77,000	2.00	3.50	2000	F ½;	S .50
Baylor	80,000	2.00	3.50	1400	F free;	S free
Texas	63,000	2.00	3.00	0	F free;	S free
Texas A&M	55,000	2.00	3.00	750	F free;	S free
SMU	48,000	3.00	3.00	1000	F free;	S free
TCU	44,000	2.00	3.00	500	F free;	S free
Tulane	39,000	2.50	4.00	200	F 1.00;	S free
Rice	39,000	2.00	2.50	100	F Nom.;	S free
Arkansas	39,000	1.50	3.00	300	F ½;	S free
Mac Murray	5,000	1.00	1.00	25	F free;	S free
OCU	22,000	2.00	2.50	400	F free;	S free
UNO	13,000	2.50	2.50	160	F free;	S free

Financial data for the various schools were difficult to come by. There were only two schools who made a yearly profit from basketball—Texas Tech and Hutchinson Junior College. The financial data estimates were as follows:

Table 9-7

UNIVERSITY	NET PROFIT (NET LOSS)	UNIVERSITY	NET PROFIT (NET LOSS)
Texas Tech	$25,000	Arkansas	(100,000)
Hutch Juco	14,000	OCU	(105,000)
SMU	Breakeven	Tulane	(150,000)
Mac Murray	(21,000)	TCU	(loss)
UNO	(26,000)	Rice	(loss)
Creighton	(30,000)	Texas	??
Baylor	(50,000)	ORU	??
Texas A&M	(60,000)		

A 10 to 15% price inflation had occurred during the past year. Consequently an additional price hike at home games in Fayetteville could be justified. Matthews suggested a price of $3.50 for a reserved seat while Sutton thought that $4.00 for a reserved seat could be charged. If a season ticket for twelve home games were priced at $40, Sutton argued that such a price discount would be a bargain for any season ticket purchaser. Matthews thought that a season ticket price of $35 would be appropriate. Faculty would pay half price for two season tickets, full price for any more than two. General admission would be a little more than half the price for reserved seats.

Wilson Matthews suggested that first priority to purchase season tickets be given to the 6,400 Razorback Club members. Wilson stated, "Razorback Club members are ardent supporters of our athletic program. They will pay any price for a ticket. Once they buy their tickets, the demand for tickets to the general public will be established, and we can sell the tickets at a fairly high price to get additional revenue for our basketball program." Eddie Sutton replied, "Well, that strategy might work. We surely could put the program in a solid profit situation if we could sell 2,600 season tickets to our home games. As you well know, our basketball program lost about $125,000 two years ago and $140,000 this past year. With a little promotion, with a high quality team, and with loyalty from our Razorback supporters, we could make a profit on our basketball program and not have to rely on our football team to generate sufficient revenue and profits to support us. They've been doing so for the past 25 years. Boy, if we could sell 2,600 season tickets, for say $90,000, we'd be on our way."

Wilson replied, "We could do it in Fayetteville, and we could do it in Little Rock. For example, if we could sell 1,200 season tickets for $40, 1,000 tickets for $35, and 400 tickets for $25, we could generate $93,000 in revenue here in Fayetteville. Let's say we sell $70,000 worth of tickets in Little Rock, which I think we could do by selling most of them to Razorback Club members, then we can put basketball on a paying basis."

Eddie replied, "Wow! That would be great. But can we sell that many season tickets? We've only sold about 300 season tickets each year during the past five years. Would the Razorback Club members support such a ticket sale? Would the general public buy season tickets in Little Rock, particularly in light of our past failures?"

The two men's enthusiasm seemed warranted and they departed to meet again. The next time their conversation turned to more practical matters. Wilson Matthews asked, "What about competition? As you know, we have a monopoly here in Fayetteville. In Little Rock we'd be competing with all the high schools, with the University of Arkansas at Little Rock, University of Central Arkansas, and other small colleges. In addition, we'd be competing with other forms of entertainment."

Sutton replied, "That's true, but we would have no major competition at our level. There are no major universities in Division I of NCAA in Little Rock. We still would retain our monopoly position as far as I'm concerned. I think our fans would pay a pretty high price to see the University of Arkansas in Little Rock. When Indiana plays basketball in Indianapolis, not in Bloomington, the price is at least $5.00 for a reserved seat. When North Carolina State plays a "home" game away from campus, the price is at least $5.00 a ticket. The same holds true for other major universities. Competition from high schools and smaller colleges would not affect us in Little Rock."

Matthews said, "But maybe we should ease our way into the Little Rock market area with a low price, build a fan following, and then raise the price next year." Eddie replied, "No I think with our quality team, our promotion and our fan loyalty we should not set a low price. People will be willing to pay a high price for our product."

"What's the seating capacity of Barton Coliseum in Little Rock?" Sutton asked. "Approximately 7,000," Matthews replied and further stated, "We could differentiate those seats like this: 3,000 seats at $5.00 each, 2,000 at $4.00, and 2,000 at $3.00. We could charge $13.00 for three tickets, $10.00 for lesser priced seats, and $7.00 for the end zone seats. What do you think?"

Eddie Sutton pondered the question. "Let's think about it before we make our recommendation to Frank Broyles."

Case 9-4 THE NAME OF THE GAME IS FOOD*

Feeding American sports fans isn't peanuts. It's a billion-dollar business that has to pay attention to such factors as ethnic and regional tastes, the weather, and the differing eating patterns of baseball, football and basketball devotees.

"The old days when you could give 'em a hot dog, a Coke and a bag of peanuts are gone," says William Connell, chief executive officer of Ogden Food Services, one of the country's largest and busiest sports and recreational feeding concerns. "Tastes are much more sophisticated today. People at the ball park may not be looking for a balanced diet, but they appreciate good food. You can't just tell them: 'This is what you're gonna get, and that's it.' "

What About Knishes?

An essential part of Connell's business is knowing what stadium crowds will and won't eat in various parts of the country. "Take knishes," he says, referring to a kind of hand-held potato pudding popular in the New York area. "Knishes go great in Yonkers Raceway, but you couldn't give them away in New Orleans. There you've got to have oysters and eggs. In Maryland they want crabcakes. In Boston it's Italian sausages, and in Buffalo Polish sausages. You even have to color hot dogs differently depending on the area—dark brown in the Northeast, bright red in the South."

Besides recognizing gustatory regionalism, stadium food purveyors analyze the eating habits of different kinds of fans with the intensity of anthropologists studying the tribal patterns of aborigines. Connell says that the type of sport being played has an important bearing on how much is eaten and how much is spent on food during a game.

He even has devised a basic table that shows the amount a typical fan will lay out on food, drink, and souvenirs during various sporting events:

Football	90 cents to $1
Basketball	$1 to $1.10
Ice Hockey	$1.25 to $1.50
Horse Racing	$1.75 to $2
Baseball	$2

* Herbert Kupferberg, "The Name of the Game Is Food," *Parade Magazine,* March 9, 1975, pp. 8–9.

"It's not that football fans lack money," says Connell. "In fact, judging by ticket prices, they're probably the most affluent of all. But it's a game that rivets the attention constantly. No football fan would dream of leaving his seat during play. The time-outs aren't that long, and there's only one 20-minute intermission with a spectacular show including floats, fireworks and a band. Who can eat?

"At baseball games, on the other hand, there's constant movement up and down the aisles. There's no compulsion to sit there every moment of the game. That doesn't mean it isn't as good a sport. But the way of life is different."

Connell says that ice hockey, which also is an attention-riveting sport, manages to do better in food sales than football or basketball because it has two intermissions rather than one "And there's nothing going on during the breaks," he adds. "All you can do is watch the Zamboni machine going around scraping the ice."

Racetrack spending, Connell says, is likely to depend on how an individual is making out on his bets. But with eight or nine races, and intervals up to half an hour between them, horse fans manage to average almost as much as their baseball brethren. "The essential thing for racetrack food is that you be able to eat it with one hand," he says. "The other has to be free for holding the form sheet. At Suffolk Downs in Boston we've developed what we call an Italian Sausage Roll—a sausage jammed into a hollow roll flavored with pizza sauce. It does very well."

Weather Factor

Weather plays an important part in determining what items sell. "The crucial point is the 45-degree mark," says Connell. "Above that you sell cold drinks; below, hot drinks. In Buffalo, for example, when the temperature goes down it means you're selling coffee at 30 cents a cup instead of beer at 60 cents. That hurts. Venders can make a difference, too. It takes a while to separate the sellers from the lookers. Some guys sell their first load of stuff and then sit down to watch the rest of the game."

Connell's company, like others in the business, is trying to expand old concepts of sports and recreational feeding. They're going into movie theaters with refreshment stands and elaborately stocked vending machines. "Movie fans are like football fans," says Connell with a sigh. "They don't leave their seats. We're trying to bring about short intermissions, between the pictures of a double feature, or after the cartoon."

The sports foods experts are also placing more emphasis on the "Diamond Clubs" and similar white-tablecloth restaurants that are built into the newer stadiums and superdomes. They're going into the convention hall business, feeding as many as 6,000 people at a time at luncheons and banquets.

Unlike food sold in the aisles at ballparks, which is brought in from the outside, meals offered at stadium clubs and convention halls are prepared in kitchens on the premises by a small army of chefs.

"It isn't easy," says Bill Connell, "but at least they've got equipment and facilities, including timing devices, that can do the job. And they haven't got four children running around the kitchen at the same time, the way a housewife does. As I tell my wife, sometimes it's harder to cook for six people than for 6,000."

QUESTION:

1. Comment on the article.

FOOTNOTE

[1] Presented at a Case Workshop and distributed by the Intercollegiate Case Clearing House, Soldiers Field, Boston, Mass. 02163.

10

MARKETING THE ATHLETIC PROGRAM TO ITS FANS (continued)

PROMOTION STRATEGIES FOR MARKETING

Marketing is focused around the promotion of various products and services. To become successful, an athletic program probably needs more promotion than any product does. Since sports are a service, not a product, they are fleeting in nature. They can only be remembered, not stored for future use. They are usually considered to be inexpensive and relatively free. They must be brought directly to the fans, or the fans must go directly to the sports. This involves few middlemen. Sports are a luxury rather than a necessity. Thus, sports should be promoted in various ways—by personal selling, advertising, and sales promotion.

Personal selling involves persuading people to buy a product or service. There are three different types of salespeople who are involved in selling the products and services of the athletic program—creative salespersons, service salespersons, and supportive salespersons. One is an order getter, another is an order taker, the other an order helper. They will be discussed in more detail later on. However, personal selling is probably the most effective way to promote a program.

Another way to sell the products and services is through product advertising. This is a nonpersonal, group presentation of current information about the athletic program. To be effective, it must be directed to a mass market, and it must supplement other forms of promotion.

Television is the best medium for national exposure. It helps with recruiting and increases the public's financial donations and general support for an athletic program. Its chief advantages are sight, sound, motion, and regional and national coverage; it is one of the biggest sources of revenue for college and professional teams.

Radio is less costly than television, it is more timely, and it offers frequent delivery locally and regionally. However, its lack of a picture and action (both so important to sports activity) is a chief drawback.

Printed material is also used to advertise athletics. Newspapers offer intensive coverage and local exposure. Through newspaper coverage, frequent, updated references to athletic events can be circulated to the public, usually at no cost to the program.

Magazines and printed programs offer some special advantages. They provide leisurely reading, superior reproduction, and perhaps national exposure. However, magazines do not reach a high percentage of the population; they are published infrequently, and their information is quickly outdated.

Direct mail offers regional, national, and special exposure to a select group of fans at a fairly reasonable cost. It can be made fairly timely and with a good quality reproduction.

Other forms of advertising may also be used—billboards and films, especially.

Consistent exposure, through the right combination of advertising media and other forms of promotion, adds a great deal to an athletic program.

Other types of promotion activities include public speaking at banquets and point of purchase displays. Speaking at banquets or other functions is routine for most athletic administrators. However, if an administrator is not adept at public speaking, he/she is urged to select someone on the staff to provide the entertainment and the special purpose message of the banquet or public appearance. It is imperative for a successful program to generate fan support through speeches at banquets, booster clubs, and other special events.

Window and interior displays are forms of point of purchase (P-O-P) promotions. It is excellent to use team schedules for point of purchase promotion, expecially if the current win-loss records are kept. Game programs and other current literature should be provided so fans can identify players. Special signs should be made for special purposes, usually at the point of sale.

Special promotions are sometimes used by athletic programs. For example, bat days, premiums, contests, two-for-one sales, demonstrations, and special honors are used to promote attendance, particularly in highly competitive entertainment situations. These promotional activities provide local exposure desired, appeal to specific groups of fans, and publicize the team's present status.

The three forms of promotional activities—personal selling, advertising, and specials—support each other and should be used together. An athletic administrator can compare his/her program to the following chart to evaluate the program's strengths and weaknesses.

Objective: To Determine Proper Promotion Media

Theory of Media Strategy

	Personal Selling	*Newspaper*	*Radio*	*Television*	*Direc Mai*
1. Nature of Audience					
1.1 Local Exposure Desired	x	x	x		
1.2 Regional Exposure			x	x	x
1.3 National Exposure				x	x
1.4 Special Exposure	x				x
2. Nature of Product and Service					
2.1 Low Cost Desired		x	x		x
2.2 Appeals to Sight	x	x		x	x
Sound	x		x	x	
Action	x			x	
2.3 Timeliness	x	x	x	x	x
2.4 Reproductions					x
3. Other Factors					

Overall Evaluation:

Message Strategies in Promotion

The use of media plays an important role in promotion, but the most important part of a sound promotion program (or a public relations program) deals with the information conveyed to the fans and general public. If the PR function is to play a significant role in promoting a good image for the athletic program, in generating ticket sales, or in promoting growth of the program, then a sound message strategy must be followed.

For example, if the aim of promotional activities is to increase the public's faith in an athletic program, then the sports information director must convey messages that are truthful and convincing. Truthfulness is at the heart of credibility. To be convincing a message has to be built on truth, not falsehood. If the public finds one misstatement in a release of information, the remaining statements will also be suspect. Information must be factual, honest, and correct.

Another characteristic is sincerity, that priceless ingredient which indicates whether a person really believes in what he is doing. Sincerity keeps the confidence of other people.

Another strategy is to use a positive approach in releasing information. It is wise to avoid negative comments; the director should emphasize what

a- s	*Speaking at Banquets*	*Point of Purchase Displays*	**Special Promotions**	→ **Compared to**	→ **Actual Situation**	→ **Evaluation** *Strength*	*Weakness*
	x	x	x				
		x					
	x	x	x				
	x	x					
	x	x	x				
	x						
	x						
		x	x				
		x	x				

can be done to correct a poor situation. Emphasizing what can be done or what is being done is much better promotion than emphasizing what is not being done. However, it is not wise to mislead by being too positive. If negative factors are being discussed, it is wise to sandwich them between two positive comments.

Losing one's cool is not good public relations. Anger and flying off the handle is a costly form of promotion because it loses friends, causes antagonism, and usually costs money, time, and effort. A negative attitude is often expressed through scolding, demanding, condemning, preaching, and bragging. Any information suggesting a negative or angry tone will cause problems for an administrator.

Using human interest stories in news releases is often effective. Referring to people, using informal language, and being oneself are good strategies to follow in this case. Likewise, making the outcome of a game uncertain—causing suspense—will make the information interesting to fans.

Emphasizing the team is a sound strategy since teamwork is fundamental to winning. But if the team is not doing too well, then emphasis on individual players could be employed.

These and other message strategies can be used in a successful promotion program.

Objective: To Develop Message Strategies

Strategies	Strength	Weakness
1. Are the messages credible?		
1.1 Are they truthful		
1.2 Are they factual		
1.3 Are they honest		
1.4 Are they correct		
1.5 Others		
2. Are the messages sincere?		
3. Are the messages positive?		
3.1 Do they avoid negatives		
3.2 Are negatives sandwiched with positives		
3.3 Others		
4. Are messages "angry"?		
4.1 Are they condemning		
4.2 Are they bragging		
4.3 Are they scolding		
4.4 Are they preaching		
4.5 Are they demanding		
4.6 Others		
5. Are the messages interesting?		
5.1 About people		
5.2 Informal		
5.3 Suspenseful		
5.4 Others		
6. Emphasis on team?		
7. Others		
Overall Evaluation:		

Sales Personnel Strategy for Selling Goods and Services

The athletic administrator must decide what type of person is best suited to sell each of the various goods and services marketed by an athletic program. There are three alternatives facing an athletic administrator. The first is the creative salesperson who aggressively seeks out people to become fans or customers of the athletic program's services. He/she is sometimes called an order getter. The second is the service salesperson, sometimes called an order taker, who usually takes or services orders. The third type is the supportive salesperson, who performs missionary work or technical work for the athletic program. This is the order helper.

Different selling situations call for different types of sales personnel. For example, if an athletic program needs to sell itself to the general public or *tive: To Determine Proper Sales Personnel Strategy*

Factors →	**Theory →** *Personnel Needed*	**Compared to →**	**Actual Situation →**	**Evaluation** *Strength*	*Weakness*
onsumer goods					
1 Convenience					
1.11 Staple	Service				
1.12 Impulse	Service				
1.13 Emergency	Service				
2 Shopping	Creative				
3 Specialty	Creative				
4 New good	Supportive & Missionary				
5 Unsought	Creative				
dustrial goods					
1 Installations	Creative & Supportive				
2 Major equipment	Creative & Supportive				
3 Accessory equipment	Creative & Service				
4 Raw materials	Creative & Service				
5 Component parts	Creative & Service				
6 Supplies	Creative & Service				
ature of buyer					
1 Industrial buyer	Creative & Supportive				
2 Wholesaler and retailer	Creative & Service				
3 Ultimate consumer	Creative & Service				
roduct life cycle					
1 Development	Missionary & Creative				
2 Growth	Creative & Supportive				
3 Maturity	Service				
4 Decline	Service				
thers					
verall Evaluation:					

to a particular organization, which is wavering in its support of the athletic program, a creative sales approach would be most appropriate. On the other hand, if soft drinks, popcorn, candy , and peanuts are to be sold to a captive audience, then order takers or service sales personnel would be most appropriate. So the question usually arises as to what factors are to be considered in determining the proper sales personnel strategy.

One fundamental factor is the nature of the product and service to be sold. A consumer product or service—a convenience, a shopping good, or a specialty good—requires a different selling strategy than an industrial good or service. A convenience good or service is a staple, an object bought on impulse, or a product (or service) needed in emergency situations. As such they would require some service type sales personnel (normally concessions would be considered convenience goods) to sell them. In contrast, people compare different shopping goods before buying. A creative salesperson should be employed to sell them. A special or uncommon effort must be made to sell specialty goods and services. This effort requires creative sales personnel. If the good or service has just been marketed, perhaps missionary and supportive sales personnel would be needed. If the good or service is normally unpopular with consumers, then a creative salesperson should be employed.

To sell an industrial product or service, usually a combination of creative and supportive personnel are needed. If a major installation (such as land, building, standard or custom-made equipment) is to be sold, then the job should go to a combination creative and supportive salesperson. The same is true for accessory equipment.

The sale of raw materials, component parts, supplies, and other industrial services would normally require a combination of creative and service personnel—probably a creative sales strategy to sell initially, and a service strategy to take succeeding orders.

Another major factor in determining the type of sales personnel to be used is the nature of the buyer. Selling to an industrial buyer usually requires salesmanship of the highest order. Here both creative and supportive personnel are needed. Selling to retailers, wholesalers, and certain types of consumers requires both creative and service personnel. Sales to the ultimate consumer would also require both creative and service sales personnel.

Another factor is the stage of the product or service in its life cycle. If it is at the development stage, then missionary and creative personnel are needed. If the product or service is in its growth stage, then creative and supportive sales personnel are appropriate. Only service sales personnel are needed if the product or service has reached the maturity or decline stage.

These factors may be analyzed in an evaluation of the sales personnel strategy. The administrator can compare the actual situation to theory, then determine the strengths and weaknesses of his own athletic program for each of the varied products/services which it sells.

The Pecuniary Strategy for Marketing

The financial strategy for marketing a program's products and services is usually confined to four fundamental strategy decisions: (1) whether to use a sales or revenue budget for the products and services sold; (2) whether to sell on credit, and if so, what type of collection system to use; (3) whether to sell preseason tickets; (4) pecuniary strategy considering product's stage in the product life cycle.

Effective administrative strategy is built on the notion of the marketing activities generating sufficient sales revenue to cover the costs of producing the goods and services. Consequently, the administrator must prepare a sales or revenue budget for an athletic program's revenue-producing activities. He must project how much revenue will be made from ticket sales, since tickets provide the greatest source of revenue for the program. In his projection, the administrator must consider the previous seasons' win-loss records, as well as what he expects the coming season to bring.

Revenue from radio and television has become increasingly important to most athletic programs. Also, revenue from concessions is increasingly important. Sometimes interest income on advance ticket sales and dividends from investments are also included in a revenue budget. Revenue from parking might be included. Other forms of revenue are donations from interested fans, booster club donations, and miscellaneous forms of income, such as transfer of funds from other sources. In any event, it is imperative for an administrator to prepare a revenue budget.

Another pecuniary strategy is whether to sell goods and services on credit. Since most revenue is generated from the sale of services rather than products, most athletic programs do not use a credit strategy. However, if

Objective: To Prepare a Revenue Budget

Strategies	Strength	Weakness
1. Does the athletic program prepare a revenue budget?		
1.1 Ticket sales		
1.2 Radio and television		
1.3 Concessions		
1.4 Investment income		
1.5 Parking		
1.6 Donations		
1.7 Transfer of funds		
1.8 Other sources		
Overall Evaluation:		

Objective: To Determine Credit and Collection Policies

Strategies	Strength	Weakness
1. Does the program sell on credit?		
1.1 Credit terms		
1.2 Source of credit approval		
1.3 Others		
2. Collection policies		
2.1 Collection procedures		
2.2 Final actions		
2.3 Others		
Overall Evaluation:		

credit is used, two subdecisions have to be considered—what the credit terms will be and who approves credit sales.

If the use of credit is approved, then the collection strategy follows. Normally the collection procedures, repossessions, and final actions have to be considered.

As suggested before, the pecuniary strategy to be followed must be determined in light of the product life cycle for each sport or other revenue-producing activity. For example, if a product or service is in the introductory stage, the program must be willing to lose money, even with a high profit margin on the goods and services. Lack of volume is the chief reason for losing money. During the growth stage the product or service has to make it big. A fairly large profit can be expected, but with slightly lower profit margins. Occasionally, in the maturity stage, products and services might sell for losses. Breakeven analyses and financial ratio analyses need to be made at this time, and other financial strategies should be considered. During the decline stage, the program must be able to suffer financial losses, to have adequate financial reserves, to consider tax write-offs (if a professional program), and to appeal to other sources of money. When determining pecuniary strategies, marketers and administrators must consider the program's stage in the product life cycle.

Sales of Preseason Tickets

Selling preseason tickets is important to a program's success. Perhaps preseason ticket sales are the best indicators of fan attendance, of possible growth, of a program's image and entertainment value. In addition, preseason ticket sales almost guarantee some degree of financial security for the coming year. Once in hand, the money belongs to the athletic program even if the fan is unable to attend, because of the weather, illness, personal reasons or whatever. Once in hand, the money can be invested in short-

Objective: To Determine Pecuniary Strategies in a Product Life Cycle

Strategies	Strength	Weakness
1. Does the marketing activity practice the following pecuniary strategies for different products and services?		
1.1 Introductory stage		
1.11 Be willing to lose money		
1.12 High profit margins		
1.13 Others		
1.2 Growth stage		
1.21 Large profits		
1.22 Still high margins		
1.23 Others		
1.3 Maturity stage		
1.31 Willing to suffer occasional losses		
1.32 Make breakeven analyses		
1.33 Use ratio analyses		
1.34 Others		
1.4 Decline stage		
1.41 Willing to suffer losses		
1.42 Have adequate reserves		
1.43 Consider tax write offs		
1.44 Search for other sources		
1.45 Others		
Overall Evaluation:		

Objective: To Promote Sale of Preseason Tickets

Strategy	Strength	Weakness
1. Does the athletic program consciously try to sell preseason tickets?		
1.1 Is the advanced ticket money invested in temporary securities?		
1.2 Other implications		
Overall Evaluation:		

term securities to yield investment income, either as dividends or as interest. These reasons usually are sufficient to overcome the ticket selling campaigns, and hard work, and time associated with preseason ticket sales.

CHAPTER SUMMARY

To market an athletic program, there must be promotional activities. Promotion can take three forms: personal selling, advertising, and special promotion.

Television, radio, newspaper, magazines, and direct mail can be used to dispense information. Each has its advantages and disadvantages in various situations. Special promotions are sometimes used in highly competitive situations. They include public speaking at banquets and other events; window displays; and specials such as bat days, contests, and two-for-one sales. To be effective, all types of promotion should complement each other.

The message strategies for effective promotion should be characterized by credibility, sincerity, positiveness, courtesy, human interest, and emphasis on team success. These are necessary to promote an intelligent PR program based on the release of information and personal contact.

There are three types of personnel necessary to sell products and services: the order getter, the order taker, and the order helper. Which type to use depends on several factors, such as the nature of the product and service, the nature of the buyer, the product's stage in the life cycle.

The pecuniary strategies relate to making a sales or revenue budget for the products and services sold. Some type of decision must be made concerning credit. In addition, the sale of preseason tickets should be considered. Finally, general financial strategies based on the product's stage in the life cycle must be considered.

Case 10-1 EASTSIDE, WESTSIDE! THE EFFECT OF WINNING ON FOOTBALL AND BASKETBALL REVENUE: A CASE IN POINT*

If you were to ask a coach what factors affect game revenue in football and basketball, he would immediately answer, "Winning!"

The rationale behind the win-loss factor in producing revenue probably goes like this: if the team wins, it attracts more fans who will spend more money on tickets, buy more hot dogs and candy and pop to increase revenues from concessions, buy more programs, and generally cause an increase in total revenues. How true is this rationale?

*This case was adapted from information presented in the article, "The Effect of Winning on Football and Basketball," Bill Stancil and Robert D. Hay, *Arkansas Journal of HPER*, June, 1978.

Table 10-1 Football Revenues and Win-Loss Records

Eastside

YEAR	GAMES HOME	GAMES AWAY	SEASON RECORD	WIN-LOSS PERCENTAGE	PERCENTAGE TIME NO. OF HOME GAMES	TOTAL REVENUE
6 yrs ago	7	4	9–2	.82	5.7	$34,080
5 yrs ago	7	4	8–3	.73	5.1	33,947
4 yrs ago	7	5	11–1	.92	6.4	38,810
3 yrs ago	6	5	5–5–1	.50	3.0	24,736
2 yrs ago	5	6	6–4–1	.54	2.7	27,626
last year	7	5	3–9	.25	1.8	27,873
this year	5	6	5–6	.54	2.7	25,168

Westside

YEAR	GAMES HOME	GAMES AWAY	SEASON RECORD	WIN-LOSS PERCENTAGE	PERCENTAGE TIMES NO. OF HOME GAMES	TOTAL REVENUE
6 yrs ago	6	4	5–5	.50	3.0	$17,955
5 yrs ago	5	6	6–5	.54	2.7	19,678
4 yrs ago	6	6	5–7	.42	2.5	19,005
3 yrs ago	6	6	7–4–1	.58	3.5	21,154
2 yrs ago	6	6	7–4–1	.58	3.5	28,919
last year	5	5	5–5	.50	2.5	25,302
this year	5	5	7–2–1	.70	3.5	25,684

Let's analyze four specific high school athletic case situations and see what we can conclude, recognizing of course that just four situations do not make a generalization true or false.

This school system's athletic program consists of two high schools, Eastside and Westside, plus four junior highs. The information that follows is presented to see if there is any correlation between winning and revenues in football at the two high schools.

QUESTIONS:

1. Use a Pearson correlation to determine if there is any significant correlation between football revenues and wins, between football revenue and win percentage, and between football revenues and number of home games × win percentage. If possible, use the SPSS-Version G on the computer. If you cannot use a computer, try the manual method.
2. Determine the coefficient of correlation (r), and coefficient of determination (r^2) and interpret the data for football revenues and winning.

Let us take a look at basketball revenues for the two high schools to see if there is any significant correlation between winning and basketball reve-

Table 10-2 Basketball Revenues and Win-Loss Records

Eastside

YEAR	HOME GAMES	AWAY GAMES	SEASON RECORD	WIN PERCENTAGE	NO. OF HOME GAMES TIMES PERCENTAGE	TOTAL REVENUE
6 yrs ago	11	13	20–4	.83	9.1	$ 9,748
5 yrs ago	13	13	23–3	.88	11.4	10,743
4 yrs ago	13	15	16–12	.57	7.4	9,740
3 yrs ago	13	13	20–6	.77	10.0	13,139
2 yrs ago	13	17	30–0	1.00	13.0	18,893
1 yr ago	14	12	14–12	.54	7.6	11,388

Westside

YEAR	HOME GAMES	AWAY GAMES	SEASON RECORD	WIN PERCENTAGE	NO. OF HOME GAMES TIMES PERCENTAGE	TOTAL REVENUE
6 yrs ago	11	13	20–4	.83	9.1	$ 5,686
5 yrs ago	13	11	20–4	.83	10.8	6,636
4 yrs ago	11	14	9–16	.36	4.0	7,251
3 yrs ago	13	13	14–12	.54	7.0	7,187
2 yrs ago	10	21	16–15	.52	5.2	8,947
1 yr ago	11	18	19–10	.65	7.2	10,133

nues. The following information in Table 10-2 is presented to determine if there is a correlation:

QUESTIONS:

1. Correlate the basketball revenues with winning for the two high schools.
2. Use an r and r^2 to interpret the data for basketball revenues and winning.
3. What variables, other than winning, affect the revenues?

Case 10-2 PUBLIC RELATIONS FOR INTERSCHOLASTIC ATHLETIC PROGRAMS*

Dick Karlgaard, Director of Athletics
Bismarck (N.D.) Public Schools

Relations with the public in any part of our educational enterprise is an ongoing, incidental, and sometimes preplanned occurrence. The very nature of the profession calls for a high frequency of contacts with stu-

* From the proceedings of an Interscholastic Athletic Administration Conference.

dents, fellow professionals, and lay patrons of the school district. In the area of athletics, this frequency of contact is compounded by a greater emotional involvement on the part of the patrons and by exposure presented through the news media.

In the administration of interscholastic athletic programs, therefore, we need to recognize our unique position in this educational community and plan a philosophy about relations with the public that covers both the daily, incidental contacts and a planned program of interpreting our activities to the public at large. The development of this philosophy and the planning of effective programming should be a task shared with members of your athletic staff. However, individual responsibilities of implementing this planning should be defined.

The athletic administrator must take the leadership in involving and directing his staff toward their responsibilities and should develop a personal checklist in bringing about its implementation. Several specific obligations of the athletic director follow.

Patrons of the district should be made aware of the total sports calendar for the year and should be presented with seasonal and weekly reminders of these events as a follow-up. In Bismarck, we pursue these tasks in the following manner:

An identification of each sports activity including sophomore, junior varsity, and varsity are made a part of the Bismarck High School yearly calendar of events. In that way all students are made aware of these happenings through their student handbook. The Chamber of Commerce is advised of our varsity activities in the sports areas that are best attended and these schedules are incorporated into a monthly greeter magazine that finds its way into all of the eating and housing establishments of the community. Our local newspapers are also given this calender so that they might incorporate it into a daily feature that identifies what's happening in Bismarck.

Seasonal schedules are sent to all of our local and state-wide sports media so that our activities are presented in their weekly calendar of events. We also prepare a rather extensive brochure for our fall and winter activities. We include the schedules for every activity of that season and embellish it with team and individual pictures along with some historical background on some sports.

Each Friday, we mail out our weekly "Sports Publicity Bulletin" which identifies all of the activities on the next week's athletic calendar for grades 7-12 in the Bismarck Public School District. Some of the highlights of that week's program are described and will include items of historical interest which may provide additional copy for the media. All of our local sports media, state-wide services, and the media of the communities whose schools we're playing are included in this mailing. Our administrative staff, our district school board, and certain lay people of our town are also on our mailing list. We change the membership of our list of lay people from year to year and have found this to be a particularly effective means of public relations.

A program of communications with the spectators at home contests is also a very serious consideration in your efforts towards better public relations. A complete roster of participants and the way in which they can be identified—by number, weight class, etc.—must be available for those in attendance. Other descriptions of them, including pictures, are some additional elements to be considered in the makeup of your program.

This program of communications also includes a need to have an effective public address system and an announcer who can be descriptive without talking too much. The selection of the public address personnel is one we make with a great deal of care because this is a very noticeable part of your home contest preparations. Voice quality, a knowledge of the activity, and the ability to sense just how much the public wishes to hear are basic requirements of the people we select. From our experience, we might point to your consideration of members of the broadcasting industry and vocal music people from your school district who have some sports background. For new people whom we consider using, we provide an orientation session to describe what information we consider to be meaningful.

A public relations program at home contests extends beyond the means of communication and includes plans for making the spectator comfortable. This comfort begins with a concern for convenient parking at the site of the contest and continues with the provision for easy accessibility to purchasing tickets of admission. From this point, the customer has the right to expect his routing into the stadium or gymnasium will be made expedient and the location of his seat will be very apparent. The existing procedure at the conclusion of the contest should be given the same consideration.

Our community contains two daily newspapers, three radio stations, and two television stations. The establishment of a fair and candid relationship with the sports staff of these news media is a task to which we give considerable attention. When a mutual respect for candor has been developed, many of the rumors that sometimes appear in print can be curtailed. If we have an impending news release of some considerable local or state-wide interest—e.g., the dismissal or hiring of a coach—we will bring the media into our confidence well in advance and explain what possibilities we may be encountering. We ask this information be held in confidence and solicit their wishes as to how they would like to have the story released to them. We have found these people are appreciative of this approach and, while not violating our confidentiality, they have been put in a position where they can background the story in preparation for the release date.

Daily relationships with students and school patrons probably offers you the most frequent opportunity to practice good public relations. Our major consideration in this ongoing relationship is attempting to anticipate potential problems. Of prime concern is the effort to make our position defensible in all facets of the athletic program. This implies that, in everything we do, we must have the best educational interests of our athletes in mind. When our position has been poorly established, we must have the integrity to admit our errors and see to their early correction. If we sincerely approach our program with this objective we won't have to apologize for our efforts and won't be looking over our shoulder in fear of public reaction.

The coaches on your athletic staff must also be made aware of their responsibilities in the area of public relations. They should realize that the measure of their positive relationships with the patrons of the community is directly proportional to the relationships that they have with their athletes. Honesty and fairness should describe their position as they attempt to provide a sports education for the boys or girls in their program.

We feel our coaches have an obligation to make themselves available, whenever possible, for television appearances, service club talks, and at our weekly Saturday morning radio program called "Coaches Corner." The coach will not only give an insight to the public on his particular athletic area but will usually eliminate some public irritations that are based on misinformation. Candor with the sports reporting professionals should be given the same consideration as that suggested for the athletic director. The quality of people in the sports media has changed in the past few decades and, whereas they used to take the role of a cheerleader for the local sports enterprises, they are now more objective in their reporting. Anything less than honesty in the coach's relationship with these people will ultimately hurt his credibility and will possibly destroy a good relationship that the coach may find useful at some point in time.

In summary, good public relations must be planned for and be based on an honest, fair relationship with the public. The basic planning must include a sound program of athletic administration in which the director identifies the educational responsibilities entrusted to him. The coach is a teacher of an athletic activity which should have the same educational philosophy as any area of the curriculum. Beyond this, he has an opportunity, unique with sports, to bring about other positive modifications of the youth's behavior. Positive behavior attitudes along with sports skills should be a significant part of this educational philosophy. A program of athletic activities based on these principles will lead quite naturally to a good relationship with the public.

Case 10-3 PENN STATE'S TV REVENUE OF $1.1 MILLION*

The magic eye of television has made football a big-time business on the college campuses of America.

Penn State University, for example, will earn more than $1.1 million this season from four football games—two regionally telecast games worth $180,000 each, a Thanksgiving night game against the University of Pittsburgh in Three Rivers Stadium will pay $244,000, and a Jan. 1 Cotton Bowl date worth more than $500,000.

The Thanksgiving night game against Pitt was originally scheduled on the following Saturday at Pitt Stadium. By switching sites and allowing television to tune in, both schools will clear more than $200,000 in profits, considerably more than they could have expected to earn at Pitt Stadium.

The key word is television.

Pitt and Penn State will be providing perhaps three hours of prime-

* Hal Bock, an AP sports article, *The Nashville Banner*, November 14, 1974, p. 47.

time entertainment and, at today's rates, the half-million dollars or so that goes to the two schools is a reasonable price for filling that much network time.

"We figure about $200,000 per hour to produce a regular filmed show," said one television executive.

Television, of course, will also be looking in on New Year's Day when the college football season concludes with the major bowl games. And the teams participating in those extravaganzas will also be taking home healthy-sized paychecks. Just how much is in those checks depends mostly on whether the teams come from conferences or are independents.

Conference teams must share their bowl spoils with their sister schools. For example, the University of Texas earned $475,092.61 as its share of the Cotton Bowl last year. The school kept $100,000 and then divided the remainder among the eight Southwest Conference schools. That meant that each SWC school, Texas included, received about $45,000 for the Longhorns' Bowl appearance.

As the number of schools in a conference increases, the bowl take for the conference representative goes down. The Rose Bowl's net revenue of about $2.5 million is divided evenly between the Pacific Eight and Big Ten Conference representatives. Thus each Pac-8 team gets about $150,000 annually, while the Big Ten, dividing the same income among more schools, realizes about $125,000 a team.

Independent schools do better financially. The 1975 Orange Bowl, for example, matches Alabama and Notre Dame. The game is a sellout and each school will receive about $600,000. Notre Dame keeps all of its income while Alabama must divide it among other members of the Southeastern Conference. The same thing happened when the same schools met in last year's Sugar Bowl. That paid $452,000 a team.

Joe Katz, director of the Sugar Bowl, said much of the bowl payoff depends on ticket sales.

"When you do not fill the stadium, then your payoff to the teams drops and you don't become competitive with other bowls," Katz said.

Payoffs to the teams are by no means the only expenses involved in operating a bowl. "There are many hidden costs," Katz continued. "Traffic control, security; everybody is paid nowadays. At one time it was a civic endeavor. But we don't get the freebies that we got from the community in the past—decorations, ushers, ticket takers. As time goes on, it costs more to operate a bowl."

In Houston, the Astro-Bluebonnet Bowl is billed as a charity affair. Last year, it collected $587,356 in revenue of which a mere $15,100 went to 22 local charities. The participants, Tulane and the University of Houston, each received $213,870. The remainder went to stadium rental and expenses.

"With a few exceptions, teams always look first at the amount of money you can pay," said Joe Eason, a Houston insurance man who serves as president of the Astro-Bluebonnet Bowl. "There are only two ways we can pay more—increase the cost of tickets or get a larger television contract."

Houston has been invited back to the Astro-Bluebonnet Bowl again this year and athletic director Harry Faulk says the income from that appearance will help balance his department's budget, which ran about $1.75 million this year. Faulk called the appearance a welcome but not a vital element in the budget.

In financial order, the four major bowls appear to line up this way: Rose, with a payoff of approximately $1.25 million apiece to the Pacific Eight and Big Ten Conference representatives; Orange, with a sellout guaranteeing a payoff of about $600,000 each to Notre Dame and Alabama; Cotton, with a 37½ percent payoff of game receipts guaranteed to each team totally, almost $500,000 last year; Sugar, which paid $452,000 to competing teams last year.

11

LONG-RANGE PLANNING FOR ATHLETIC FACILITIES: MAKING AN ENVIRONMENTAL ANALYSIS

Athletic facilities provide the place and time utilities so necessary for fan entertainment. They also provide the time and place utilities for athletes to engage in the everyday practices so necessary to produce winning teams. Athletic facilities also represent large financial commitments for twenty to forty or more years, and who knows what will happen twenty years from now? For this reason, it is necessary to make long-range plans for the construction and maintenance of athletic facilities. Administrators have attempted to plan for long-range goals by constructing planning models. The factors in one such model are presented in the chapter which follows.

Long-range planning for athletic facilities is affected by three major factors: (1) the philosophy of the administrator, (2) an environmental appraisal of the factors affecting athletic facilities, and (3) the subsequent administrative strategies developed from an analysis of the environmental factors and from the administrative philosophy. It is necessary to take a more detailed look at the three major variables (see Figure 11-1).

PHILOSOPHY OF THE ADMINISTRATOR

Philosophy may be defined as a set of personal values which a person holds dear and which guide a person's thinking and actions. These values are derived from a variety of sources and may be classified in a number of ways. One way is to analyze how the sociocultural values of an administrator affect his/her thinking and actions. For example, the administrator born in the South may have a different set of values about black athletes

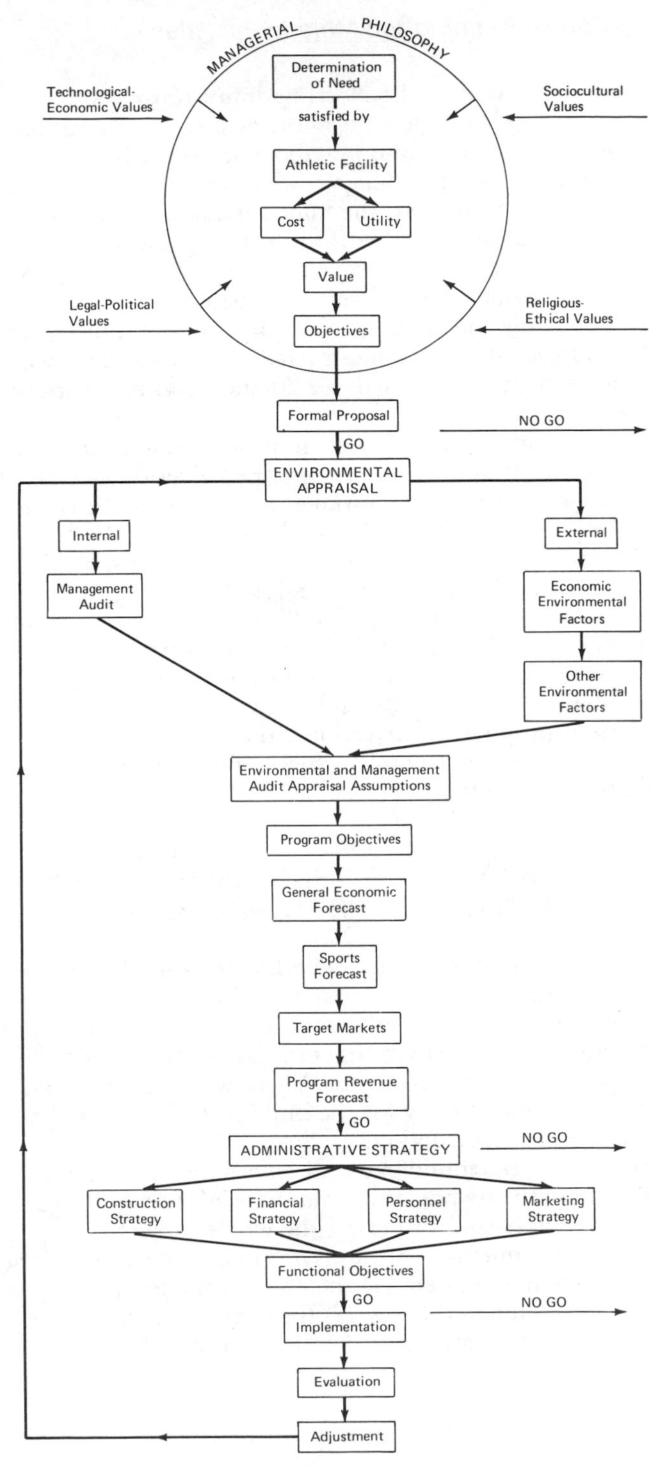

Figure 11–1 Managerial Philosophy

than one born and reared in the North; administrators' values may differ about male and female facilities. Technological-economic values might influence an administrator's philosophy about spending money or encouraging innovations. The legal-political values of an administrator may differ according to his team affiliation—he may think one way if his program depends on tax revenues, and another if his team is professional. An administrator's ethical-religious values are expressed through his honesty and integrity. A combination of all these values determine the administrator's philosophy. Following his own philosophy, an administrator decides, among other things, whether athletic facilities are needed, what designs should be followed, how they will be financed, and a variety of other decisions.

The administrator's values play an important role in long-range planning. They influence how an administrator perceives the need for facilities, the types of facilities needed, the initial estimated costs, the economic utilities that will be created, the value of the facility, and why the facility should be constructed. The administrator's values determine his answers to these questions; from the answers, he decides whether to propose that a new facility be designed, built, financed, and used. If an administrator's value system tells him/her subjectively that a new facility is not a worthy venture, chances are good that a new facility would never be constructed. On the other hand, if an administrator subjectively decides that he/she ought to make a formal proposal to investigate the feasibility of a new facility, then the first major hurdle is passed which influences the long-range planning for an athletic facility.

THE FEASIBILITY OF A PROPOSED FACILITY: APPRAISING THE ENVIRONMENT

If an administrator must decide whether to construct a new facility, he/she should analyze both the internal and external environments. Which external factors affect the proposal to build or not to build a new facility? There are several economic environmental factors that affect the decision. How much will the new facility cost? Where will the revenue come from and how long will it take to pay for the building? Where are the sources of capital to finance the construction?

There are also noneconomic external environmental factors to be considered. Problems with any one of the many social, cultural, legal, political, or technological factors could forestall the whole project.

An internal environmental appraisal must be made as well. The following factors must be investigated: (1) the objectives and philosophy of other administrators concerning athletics, (2) the strengths and weaknesses of the existing athletic program, and (3) a detailed forecast of various factors that will affect the proposal.

Administrative Strategies

After analyzing the internal and external environmental factors, assuming the "go" signal is on, the administrator must formulate a series of strategies. This includes all financial strategies, personnel strategies, and marketing strategies that affect the proposed facility. Once these have been formulated, the administrator must step back and decide whether to proceed in planning and executing the proposal.

MORE DETAILED ANALYSIS OF EXTERNAL ENVIRONMENTAL FACTORS

Let us take a more detailed look at some of the external environmental factors that should be considered by an athletic administrator.

Cultural Factors

Some cultural factors could determine whether or not to build an athletic facility. There is a trend for people to become active participants in athletics for life-long use. The participation in lifetime sports such as tennis, golf, and bowling would suggest that facilities would have to be constructed to take advantage of this trend for people to become active participants (not just observers) in athletics for a lifetime (not just temporarily while they are in school).

Another factor is society's concern for physical fitness. Nowadays people like to look healthy and to be healthy. Thus, people are enrolling in physical fitness programs; this indicates that additional athletic facilities should be built.

In addition, people in our society view athletics as a form of entertainment that will help them escape the pressures of life. A physically and emotionally healthy person needs some form of release from the pressures of work, home, and school. Consequently, an increasing interest in athletics as a form of entertainment indicates a possible need for additional facilities.

There is a trend for the members of a community to become involved in campus activities at the high school and college levels. There is an increased demand by the community for extracurricular activities in politics and music, for exhibitions, and for entertainment. This increases the pressure for new multipurpose athletic facilities to house such activities.

The movement away from mandatory physical education classes for students is a negative factor to be considered before building a new facility. However, the slack is being taken up by students engaging on a voluntary basis in intramural sports which require additional facilities.

Now, both males and females are involved in athletic activity. If female sports become as prevalent as male sports, demand for athletic facilities should double, and pressure for long-range planning of athletic facilities will increase. From these examples, it is evident that cultural trends do affect the construction of athletic facilities, and that the administrator can do little to change the course of cultural trends.

Social Factors

Some social trends also affect long-range plans for athletic facilities. Changes in population—the market target for athletics—affect the demand for athletic facilities. The number of people, the composition of the population, and the movement of population all affect the long-range plans for facilities. The enrollment trends at schools—the number, movement, and composition of the student body—affect the amount of participation and spectatorship at athletic events. Whether there is growth in population (or enrollment) indicates whether new facilities ought to be built.

Legal Factors

Some legal factors also affect the long-range planning. The most recent has been the passage of Title IX of the Health and Education Act, providing for equal opportunity for males and females in competitive athletics. Since most athletic facilities have been designed for males, the passage of the Title IX legislation will require modification of old facilities or construction of additional facilities.

Court-ordered integration of black and white students will also affect the construction of facilities, positively for some programs and negatively for others, depending on the racial balance achieved.

The protection from antitrust laws in the case of professional baseball has a significant effect on building of baseball facilities in that the baseball leagues control the franchises for baseball teams and the resulting construction of facilities.

Political Factors

In some collegiate athletic programs, state political activity has a bearing on long-range plans. It has been a widely held opinion that a state legislature's generosity is often contingent on the records of state-supported athletic teams. Since athletic programs are good public relations for a state, a winning program has an excellent chance of getting money to build athletic facilities. This view is often expressed by those legislators friendly toward a collegiate program.

Many politicians recognize that by supporting athletic programs, they could collect a number of votes. In exchange for votes, the governor and the legislative authority could appropriate revenue-sharing funds for construction of athletic facilities. Or perhaps the governor and legislators could lend their personal support and prestige to recruiting and fund-raising activities.

Sometimes logrolling exists for capital expenditure projects for athletic purposes. If the state funds an athletic complex for one institution, it is not unusual to find another institution requesting funds for a similar project the next year. This process, logrolling, is common among athletic programs in need of funds.

In one state, a comprehensive schedule for reporting fiscal data has been incorporated into the college budget. This could start a trend toward a statewide board of athletics, or it may inspire the development of a five-year plan for athletic programs, which includes a schedule for the construction of athletic facilities. State politics will probably become an increasing factor to be reckoned with.

Technological Factors

There are some technological factors that also affect the long-range planning of facilities. For example, modern roofing methods make available maximum space at minimal clost. The development of high quality synthetic surfaces that cost the same as traditional surfaces gives a facility flexibility; one can use the new building for a variety of purposes. Retractable, movable theater seats provide flexibility: the administrator can quickly and easily change the orientation of a facility, catering to either spectators or participants. Modern acoustical systems and public address systems allow a facility to be changed from a participative-type one to a spectator-type facility. This flexibility is very important in designing a multipurpose complex. Climate control has made it possible to provide practically any type of climate—warm or cool, moist or dry—for spectator comfort.

Economic Factors

An economic factor affecting the long-range plans is the trend toward recognition of athletics as a profit making entity, separate and apart from the physical education program. This economic trend is noticeable in communities where taxpayers have rebelled against higher school taxes. As a result, athletic programs are now considered self-supporting extracurricular activities. Taxpayer money can no longer be used for any type of entertainment, including athletic programs.

A community's general economic condition might determine whether a new athletic facility will be financed. If the per capita income in a community is declining or at a standstill, it is unlikely that the community will finance an athletic facility. Other factors to be considered are construction costs and interest costs of capital.

The nature of the competitive position of the athletic program is another economic factor that affects long-range planning. If the program competes with other local athletic programs for fans—at the professional, college, or high school level—it is improbable that athletic facilities will be expanded.

Another factor to be considered is the professional team's franchise position. Professional leagues will grant only one franchise in a particular location. This franchise is generally an exclusive right to attract fans in the community, and to avoid having competing teams in the same league. With only one major team bidding to lease a facility, the city or county governmental unit has little leeway in negotiating. As a result, the taxpayers must normally subsidize the facility by either approving a bond issue or paying property taxes. Whether to build an athletic facility for a major professional team must be decided by the members of a community.

Pooling broadcasting rights does not allow competing networks to broadcast games. If there were freedom in broadcasting, an increased number of fans would attend athletic events, and more professional teams could coexist in a particular community. This would call for further expansion of athletic facilities.

The fundamental economic principles of supply and demand, and freedom of the competitive situation, and their consequent subfactors, are important factors in long-range planning.

External environmental factors affect long-range planning. However, an administrator cannot control these factors; the best he can do is to recognize them and plan accordingly.

MORE DETAILED ANALYSIS OF INTERNAL ENVIRONMENTAL FACTORS

One factor affecting an athletic program's building activity is the higher administration's philosophy concerning athletic programs and their objectives. This is particularly important in schools and colleges. The athletic administrator must determine the administration's priorities in relation to the following activities: competitive athletics versus compulsory or voluntary physical education; intramural sports versus leisure-time activities for faculty, staff, and families; club sports versus off-campus use of athletic facilities; male versus female competitive athletics. These athletic activities compete for time and money with each other. For example, if the higher administration is concerned about male *and* female competitive sports, then the male sports will suffer unless additional resourses are made available. If the higher administration feels that curricular physical education programs have higher priority than competitive athletics, then the extracurricular athletic program will be slighted as far as resources and facilities are concerned.

Unlike physical education programs, club sports, intramurals, leisure-time activities, and extracurricular athletic programs are self-supporting. Because it is financially independent, an athletic program can justify its existence in a special way and receive top priority from higher administration. An athletic program satisfies more people—fans, players, community, the organization, society—than does a physical education program. Physi-

Objective: General Environmental Appraisals for Long-Range Planning for Facilities

Factors	Strength	Weakness
1. Do any of the following values affect the athletic administrator's philosophy about facilities?		
1.1 Socio-cultural values		
1.2 Technological-economic values		
1.3 Legal-political values		
1.4 Ethical-religious values		
1.5 Others		
2. Has an appraisal been made of the external environmental factors affecting facilities?		
2.1 Economic		
2.11 Costs		
2.12 Revenues		
2.13 Sources of capital		
2.14 Competition		
2.2 Cultural factors		
2.3 Social factors		
2.4 Legal factors		
2.5 Political factors		
2.6 Technological factors		
2.7 Others		
3. Has an appraisal been made of internal environmental factors affecting facilities?		
3.1 Objectives and priorities of the administration affecting facilities		
3.2 Management audit of strengths and weaknesses		
3.3 Forecasts of factors affecting facility		
4. Have the following administrative strategies been formally made?		
4.1 Financial		
4.2 Personnel		
4.3 Marketing		
4.4 Others		
Overall Evaluation:		

cal education programs exist to satisfy only needs of students and faculty. Intramurals and club sports tend to satisfy only the needs of students. Leisure-time programs tend to satisfy the needs of students, faculty, and their families. Off-campus programs satisfy the entertainment needs of the community and on-campus groups. An athletic program, more than any other type of physical education activity, satisfies the needs of a diverse group of people. It is crucial to recognize this when determining what type of athletic facilities should be constructed.

Another internal factor important in long-range planning is the management's audit of an athletic program's strengths and weaknesses. One can formulate a strategy to build on the program's strengths; one can formulate a strategy to correct a program's weaknesses. These audits can be important tools in planning the administrative strategies used for athletic facilities.

The administrative strategies, based on the administrator's philosophy and his appraisals of the environment, can serve as guides when one is planning the construction, the financing, the staffing, and the marketing of athletic facilities. This is the subject of the next chapter.

The athletic administrator can evaluate the strengths and weaknesses of the environmental appraisal for a general long-range plan for athletic facilities by using the analysis on p. 239.

A review of Figure 11–1 will give an overall view of the requirements for long-range planning for an athletic facility.

CHAPTER SUMMARY

The introductory chapter about long-range planning considers the three variables that affect plans for athletic facilities—the philosophy of the administrator, the internal and external factors, and the resulting administrative strategies.

First, the values that make up the philosophy of the athletic administrator must be identified. If the administrator's values are not conducive to the construction of facilities, new facilities will probably not be built. He/she initially determines the need for facilities, the types needed, the initial costs, the value of the facilities, and the objectives to be pursued by constructing a new building. He then makes a formal proposal for additional facilities.

Second, the administrator must analyze the internal and external environmental factors affecting a facility. The external appraisal includes the following factors: economic, social, cultural, legal, political, and technological. The internal factors include administrative priorities and management's audit of the strengths and weaknesses of the athletic program.

Third, administrative strategies—financial, personnel, and marketing—resulting from the first two analyses, must be formulated. These are discussed in detail in the next chapter.

Later in the chapter, the environmental factors that could affect the construction of athletic facilities were considered at length. Cultural factors include the popularity of lifetime sports, the concern for physical fitness, the need to escape everyday pressures, the interest of men and women in organized sports, and the community's involvement in athletics. Social trends include population and enrollment figures. Economic trends include the profit-making ability of athletics, and the general economic conditions affecting supply, demand, and competition. Technological innovations include improved encapsulation, synthetic surfaces, retractable seating, acoustics and communications, climate control, and special lighting. Legal factors include passage of Title IX, racial integration, and antitrust exemption.

The administrator's priorities concerning different types of physical education and athletic programs must be determined. A review of the long-range planning process is seen in Figure 11–1.

Case 11-1 SPORTS HAS ENOUGH CENTS TO COME IN OUT OF THE RAIN*

The year 1975 might go down in sports history as the season when football got enough cents to come in out of the rain.

Of course, the University of Houston, the National Football League's Oilers and the Bluebonnet Bowl did it 10 years ago in Houston's Astrodome—the world's first roofed arena. It will take more cents there, though, to repair the leaky roof that's letting rain catch up with the game.

At least three new domed stadiums opened for business this year, and two more are scheduled for completion in time for the 1976 season.

There is a major problem, however, directly related to the dollar. And that is why there are no new domed stadia on the drawing boards.

All the new stadiums were conceived during the sports boom of the late 1960s—a boom which is tailing off, as witnessed by no-shows, the National Collegiate Athletic Association's economic problems, and the financially troubled World Football League.

But the stadiums are there, in their multimillion dollar splendor, whether the games they were built to house survive or not.

Weather had something to do with the building of domes, but not everything. Roofed buildings stand in the blustery snows of Pontiac, Mich., in the mists of Seattle's autumns, and the monsoons of New Orleans winters.

They range in size from the 12,000-seat dome on the campus of East Tennessee State to the 80,000-seat bubble at Pontiac. They range in cost from the $164 million Louisiana Superdome to $8.5 million for the East Tennessee State dome.

They survived labor squabbles, lawsuits, and spiraling costs.

Two of them, the King County Stadium (Kingdome) in Seattle and a much smaller dome at the University of Northern Iowa, are not yet complete.

* *Tulsa Daily World,* October 26, 1975, sec. 5, p. 12.

Why were they built in the first place? Money.

"I talked to a fellow from New Orleans just a week ago, and he was saying that the Superdome, even without the stadium being completed, brought about $25 million into the city during the Super Bowl period," said King County Executive John Spellman of the Kingdome.

Domes and dome-related events draw tourists, and tourists bring money. "In the late 60's, we were a typical old core city with increasing crime, increasing public apathy, and deteriorating downtown business," said Robert Rummel, executive director of the Pontiac stadium (Ponmet).

"We were in need of some vehicle that would revitalize the city and we became aware of what new stadiums had brought to other areas in the way of business and in the way of pride and image."

"Look what was there before," said Billy Connick, secretary treasurer of the Superdome, gesturing toward the spot where a big hotel rises beside the dome on what was once a warehouse district.

What Rummel and Connick said, in brief, is that replacing old property with new raises property values, which raises property tax income, which means more money in the city kitty.

Good football players mean good seasons, and that means more fans in the stands which means more bucks in the bank.

With all the economic benefits to be derived, why are no more of the big buildings on the drawing boards, especially in cold weather cities?

Money again. With most stadiums costing far more than originally thought, with the inflation crunch pinching almost all areas of athletics, with cities becoming more and more reluctant to commit tax dollars to sports, with the peaking of the sports boom in many areas, most entrepreneurs have begun to view such undertakings as risky projects.

QUESTION:

1. Comment on the article.

12

ADMINISTRATIVE STRATEGIES FOR BUILDING ATHLETIC FACILITIES

Let us assume that both internal and external appraisals have been made, and that the administrator has determined his priorities. What administrative strategies should be considered in planning for facilities? First, how can new athletic facilities be justified?

One way to justify them is to analyze the organizational objectives and their relationship to the athletic facilities. If the major objective is to produce a winning team to satisfy the entertainment needs of our fans, the facilities are necessary to help players practice and to produce a winning team. In addition, excellent facilities attract fans. If the team's objective is to develop the athletes' characters, facilities are necessary to attract athletes and to build their morale. If an objective is to improve the program's image, athletic facilities are necessary to create a good image by their clean and well-designed physical appearance. If profit is an objective, facilities are necessary to provide the sales revenue from the fans who attend. If growth is an objective, facilities will stimulate an increase in fan attendance and player participation. If improving the quality of life is an objective, facilities will help people to enjoy the good life by watching or participating in a form of entertainment integral to emotional and physical well-being. Facilities also help to satisfy some of the needs of employees, creditors, suppliers, members of the community, government, fans, players, and administrators, all of whom are part of society. It may be concluded that facilities are needed if various athletic program objectives are to be accomplished. Therefore, an administrator can justify the need for facilities in a number of ways to various groups of people.

ECONOMIC FORECASTS

A series of economic forecasts must be made to determine whether sufficient revenues can be generated to support a new facility. If an athletic program is more or less financially self-contained, then it must generate the revenue needed to pay for its facilities. If the program depends solely on tax money, a revenue base may not be necessary if taxpayers are willing to support the facility. Even in this situation it may be a wise strategy to determine whether economic conditions indicate that taxpayers will support construction.

First, a general economic forecast is needed. The gross national product (GNP) and the personal disposable income can be plotted, and a crude forecast can be made to determine whether the economic condition warrants a continuation of plans to construct a new facility. A regional economic forecast is also necessary, especially if the athletic program generates revenue from its location. One must rely on income per capita figures and other indicators when forecasting regional economic conditions. Economic information can be found for a standard metropolitan statistical area (SMSA) in the census data. It is also advisable to get a local economic forecast from the chamber of commerce or any other source. These general economic forecasts—national, regional, and local—will hopefully provide an optimistic picture of economic conditions necessary for providing an economic base to support the financing of an athletic facility. However, if the analysis is not optimistic, it is unlikely that a new facility will be constructed to house an athletic program dependent on outside revenues.

An industry or sports attendance forecast must also be made. This forecast determines the rate of increase or decline, on a nationwide basis, of those attending or participating in the sports that comprise an athletic program. Data described in the first chapter should serve as industry data; it should help to determine the present and future trends of a sport. The administrator should correlate the economic forecasts with the industry forecasts and note any significant relationships.

Next, the administrator should make a sport-by-sport forecast to determine whether there is a growth or decline in attendance/participation where the athletic program is located. This information can be obtained from the athletic program's conference. Other regional conference attendance/participation figures should be obtained to see if any trends are evident.

Once the general economic forecasts and the industry forecasts have been made, the athletic administrator must determine which sports to include in his program. He must decide whether a circular growth strategy or a horizontal growth strategy will best suit his program. The administrator must determine whether the sport is revenue-producing and entertaining enough to attract paying customers. Sports that do not produce revenue will not help to support an athletic facility. Football, and sometimes bas-

Objective: Administrative Strategies to Plan for an Athletic Facility

Factors	Strength	Weakness
1. Can the plans be justified? Are facilities needed for		
1.1 Players to practice for winning		
1.2 Fan attendance for entertainment		
1.3 Building morale for players		
1.4 Recruiting players		
1.5 Creating an image of well-designed physical appearance		
1.6 Providing revenue for profits		
1.7 Increasing fan attendance		
1.8 Increasing athlete participation		
1.9 Improving the quality of life for multipurpose use of		
1.91 Fans		
1.92 Players		
1.93 Employees		
1.94 Creditors		
1.95 Administrators		
1.96 Government		
1.97 Suppliers		
1.98 Community		
1.10 Other values		
2. Have a series of economic forecasts been made?		
2.1 General economic forecast		
2.2 Regional economic forecast		
2.3 Local economic forecast		
3. Have sports attendance/participation forecasts been made?		
3.1 National forecast for all sports involved in the program		
3.2 Conference forecasts/area forecasts		
4. Has determination been made as to types of sports to be offered?		
4.1 Revenue-producing sports		
4.2 Non-revenue sports		
5. Has market target been determined?		
6. Has a revenue budget been made to determine payback?		
Overall Evaluation:		

ketball, must often bear the financial burden of scholastic athletic programs. In the professional ranks, if it is to exist, each sport must pay for itself or otherwise it will go out of existence.

In addition, a market target must be determined, to insure sufficient local and regional revenue to support the athletic facility. Once a market target has been defined, the program must make a revenue budget. From this budget, the administrator can decide whether it is justifiable to spend hundreds of thousands and sometimes millions of dollars on an athletic facility.

The athletic administrator can evaluate the administrative strategies for a facility by using the analysis on the preceding page.

FINANCIAL STRATEGIES

Two fundamental problems face the administrator planning to finance an athletic facility: the existing shortage of capital and the competition for available funds. Most scholastic institutions have had to cut back or at most hold their own regarding financial resources. In addition, students and faculty are reluctant to commit funds for athletic facilities to be used exclusively by athletes. Sometimes the administration, faculty, students, and alumni believe that athletics is a highly profitable extracurricular business not justified in seeking funds normally used for curricular matters. As a result, some type of financial strategy must be developed to overcome the shortage and the competition.

Internal and external factors must be considered by the administrator as he devises a financial plan. A projection of the demand for facilities is required, as suggested in the previous pages. Some estimate should be made of the size of the facility, the cost, and the revenue necessary to support the cost for the next 20 or 30 years.

An administrator should become familiar with the facilities and the successful financial plans of comparable institutions. Conferences with other administrators, trips, personal visits, and other contacts will make the administrator aware of the financing strategies used by other athletic programs. All kinds of evidence should be obtained—photos, motion pictures, testimonials, and budgets.

An athletic administrator has to recognize that alone it is impossible to procure the necessary funds for construction. Consequently, it is wise to seek the help of all departments that could use the proposed facility. This is especially true in the preplanning stage of the facility. For scholastic programs, the facility could be used by those who participate in physical education, recreation, intramurals, drama, music, and student and community activities. As suggested, since competition for funds is severe, it is wise to seek a broad base of support; without the support of a number of departments, it is unlikely that the project will get off the ground.

Another area to be investigated deals with using the facilities jointly, for both school (or professional team) and community. It is often possible to rrange lease-back agreements in which an athletic program helps to build facility for a community with the right to lease it. Several professional eams use a lease rather than build an expensive facility with no possibility f it paying for itself. Most athletic facilities are used infrequently; they eldom generate sufficient revenue through athletic events to pay for them-elves. Therefore, joint sponsorship of a multipurpose facility is a wise strat-gy to follow. A high priority for financing can be obtained through joint ise. This strategy makes sense to most athletic administrators.

In addition, the administrator must estimate the capacity of the new fa-ility and the amount of equipment needed. Until an architect's plans have een made, the administrator's initial plans should include the size of the acility, the type of equipment needed, the location, and the materials. It nay be wise to divide construction into stages, then schedule when each tage should be completed.

Estimated costs of the project have to be made in order to determine ossible sources of funds. Architects should be able to give a preliminary stimate before bidding begins.

Finally, one must consider possible sources of funds for the facility. The nain source of money will probably come from a bond issue. This is a nor-nal way to raise money for a long-term asset. The administrator must de-ermine ways to repay the bonds as well as interest for a period of 20 to 30 ears.

One way to raise money is to rely on tax revenues from the taxpayers of he community. Even with professional teams, taxpayers are the ultimate ource of revenue; taxes often finance athletic facilities that are leased to rofessional teams. When a school or college uses the bond route, tax noney is used to repay the bond. This is usually voted on by the local itizenry.

Another common source of funding is student assessments and fees. ince most scholastic organizations charge a fee for student activities, a ortion of this fee may be set aside to pay off bonds. Although student fees re not sufficient to pay off the debt, a combination of sources can be used.

The sale of preferential seats is another way to finance the indebtedness. One can promote a campaign among the supporters of the athletic pro-ram to donate a large amount of money for five to ten years in exchange or preferred seats in the facility. Even this source must usually be supple-nented by other means.

Another method is to levy a special tax on all tickets sold. This special evy is then used to pay off the bonds.

Often donations from supporters of the athletic program are sought. Most supporters, however, expect something in return for their donations. Donations to scholastic organizations are deductible for income tax pur-oses. Further, if businesses donate money, their donations may be de-lucted as advertising or promotion expenses. Some colleges have each mployee's contribution matched by the employer. The alumni provide a lonation and are matched by their employers, who can contribute a tax leductible contribution to a nonprofit educational institution.

The ultimate "sources" of money for financing an athletic program are the supporters or fans, either as ticket buyers, preferred seat buyers, donators, or taxpayers. Usually bonds are the main source of revenue; administrators pledge to pay off the bonds through ticket sales, special levies, assessments, and donations.

An administrator can evaluate the financial strategies of an administrative plan with the following analysis.

Objective: To Determine a Financial Strategy for Planning Facilities

Factors	**Strength**	**Weakness**
1. Does the administrator recognize financial limits?		
1.1 A capital shortage problem		
1.2 Competition for funds exists among other groups		
2. Has an appraisal of external environmental factors been made?		
3. Has an appraisal of internal environmental factors been made?		
4. Have the projected demand and revenue been determined?		
5. Is the administrator familiar with other place's facilities and financial plans?		
6. Have joint facilities been investigated?		
7. Has a detailed estimate of capacity and other equipment been made?		
8. Has a cost estimate been made?		
9. Have possible sources of bond funds been investigated?		
10. Have possible sources of revenue to pay back bonds been investigated?		
10.1 From tax funds		
10.2 Student fees and assessments		
10.3 Sale of preferential seats		
10.4 Special levies on tickets		
10.5 Donations from boosters		
10.6 Others		
Overall Evaluation:		

PERSONNEL STRATEGIES

The key personnel strategy is to get various personnel to participate in the planning and design of athletic facilities. Participation forces people to commit themselves, guaranteeing support for athletic facilities. The principle of personnel participation is a powerful tool that every athletic administrator should recognize. By involving a number of people, valuable ideas are generated and used in planning the facilities.

The governing board must support the project or it will fail. Since the board represents the taxpayers of the community, their approval is essential. If the board members are split in their support, the community will offer only partial support to the project. It is unlikely that a bond issue or any other type of financing will be approved.

The key executive is the president of the organization; his support is vital. If the president is hesitant, the project will drag on and eventually lose the support of other people. The president or superintendent makes the decisions vital to the success of the project.

If the president cannot make the plans, a planner usually is appointed as project director. The president must rely on expert advice from several people and interpret all the information that flows through the project director.

The faculty or employees of any organization should become involved in the plans since they will be employed in the new facility. They can be helpers, providing ideas, conducting surveys, visiting other places, and supplying advice to the project director before the plans are drawn.

The architect should be a member of the planning group. The architect must review preliminary plans and specifications; estimate the costs; approve change orders; inspect construction; advise the project director; and design the blueprints for the project, including materials, the various subsystems of climate control, lighting, acoustics, and mechanical and electrical plans.

Sometimes an equipment planner becomes very useful in determining the equipment and machinery necessary for athletic facilities. The equipment planner coordinates the equipment requested by coaches, employees, administrators, and other community personnel who have an interest in the project.

A legal advisor is also a necessity for most projects. Assistance on bond legalities, land purchases, contracts, and other legal matters is essential.

Sometimes a person is employed to search for building sites, to plan traffic routes and utility services, to purchase land, and to perform other related duties.

The general contractor, a private entrepreneur, works directly with the project architect. He/she can offer excellent advice on materials and labor for the project.

A citizens' committee can also be valuable. This committee can provide community relations contacts, financial support, and general promotion of the facility. It is particularly helpful if it represents the varied groups having an interest in a multipurpose facility.

Governmental agencies may also play a part in planning the facility. Zoning agencies, libraries, and state and regional planning agencies have a direct interest in the proposed facility.

The preceding people usually serve on the project committee, which becomes the chief decision-making body for the project. The project director becomes a key person on this committee because through him/her all the plans are submitted, although he/she may not have final authority to make the key decisions.[1]

MARKETING STRATEGY

The two fundamental promotion strategies—message and media—are used extensively in the promotion of a new athletic facility. The messages and media selection must be geared to receiving a positive vote in a bond election, in the state legislature, or in the form of a financial contribution from an interested fan.

The message strategy can be hand-tailored based on all the information received in the planning process as suggested in this chapter. The external and internal appraisal of environmental factors supplies the information necessary for speeches, for newspapers, and for direct mail to interested fans.

The booster clubs can also play an influential role in promoting the construction of a new facility. Through a planned program, each member can use his/her influence to talk with influential people in the community.

When planning the promotion program, one must anticipate opposition to the proposal. Consequently, a strategy to overcome resistance should be planned. One must promote a multipurpose facility that will serve various community groups; this should overrule the objection that the community is overemphasizing the importance of athletic programs by constructing a new facility.

A variety of media should be planned for in advance of the announcement for the facility. Before publicly proposing the new facility, media should be planned. The following should be available when the proper time arises.

Artist's drawings
Models
Possible photographs
Testimonials
News releases
Radio and TV programs
Speaking engagements
Endorsements
Other media

A general selling strategy should be based on the fundamental sales formula of first creating attention and interest in the facility. Normally this is accomplished by stating the unfulfilled needs of people who would be interested in a multipurpose complex. The second step involves making people desire the construction of a facility. This can be accomplished by emphasizing how a multipurpose facility can improve the community. The third stage normally involves the conviction or the proof of the proposal. Testimonials, experiences of other athletic programs, and endorsements play a part at this stage. Finally, action is emphasized—a person should

Objective: To Develop Personnel and Marketing Strategies for Planning Facilities

Factors	Strength	Weakness
1. Have the following personnel been actively participating in the plan?		
1.1 Board		
1.2 Executive		
1.3 Planner		
1.4 Faculty/Employees		
1.5 Architect		
1.6 Equipment planner		
1.7 Legal advisor		
1.8 Site finder		
1.9 Contractor		
1.10 Citizens' committee		
1.11 Governmental agencies		
1.12 Project committee		
1.13 Others		
Overall Evaluation:		
2. Have the following selling strategies been considered?		
2.1 Attention and interest stage		
2.2 Development of desire stage		
2.3 Conviction or proof stage		
2.4 Action stage		
2.5 Message strategy		
2.6 Media strategy		
2.7 Opposition strategy		
2.8 Booster club		
2.9 Other		
Overall Evaluation:		

vote, send in money, talk to people. These four steps (attention and interest, desire, conviction, and action) are tried and true for most sales efforts.

An administrator can evaluate the personnel strategies and marketing strategies of an administrative plan by using the analysis on the preceding page.

CHAPTER SUMMARY

First, internal and external appraisals of the environment must be made; then the administrator can devise his strategies. Justifying the facilities is the first step. This can normally be done by relating the reasons for facilities to the various organizational objectives: for players to practice to produce a winning team; for fan attendance so the team can entertain and increase revenue; for recruiting players and building player morale; for improving the program's image; and for improving the quality of life for society through a multipurpose facility.

A financial strategy is needed to overcome the capital shortage problem and the competition for funds. The administrator can take steps to alleviate this problem. He can make an external and internal appraisal, project the demand for facilities, familiarize himself with other places and financial plans, consider joint facilities with other communities, make a detailed estimate of capacity and costs, consider a bond issue, consider possible sources of revenue to pay off the bonds—from tax funds, student fees and assessments, sale of preferential seats, special levies on tickets, or donations from boosters.

Various people must actively support the project. These people include the board, the chief executive, planners, faculty/employees, the architect, the equipment planner, legal advisors, contractors, citizens, governmental agencies, and the project committee and possible subcommittees.

Finally, it is vital that the facility be promoted and sold to voters, administration, and fans. Various stages of selling the facility are fundamental—the attention and interest stage, the desire stage, the conviction or proof stage, and finally the action stage. A selling plan should include messages and media strategy and opposition strategy. Booster clubs are also an excellent means of promotion.

Case 12-1 STRATEGY TO FINANCE THE NORTHWESTERN STATE BASKETBALL FIELDHOUSE*

Fred Barber, Northwestern State University Athletic Director, Walter Matthews, Assistant Athletic Director, and Edward Sullivan, Head Basketball Coach, met in June to discuss their plans to improve the performance of Northwestern's basketball program.

* This case was adapted from a case prepared by L. Joseph Rosenberg, University of Arkansas, Fayetteville. This case is designed to be used as a basis for class discussion rather than to illustrate either effective or ineffective handling of an administrative situation.

Sullivan had been at Northwestern State only a year, replacing Larry Egan, former basketball coach, who had resigned. Sullivan's win-loss record for his first year on the campus was 73% wins, compared with the previous five-year record at Northwestern State of only 35% wins.

When Sullivan, the former basketball coach at Weston State, an independent college, was hired, he promised Athletic Director Fred Barber that he would turn the basketball program around. Barber was pleased with Sullivan's first-year performance, because Sullivan, who had an outstanding winning record at Weston, joined Northwestern State as the third highest paid basketball coach in the conference.

The University administration stated that it wanted the basketball program to operate on a comparable basis to that of the University's football team. They wanted the basketball program to grow, in fan attendance, in player talent, in coaching staff, and promised whatever it took to develop a winning team in the conference and on a national basis.

Fred Barber was in full accord, stating that as NW State's Athletic Director, he would, given adequate support, do the same for the basketball team as he had for the football team. Barber pointed out that the basketball team played its home games in the fieldhouse, built over 25 years ago at a cost of $500,000, with seats for only 5,200, of which over 3,000 were reserved for students; and that if the program moved, the physical facilities would have to be renovated or replaced. Part of the agreement with Sullivan when he was hired was that Northwestern State would back a plan to help remodel or replace the existing fieldhouse if a winning season indicated the need for additional facilities.

One of the selling points that Barber used to convince Coach Sullivan to come to Northwestern State University was the assurance that improved physical facilities would be developed. Barber recognized that the basketball coach must show or promise the potential players first-rate basketball facilities. The various factors were mutually supporting if a winning basketball system was to be operated on a continuing basis.

The principal topic discussed by Barber, Sullivan, and Matthews at their meeting involved physical facilities. The fieldhouse had a basketball court placed on a mounting in a dirt-filled facility that was also used for football, baseball, and track during inclement weather. The three agreed that larger facilities were necessary, since many of the 13 home games during the previous year had been oversold. The general public found it almost impossible to purchase tickets.

Several critical questions were raised at their informal meeting. Specifically, they finally stipulated a benchmark that seating capacity for basketball games should be set at approximately 9,000 people. Then came a series of specific questions such as, Should the basketball facility continue to be a multipurpose structure? Should the fieldhouse be renovated or should a new building be built? How should it be financed?

Walter Matthews, who specialized in promotional and financial aspects of the athletic program, said that he would like to think out loud and would appreciate the reaction of Barber and Sullivan to his comments. He reminded them that tens of thousands of students had used the facilities of the fieldhouse during its 25 years of existence. Matthews noted that the building was located on the athletic complex and would not just go away if a new fieldhouse were constructed.

Further, Matthews recalled the statewide outcry when it was proposed that the former administration building be demolished. Instead, state funds were obtained and it was in the process of being renovated. At this point Athletic Director Barber reminded Matthews that state funds were not provided to athletic activities on the campus; that indeed, the income from football was not only financing football, but all other athletic activities of Northwestern State. Matthews agreed.

Matthews, himself, was well-known throughout the state. He serves as executive director of the 6400-member Booster Club. While it totally cooperates with the NW State Alumni Association, the Booster Club and its various chapters have members who, in addition to traditional support of the University, have a special interest in one or more of its eight intercollegiate sports. Numerous individuals who attended other colleges or did not go to college are active participants and financial supporters of the Booster Club. Funds raised by the Club are used to provide athletic scholarships and for other sports purposes since the Department of Athletics receives no tax funds for its operations. As Matthews continued talking, he recalled that NW State had the authority, with approval by the Board of Trustees, to issue construction bonds, with debt service to be met by gate receipts or gifts. Should there be a plan to renovate the fieldhouse or to build a new building, some funds could be made available from that source. Matthews remarked that within the prior two years the Booster Club had raised sufficient funds to provide for an outdoor track, a baseball field, and for a new football and administrative facility at the north end of the stadium. He felt that the timing was right to raise funds to improve or replace the fieldhouse.

Matthews noted that the fieldhouse was used regularly as an arena for visiting speakers, that symphony orchestras performed in the fieldhouse, and that in the event of inclement weather, graduation ceremonies were conducted in the structure.

Coach Sullivan reminded both Barber and Matthews that he could not be expected to recruit outstanding young basketball players unless something was done, promptly. He had used the ploy of recruiting last year based on a promise of improved facilities. He urged that a viable program be developed promptly. He noted that more seats meant more revenue. An average of 39,000 fans per year had attended NW State games the previous five years. The ticket price during the previous year was $1.50 for general admission; reserve seats were $3.00 each; students were admitted free; faculty could purchase tickets on a ½ price basis.

Matthews reflected that the outstanding performance of the team under Coach Sullivan had resulted in students and faculty filling the present fieldhouse to such an extent that the general public was, for all practical purposes, unable to attend Northwestern State games. His studies indicated that almost all of the student and faculty market with an interest in basketball were being accommodated because they were given priority in the purchase of tickets.

Enlargement of the fieldhouse seating capacity, from 5,200 to approximately 9,000 would permit an additional 3,800 local fans to attend basketball games. Based on available statistics Matthews prepared the following information:

Proposed Additional Reserved Seats	Seat Price Per Game
3,800	$3.50

Matthews noted that additional revenue for each of the 13 home games should result in elimination of the $100,000 annual loss incurred by basketball activities.

Barber said that the three men had other activities scheduled and it would be necessary to conclude the meeting. He asked Matthews to think through the various topics discussed and a meeting was scheduled for one week later, at the same hour.

Matthews returned to his office and began to consider the situation. He noted that his mail included a letter from an architect confirming a previous estimate of $4½ million as the cost to remodel the fieldhouse. The figure included 5,000 new theater seats, room for more than 9,000 fans totally, improved sound facilities, better lighting, a more attractive exterior, and a building able to more adequately meet students' needs for graduation, speakers, meetings, entertainment, as well as sports activities. It would also include ten classrooms. The cost of a new structure with comparable facilities had been estimated at $10–12 million.

Thinking of a strategy to help finance the proposed facility, Matthews recalled that six years ago Northeastern University, in Foxboro, had gone to the state legislature with a plan for a new football stadium. Northeastern proposed that the legislature appropriate $750,000 for a stadium if Northeastern could raise $750,000 matching funds. The legislature approved the plan and appropriated funds for Northeastern to construct a stadium.

Matthews knew that it would be awkward for the legislature to deny a similar request for Northwestern State University. Thus, Athletic Director Fred Barber felt assured of legislative support. Matthews recalled that during the previous year about 40 activities, other than basketball games, were held in the present fieldhouse. Plans provided for the fieldhouse to include facilities for a women's intercollegiate athletic center. NW State expected to field a women's intercollegiate basketball team upon completion of the improved facilities. Further, the increased attendance at the basketball games would provide additional revenue each game to help cover the financial obligations. Matthews thought that basketball ticket prices would continue to increase during future years since the current prices were about twice the level of those charged ten years earlier.

Matthews had already secured agreement for the price of reserved basketball seat tickets to be increased fifty cents for next year. He knew that at colleges with a high win-loss record, tickets were priced fifty cents to one dollar above that of other schools, suggesting a possible price inelasticity at universities with winning basketball teams.

Matthews made an appointment with Vice President for Fiscal Affairs. He reviewed his plans to raise $1,000,000 from Booster Club members. The V. P. also estimated the income necessary to service bonds in various amounts. The two executives looked at the financial report of NW State for the most recent five years.

The V. P. prepared a table showing the debt service requirements from University general funds for the last five years:

Northwestern State University Summary of Annual Debt Service Requirement

June 30 year	*Principal*	*Interest*	*Total*	*Unliquidated principal*
5 yrs ago	$658,900	$1,314,485	$1,973,385	$32,328,000
4 yrs ago	683,000	1,336,908	2,019,908	31,565,000
3 yrs ago	814,500	1,264,508	2,079,008	30,666,000
2 yrs ago	798,500	1,412,131	2,210,631	32,780,000
last year	920,000	1,464,165	2,384,165	32,571,000

The V. P. commented on the statement of bonds outstanding, noting interest rates paid during the most recent five years:

Northwestern State University Statement of Bonds Outstanding

Description of bonds	*Amount of original issue*
6¼–6½–6¾–7 Stadium Improvement Bonds	$416,400
5.0–6.0–5.8–7.0 Academic Building Bonds	$6,500,000
6½–5.80–5.90–6–5 Improvement Bonds	$3,000,000
6.25–5.50–5.25 Academic Building Bonds–Law School	$800,000

A Schedule of Revenue and Expenditures was prepared for the intercollegiate athletic program of the University. Both men examined several items for the last three years.

Northwestern State University Schedule of Revenues from Intercollegiate Athletics

Year ended June 30	*Revenue basketball only*	*Expenses basketball only*	*Athletic fund balance total cash*
two years ago	$31,980	$150,000	$ 5,908
one year ago	$35,702	$160,000	$ 95,440
last year	$54,509	$150,000	$160,394

Both men considered what strategy should be planned. What type of facility—a new structure or a refurbished one? Could the necessary money be raised? How?

Case 12-2 MONEY-MAKING PLANS FOR N. U. REJECTED*

Proposals to raise money for a possible stadium expansion for the University of Nebraska and to give the Huskers a better break on football gate splits were rejected by the Big Eight athletic directors, Nebraska's Bob Devaney said Saturday.

The defeats all but scuttled plans for a stadium expansion for this fall, but the door was opened for a possible addition the following year.

"I don't think we could do it by this fall anyway. I think the (Board of) Regents are figuring on 1978 now," the Nebraska athletic director said.

Devaney presented the proposals at the meeting in Kansas City at the request of the regents.

Devaney was the only member to vote for a proposal for Nebraska to keep all the income from 8,000 seats in a proposed expansion until the addition is paid for.

The directors also voted down, 7–1, another Nebraska suggestion to limit to $150,000 the amount a visiting school could receive. Visiting schools collect above $166,000 from Nebraska, Devaney said.

"We got a break this year, but we''ll go to the $8 split next year. At least we won't have to dig our people again with a surcharge (to finance construction)," Devaney said.

Nebraska will levy a $1 surcharge for four nonconference games (up to $9.25) to pay for a new AstroTurf playing field this fall.

The athletic directors gave Nebraska a break, however, by holding the line on splitting football gates based on a $7 ticket rate instead of going ahead with a previously planned $8 split.

The difference, Devaney said, means Nebraska will be $78,000 ahead because it has the largest stadium—76,400 seats—in the Big Eight.

Devaney arrives at the $78,000 this way:

Nebraska will charge $8.25 a seat for 50,000 nonstudent or faculty seats this fall, the same as a year ago, for conference home games against Iowa State, Kansas, and Colorado.

Under the Big Eight's 50–50 split on $7 arrangement, the Huskers will get to keep the extra $1 per seat (the additional 25 cents is for tax), or $50,000 per game. For three games, that would be $150,000 more than Nebraska would receive on an $8 split.

Nebraska will receive 50 cents less for an estimated 145,000 seats on four conference games on the road, or about $72,000. The net gain would be $78,000, Devaney said.

That plan came on the fourth vote and carried, 5–3, Nebraska voting with the majority, Devaney said.

Devaney also said he recently renegotiated the two-year home-and-home contract with Alabama, which starts with the Crimson Tide visiting Nebraska for the second game this fall.

Instead of the original $166,000 Alabama would have received under the 50–50 plan, Bear Bryant's team will take home a flat guarantee of $125,000. Nebraska will get the same in Tuscaloosa next year.

* *Omaha World Herald*, March 6, 1977.

QUESTION:

1. Comment on the article.

Case 12-3 PLAY TENNIS AT ICHIBAN?*

Frank Broyles, Athletic Director at the University of Arkansas, pondered over a written request he had received from Tom Pucci, the newly appointed first-year tennis coach. The request involved changing sites for the tennis matches to be played from the present University tennis courts to Ichiban Recreation Complex in Rogers, 20 miles away.

As Frank sat there he recalled that he had seen Ichiban being built during the past two years. Ichiban was a huge recreation complex built on the outskirts of Rogers, whose population was less than 20,000. Ichiban included five indoor tennis courts, with a seating capacity for 2,500 people. It was a plush place where members could witness a tennis match while sitting in cushioned chairs behind a glass partition on the second floor overlooking the five beautiful courts, sipping a drink, watching the action, and listening to an announcer describing the results of the matches. In addition, Ichiban had a regular size gymnasium, with the most recent gymnastic equipment. It also had the only handball court in Northwest Arkansas and a paddle court. It was touched off with a Chinese restaurant and a pro shop. All in all, Ichiban was an athletic oasis in an area where private athletic facilities were at a minimum.

Ichiban was built by a retired businessman who had moved to northwest Arkansas. He was looking for a new challenge in life and also some activity that could be used as a tax write-off. The recreation facility, which he called Ichiban, had a Chinese motif in appearance. It was built without any consideration for economy or for the market. Only the best quality equipment and materials were designed and built into the facility. Ichiban was managed by a retired general who had acquired a staff of employees to help him, one of whom was a new tennis director.

Tom Pucci, a young Ph.D. from New Mexico University was hired to teach physical education classes this past spring. One-third of his class load was devoted to being the Razorback tennis coach, replacing the former coach who had resigned to become a pro at a tennis club back East. Tom was an eager tiger, according to Frank Broyles, and was enthusiastic about his new job as tennis coach. He was looking for ways to improve an already growing tennis program at the University. In fact, this coming tennis season, the University of Arkansas Razorback tennis team was approved to play as a member team in the Southwest Conference, the first time in history for the tennis team to play other Southwest Conference schools in tennis. Frank was concerned about this move because the previous tennis teams had very seldom played national tennis powers. The Southwest Conference, however, was consistently one of the toughest in the nation. This past year, he remembered, three Southwest Conference tennis teams

* This case was written and researched by Robert D. Hay and Tom Pucci of the University of Arkansas. It is not intended to portray correct or incorrect administrative practices, but it is to be used as a teaching tool.

ranked in the top twelve of the nation. How could his Razorbacks compete against such powers?

The facilities for playing varsity tennis matches on campus were marginal at best. There were only four outdoor courts which were fit to play matches with top-notch schools. There were no permanent seating facilities. In the past years, no more than 50 spectators would attend a dual match and those were friends of the players. Many times the weather was inclement, especially in the spring, and matches had to be cancelled. Practices were limited because of weather conditions. Sometimes the tennis team laid out one court in the men's gymnasium to practice indoors.

As Frank Broyles thought about the request, he again read the memo from Pucci:

TO: Frank Broyles
FROM: Tom Pucci, Tennis Coach
SUBJECT: Playing All Home Matches at Ichiban Tennis Center

Tom Adkins, corporate counsel and acting Tennis Director of Ichiban Sports Center, Rogers, has approached me with the offer of all the tennis team's home matches to be played at the Ichiban Tennis Center. After due consideration, I strongly recommend we accept such offer. The following are my considerations and arguments in support of my recommendation:

1. By playing all home matches indoors at Ichiban, we shall necessarily alleviate any future worry about possible inclement weather cancelling matches.

2. By playing indoors, we shall be able to reschedule all home matches to weekend evenings (i.e., Friday or Saturday evenings) beginning at approximately 6:30 p.m. The players would be out of school and would not have to miss any classes. Further, members of the public who desire to attend such matches would easily be able to do so. Also, selected matches would be scheduled for Saturday evenings since I have substantial assurance from Razorback tennis fans in Little Rock that there is a probability that a chartered bus full of Razorback tennis fans would come to Ichiban from Little Rock to attend such Saturday night matches. The Rogers Holiday Inn is just up the highway from Ichiban to accommodate any such out-of-town tennis fans who would desire to spend the weekend in Northwest Arkansas.

3. Admission would be charged for all such matches at a percentage split mutually agreeable between Ichiban and the University. In addition, we hope to attract, in the reasonable foreseeable future, big name nonconference perennial tennis powers (e.g., Southern California, Trinity, etc.) to play against the Razorbacks at Ichiban; and as a result, considerable revenue would be realized by the University.

4. I strongly believe if students are interested they wouldn't mind a 20-minute drive to Rogers to watch a tennis match. We must get people involved and following our tennis program. The last four months I have worked very hard attempting to sell our product. Now we must have a great facility to play in where people are comfortable. We are so lucky that these fine people of Ichiban want to promote the sport

this way. We must take advantage of the opportunity or build a tennis facility on our campus. Actually, I am scared stiff to bring in a recruit and show him our own campus facility. TCU, Rice, Houston, Texas, every school in the Southwest Conference has far better facilities than we have. If we use this facility in Ichiban, though, we will have the best facility in the league.

I have set my goal to be the best in the nation. We must be creative, imaginative, and motivative in our thinking and plans to get us to that great goal. Playing our matches at Ichiban is the first giant step we must take.

I would love to play our matches on campus, but where do I play them? You must remember we are in the Southwest Conference, one of the toughest conferences in the nation. Three teams last year were ranked in the top 12 in the nation. In order to compete with the established programs, we must work harder and be creative. Playing on campus on the varsity courts with two small sets of bleachers, grass growing on the courts, and the dormitories located extremely close to the courts which creates a noise factor is not the atmosphere that is conducive to big time tennis. Added to this is the fact that we only have four courts to play on for tournaments where every school in the Conference and 99% of the major colleges in America have the regulation six.

5. The last point is I think the most important of all: that is recruiting. At the present time we have a good team if everyone can get healthy, but I strongly believe our program is at a crossroads. Last year we had a good recruiting year. Buddy Bowman was ranked fourteenth in the nation and is by far the best recruit we have. Rumery is going to become a good player, and we won't see Hawking until January 5. This year we are going after the best; because of Buddy we can do that. We will get John Bailey of Little Rock who has a good chance of being ranked high nationally. We are going after the following and all have expressed interest.

1. Nial Brash—ranked #3 in Boys 18 nationally from Palo Alto, California.

2. Cary Stansbury—ranked #2 nationally Boys 16 nationally from Tiburan, California.

3. Peter Rennert—ranked #7 in Boys 16 nationally from Great Neck, New York.

4. Eric Iskersky—ranked #6 in Boys 18 nationally from Rossford, Ohio.

5. James Boustany—ranked #32 in Boys 18 nationally from Lafayette, Louisiana.

All of these boys are being recruited by every school in the nation, but with the facility at Ichiban and the knowledge that all home matches will be played there, I promise you we will get at least two of them. The utilization of this facility will give us the advantage to get us established. If we don't recruit well, we are really in trouble, as we'll continue to stay the same or decline. This is a big year for us, sort of the make it or break it year for the tennis program. I am sure you have had recruiting years like that in football.

6. If we get these recruits and develop a following, there is an un-

tapped group of *donors* out there that we can get to. There are people in Arkansas with money who love tennis. We must get these people involved in the program. The owner of Ichiban is one fine example of what I am talking about. Thus playing in a nice facility in the evening will be the first step; then we must *win*.

7. The last point I want to use is in a question. If the football team had a 5,000 seat bleacher stadium on campus but could play in a beautiful 50,000 new stadium 15 miles away at no charge to the program, where would you play your games? I think I know the answer. This is the situation that we are confronted with.

The 1976 tennis schedule called for 24 matches, eight of which would be played at home. The tennis team could use the Athletic Department mobile vans to travel to and from the campus. The four vans, which were donated to the Athletic Department by auto dealers over the state (actually used as demonstrator models each year), would not cost much, only gas and oil and tires to and from Rogers.

The University cooperated with the NCAA in purchasing travel insurance for all of its athletes to and from athletic events. The Department, however, did insure the four vans for collision and liability just as any other motor vehicle.

As Frank Broyles surveyed the financial operations, he pondered what he would recommend to the faculty athletic committee when it planned to meet next week.

Summary of Financial Data of the Athletic Department
for the Year 74–75

Revenues	
Ticket sales—all sports*	$1,260,000
Other revenues (TV, concessions, investments, donations, misc.)	926,000
Total	$2,186,000
Expenses	
Tennis**	19,500
Other sports	1,468,000
Administration and other	633,500
	$2,121,000
Net	$ 65,000

* *$1200 collected from other minor sports. None from tennis.*
** *Tennis was budgeted for approximately $15,000. Actual expense was approximately $19,500.*

FOOTNOTE

[1] See also Robert T. Bronzan, "New Concepts in Planning and Funding Athletic, Physical Education and Recreation Facilities" (St. Paul: Phoenix Intermedia, 1974). This book is an excellent source of information about scholastic athletic facilities.

13

DESIGNING AND EVALUATING ATHLETIC FACILITIES

One major strategy involves the design of athletic facilities. To design a facility, it is necessary to evaluate the strengths and weaknesses of the present facilities, or to evaluate comparable facilities of other institutions to get ideas about the needs required. An architect should know the administrator's requirements for the proposed facility. This chapter considers the factors integral to designing athletic complexes.[1]

SELECTION OF AN ARCHITECT

It is advisable to appoint a committee to select an architect. This prevents administrative bias, favoritism, or poor judgment. What are the factors to be considered when selecting an architect?

The first is the professional status of an architect. Licensing, professional ranking by peers, publication of articles, and professional honors signify some degree of professional status.

Experience is another consideration. Subfactors such as areas of specialization; number of projects completed; sizes, types, and costs of completed projects; and nearby projects should be examined.

The architect's professional staff is also a factor. The size, quality, organization, location, and availability of staff should be considered.

The methods of operation should also be a significant factor in the selection process. Responsibility for damages, emergency measures, and definition of procedures are all important.

Interest in the project should also be considered. Is the architect sincerely interested in helping or is his motive purely selfish?

Past performance should be considered. Determine the quality of his/her completed work in terms of creativity, functionalism, and beauty.

References should be evaluated. These may be obtained from previous clients, contractors, and others who know the architect.

These factors can be arranged into a weighted decision matrix.

Objective: To Select an Architect

Factors	**Weight**	*Architect #1*	*Architect #2*	*Architect #3*
1. Extent of professional activities				
2. Professional experience				
3. Professional staff				
4. Operational methods				
5. Interest in the project				
6. Past performance				
7. References				
8. Others				
Overall Conclusion:				

After the architect is selected, he should provide a number of services for the athletic program. After conferring with the project director or athletic administrator, the architect should present pre-design plans, usually in writing. Then a schematic design in graphic form should be prepared. Once the schematics have been approved, the architect prepares more detailed plans. After the plans are approved, he/she writes electrical, mechanical, and structural construction documents. Then the architect assists in the bidding process. Once the construction bid is approved, the architect evaluates the contractor's work as it is completed. Finally some additional services must be performed—selecting equipment, making appraisals, approving change orders, and securing required documents. All of these professional services are performed by the architect.

EVALUATION OF INDOOR FACILITIES

The following checklist includes factors to be considered when designing indoor facilities. An athletic administrator can use them to evaluate the strengths and weaknesses of present facilities in order to determine needs not met. The administrator can also use them to consider the design of a new facility.

Objective: Factors to be Considered When Designing Indoor Facilities

Factors	Strength	Weakness
1. *General Factors*		
1.1 Future needs: capacity for fans, participants, male, female, community groups, based on trends		
1.2 Expansion available		
1.3 Can be used for athletics, physical education, intramurals, club sports, recreation, other extracurricular benefits such as music, dancing, theatre, and conventions		
1.4 Teaching stations available		
1.5 Site near fans, participants, and community residents		
1.6 Feeder streets		
1.7 Parking areas		
1.8 Electricity available		
1.9 Water		
1.10 Natural gas		
1.11 Sewage		
1.12 Storm drainage		
1.13 Zoning		
1.14 Handicapped parking, loading, and ramps		
1.15 Soil tests		
1.16 Security and lighting		
1.17 Outdoor hallways		
1.18 Maintenance easy		
1.19 Rooftops can be used		
1.20 Fire walls		
1.21 Escape systems		
1.22 Proper window heights		
1.23 Minimize maintenance costs of Lighting, PA systems, Plumbing, Climate control, Cleaning		
1.24 Odd-shaped rooms eliminated		
1.25 Wall surfaces		
1.26 Colors acceptable		
1.27 Beauty		
1.28 Others		

Factors	Strength	Weakness
2. *Main Activity Area*		
2.1 Adequate floor area for athletics offered		
2.2 Buffer zone between activity areas		
2.3 Solid walls		
2.4 Wall surfaces		
2.5 Ceiling height		
2.6 Retractable backboards		
2.7 Movable partitions		
2.8 Contiguous storage rooms		
2.9 Acoustics		
2.10 Adjustable lighting for		
Intensity		
Area		
Spot		
Color		
Emergency		
Telecasting		
2.11 Quality public address		
2.12 Motion picture booth		
2.13 Closed circuit television		
2.14 Telecasting facilities		
2.15 Press box		
2.16 Scoreboard		
2.17 Time clocks		
2.18 Portable stage and backdrops		
2.19 Climate control		
2.20 Floor plates		
2.21 Wall hangers		
2.22 Ceiling attachments		
2.23 Doorways and hallways		
2.24 Storage for large items		
2.25 Signs		
2.26 Service elevators		
2.27 Lock-keys for rooms		
2.28 Others		
3. *Fan Accommodations*		
3.1 Comfortable seats		
3.2 Temporary seats		
3.3 Maintenance of seats		
3.4 Line of sight for seats		
3.5 Color keyed seats		
3.6 Aisles, stairways		
3.7 Lavatories		
3.8 Drinking fountains		
3.9 Foyer		
3.10 Concession stands		
3.11 First aid rooms		

Factors	Strength	Weakness
3.12 Ticket sales facilities		
3.13 Ticket collections		
3.14 Lighting		
3.15 Acoustics		
3.16 Climate		
3.17 Public address		
3.18 Others		
4. *Surfaces*		
4.1 All-year use		
4.2 Multiple uses		
4.3 Dust resistant		
4.4 Stainless		
4.5 Inflammable		
4.6 Nonabrasiveness		
4.7 Aesthetics		
4.8 Durability		
4.9 Resiliency		
4.10 Safety		
4.11 Maintenance		
4.12 Cost per use		
4.13 Others		
5. *Foot Traffic*		
5.1 On and off ramps		
5.2 Foot traffic patterns		
5.3 Noise		
5.4 Safety		
5.5 Dirt, mud, moisture		
5.6 Others		
6. *Administrative Unit*		
6.1 Accessible with privacy		
6.2 Telephone and internal communication system		
6.3 Secretary's office		
6.4 Secretarial work room		
6.5 Visitor room		
6.6 Storage space		
6.7 Staff drop-in area		
6.8 Central control system for Communication Climate control Lighting		
6.9 Others		
7. *Team Room*		
7.1 Located close to activity area		
7.2 Lockers around		
7.3 Open center		
7.4 Exhaust system		
7.5 Climate control		

Factors	Strength	Weakness
7.6 Blackboards		
7.7 Bulletin boards		
7.8 Motion pictures		
7.9 Electrical outlets		
7.10 PA system		
7.11 Floors		
7.12 Walls		
7.13 Security		
7.14 Others		
8. *Coaches' Room*		
8.1 Adequate size		
8.2 Close to activity area		
8.3 Lockers		
8.4 Floors		
8.5 Climate control		
8.6 Intercommunications		
8.7 Telephone		
8.8 Bulletin board		
8.9 Blackboard		
8.10 Clock		
8.11 Toilets		
8.12 Others		
9. *Locker Rooms*		
9.1 Located near activity area		
9.2 Adequate size for peak loads		
9.3 Climate control		
9.4 Exhaust system		
9.5 Floor surface		
9.6 Floor pitch		
9.7 Drain openings		
9.8 Hose taps		
9.9 Waterproofed electrical switches		
9.10 Lockers mounted		
9.11 Bulletin boards		
9.12 PA system		
9.13 Contiguous to showers		
9.14 Toilets		
9.15 Fountains		
9.16 Grooming area		
9.17 Others		
10. *Shower Room*		
10.1 Sufficient size for peak loads		
10.2 Hot and cold water supply		
10.3 Height and angle of shower heads		
10.4 Exhaust system		

Factors	Strength	Weakness
10.5 Soap supply		
10.6 Surface material		
10.7 Toilets contiguous		
10.8 Drying room		
10.9 Corners rounded		
10.10 Water taps		
10.11 Drainage		
10.12 Others		
11. *Training Room*		
11.1 Adequate size		
11.2 Floors		
11.3 Walls		
11.4 Room drainage		
11.5 Climate control		
11.6 Internal and external telephone		
12. *Equipment Room*		
12.1 Counters		
12.2 Adequate size		
12.3 All utilities		
12.4 Storage		
12.5 Adjustable shelves		
12.6 Repair center		
12.7 Record keeping		
12.8 Drying room contiguous		
12.9 Security		
12.10 Others		
13. *Laundry Room*		
13.1 Contiguous to equipment		
13.2 Near plumbing		
13.3 Floor pitched		
13.4 Drain vents		
13.5 Large doors		
13.6 Electrical outlets		
13.7 Drying room		
13.8 Others		
14. *Exercise Therapy Room*		
14.1 Adequate space		
14.2 Climate controlled		
14.3 Damage-resistant floor		
14.4 Adequate walls		
14.5 Security		
14.6 Drinking fountain		
14.7 Cuspidor, with running water		
14.8 Spectator space		
14.9 Blackboards		
14.10 Bulletin boards		
14.11 PA system		
14.12 Others		

Factors	Strength	Weakness
15. *Officials' Room*		
15.1 Adequate space		
15.2 Lockers		
15.3 Showers		
15.4 Drying		
15.5 Toilet		
15.6 Utilities		
15.7 Time clock		
15.8 Blackboard		
15.9 Others		
16. *Visitors' Rooms*		
16.1 Adequate size		
16.2 Adjustable size		
16.3 Security		
16.4 Shower, drying, locker, toilet, dressing		
16.5 Blackboards		
16.6 Time clock		
16.7 Others		
17. *Lecture and Group Meeting Rooms*		
17.1 Adequate size		
17.2 Partitions		
17.3 Colors		
17.4 Adjustable lighting		
17.5 Climate control		
17.6 Motion pictures		
17.7 Closed circuit TV		
17.8 Soundproof		
17.9 Seating		
17.10 Blackboards		
17.11 Storage		
17.12 Light refreshment facilities		
17.13 Others		
18. *Library, if desired*		
19. *Lounge, if desired*		
20. *Trophy Room*		
20.1 Accessible to fans		
20.2 Shelves and cases		
20.3 Lighting		
20.4 Security		
20.5 Others		
21. *Custodial Rooms*		
21.1 Centrally located		
21.2 Auxiliary rooms		
21.3 All utilities		
21.4 Storage		
21.5 Others		
Overall Evaluation:		

There may be special purpose activity rooms, such as handball courts, judo rooms, or wrestling rooms. The preceding analysis should help an administrator decide on the types of facilities needed when he/she confers with the architect. The special considerations given to a swimming pool are not covered here.

EVALUATION OF STADIUM FACILITIES

Since football is the greatest revenue producer for an athletic program, some attention should be given to the stadium facilities because these are the facilities that customers will pay for through their ticket purchases.

The strengths and weaknesses of the following factors may be evaluated from the viewpoint of either improving existing facilities or designing new ones.

Objective: Factors to be Considered When Designing a Stadium

Factors	Strength	Weakness
1. *General*		
1.1 Capacity		
1.2 Multipurpose		
1.3 Expansion available		
1.4 Site available to fans		
1.5 Site near lodging, eating, and drinking		
1.6 Soil tests		
1.7 Feeder streets		
1.8 Parking		
1.9 Regulatory standards		
1.10 Utilities available		
1.11 Surface		
1.12 Aesthetics		
1.13 Scoreboard		
1.14 Others		
2. *Seating*		
2.1 Permanent seats		
2.2 Temporary seats		
2.3 Line of sight		
2.4 Cleaning costs		
2.5 Drainage		
2.6 Color-keying		
2.7 Access to seats		
2.8 Riser heights		
2.9 Emergency evacuation		
2.10 Others		

Factors	Strength	Weakness
3. *Lighting*		
3.1 Night lights		
3.2 TV availability		
3.3 Maintenance		
3.4 Emergency lighting		
3.5 Adequate security lighting		
3.6 Decentralized control		
3.7 Others		
4. *Ticket Sales/Collections*		
4.1 Booths adequate size		
4.2 Strategic alley located		
4.3 Utilities		
4.4 Maintenance		
4.5 Security		
4.6 Protection of fans against weather		
4.7 Other		
5. *Concessions*		
5.1 Sufficient number		
5.2 Adequate size		
5.3 Traffic flow		
5.4 Utilities		
5.5 Maintenance		
5.6 Storage		
5.7 Fan protection from weather		
5.8 Security		
5.9 Other		
6. *Lavatories*		
6.1 Sufficient number		
6.2 Adequate locations		
6.3 Traffic flow		
6.4 Maintenance		
6.5 Security		
6.6 Other		
7. *Press Box*		
7.1 Working news space		
7.2 Guest and VIP space		
7.3 Climate control		
7.4 Toilets		
7.5 Food service area		
7.6 PA system announcer		
7.7 Field microphone system		
7.8 Telephone connections		
7.9 Scoreboard operators		
7.10 Scouts' space		
7.11 Coaches' space		
7.12 TV space		

Factors	Strength	Weakness
7.13 Radio space		
7.14 Elevator		
7.15 Staircase		
7.16 Others		
8. *Other Facilities*		
8.1 First aid		
8.2 Drinking fountains		
8.3 Large vehicles		
8.4 Perimeter fence		
8.5 Others		
Overall Evaluation:		

It is a wise strategy to push the strengths of an athletic program. If a football stadium is the chief revenue producer, it should be given top priority for being a quality facility.

CHAPTER SUMMARY

This chapter stresses three strategies regarding the design of facilities: how to select an architect and the services to be rendered, how to determine the design of indoor facilities, and how to determine the design of a stadium. A checklist approach has been used so an administrator can evaluate the strengths and weaknesses of present or proposed facilities.

13-1 EVALUATION OF YOUR ATHLETIC FACILITIES

The most obvious case for this chapter is to have a team of people evaluate the athletic facilities of a high school, junior college, college, or professional athletic program.

Using the checklist in this chapter, the team can evaluate the strengths and weaknesses of the facilities, discuss their findings in class, and then prepare a report for the athletic administrator.

The report should include not only the findings, but might suggest other aspects such as architects, long-range plans, financing, personnel, and marketing strategies.

FOOTNOTE

[1] See also Robert T. Bronzan, *New Concepts in Planning and Funding Athletic, Physical Education, and Recreation Facilities* (St. Paul: Phoenix Intermedia, 1974) This book provides an excellent analysis of design factors.

14

ADMINISTERING ATHLETIC EQUIPMENT AND SUPPLIES

First-class, top-notch, safe equipment and supplies are needed to produce a winning athletic program and to develop the abilities of the athlete. The administration of this important facet requires the existence of a reciprocal exchange of contributions between the equipment suppliers and the athletic program. Both the suppliers and the athletic program must achieve their objectives if this mutual exchange is to be beneficial.

What must the suppliers contribute to the athletic program? First, they furnish the needed equipment and supplies for the program, in the proper quantities and at a fair price. In addition, the supply should be available at the right time and place. Supplies and equipment must be high quality and safe. The supplier must provide truthful information and proper service. If these contributions are made by a supplier, then the athletic program objectives may be accomplished.

In return, the athletic program must make certain contributions to their suppliers. For example, the supplier must be paid promptly for the supplies furnished. In addition each supplier expects to be given an equal opportunity to present his/her selection of supplies to the athletic administrator along with competing suppliers. A supplier needs adequate lead time when ordering equipment and supplies so that production and delivery can be made. An athletic administrator must make clear specifications on orders. Fair treatment regarding competitors is also a desired objective. Most suppliers would like to sell their supplies at a reasonable price to make a profit. They also expect to receive truthful and adequate information about the athletic program. Finally, they want a chance to grow with the athletic program. All of these objectives must be realized by suppliers if there is to

Objective: To Have a Reciprocal Exchange of Contributions Between Suppliers and the Athletic Program

Factors	Strength	Weakness
1. Do the suppliers contribute the following to the athletic program:		
1.1 Needed supplies and equipment in proper quantities		
1.2 At a fair price		
1.3 At the right time		
1.4 At the right place		
1.5 With right quality		
1.6 With safety in mind		
1.7 With truthful information		
1.8 With proper service, if necessary		
1.9 Others		
Overall Evaluation:		
2. Does the athletic program contribute the following to its suppliers:		
2.1 Payment on time for supplies furnished		
2.2 Equal opportunity to present supplies		
2.3 Adequate lead time		
2.4 Clear specifications		
2.5 Fair treatment with regard to competitors		
2.6 Reasonable price to make a profit		
2.7 Truthful and adequate information		
2.8 Chance to grow with the program		
2.9 Others		
Overall Evaluation:		
3. Is there an equitable exchange of contributions between		
3.1 The program and the suppliers		
3.2 Vice versa		
Overall Evaluation:		

be a mutual exchange of contributions between the suppliers and the athletic program.

PURCHASING STRATEGIES TO ACHIEVE ATHLETIC PROGRAM OBJECTIVES

If an athletic administrator is to produce a winning team and satisfy fans, he must buy the goods and services that appeal to fans rather than those he personally wants. Fans are the ultimate contributors to a successful program; if they are not satisfied, then the program will not succeed.

Two fundamental strategies must be followed to develop the athlete. The first is to buy safe equipment to reduce or prevent injuries. The second is to buy top-notch equipment and supplies to increase player morale.

If a program is to make a profit, there are two major strategies to follow. First, the administrator must minimize purchasing costs. Then he must determine whether to buy the equipment and parts or to make the equipment and parts. The minimizing approach involves keeping an adequate inventory to satisfy the needs of fans and athletes rather than ordering haphazardly. The make-or-buy decision is discussed later.

If growth is a program's main objective, it is essential to make a forecast of the equipment and supplies needed. From a revenue forecast, administrators and coaches can make a fairly accurate projection of the equipment and supplies needed.

If an improved image is the objective, there are two major strategies to follow. The first is to buy only first-class equipment and supplies which are revealed to a discerning athlete or fan. Second-rate materials usually indicate a second-rate athletic program. Another related strategy involves buying from "friends" of the athletic program.

If continuity of the program is desired, two basic strategies may be used: (1) having a sufficient supply of materials on hand, so that the program never runs out of the materials when and where the fans and athletes desire them, (2) having more than one source of materials—even if the source dwindles, the program will not dwindle.

If the program's goal is to improve the quality of life for society, two strategies can be followed: (1) buying the materials from minority businesses whenever possible, and (2) buying art and cultural objects to support people in the arts.

In summary form, an athletic administrator may evaluate the purchasing strategies used in his/her program by analyzing the chart on the next page.

MAKE-OR-BUY DECISION

The athletic administrator is often faced with the make-or-buy decision regarding products and services. For example, should a program make its own equipment or should it buy the equipment? Should we do our own

Objective: To Devise Purchasing Strategies to Accomplish Athletic Program Objectives

Strategies	Strength	Weakness
1. Entertainment for fans		
1.1 Buying what the fans want rather than following personal preference		
1.2 Others		
2. Development of athletes		
2.1 Buying safe equipment to prevent/reduce injuries		
2.2 Buying first-class materials to increase morale		
2.3 Others		
3. Making a profit		
3.1 Minimize purchase costs		
3.2 Make-or-buy decision		
3.3 Others		
4. Growth		
4.1 Forecast equipment and supplies needed		
4.2 Others		
5. Image		
5.1 Buying only first-class materials		
5.2 Reciprocity in buying		
5.3 Others		
6. Continuity		
6.1 Sufficient inventories on hand		
6.2 Having more than one source of supply		
6.3 Others		
7. Improving quality of life for society.		
7.1 Purchase from minority groups		
7.2 Buy art and cultural objects		
7.3 Others		
8. Others		
Overall Evaluation:		

laundry or should we have it done elsewhere? Should we perform the concessions function or should we hire an outside firm to do so? Should we train a member of our staff to do a job or should we employ someone new? Should we do our own broadcasting or should we hire outsiders? All of these decisions involve a fundamental make-or-buy proposition. What factors influence whether we make or buy products and services?

The first and major factor is the source of supply. If the athletic program has a strong source of supply, then products and services should be bought. If the source of supply is weak, then the equipment, supplies, or services should be produced by the program. If the source of supply is undependable, then, providing there are no obstacles, it is best for the program to make its own equipment. If the source of supply is a dependable and strong one, we should use it unless a strong case can be made for not doing so. There are several factors to support this view.

If buying will simplify administrative tasks, then it is wise to purchase supplies. This is important since administrative tasks—planning, acquiring resources, organizing resources, leading people, coordinating efforts, evaluating events—are so complex. Normally, an administrator tries to simplify his tasks, and buying a product or service is simpler than making it.

If attention must be focused on more important things, then the administrator should decide to buy equipment. Normally attention should be devoted to a major objective rather than minor ones of making some product or service which is a part of the major one.

However, if the management of a program is adequate, and the manager's expertise includes experience and a willingness to make the product or service, the program should take advantage of the opportunity to produce its own supplies.

Another related factor is the availability of technological competence in the organization. If the people in the athletic program do not have the competence to make the product or service, then it is necessary to buy from other sources.

Reducing the financial investment is another factor favoring the decision to buy. If an administrator decides to make his own products and services, then some type of financial resource becomes necessary. However, if that money is not available or if the financial investment must be reduced, then the better alternative is to buy.

Flexibility—both organizational and financial—requires a buy decision. If the program is channeling its revenue into making a product or service, then the program's financial flexibility is hampered. If the organization has other resources—people, machines, space, and time—tied up in making a product or service, it cannot take advantage of passing opportunities. If flexibility is desired, then the decision to buy should be made.

If it is difficult for the program to coordinate with an outside supply source, then it is best to make the product or service. Coordination with outsiders is time consuming, expensive, and frustrating. When these occur, it is best to make the product or service.

Objective: To Decide Whether to Make or Buy Products and Services

Factors →	**Theory →**		**Compared to →**	**Actual Situation →**		**Evaluation**	
	Make	*Buy*		*Make*	*Buy*	*Strength*	*Weakness*
1. Strong source of supply		X					
2. Weak source of supply	X						
3. Simplifying managerial tasks		X					
4. Focusing managerial attention on more important things		X					
5. Inadequacy of management		X					
6. Adequacy of management	X						
7. Reducing investment		X					
8. Flexibility desired		X					
9. Technological competence available	X						

10. Coordination with outside sources is difficult	X				
11. Large volume needed	X				
12. Supplier is unwilling to furnish special services	X				
13. Others					
Overall Evaluation:					

If a large volume of products and services is needed, then the decision should be to make the supplies. Economies of scale would suggest that expenses could be reduced by making your own. However, if a large volume is not needed, then a buy decision is the best alternative.

If a supplier is unwilling to furnish special services such as speedy service or oddball sizes, then the program should make its own supplies. When the supplier exhibits a poor attitude, it is a good idea to rely on the program's own resources.

Other factors may be considered in a make-or-buy decision, but the key ones are suggested in the model that is shown. When theory is compared to an actual situation, its strengths and weaknesses can be evaluated.

This fundamental decision model is used in a variety of situations that affect profitability, growth, entertainment, and other program objectives.

DECIDING THE NUMBER OF SUPPLIERS

Another typical purchasing decision involves the number of suppliers needed. Should an administrator buy from only one supplier or from a large number of suppliers? To maintain continuity, the program should have a number of suppliers. If the program relied on only one supplier, what would happen if that one supplier went out of business for any variety of reasons? If there is a possible failure of supply, it would be wise to buy from a number of suppliers.

Another factor to consider is whether low prices are desired. Using a number of suppliers will increase competition and lower prices.

If a variety of products and services is desired, then the program should buy from many suppliers. Commissioning several suppliers, each with his/her own line of supplies, insures a wide variety of products and services.

If good business relations are desired in the purchasing function, it is wise to use only a few suppliers. In this case, excellent relations usually exist between the buyer and seller since they are in constant contact.

Few suppliers should be used if high quality products and services are desired. If a supplier knows that he will receive a large number of orders from the athletic program, he will design high quality requirements into a product.

If a product or service has special requirements, only one or a few suppliers should be dealt with. The supplier who realizes that he is the program's only source will usually bend over backwards to fulfill special requirements for the products and services needed by an athletic program.

The administrative decision as to the number of sources of supply usually varies from one product/service to another.

Objective: To Select the Number of Suppliers

Factors	**Theory →** *Number of suppliers*		**Compared to →**	**Actual Situation →**		**Evaluation**	
	Few	*Many*		*Few*	*Many*	*Strength*	*Weakness*
1. Possible failure of supply		X					
2. Low prices desired		X					
3. Large variety required		X					
4. Good business relations desired	X						
5. High quality desired	X						
6. Special services required	X						
7. Others							
Overall Evaluation:							

Objective: To Determine Purchasing Strategies to Accomplish Supplier Objectives

Factors	Strength	Weakness
1. What methods of purchasing are used?		
1.1 Purchase orders		
1.2 Bids		
1.3 Unsolicited orders		
1.4 Other		
2. When is the time of purchases?		
2.1 Hand-to-mouth		
2.2 Forward buying		
2.3 Speculative buying		
2.4 Other		
3. Is there a dollar limit on purchasing?		
3.1 Equipment		
3.2 Supplies		
3.3 Other		
4. Who establishes specifications?		
4.1 User		
4.2 Buyer		
4.3 Seller		
4.4 Other		
Overall Evaluation:		

PURCHASING STRATEGIES TO ACCOMPLISH SUPPLIER OBJECTIVES

The methods of purchasing from suppliers are usually varied; these three are the most common: purchase orders, bids, and unsolicited purchases.

The use of purchase orders enables a supplier to accomplish some of his/her objectives; purchase orders guarantee clear specifications on orders, adequate lead time, and an opportunity to sell at a reasonable price. The use of purchase orders is probably the most common way for an athletic program to order products and services.

Bids are normally presented on orders involving a substantial sum of money. Potential suppliers are given equal opportunities to present their bids to an athletic program. Bids also ensure adequate lead time and clearly specify what is being purchased. The fair treatment given to potential suppliers induces other suppliers to enter the market. Bids allow most suppliers to sell at a reasonable price and to make a profit. If awarded, bids also give the supplier a chance to grow with the program. Bids usually assure the program a low price for the product or service, although sometimes a low price may not be the key factor in accepting a bid. Other factors might include fast delivery time, quality, reputation, sales terms, technical service, and reliability.

The use of unsolicited orders allows an athletic program flexibility in buying items at the right time and place and with proper service. The use of petty cash funds and unsolicited orders allows an athletic administrator some discretion in buying small items.

The date of purchase is also important to suppliers, particularly if adequate lead times are necessary. A hand-to-mouth purchasing practice might be advantageous to a program, but it plays havoc with most suppliers. Forward buying is usually desired by suppliers because it allows enough lead time to make, pack, or deliver the items on a purchase order or bid. Speculative buying is risky for an athletic program; usually items are not purchased in large enough quantities to justify using a speculative buying practice.

Normally there is a monetary limit on buying larger items. Such a practice protects against unwarranted purchases.

The specifications desired by suppliers should be clear, complete, and correct. It is very difficult for a supplier to make and deliver an item when there is no meeting of the minds between buyer and seller as to the specifications desired. The best practice is to have the users of the product or service, the purchaser, and the supplier make suggestions and determine the specifications.

Some purchasing strategies may be evaluated by using the preceding analysis.

EQUIPMENT AND SUPPLIES: STORAGE AND MAINTENANCE

Adequate storage space must be available for a variety of purposes. First, there should be room to organize supplies, permitting the use of older supplies first (first in, first out). Unused supplies deteriorate and lose their effectiveness. Second, there must be sufficient room to allow movement of handling equipment for receiving initial and subsequent orders. This is particularly true in the case of fork lifts and large dollies, which are necessary to move large pieces of equipment. Third, people must be able to move around comfortably in the storage space, so they can take inventory accurately. Fourth, storage areas should contain a special area for uncommon functions, such as drying equipment and supplies after storms and after practices. There must be adequate space to issue supplies and equipment. In addition, space is needed to mark and identify individual pieces of equipment for players. Finally, space is needed for the repair and maintenance of costly equipment.

If the adequate space is not available, supplies and equipment will not be under proper control. Supplies could be lost, stolen, or deteriorating. In

Objective: To Store and Maintain Equipment and Supplies

Factors	Strength	Weakness
1. Is adequate storage space available to		
1.1 Permit use of older supplies		
1.2 Prevent physical deterioration		
1.3 Allow proper handling equipment to move		
1.4 Take accurate inventory		
1.5 Allow for peculiar storage requirements		
1.6 Others		
2. Is adequate space available to		
2.1 Allow issue upon signature		
2.2 Identify and mark properly		
2.3 Repair and maintain equipment		
2.4 Other		
Overall Evaluation:		

this case, program objectives—producing a winning team, developing athletes, making a profit, keeping a good image, and maintaining continuity of the program—would not be effectively accomplished.

INVENTORY CONTROL METHODS

One of the easiest ways to lose money, to frustrate athletes, to run out of inventory, and to create a poor image is by not having an inventory control system for the many types of inventory which an athletic program carries. An inventory control system is particularly important for concessions and for athletic equipment and supplies.

Fundamental to good inventory control is the task of taking an inventory; if inventories are taken frequently, it is easy to keep track of losses, gains, and usage.

Records must be kept to maintain a good inventory control system. Usually an individual sheet for each piece of equipment is necessary. This sheet should have a record of the beginning inventory, the receipts, the issues, and the ending inventory. It is also wise to record the losses and reorder points, as well as the purchase orders. Such records, meticulously kept, serve as protection against losses, theft, run outs, and rush orders.

Also needed is some type of security system against theft for all the supplies and equipment. Marking of equipment for identification purposes is necessary. In addition, items subject to theft should be stored in a locked place.

Objective: To Institute an Inventory Control System

Factors	Strength	Weakness
1. Does the athletic program have an inventory control system for		
1.1 Equipment		
1.2 Supplies		
1.3 Concessions		
1.4 Other		
2. Are inventories regularly taken for		
2.1 Equipment		
2.2 Supplies		
2.3 Concessions		
2.4 Other		
3. Are adequate records kept showing		
3.1 Beginning inventory		
3.2 Receipts		
3.3 Issues		
3.4 Ending inventory		
3.5 Purchase orders		
3.6 Reorder points		
3.7 Losses		
3.8 Other		
4. Do supplies and equipment have		
4.1 A security system		
4.2 Identification		
4.3 Other		
Overall Evaluation:		

CHAPTER SUMMARY

There must be a mutual exchange of contributions between the suppliers and the athletic program if administration of equipment and supplies is to be successful. The supplier should contribute the equipment at a fair price, and at the right time and place. Merchandise should be high quality and safe. The suppliers should be truthful and supply proper service. In return the athletic program must pay the supplier on time, give all an equal opportunity to present their wares, allow adequate lead time, delineate adequate specifications, pay a fair price, provide adequate information, and give the suppliers a chance to grow with the program.

There are several purchasing strategies used to accomplish the program objectives. First, it is necessary to buy supplies that will satisfy the users rather than the administrator. Purchases must consist of safe, first-class equipment and supplies. It is important to minimize purchase costs and to determine the proper make-or-buy decision. A forecast of the supplies needed is fundamental. It is sound strategy to have a sufficient quantity of supplies on hand, and to have more than one source of supply. The administrator might also decide to buy from minority enterprises.

A make-or-buy decision is influenced by many factors. Those that favor buying are a strong source of supply, a need to simplify managerial tasks, a need to focus managerial attention on more important things, an inadequate management, a need to reduce investment, and a desire to maintain flexibility. Those factors suggesting a "make" decision are weak source of supply, an adequate management, the availability of technological competence, some difficulty in coordinating the administration with outside sources, the need for a large volume, or a supplier unwilling to furnish special services.

A further decision of how many suppliers to use is influenced by several factors. Those suggesting a large number of suppliers include a possible failure of supply, a desire for low prices, and the need for a large variety. Those factors indicating that the number of suppliers should be limited are a desire for good business relations, the need for high quality equipment, and the importance of special services.

There are several other purchasing strategies to be followed if the program is to satisfy the suppliers' objectives as well as its own. Purchasing methods include bids, purchase orders, and unsolicited orders. The timing of purchases includes forward buying, speculative buying, and hand-to-mouth buying. Sometimes there is a dollar limit on purchasing. Specifications should be jointly decided on by the user, buyer, and seller.

Every effectively administered athletic program has to provide space for the maintenance and storage of equipment and supplies. In addition, there must be an adequate inventory control system for equipment, supplies, and concessions.

Case 14-1 FOOTBALL CONCESSIONS AT NESU

Fred Baker, Athletic Director for Northeastern State University, gazed at a proposal regarding the concessions at NESU. The proposal was in the form of a letter from John Powell, manager of the local MacDonald's Hamburger franchise, who stated that his fast food restaurant would be interested in selling the hot dogs, cokes, coffee, and candy at the home football games which NESU played in its 41,000-seat stadium on Saturdays. The letter stated that in exchange for MacDonald's rights for the concession that Powell would guarantee NESU a fee of $8,000 a game plus 10% of the revenues from concessions after the $8,000 minimum net profit was achieved. That offer was attractive to Fred Baker who was a good friend of Powell. In fact, Powell was a staunch financial supporter of NESU, who always attended the games, advertised in the game programs, provided jobs for players, and contributed to the Booster Club.

Fred Baker then called a meeting of Abe Lincoln, the Business Manager for NESU; William Mather, the Associate Athletic Director; and Lanny Ferguson, the Assistant Athletic Director for Administration. The four of them discussed the MacDonald proposal.

Abe was the first to comment on the proposal. "I've been handling the concessions for our football games for the past sixteen years. During that time our concessions have contributed three-quarters of a million dollars to our athletic program funds. Not one year have we ever lost money. For example, last year our net revenues from concessions were $100,000 and our merchandise costs were $45,000, netting us $55,000. The year before our net revenues were $95,000 and costs were $40,000. Three years ago, they were $83,000 and $37,000. Four years ago they were $77,000 and $39,000. Whew, in the past four years we have netted $194,000. Why should we change from what we've been doing?"

Lanny remarked, "Fred, Abe is correct. In fact, our net program profits for the past four years have been approximately $10,000, $69,000, $65,000 and $90,000. Without the concessions, we would have been barely able to net any money."

"Yes, but what about all the hassle that goes into running those concessions for our three home games?" William Mathers countered. "Abe, since you run the concessions, don't you admit that you could focus your managerial attention on more important things, such as keeping the books, making reports, preparing budgets, and other administrative matters?"

"Well, that depends on what you consider important," Abe replied. "Personally, I consider making that $50,000 a year on three games pretty important for our athletic program. Sure, it's a lot of hassle on my part, but I'm willing to do it. In fact, I've been training Ed Russell, our track coach, to help me."

"Well, it seems to me that we could simplify our managerial tasks if we farmed out the concessions to MacDonald's," Fred remarked. "Just think, no long hours getting ready to sell everything. No ice hauling, no getting organizations to help us, no counting of money, no worry about getting robbed. Those are headaches."

"Yes, but we have the managerial expertise to handle those chores,"

Abe replied. "Ed and I have been taking care of those tasks for our football games, our basketball games, our track meets, our baseball games, whenever our services have been demanded for the past sixteen years and we've been doing fairly well at it."

"There's no denying that, Abe," remarked William. "But you are retiring this July. Why don't we get out of the concession business when you retire and let MacDonald's handle it? None of us, then, would have to worry about concessions. Heaven knows that we're all too busy worrying about other affairs."

Lanny said, "Now wait a minute. Ed Russell, our track man, has been working with Abe for five years. Ed is very conscientious and qualified to take over and manage our concessions. He would do a good job for us."

"That's right," said Abe. "If Ed takes over the concessions, I'll have enough work to go on half time. Someone has to handle the bookkeeping of all of our expenses, prepare reports, purchase equipment and supplies, take care of the scholarship payroll, type employee contracts and hourly help payrolls, be a money courier, and the like."

"Yes, okay, but . . ." William Mather remarked, "How much investment have we tied up in our concessions business? If we got out, we could reduce our investment and use that money for scholarships."

"Well, our stock room is always full. I just took inventory last month and it amounted to $10,000 at cost. Stocking is a big job and we have lots of potential problems in inventory control if I don't stay on top of it. When I first took over the concessions, I installed a simple inventory control system. Boy, do I remember the results!" Abe commented.

"What happened?" Fred asked.

"Well, before I was put in charge, each hawker was given a tray full of peanuts, cokes, candy, and so forth. When he returned to get filled up, he would give me the money, and go out and sell some more. There was no control on his beginning inventory, what was added, an ending inventory, and what he sold. All each hawker did was to sell what was given him and return the money. When I took over, I gave each hawker a list of items in his tray. When he came back to get more, I added to his list. When he returned to check in, I asked him to give the required amount of money, based on the beginning, ending, and what he had refilled. I paid him a commission of 20%. Do you know what happened?" Abe continued.

"After the first game of demanding the money or inventory, sixty people quit. They had been stealing us blind because they had not been held accountable for their actions! I instituted that simple inventory control system and since that time, our losses have been minimal," Abe continued.

"Do you have qualified people to help you sell to 40,000 people on a Saturday afternoon?" Fred asked.

"I surely do," replied Abe. "I get volunteer groups to do the selling. I pay them a minimum guarantee of $100 a game plus a commission of 14% of their gross, whichever is higher. Any shortages are docked from their commissions. I guess that 300 to 330 hawkers and support personnel are required on a big day. And I've recruited good groups who are willing to sell to make some money for their cause. For example, I recruited Boy Scout Troop #2, the Explorer Scouts, a Foreign Language Club from the high school, the Farmington Methodist Women's Club, The First Christian Church, Gamma Xi of Geta Gamma Phi, the Latter Day Saints, The United Presbyterian Church Women's Club, the high school Choralettes, Arnold Air Society, and others. Each group is assigned to an area, stocked with merchandise, sells, renders a report, and receives a commission. All of them require a great deal of coordination on my part to see to it that selling goes off okay. It's a job."

"And we have a large volume of merchandise that is sold. For example (Abe hands out a sheet), here's what we sold last year just at our three home football games (see next page).

"In addition, our novelty sales, advertising, cushions, and programs sold for $48,000 and netted us $24,000 profit."

"This is big business, isn't it?" remarked Lanny.

"Yes, it is, and I surely don't want some outside seller coming in here to take it away," stated Abe. "And I'm sure that several outside concessionaires would be willing to bid on our concessions business if we decided to go in that direction. In addition to MacDonald's, I know of Wendy's Hamburgers, a traveling concessionaire down state, a group from the neighboring state, and another who would be very much interested in our gross revenues from concessions.

"If we brought in an outside concessionaire, keep in mind another factor. A friend of mine has been in the concessions business for forty years. He has told me many, many times, 'Abe, keep in mind, an outside concessionaire has the first count when it comes to computing the percentage for a fee. He has the first count and you have no way of checking whether 15–20% comes off the top before your split.' "

Lanny said, "If we let MacDonald's handle the concessions, I know that 10% of gross revenues goes to the home office for their franchise fee, plus probably 15% for profit. As a result their prices will probably be higher than ours."

"That's right! And practically any outside concessionaire has personnel who portray a carnival type spirit. I don't believe our fans want that. They would prefer local hometown folks to buy from," stated Abe.

"Regarding prices for soft drinks," Fred interrupted, "what are the chances of raising them from 25¢ to 50¢? We need to make more money to pay off our bonded indebtedness. One way to do it is to make more money out of our concessions."

"Our present prices for concessions are fairly reasonable," stated William Mather. "For example, cokes are now 25¢. Candy is 25¢. Cigarettes are 75¢. Peanuts are a quarter as are Cracker Jacks. Fifty cents for hot dogs and 60¢ for sandwiches. Couldn't we raise the price for cokes to 50¢? And sandwiches to $1.00? And 50¢ for Cracker Jacks?"

"Well," stated Abe, "we do sell the highest quality food available. Cokes are top quality drinks. Our sales hawkers are top quality local people. However, I don't want to gig the customers. There's a moral issue here. I don't think our fans would stand a dollar for a hot dog or fifty cents for Cracker Jacks. Hot dogs in town are priced at 50¢, Cracker Jacks at 15¢, Cokes at 30¢, cigarettes at 60¢, sandwiches at 70¢, peanuts at 20¢, candy bars at 20¢."

Football Concessions

		Sales		Merchandise costs
Drinks	Sold by Hawkers	$ 17,824		$ 3,743
	Sold in Stands	40,560		10,140
	1st Game Total	$ 58,384	(Hot Weather)	$13,883
	Hawkers	$ 19,558		$ 4,107
	In Stands	38,381		9,595
	2nd Game Total	$ 57,938	(Hot Weather)	$13,702
	Hawkers	5,094		$ 1,069
	In Stands	11,909		2,977
	3rd Game Total	$ 17,003	(Cold Weather)	$ 4,046
	Grand Total Drinks	$133,325		$31,631
Candy		$ 3,053		$ 763
		1,657		414
		3,698		924
		$ 8,408		$ 2,101
Cigarettes		$ 596		$ 447
		408		306
		397		297
		$ 1,401		$ 1,050
Peanuts		$ 4,319		$ 985
		3,309		753
		4,782		1,097
		$12,410		$ 2,835
Sandwiches		$ 918		$ 688
		703		527
		852		639
		$ 2,473		$ 1,854
Hot Dogs		$ 7,461		$ 3,730
		5,574		2,787
		7,694		3,847
		$ 20,729		$10,364
Cracker Jacks		$ 2,196		$ 658
		1,042		420
		2,055		616
		$ 5,293		$ 1,694
Grand Total		$184,039		$51,529

"Yes, but at a football game we've got the only show in town when it comes to concessions," stated William.

"Yes, but I don't want to gig the public," retorted Abe. "For example, Fred, we now sell a hot dog for 50¢. It costs us 15¢ for a hot dog and bun. Since we make them ourselves, we do not have much spoilage. If we let the Student Union make 3,000 ¼ pound hot dogs, they will cost us 60¢ each. That's 40¢ gross on each one versus 35¢ gross on our present price. And who knows if we can sell 3,000 hot dogs on one day? If we don't, we've got lots of spoiled hot dogs on our hands."

Lanny stated, "I think we should let Ed Russell handle our concessions from now on and let Abe help him."

William said, "No, I think we should let an outside concessionaire handle it."

Abe stated, "I think Ed could do it."

Fred pondered about that decision and the prices. "Let's adjourn and think about it some more."

Part V

Financing An Athletic Program

Athletic programs use a number of financial strategies to achieve their objectives. These strategies include ways to plan for money, sources and methods of acquiring money, and evaluations as to how money is used.

15

ADMINISTERING THE FINANCES OF ATHLETIC PROGRAMS

There must be a reciprocity between the athletic program and the contributors of capital if the program is to be well administered. Those who provide capital hope to satisfy their personal objectives through financial contributions to the athletic program. For example, most capital providers would like to get an adequate return on their investment. In addition they would like to receive a continuous return on their investment. Further, they expect to receive adequate information concerning the administration of their financial investment.

Those who invest in the athletic program wish to accomplish other, more difficult objectives. Safety of their investment is a desirable objective. The marketability of their investment is a desirable objective, that is, the ability to buy and sell their investment in the marketplace. Further, they would like to have their investment appreciate in value.

In exchange for the satisfaction of their personal objectives, capital providers contribute certain things to a successful athletic program. The program needs capital to operate its activities. Both long-term capital—for the construction of facilities—and short-term capital are necessary to fund the operations of an athletic program. In addition to money, the program needs moral support from the investors. This is particularly true when the team is not winning.

The local school board for high schools, the board of trustees for a college, or the owners of a professional team could all invest in the athletic program with the same objectives: to receive continuous, adequate return on their investment, and to obtain information about the program. In addition, if they are private owners they hope to have a safe, marketable investment that will appreciate in value. They will generally support the program if they are compensated in return.

Objective: To Achieve Reciprocity Between Suppliers of Capital and the Athletic Program

Factors	Strength	Weakness
1. Is there an equitable exchange of contributions between the capital providers and the program? Do the capital providers receive the following:		
1.1 Adequate return on their investment		
1.2 Continuous return		
1.3 Adequate information about their investment.		
In addition, if the owners are private:		
1.4 Safety of investment		
1.5 Marketability of investment		
1.6 Appreciation of value		
1.7 Others		
2. Does the program receive the following, when necessary:		
2.1 Long-term capital		
2.2 Short-term capital		
2.3 Adequate support		
2.4 Others		
3. Is the exchange satisfactory		
3.1 To the program		
3.2 To the capital providers		
Overall Evaluation:		

FINANCIAL STRATEGIES TO ACCOMPLISH ATHLETIC PROFIT OBJECTIVES

Most athletic programs hope to make a profit, to have more revenue than expenses. If a profit is made, then short-term needs for capital are usually satisfied, unless some special short-term need is urgent. The financial strategies associated with the profit objective are limited because profit is made by producing and marketing a team. However, some financial strategies may be used.

First, it is necessary to have financial statements available on a monthly and yearly basis to determine if profits are being made. Financial statements differ according to the program, but the most common ones are a statement of income and expenses, a statement of financial condition, and perhaps a cash flow statement. If the program operates on a cash basis, rather than accrual, then a cash flow statement may not be necessary.

A second financial strategy is to invest excess funds so they will generate additional revenue. This is true of the revenue received from advance season tickets sales. Money received six months in advance can be invested in short-term securities to receive interest or dividends. If excess funds exist from past operations, it is wise to invest them. Donations should also be invested until the cash is needed.

Another strategy is to minimize expenses. For example, one should not have an excessive inventory of supplies on hand. Having too many petty cash funds will not help to minimize expenses. On the other hand, taking advantage of supplier discounts is another way to minimize financial expenses.

Another financial strategy is to use conservative or liberal accounting practices, depending on how they affect profits. Normally, a conservative approach is to use a fifo method (first in, first out) in accounting for inventories. Such a method decreases the costs of using inventory and increases profits in times of inflation. If profits were desired to be lower, then a lifo method (last in, first out) could be used. Or if assets are depreciated, a straight-line approach, normally a conservative method, often increases the profits in a given year. If profits were desired to be lowered, a sum-of-the-digits depreciation method could be used. There are other methods in accounting which can be used in either lowering or increasing profits in a given time period.

Financial Strategies for Growth

Long-term growth is another athletic program objective which is a common organizational goal. The administrator must determine how to finance growth. Normally, the profit made by an athletic program is used to finance yearly operations. Ordinarily an athletic program will not make enough profit to finance long-term growth, especially if it involves the construction of facilities. Consequently, growth, expressed in terms of additional assets needed, is usually financed by bonds, stocks, or a combination of both. A high school or college athletic program cannot issue stock. Therefore, their alternatives are bonds, donations, or supplements from the scholastic operating funds. Since most schools are reluctant to issue scholastic operating funds for athletics, programs are limited to issuing bonds and seeking donations. However, a professional team can utilize both stocks (or equity capital from the individual owner) and bonds.

What factors determine whether to use stock (equity capital) or bonds (creditor capital)? The nature of the organization is an important factor. If the organization is a manufacturer requiring heavy fixed assets, bonds should be used because the fixed assets can usually be mortgaged. Both retailers and service organizations should use stocks; normally, they do not have sufficient long-term assets (except perhaps land or buildings) that can be mortgaged by issuing bonds.

A stable sales pattern indicates that an organization can use bonds; the organization can pay interest regularly from its relatively stable income stream. If the sales pattern fluctuates from time to time, the organization probably has to use stocks, for which dividends do not have to be paid on a recurring time basis.

Using financial leverage (sometimes called trading on the owners' equity)—financing the organization with creditor capital as well as owner capital—indicates that long-term growth is financed by a combination of bonds and stock.

If the cost of issuing bonds is high in proportion to the amount of money received, then it is wise to use stocks. On the other hand, if the cost of issuing stocks is high in relation to the amount of money received, then it is wise to finance long-term growth with bonds.

Another factor to be considered is the high income tax rate on profits. Since most corporate income taxes are roughly 50 percent, it is common to use bonds—interest is a deductible item in computing profits, whereas dividends are not deductible for income tax purposes.

A major factor is the conservative philosophy of most managers in dealing with money. Most owner-managers would rather not use other people's money but would rather use their own to finance growth. Their philosophical value system would suggest that owing money to other people is bad. If their own money is used rather than borrowed from other people, no interest expense is incurred, there is no repayment of the principal, and dividends need not be paid. These conservative philosophical values dictate that stocks be issued rather than bonds. However, one factor might offset this conservative philosophy: when additional stock is issued, the owners' equity might be diluted.

There are other factors to consider when determining whether to use owner capital (stocks) or creditor capital (bonds/notes). The key factors have been discussed in this chapter. They may be arranged in a model to help the administrator make the proper decision or to evaluate the present financial position of an existing program.

A scholastic administrator can substitute "donations" in place of "stocks" and use the model to determine how to finance long-term growth.

Another strategy sometimes used to improve the weak financial position of a team or a league is to merge with a stronger team or league. This strategy has worked with football leagues, hockey leagues, and basketball leagues. When teams are merged, then organizational growth occurs.

Objective: To Finance Long-Term Growth by Stocks and Bonds

Factors	**Theory →**		**Compared to →**	**Actual Situation →**		**Evaluation**	
	Stocks	*Bonds*		*Stocks*	*Bonds*	*Strength*	*Weakness*
1. Nature of Organization							
1.1 Manufacturer with heavy fixed assets		X					
1.2 Retailing	X						
1.3 Service	X						
2. Sales Pattern							
2.1 Stable sales		X					
2.2 Fluctuating sales	X						
3. Financial Leverage	X	X					
4. Costs to Issue							
4.1 High cost of bonds	X						
4.2 High cost of stocks		X					
5. High Income Tax Rate		X					
6. Conservative Philosophy of Management	X						
6.1 No interest to be paid	X						
6.2 No repayment of principal required	X						
6.3 No dividends absolutely required	X						
6.4 Possible dilution of owners' equity		X					
7. Others							
Overall Evaluation							

Financial Strategies for Continuity of the Program

Most athletic programs fail because of an immediate lack of money. Of course, money is the result of other factors which are the real culprits causing failure. However, since money is such a vital resource for maintaining continuity of any athletic program, it behooves any administrator to utilize at least three strategies to help preserve continuity: (1) having adequate financial reserves, (2) maintaining depreciation accounts, and (3) maintaining an insurance program.

Adequate cash reserves are necessary in case of losing seasons, prolonged casualties, or unexpected emergencies. Having sufficient savings or cash invested in marketable securities helps a team to weather the storms of adversity. Of course, having plenty of cash reserves depends on making a profit or having wealthy donors; it is most likely that fans and benefactors will support a winning team over a loser. Large cash reserves are most often maintained by winning teams.

Another way to maintain adequate reserves to help replace long-term

Objectives: To Devise Financial Strategies to Achieve Athletic Program Objectives

Strategies	**Strength**	**Weakness**
1. Making a Profit		
1.1 Use of timely financial statements		
1.2 Minimize financial costs		
1.3 Invest excess funds		
1.4 Use of liberal/conservative accounting practices		
1.4 Other		
2. Growth Objective		
2.1 Use of bonds/stocks to finance growth		
2.2 Mergers		
2.3 Others		
3. Continuity of the Program		
3.1 Having adequate financial reserves		
3.2 Maintaining depreciation accounting		
3.3 Adequate insurance program		
3.4 Others		
Overall Evaluation:		

assets is to use depreciation accounting. Merely depreciating an asset does not provide cash reserves. However, when an athletic administrator recognizes depreciation as a true expense of assets wearing out, and when this depreciation expense is recorded in the account books, then the administrator will not be misled into believing that plenty of money is available for the replacement of equipment, astroturf, buildings, or tracks. If the actual depreciation of an asset is set aside into a fund, then the money will be available to help replace the asset when it wears out. However, the administrator must reckon with inflation as well as depreciation. Today the asset cannot be purchased at the price charged ten years ago.

A further strategy to maintain some degree of asset continuity is to insure the major assets against fire, wind, storms, theft, and floods. Insurance will help to replace assets, at least partially, if a disaster strikes. In addition to physical assets, even the lives of key executives or players can be insured.

On the preceding page is a summary of the major financial strategies an administrator can use if continuity, growth, and profits are desired objectives.

Financial Strategies to Accomplish Investor's Personal Objectives

As mentioned previously, those who provide athletic programs with capital have certain personal objectives which they wish to accomplish. Which financial strategies will help them achieve their goals? First, they hope to receive a financial return on their investment, usually in the form of dividends. Dividends can be in the form of cash, assets (in the case of private ownership), or another kind of compensation (in the case of schools). Dividend payments must be paid regularly, regardless of profits, to satisfy the owners' objective of achieving a continuity of return. Regular dividend payments may not be possible all the time, but they are a main objective of investors.

Capital investors want to know how their investments are being managed. The obvious strategy, then, is to provide them with at least an annual financial report as to the financial position and financial operations for the year.

Investors are concerned about the safety of their investment. Two strategies can be followed to provide a degree of safety for the investors: (1) use financial reserves to protect the investors' equity in case of emergencies, (2) maintain an insurance program to protect the assets.

The marketability desired by investors can be accomplished by having a public issue of stocks or bonds in a market where trading can take place. Of course, investments can be marketed only in the case of privately owned athletic programs such as the Milwaukee Bucks of the NBA.

Investors also hope their investment will appreciate in value. Reinvesting profits in the program rather than paying dividends increases the book value of an investment. An increase in the book value as well as an increase in profits each year usually means an appreciation of the investment.

If the athletic program is privately owned, its ability to accomplish the investors' objectives may be evaluated by the following:

Objective: To Devise Financial Strategies to Accomplish the Investor's Objectives

Strategies	Strength	Weakness
1. Return on investment		
1.1 Pay dividends		
1.2 Other		
2. Continuity of Return		
2.1 Pay regular dividends		
2.2 Pay regardless of profits		
2.3 Other		
3. Information		
3.1 Issue annual financial report		
3.2 Other		
4. Safety of Investment		
4.1 Use of financial reserves		
4.2 Insurance program		
4.3 Other		
5. Marketability		
5.1 Public issue of stocks/bonds		
5.2 Other		
6. Appreciation		
6.1 Do not pay dividends		
7. Others		
Overall Evaluation:		

SUMMARY

For successful administration of a program's finances, there must be a reciprocity between the needs of the athletic program and of those who provide the financial capital. Investors expect an adequate and continuous return on their investment. They also expect information about their investment. If they are private capital contributors, they expect safety, marketability, and an appreciation of their equity capital. In return, the athletic program expects long-term and short-term capital, as well as financial support to be provided for the program.

There are various financial strategies used to accomplish program objectives. To make a profit, it is important to use updated financial statements, to minimize financial costs, to invest excess funds, and to use liberal or conservative accounting practices. If growth is an objective, the program can use stocks or bonds to finance expansion. Mergers can also be used. If he program desires continuity, there are at least three effective financial trategies—accruing adequate financial reserves to draw on, maintaining lepreciation accounts, and maintaining an adequate insurance program. These strategies can also be used to accomplish the personal objectives of he investors.

Case 15-1 FINANCING THE TOTAL ATHLETIC PROGRAM*

The Third Central Regional Conference on Secondary School Athletic Administration was held at the Holiday Inn Plaza, Wichita, Kansas, October 20–22, 1974. There were approximately 200 registrants from seven states.

Dr. Arzell Ball, superintendent of schools, Shawnee Mission, Kansas, was one of the convention speakers. Dr. Ball's speech follows:

Interscholastic competition is taken seriously by patrons in Kansas. As superintendent of the second largest school district in the state, I am in agreement with Kansas citizens.

In developing productive citizens, assuming quality, basic education is available, two additional key concepts are important—involvement and identity. At the present time, in our school district about 60% of the senior high students are involved in some type of extracurricular activity. A few years ago the percentage was much lower. I would hope by the mid 70's the number of students involved in extracurricular activities would be much higher, approaching 80 to 90% of the student body. The broad area of fine arts including debate, drill teams, marching bands, drama, forensics, journalism, concert band and orchestra involve over 20% of the senior high school students. Competition can be keen with large numbers of students motivated by creating contests in the areas of music, debate, journalism, etc. Show me an involved student, assuming it is a constructive activity, and you will have a youngster who will remain in school and at least tolerate the basics—math, science, social studies, and language arts.

The board and administration of a school district should be proud of an outstanding interscholastic program and look forward to an expansion involving coed sports in a wide variety of activities, including tennis, volleyball, softball, swimming, gymnastics, track and cross country, golf, and basketball. The same list of sports should be available for boys with the addition of football and wrestling.

I would like to share with you a few statistics showing the expansion of interscholastic sports in the five Shawnee Mission high schools.

In 1969, 2005 boys were participants as compared to 217 girls.
In 1970, 2680 boys were participants as compared to 502 girls.
In 1971, 2789 boys were participants as compared to 546 girls.
In 1972, 2656 boys were participants as compared to 741 girls.
In 1973, 3012 boys were participants as compared to 876 girls.

* From *The Athletic Director*, a publication of the National Council of Secondary School Athletic Directors, vol. 6, no. 2, January 1975.

In summary, in the five-year period, participants in boys sports have increased from 2005 to 3012, an increase of 50%; girls from 217 to 874 participants, a 300% increase.

The expansion of boys' and girls' varsity sports didn't just happen—no miracle occurred. Instead the board, administration, and staff developed a sound financial system for interscholastic sports, intramurals, and fine arts. We were originally thinking in terms of a five- to ten-year program. However, due to recent court decisions affecting interscholastic sports, girls arrived on the scene and our long-range planning became short, intermediate budgeting. Over the last five years only two interscholastic sports for boys have been added to the program, gymnastics and baseball. For girls, seven sports have been implemented, and basketball and golf will be included in the 1975 school year.

Oversimplified, our budget philosophy is a blend of district subsidy and local school incentives—Dads' Booster Clubs, merchandising a program of comprehensive activity tickets, improving community relations by issuing tickets to senior citizens, and season tickets.

Five years ago the district was successful in passing a $6 million bond issue to improve secondary facilities and expand athletic space in the five senior highs and one junior high. Five indoor swimming pools and an additional gym at the largest junior high school were completed, and a new 12,000-seat stadium was built for the district on the south campus. The district is now able to seat approximately 20,000 football fans on Friday night at $1.75 per adult.

At the local level, the senior high activity fund has averaged approximately $22,000 to $24,000 a year. This money is generated primarily by adult ticket sales and student activity tickets, selling at $8.50 each this year. Last year, the senior high gate receipts and activity tickets produced a total of $157,810.00. The Board of Education directly and indirectly subsidized the athletic program in the amount of $249,372.00.

The Board of Education paid for the following services:

Police officers (crowd control)	$ 15,000.00
Coaching salaries	125,000.00
Equipment & supplies for new athletic programs	
baseball and softball equipment	10,440.00
baseball and softball operations	6,700.00
baseball and softball practice facilities	10,000.00
Football buses	900.00
Stadium sound system repair	128.00
Stadium–field preparation	9,284.00
Jr. varsity and sophomore field preparation	14,220.00
Track facilities	7,700.00
Ticket takers and sellers	50,000.00
	$249,372.00

As you can see, the interscholastic program last year was heavily subsidized by the Board of Education. However, we talk in terms of a self-supporting program, meaning a local school athletic program which pays for athletic equipment, referees' fees, and other miscellaneous expenses. In summary, the Board of Education pays for all coaching salaries, original athletic equipment, all new facilities and maintenance, the maintenance on two stadiums and the various practice fields, crowd control, and the initial cost involved in the implementation of a new program.

To further explain the financing of the athletic program, the general activity account in each senior high school is divided into Groups II and VII. All interscholastic activities are included in Group II and administered by a vice principal and, as previously stated, financed from activity tickets and gate receipts. Each school is encouraged to establish a balance of $3,000 to $5,000 in order to cope with emergencies.

The Board of Education subsidizes fine arts (Group VII) at the district level, $70,000 annually. Each senior high school receives a total of $14,000 to finance their fine arts program. The fine arts students are required to purchase activity tickets. Although the fine arts department in each senior high is subsidized, programs are expected to be partially self-supporting. For example, the journalism program is subsidized on a 45–55 plan—45% of the program supported by subsidy and 55% by advertising sales. Separating the two units, athletics and fine arts, has greatly improved our public relations. A football coach can no longer say he is paying for the band, the drama department, and drill team.

This year, the Board of Education has supplied additional funds to enable the district director of athletics in the central office to give additional subsidy to the small senior high school and to assist financing the ten junior high 8th and 9th grade boys' basketball and 8th and 9th grade girls' volleyball programs. The subsidy amounts to a total of $70,000. The major share of the additional funds was appropriated primarily for senior high girls' sports. At the present time, we do not charge admission for girl's sports so it is impossible to make them self-supporting.

With outstanding leadership and salesmanship at the local level, the activity fund may be improved by good merchandising. For example, in one of our senior highs last year, 95% of the student body purchased activity tickets as compared to another high school selling only 76% of the students a $6 activity ticket. This year the percentages remain about the same. However, the ticket has been increased from $6 to $8.50 per student.

It is the responsibility of the district director of athletics to equalize athletic opportunities among the five senior high schools. I will admit it is a delicate balance between subsidy and local initiative. However, over the last five years the larger senior high schools required very little, if any, direct subsidy. Good business procedures have been practiced and in-service is provided for the five directors of athletics. The in-service program includes budgeting, merchandising, and a conference with the district auditors at the beginning of each school year. A complete accounting of expenditures is available to each director at the end of the month. These reports are supplied by the data processing department.

To be a winner you must start early. The Board of Education subsidizes a K–12 intramural program in the amount of $70,000.00 annually. The intramural budget enables elementary students, primarily from fifth and sixth grades, to have three intramural sessions a week after school. In some elementary schools up to 90% of the upper elementary grade students participate in some kind of intramural activity. Junior high schools offer intramurals five days a week before and after school, and swimming is available on Saturday mornings at the five senior high schools. Last year 71% of the boys and 62% of the girls participated in junior high intramurals. Senior high intramurals are offered after school and in the evenings. Intramural supervisors are paid $5.00 an hour. In addition to the junior high intramural program, extramural sports are popular in the areas of track, cross country, swimming, gymnastics, wrestling, and volleyball. This fall, in Shawnee Mission, the YMCA and a private organization called Olympia have suited over 150 football teams, grade five through nine. The YMCA has over 3,000 boys playing football at the south complex each weekend. Ten games are played simultaneously. Over 1500 girls are cheerleaders, grade five through nine.

The typical Dad's Booster Club and several groups for athletics and fine arts would average approximately 300 members at each school. Isn't it logical to assume youngsters and adults who are directly involved in sports will attend sporting events?

All elementary youngsters accompanied by a parent are admitted free. Patrons over 65 are admitted free, and the employee is admitted free but must pay for the other members of his family or friends attending the game with him.

Each year the senior high schools distribute bumper stickers reading, "Better than Best," "State Champion," "District Champion," etc. Again, local initiative and control are encouraged, assuming activities are within board policy.

In summary, I would encourage public school districts to develop a long-range five- to ten-year plan, initiate a blend of local effort and district subsidy, and face up to the major problems in financing athletics caused by inflation, inadequate facilities, and personnel shortages. Inflation is forcing many private recreational organizations and private schools out of business. Public schools must cope with budget problems caused by inflation and expanding programs. We need help desperately from other public agencies, particularly park and recreation boards and cities. Bond issues will need to be proposed to finance adequate physical education and recreational facilities. Instructors need additional training if new programs are to be successfully implemented. Considering public relations, why not ask for full funding for girls' sports, fine arts, and junior high interscholastic activities. Maybe—just maybe, senior high boys' interscholastic sports can be "self-supporting."

QUESTION:

1. Comment on the speech.

Case 15-2 FINANCING INTERSCHOLASTIC ATHLETICS*

The fiscal problems of interscholastic athletics are of two varieties. The first variety is practical:

1. Atlanta's interscholastic budget has been cut by 7% for 1975–76, while the cost of doing business has jumped at least 7% in that city. Problem: Buying the same product at a higher cost with less money.

* From *Interscholastic Athletic Administration,* vol. 1, no. 4, Fall 1975.

2. Attendance at athletic contests conducted by Elyria, Ohio's two high schools has decreased by 20% in the last two years. Student attendance is down 50%. Problem: Competing for the distracted spectator's dollar.
3. The Chicago Public Schools budget for girls' interscholastics was increased from $203,522 for 1974–75 to $1,052,168 for 1975–76, as the program was expanded from three sports to twelve. Problem: Providing girls deserved opportunities for participation in interscholastic athletics.

The second variety is a matter of perspective—the public's perspective of the role and value of interscholastic athletics and the cost of the program:

4. Cincinnati, Ohio, built a $45 million facility for football and basketball franchises while trimming the city's school budget by $15 million. Problem: Overemphasizing professional sport at the expense of public education.
5. Voters of Springfield, Illinois, defeated two referenda intended in part to remove a deficit of nearly $100,000 which results each year from conducting the interscholastic athletic program. Problem: Overestimating taxpayers' willingness to pay for public institutions and programs.
6. The Board of Education in Philadelphia proposed elimination of junior high school, junior varsity, cadet, and intramural programs in 1975–76, in order to save $686,000 in a $500 million public school budget. Problem: Underestimating the benefits of athletic competition at subvarsity levels.

Athletic directors can do little to remove the practical problems. Inflation is a factor over which they have no control; one can only mitigate its damages on the athletic budget through fund-raising and cost-saving plans, some of which are discussed in this issue. Dwindling gate receipts may be a sociological factor which is bigger than the individual athletic director. . . . And the matter of expanding girls programs should be accepted not as a problem, but as a challenge—a movement which is long overdue.

The problems of public perspective, although enormous, may be more manageable. Recent events indicate they are; for although the athletic budget has been the fiscal whipping boy for school administrators and the public in some communities, other communities have provided interscholastic athletics with resounding support in the midst of school financial woes.

In San Francisco, for example, proceeds of a rock concert and 10% of the weekend sales of four department stores were pumped into the Board of Education coffers after it announced immediate suspension of last spring's interscholastic athletic program in order to save $200,000 in a $4 million austerity drive.

Bill Graham, the rock concert coordinator, and Frank Gorny, who stimulated the department stores' donations, did not share the same perspective as members of the San Francisco Board of Education. Their "Let's keep school athletics alive" attitude is a result of the way they look upon the programs. It is their perspective which athletic directors must convey to the general public.

This can be done with emotionalism as well as reason. For example, is it not conceivable voters might become outraged when they realize they are funding a multimillion dollar stadium for a professional sport franchise owned by a millionaire, while they are cutting the education budget for their own children?

Is it not conceivable the people of Kansas City could have been made to revolt against the idea of spending $100 million on professional sports complexes while seeking donations to make ends meet in the public school athletic program?

However, we must also realize taxpayers are tired—tired because there are fewer of them in relation to the total population than at any previous time in history. There are, in fact, fewer taxpayers than public aid beneficiaries today.

Moreover, taxpayers are learning that the more they pay, the more they lose control over their own lives. Increasing government regulation of business, industry, recreation, education, and all other aspects of living demands money; and taxpayers foot the bill.

Of all the taxes the public pays, the local property taxes and referenda which support schools are most within the public's control and are, therefore, the taxes it can most easily reject when it is fed up. This is already happening in communities across the country.

Therefore, athletic directors must go beyond emotionalism to present to the public a solid, rational case—refuting arguments that give the public a perspective which is different from their own and supporting arguments which might provide the public with a new perspective.

The typical argument for elimination of interscholastic athletics is the great expense which benefits few students in a nonessential program in terms of the educational process. The argument is based on three misconceptions.

First, the interscholastic athletic program is not expensive. The portion of the total school budget allocated for athletic programs is almost embarrassing:

Atlanta, Georgia—1%
La Crosse, Wisconsin—.5 of 1%
Madison, Wisconsin—.69 of 1%
Philadelphia, Pennsylvania—.25 of 1%
San Francisco, California—.38 of 1%

A survey conducted by the National School Boards Association found the portion of the total school budget devoted to athletics to be between .6 of 1% in a wealthy surburban community to 5% in a small city.

Second, the interscholastic athletic program long ago stopped being beneficial to only a few students. Schools that typically offered two or three sports for boys in the 1940s now sponsor nine or ten sports for boys and nearly as many for girls.

Two suburban Chicago athletic directors who keep accurate records have independently found just over 50% of the student body of their schools to be involved in the athletic program either as players, managers, trainers, or cheerleaders. The National School Boards Association reports from 9.5% (industrial city) to 46% (rural area) of the student body to be actual participants in the interscholastic athletic program.

Third, the interscholastic program is as essential to the educational process of many young people as any other part of the curriculum. Some students can be reached best or perhaps only through mathematics while some are reached through music and some through football or gymnastics. Some students will mature and establish character during a disciplined study of biology, others through dedication to baseball or track.

"Sports provide a sense of belonging to something," according to Vernon Young, Athletic Director at Philadelphia's Franklin High School. "I think if kids belong to something in school, they're less likely to belong to the wrong things outside of school."

"Games are an immensely socializing influence," according to California sports columnist Charles McCabe. "At the school level it is even true, in the words of the old platitude, that they contribute to the growth of character. The experience of winning and, more importantly, of losing, is one of the most important things schooling can give."

Mission (California) High School basketball coach, Ernie McNealy, states: "At Mission, most of the youngsters come from low socioeconomic areas, poverty areas. The only thing that keeps them in class is basketball, track, or some other sport. Take that away and you're turning them back on the streets."

According to *Philadelphia Inquirer* sportswriter, Don McKee: "Sports always has been one of the great leveling influences in schools, a means of generating contacts between students of different economic, religious, and racial backgrounds."

"That, surely, is what our schools should be all about—promoting a sense of understanding about others. Sports, handled properly, is one way to accomplish that."

In addition to these socializing influences, athletics have been proven to stimulate academic achievement. Many studies substantiate this, and one of the earliest (1969) found that athletes averaged better marks than non-athletes in all subgroupings (white-collar family, blue-collar family, college-bound, non-college-bound, upper half of class, lower half of class). In fact, the researchers wrote, ". . . . the boys who usually have the most trouble in school are precisely the ones who seem to benefit most from taking part in sports."

"It would seem," the researchers also wrote, "that interscholastic athletics serves a democratizing or equalizing function. It represents a vehicle for upward mobility."

Moreover, the athletic program is a cohesive force in many communities. It stimulates interest in school activities by nonparticipating students and townspeople. An athletic event often provides the forum where the community becomes aware of other school activities and may be moved to support them. The people who support athletics tend to support the whole school program and are willing to pay for it. According to Gene Calhoun, past president of the Madison, Wisconsin, Board of Education, "If you lost athletics, you would lose one of the best supportive pillars. You would lose people who support the whole budget."

Al Cancler, Athletic Director at Philadelphia's Mastbaum High School, says, ". . . a good sports program can provide a glue for the school. It helps pull everything closer together. . . ."

Interscholastic athletic programs are not educational frills, but educational staples. The money spent on athletics is not an educational extravagance, but an educational bargain. Athletics are successful as educational tools—successful because instructors and participants interact in emotional situations where they are visibly and measurably accountable for their performances. Athletics may be the most economical way of reaching and affecting positively great numbers of boys and girls, as well as the community.

It is the duty of high school athletic administrators to present this perspective to the people of their community. The economical efficiency of educating boys and girls through interscholastic athletics can be substantiated and is something in which athletic directors can take great pride.

QUESTION:

1. Comment on the article.

Case 15-3 PETERS: NO MONEY CRISIS IN ATHLETICS*

Could a high school financial crisis happen in Little Rock?

It's no longer a joking matter. It's something to look into. It has happened in St. Louis, San Francisco, Philadelphia and now in Miami.

The San Francisco Board of Education recently cut high school athletics in a budget-saving move. They later found an error had been made in bookkeeping. The high school programs in St. Louis are very close to being eliminated. Donations and funds aided a Philadelphia crisis after athletic funds were chopped from the budget. A decline in football attendance has started to hurt Miami's program.

Why not Little Rock?

Little Rock is presently standing on solid ground. But for years the ground was steady in St. Louis, San Francisco, Philadelphia and Miami.

The financial situation is severe in many of the larger cities because the bulk of their money needed to run a high school athletic program comes from football.

"A crisis like that could happen, but not as long as we're making money," said Little Rock athletic director Raymond Peters "And this was an unusual season. The Little Rock schools finished one-and-two in both football and basketball. Attendance was up."

"The senior high level is in the black. But we'll always need some help for our junior high and middle school programs."

Why?

"They don't draw," said Peters. "The busing hurts us there. Up until then (busing) we always made our way. They don't draw, but their equipment, and they've got to have it, costs the same."

Is it possible for one school to go into the red financially?

"Yes and no," said Peters. "All of our money for our athletic programs comes out of one pot. Let's take this example: Central and Hall are operating in the black. Parkview is in the red. We keep separate

* Taken from an article in *Arkansas Gazette,* Sunday, April 20, 1975. Writte[n] by Wadie Moore, Jr.

books on all the schools, but Parkview will be able to continue on its feet until it leaves the red."

"They borrow. It's just like a bank. We'll borrow from Hall and Central but we won't show it on the black figures. That's on a separate sheet. Then when Parkview is able to operate in the black we'll return the money that they've borrowed from Hall and Central."

"That way everyone is able to operate on the same level. There's no set budget for the schools and they've been told to lean a little with what they buy."

Top-Ranked Teams

Parkview was No. 1 in the state in football last fall with an 11–0 record. Central was second in the state with a 10–1–1 mark. On at least three occasions during the football season, Quigley Stadium was at near capacity or overflowing.

The same was true in basketball. Central wound up No. 1 in the state with a 27–1 record. Little Rock Hall was second with a 22–3 mark. Capacity crowds were a natural on Tuesday and Friday for those two teams.

"Basketball can carry its way," said Peters. "Track is a total loss. Actually, we always hope to have a good football and basketball season to take care of track."

"And this year was unusual. We had some of the largest high school games since I've been here in Arkansas. They say that before my time they were pretty big when Pine Bluff and Little Rock used to play. It must have been some kind of crowd."

Has a financial crisis ever hit Little Rock's athletic program?

One Crisis Before

"Once since I've been here," said Peters, "The school district had to come to our rescue in the late 1950s. They bailed us out the year that the schools were closed."

"We didn't have a slush fund. There was nothing set aside for a crisis. At least not to my knowledge. Today I believe we could handle it."

Raymond Peters is often criticized for being a penny-pincher. He laughs about that today after hearing towns like St. Louis, San Francisco, Philadelphia and Miami.

"That's why we've got all of the money in one pot and not divided, and not with a budget," said Peters. "If a team had a certain budget they would probably try to spend every penny of that money during that school year. That's not what we're looking for. I like to see this extra money carried over into the next school year."

"We're going to face a year when one of the Little Rock schools will find it hard to operate. That's why we've got it in a pot. To help out like a bank. What I try to impress on our coaches is to save and to have some money for those lean years."

And the effect of high prices?

'Already Tough'

"With the rate of equipment costs going up, things could start to get tough on us," said Peters. "It's already tough on us. It's already tough as far as I'm concerned."

"But we've only changed the gate admission once in the last four years. We changed the adult tickets from $1.50 to $2. We left the student price at $1 at the gate and 75 cents in advance. You know the kids won't buy those advance tickets. That quarter doesn't mean that much to them."

It does to Raymond Peters. He counts every penny. That's one reason why Little Rock might not join the ranks of San Francisco, St. Louis, Philadelphia and Miami. Peters is a banker you can trust.

Case 15-4 COLLEGE FOOTBALL: THE STATE'S MULTIMILLION DOLLAR RELIGION*

It has been said that the two dominant religions in Oklahoma are Baptists and football—not necessarily in that order.

But just as devout Southern Baptists fully expect to get to Heaven, devout Oklahoma football fans fully expect their teams to win, and win big.

A "winning" season at Oklahoma is 11–0 and a victory in the Orange Bowl. There were some grumblings this season when Coach Barry Switzer went 8–2–1 while playing only four seniors on the starting teams.

But the cost is high. "Big Time" football doesn't come cheap.

In a special report for the November issue, the *Oklahoma Business* magazine took a look at the amount the two state schools shell out for winning football.

The amounts given to the magazine by the respective schools for football were surprisingly moderate—$1.9 million in fiscal 1975–76 at Oklahoma and $1.6 million for OSU in the same period.

However, both schools readily admitted the amounts all depend upon which figures are listed under which columns.

For example, all revenues from Big Eight TV and bowl games are lumped into the "general" category at OSU. So it is more accurate to look at the entire sports budget which comes to $5.1 million at Oklahoma and 2.7 million at OSU.

Football accounts for about 75% of the revenue at each school, with the remaining 25% coming from basketball, wrestling, and the other sports.

If you take the combined $7.8 million revenue at both schools, only 38 corporations in Oklahoma during fiscal 1975–76 had higher revenues.

Like any large industry, Oklahoma football has spawned many smaller feeder industries, ranging from sweatshirts to game broadcasts.

The Oklahoma news network shells out over $40,000 per year for the exclusive radio rights to the games. The group resells the games to 150 regular stations each week and up to 400 stations, including the Armed Forces Network, for special games.

Another contract gives KTUL–TV in Tulsa the rights for the OU playback, narrated by Switzer.

For OSU, WKY radio and KTVY television in Oklahoma City had the contracts for the 1976 season for the games and playbacks.

* *Tulsa Daily World,* December 5, 1976.

"We lost a few radio markets when the Communists took over Viet Nam," said ONN general manager Kenney Belford, "though we thought we might not even lose them—after all, you would think that the Big Red would fit right in."

One of the largest beneficiaries, of course, is the winning coach.

Switzer, in addition to his annual $33,000 salary from the university, has outside income that pushes his estimated total to near $100,000.

His enterprises include full rights to the OU playbacks, a daily five-minute statewide radio show; a weekly, during the season, television show, plus endorsements for products ranging from air conditioning to cars. He also is a partner in a new life insurance company. The television show alone nets Switzer a reported $15,000.

Switzer's narrated game replay is shown in Houston, Tulsa, Fort Worth, Dallas, Oklahoma City, Wichita Falls, Tex., Lafayette, La., Ada and Lawton, Okla., plus alum groups in Singapore, Lebanon, London, Brussels, Norway, Amsterdam and Tokyo.

Stanley also has a television show with a potential audience of 3.5 million, but his other benefits have yet to approach Switzer's.

The University of Oklahoma also is unique in that not one dime of legislative appropriated money goes to the athletic departments.

The department is completely self-supporting, not only in actual cash outlays but also in the fact it pays rent, utilities, and all repairs on the structures it built in the first place.

Plus the OU department foots the entire bill for women's athletics—$140,000 for fiscal 1976–77, and still pays $20,000 toward the intramural program.

The situation is somewhat different at OSU. Women's intercollegiate sports are not funded by the athletic department, being instead under the school's Physical Education Department.

Also, the school receives about $100,000 in state money to help defray salary expenses, which totaled $378,000 in 1975–76.

The department also does not do all of its own construction. Iba Hall, the athletic dorm, was built, and is run, by the university. The department also does not pay any utilities.

The attitudes of the two departments also are different. At Oklahoma, football is "big business." At OSU, the school is "big business" and football is a large share of that business.

QUESTION:

1. Comment on the article.

Case 15-5 COLLEGE SPORTS SEEKS NATIONAL REMEDIES*

Still trim and his 1950's crewcut streaked with gray, Elroy (Crazylegs) Hirsch has middle-aged gracefully and prospered professionally, head of a nearly $3-million-a-year business called the University of Wisconsin athletic department.

But like others in business, the former brilliant pass catcher is feeling

* Mike O'Brien, *Arkansas Gazette,* April 22, 1975.

a tightening economic crunch. He is convinced that unless immediate national remedies are found, insolvency or bankruptcy may drastically alter the structure and shape of major college athletics.

"I think we're going to be forced to believe that, with the money crisis the way it is, it's that (national remedies) or go broke," Hirsch said. "I think we've done about all we can do at this point. We're down to a point where if we cut any further, we'll affect the quality of the program."

Hirsch is prepared to recommend this:

Possible reduction in scholarships for income-producing sports.
Reduction, or elimination, of scholarships, for nonincome sports.
That the school, not the athletic department, finance women's sports.
A halt to scheduling of football games a decade in advance.
Sharp cuts in recruiting costs.

Wisconsin's plight may not be as severe as many other universities. The football team, which finances 95% of the athletic program, has been among the nation's top five in home attendance for several years, and the school now fields a winning team.

Projected athletic expenses for the year ending June 30 are $2.7 to $2.8 million. Hirsch projects a $40,000 to $60,000 profit, in contrast to a $200,000 deficit six years ago.

"But we're at the mercy of how good we are and the weather," he said. Even if the weatherman is kind and the Badgers win big, Hirsch believes inflation will cause costs to surpass revenues in two to three years.

"We can't keep going at the pace we are," he said. "There's no way, unless we keep raising ticket prices, and that's impossible. I think what we're going to have to do is get legislation on a national level through the NCAA so Division I colleges will all play under the same rules."

"For instance, by 1977 we all have to be down to 105 scholarships (at one time) in football. . . . There is a lot of sympathy we can go down to 90 and still put out first-class football," he said, adding he believed basketball grants could be cut from 18 to 15 and hockey from 23 to 20.

"That's the three income sports," he said. "Now, we're going to have to cut the nonincome sports. If they don't produce the revenue for you, we can't afford the grants in aid. . . . Now that's looking at it in a very cold, businesslike way."

Hirsch emphasized the last thing he wants to do is drop any nonincome sports, such as baseball, track, golf and swimming. But he is prepared to drop scholarships for them "if it went nationally."

Not an Island

"I can't be an island," he said. ". . . I'd be crucified for it. If the Big Ten went to it, I'd go along with the Big Ten."

"Now, the Big Ten may be an island and it may hurt them for two or three years, but I think the rest of the country would say, 'Look what the Big Ten did, and look, they're solvent.' I think the other conferences would go along."

He said a problem that develops is with schools which have developed strong teams in minor sports, such as Indiana and Southern Cal in swimming, Stanford in tennis, Wake Forest and Houston in golf. Of those schools, he said: "We don't have the right to go in and by legislation destroy that program. We're trying to find a formula to overcome it."

Then there is the major problem caused by pending new federal guidelines that would require colleges to offer equal athletic opportunities to women or face the loss of all federal funds.

Hirsch said he strongly favors viable programs for Wisconsin's ten intercollegiate women's sports. But he thinks the college administration, and not his department, should pay for them.

"You can't throw it on the men's program," he said. "Women deserve a program, but I think funding should come from a source other than men's intercollegiate athletics, or we're going to have to drop sports."

Scholarships Down

Wisconsin's 10 nonincome men's sports receive 20 scholarships a year, down from 34 two years ago, at a saving of $92,000.

Hirsch also dislikes the practice of scheduling football games far in advance. "Now that's ridiculous," he said.

"One thing I'm going to propose is a moratorium on scheduling and see if there isn't some legal way we can do away with all these contracts that have been made 12 to 14 years in advance. . . .

"How do you know you'll be competitive at that time?" he said. "We have no way of knowing in 10 or 12 years if we can play a Nebraska or Oklahoma or Southern Cal. . . . It would be much more intelligent for everybody to just schedule four years ahead with your present class of students you have to work with."

Hirsch adamantly disagrees with those who advocate a return to one-platoon football for economic reasons, claiming it couldn't save money unless the number of scholarships were dropped significantly.

16

FINANCIAL PLANNING, ACQUISITION, AND EVALUATION

The typical finance function of any organization can be analyzed by the managerial functions of planning, acquiring, and evaluating the financial resources. The administrator can plan for financial resources using two types of budgets—operating and capital. Since an operating budget charts the income and outgo of money, it helps an administrator plan for the revenues and expenses of an athletic program. It serves as a short-term plan (usually for a year or less) for estimating the revenue needed for survival and for allocating funds to various branches of an athletic program. After the operating budget is approved, it may be used to compare actual expenditures and revenues with budgeted expenditures and revenues and then to act accordingly in light of the desired objectives.

A high school operating budget can illustrate the revenue and expense planning for an athletic program consisting of nine sports. The operating budget is broken down into an overall budget and then detailed budgets for each sport which, when combined with each other, make up the total operating budget for an imaginary Westside High School as illustrated in Table 16–1.

Tables 16–2 and 16–3 exhibit a detailed breakdown of direct expenses for Westside's football and basketball program. Each other sport or activity has a similar breakdown of supplies expense, salaries, meals, transportation, and other miscellaneous expenses directly associated with the sport or other activity. The indirect expenses of interest costs, depreciation, concessions, maintenance, and others are not budgeted directly but may be allocated to each sport by other cost accounting methods.

The capital budget is usually reserved for major pieces of equipment

Table 16-1 Westside High School Athletic Budget for the Year

	Estimated revenues		
Football			
Season tickets		$ 6,000	
Reserved seats		14,000	
General admission		12,000	
Other jv, jr. high		8,000	
Total			$ 40,000
Basketball			20,000
Swimming			1,000
Wrestling			1,000
Hockey			4,000
Other sports			1,000
Student fees			15,000
Other income			
Parking	$1,000		
Radio	2,000		
Rental fees	6,000		
Investment income	1,000		
Other income total			10,000
Concessions			20,000
Donations from boosters			18,000
Subsidy from school board			25,000
Total			$155,000
	Estimated expenditures		
Administration		$ 20,000	
Football		30,000	
Basketball		21,000	
Swimming		6,000	
Wrestling		8,000	
Hockey		4,000	
Other sports (baseball, golf, tennis, track)		20,000	
Maintenance		9,000	
Bond interest		6,000	
Depreciation on facilities		10,000	
Concessions		15,000	
Miscellaneous		1,000	
Total		$150,000	
	Summary		
Total estimated revenues		$155,000	
Total estimated expenses		150,000	
Total estimated profit		$ 5,000	

Table 16-2 Direct Football Budget Expenditures

Supplies and minor equipment		
Game jerseys (home and away), pants, shoulder pads, helmets, hip pads, jaw pads, laces, practice jerseys, mouth guards, hats, T-shirts, cleats, travel bags, decals		$ 3,000
Other supplies		
Awards, weights, training room supplies, audio-visual aids, cleaning, laundry, films, papers, misc.		6,000
Salaries of coaches allocated to athletics		11,000
Wages paid		
Officials	$1000	
Ticket sellers	400	
Ticket takers	600	
Ushers	500	
Press box	300	
Policemen	2800	
Parking attendants	400	
Supervisors, end zone, restrooms, band, etc.	500	
Hourly help	500	
Total		7,000
Meals, transportation, lodging		
5 away games		3,000
Totals		
Supplies and minor equipment	$ 3,000	
Other supplies	6,000	
Coaches' salaries	11,000	
Wages for games	7,000	
Meals, transportation, lodging	3,000	
Total	$30,000	

improvements in facilities, and expansion of facilities. These capital im provements are long term and are financed by means other than norma operations.

ACQUISITION OF CAPITAL

For long-term purposes there are several sources of capital; most hav been discussed in the section concerning the financial strategies for athleti facilities.

The most common way to finance long-term assets that can be mort gaged is by issuing bonds or, in the case of professional teams, by addin private capital. The interest rate in floating a bond issue, the length of th payback period, and the sources of revenue that will repay the principa and interest are of major concern.

Money for major pieces of equipment and major additions to the athletic facilities often comes from private donations. These donations are usually obtained from booster clubs, from individual donors, and from the sale of ticket preferences associated with a donation.

Assessments on tuitions paid by students are another means of raising money. A nonvoluntary assessment usually provides the financial resources to be used for a variety of purposes. Normally, students have a favorable attitude toward the athletic program since it provides an appealing form of entertainment.

Some college athletic programs have trust funds or reserve funds. These funds are invested in securities that yield either interest or dividends, and serve as sources of capital for the program. Trust funds may be received as a special contribution to the athletic program from the estate of an alumnus or from any sort of donation for special athletic purposes. If the program maintains a depreciation reserve fund, the proceeds from it may be invested. Both the trust funds and other reserve funds are excellent sources of capital for long-term uses.

Another approach to long-term funding is a joint funding program, normally consisting of the school, community, and local or state government. If these organizations contribute money to finance an athletic facil-

Table 16-3 Direct Basketball Budget Expenditures

Supplies and minor equipment		
Shoes, trunks, jerseys, socks, supporters, balls, bags, laces, nets		$1,900
Other supplies		
Awards, first aid, film, cleaning, laundry, etc.		1,000
Coaches' salaries allocated to athletics		13,000
Wages paid		
Officials	$1,000	
Ticket seller and taker	500	
Supervisors	500	
Police	500	
Hourly help	600	
Total		3,100
Meals, transportation, lodging		
Away games		2,000
Totals		
Supplies and minor equipment	$ 1,900	
Other supplies	1,000	
Coaches' salaries	13,000	
Wages paid	3,100	
Meals, transportation, etc.	2,000	
Total	$21,000	

Objective: To Plan for and Acquire Capital

Factors	Strength	Weakness
1. Does the program use financial budgeting?		
1.1 Total operating budget		
1.2 Revenue budget		
1.3 Expense budget		
2. Does the program use a capital budget?		
2.1 For facilities		
2.2 For equipment		
Overall Evaluation:		
3. Does the program use any of the following sources of capital for long-term purposes?		
3.1 Bonds/stocks		
3.2 Donations		
3.3 Booster clubs		
3.4 Student assessments		
3.5 Trust funds		
3.6 Reserve funds		
3.7 Joint funding		
3.8 Private owners' equity capital		
3.9 Other		
4. Does the program use any of the following sources of capital for short-term purposes?		
4.1 Normal operating profits		
4.2 Financial subsidies		
4.3 Borrowing from banks		
4.4 Sale of season tickets		
4.5 Other		
Overall Evaluation:		

ity, they can use the facility jointly. Sometimes joint funding is the only way to build a facility since each individual organization might not justify spending the money for a huge facility that often stands idle.

Most professional teams finance a long-term asset by having the owners contribute equity or ownership capital from their private savings. If the organization is a corporation, additional capital stock can be issued to the owners in exchange for their equity capital. If the organization is a partnership or a single proprietorship, then the owners' financial contribution is credited to their owners' equity account balance.

There may be other sources of long-term capital, but the major ones are bonds or stock, donations, student assessments, trust funds, joint funding by community and state governments, and private equity capital (in case of professional teams).

To obtain short-term capital (capital usually required for less than a year), the administrator must rely on normal operating profits, sale of season tickets, short-term bank notes, or subsidies from other funds.

Operating profits are usually the major source of financing for athletic programs. It must be admitted, however, that many athletic programs rely on subsidies from other sources to maintain their continuity. Profits are the result of increasing the program's revenues and/or reducing the operating expenses of providing revenue. The strategies to increase revenue have already been discussed. Although there are ways to reduce expenses, it is much easier to increase revenue to provide the short-term source of capital needed for continuity of the program.

Financial subsidies to athletic programs are common because athletics were initially financed by either private or public subsidies. In both professional and nonprofessional sports, it is necessary to find someone to support a financially losing program. It is unlikely that fans will support a team that does not win. Consequently, if the program is to maintain continuity, capital must come from a private donor or a scholastic budget. Within the past forty years, athletics has found that it can financially support itself at the gate. Professional athletic teams have led the way, followed by self-supporting major college athletic programs; in the future probably lower division colleges, junior colleges, and high schools will be able to support themselves as well. Until that time arrives, and until the profession of athletic administration is accepted, there will continue to be some sort of financial subsidy to provide short-term sources of capital for professional and scholastic programs. Whether athletics is worth it must be determined by the local citizens. The benefit/cost analysis to determine the value of athletics (suggested in the first chapter) is a guide for that decision-making process.

Often local banking institutions will provide athletic programs with short-term loans if the athletic program can demonstrate its ability to repay principal plus interest.

The sale of season tickets six months before the season actually begins is also a source of short-term capital. Having the money in the coffers for six months provides an extra source of capital that can pay expenses occurring before a season starts.

Regardless of the source of capital—either long-term or short-term—the athletic program must be financed. Planning for and acquiring capital are major functions performed by an athletic administrator.

EVALUATION OF FINANCIAL OPERATIONS

Several traditional accounting controls help the administrator to evaluate the program's finances. The first is to have a double entry system of accounting. For every debit there must be a credit. When cash is debited (increased), there should be a corresponding credit showing the source of that cash increase. When expenses are debited (increased), there should be a corresponding credit showing the source of the expense. Money and other assets should be accounted for by a double-entry system. Otherwise there could be some shady dealings.

In addition, an annual financial audit should be made, preferably by an outside person who can render an independent opinion concerning the consistency of financial operations and the financial position of the athletic program. When an athletic administrator is handling other people's money, an audit will protect the administrator from criticism of the general public and give the general public a feeling of confidence about the financial integrity of the athletic program. A financial audit can serve both of these purposes.

If financial operations are to be evaluated, then monthly, quarterly, and annual financial statements are necessary. Proper financial planning and controls demand the availability of information for intelligent decision making and for auditing the financial operations of the program. Financial statements serve these purposes if they are properly prepared according to a double-entry system, if they are written by qualified accountants, and if they utilize generally accepted accounting techniques.

MARGINAL ANALYSES OF VARIOUS SPORTS AND ACTIVITIES

Most interscholastic athletic programs consist of several different sports, such as football, basketball, and track. The income and expense statement is subdivided according to individual sports so the administrator can determine the profitability of each. If a sport shows a loss on the income statement, the administrator must decide whether to retain or to eliminate that sport or activity. (In larger cities, the athletic director may have the income and expenses subdivided according to high schools, some showing a loss, others a profit). For example, suppose the yearly revenues and expenses were as shown on the next page.

Basketball is operating at a loss of $1,000 and football is operating at a profit of $10,000. If basketball were discontinued, the revenue would be reduced by $20,000. However, the fixed expenses of $13,000 would not be discontinued, but the variable expenses of $8,000 would be eliminated. The net effect of discontinuing basketball would be to cut the profit by $12,000 and have a combined loss of $3000 for both sports. Would this be a wise decision? No, because basketball did provide a gross margin of $12,000 to cover part of its fixed costs of $13,000. In other words, the $20,000 worth of

	Football	Basketball	Combined total
Revenues	$40,000	$20,000	$60,000
Fixed expenses	11,000	13,000	24,000
Variable expenses	19,000	8,000	27,000
Total expenses	$30,000	$21,000	$51,000
Net Profit (Loss)	$10,000	($ 1,000)	$ 9,000

basketball revenue less the $8,000 variable expenses would provide enough margin to cover part of the overhead that is going to continue whether basketball is discontinued or not. In order to arrive at this conclusion, it was necessary to make this marginal analysis.

It is necessary to establish criteria for allocating funds or expenses to each sport. Suppose a school had $15,000 revenue from student fees. How much should be allocated to football and how much to basketball and how much to other sports? One way to determine this is to add up the prices multiplied by the number of events for each sport, establish a ratio, and allocate the $15,000 on the basis of the ratio. How can a $10,000 depreciation expense be allocated to the various sports? The obvious way would be to determine the costs of the basketball, football, hockey, and other facilities, establish a ratio, and allocate funds on the basis of the relative cost. The allocation may be complicated, but it should be done to segregate the revenues and expenses of each sport and to determine a marginal analysis. The same approach can be used to allocate revenue or expenses of products and services such as concessions, radio, TV, and parking

BREAK-EVEN ANALYSIS

In a break-even analysis it is assumed that the expenses of a particular sport can be classified as fixed expenses and variable expenses. Fixed expenses, such as depreciation of the facility, coaches' salaries, and insurance, do not vary with a season's revenues. On the other hand, variable expenses, such as commissions for concessionaires, officials' salaries, and the rental of facilities, vary directly with the season's revenues. The total revenues for an entire season—including ticket sales and revenue from concessions—must exceed both the fixed and variable expenses if the sport is to make a profit. This relationship can be stated as follows: Revenues minus the sum of the fixed and variable expenses equals net profit (before income taxes). The point at which the season's revenue is exactly equal to the total of fixed and variable expenses is called the break-even point. At this point, the net profit is zero. This relationship can also be stated in a formula:

Let R = Season's Game Revenues at the Break-Even Point
Then Break-Even is at that point where:
R = Fixed Expenses + Variable Expenses

For example, if the fixed expenses for a season of 12 home games in basketball were $15,000, and if the variable expenses equaled roughly one-third of the total revenue, the break-even formula can be used to find R.

$$R = \$15,000 + \tfrac{1}{3} R$$
$$R - \tfrac{1}{3} R = \$15,000$$
$$\tfrac{2}{3} R = \$15,000$$
$$R = \$22,500$$

If the ticket prices were $1.50 each, if concessions averaged $.75 for each customer per game, and if the break-even point were $22,500, then 10,000 fans would have to attend during a season before the break-even point would be reached (approximately 875 customers per game).

If the fixed expenses increased to $21,000 and other variables remained the same, the formula can be used to determine the break-even point.

$$R = \$21,000 + \tfrac{1}{3} R$$
$$\tfrac{2}{3} R = \$21,000$$
$$R = \$31,500$$

The break-even point can be computed for each game, for game concessions, and for other sources of revenue such as parking or TV.

For an individual game, the total season fixed expenses must be divided by the number of games to determine a per game fixed expense. The officials' salary, which is more or less uniform, must be added to the fixed expense. The coaches' salaries and the players' salaries (in case of professionals) would be fixed expenses. The game supplies are also considered a fixed expense. Practically all expenses are fixed, with the exception of concession supplies, which vary according to the number of customers. Consequently, the break-even point is the approximate total of all fixed expenses per game.

The break-even analysis becomes a valuable tool to use in short-term decision making—the administrator can predict how many fans must attend for the team to break even. It may be used to predict break-even point if ticket prices are raised, if fixed expenses are cut, or if variable expenses are changed.

PERCENTAGE ANALYSIS

Another common financial tool is the percentage analysis. This is often used on the income and expense statement. All expenses are usually listed in actual dollars, and then each expense is listed as a percentage of the total revenue (100%). For example, the operating statement for a professional football league is shown in Table 16–4.

Analysis reveals that approximately 64% of the income is derived from ticket sales of regular and preseason games, as well as postseason games

Table 16-4 Professional Football League: Combined Statement of Income and Expenses for the Year (Dollars in Thousands)

Income		*Percentage*
Ticket sales	$109,200	56.8
Television and radio	63,400	33.0
Postseason games	13,500	7.0
Concessions	3,700	1.9
Others	2,500	1.3
Total income	$192,300	100.0
Operating expenses		
Player costs	81,500	42.4
Team expenses	33,500	17.4
Stadium costs	12,400	6.4
League costs	14,800	7.7
General administration	27,800	14.5
Other	2,300	1.2
Total operating expenses	$172,300	89.6
Net income before income taxes	20,000	10.4
Income taxes	$ 10,000	5.2
Net income	$ 10.000	5.2

Television accounts for 33% of the income. The remainder comes from concessions and other small enterprises.

Player costs, including salaries, bonuses, insurance, medical benefits, pensions, and other taxes, account for 42% of the total expense. Team costs (including stadium and league fees) account for 32% of the total. General administration of the teams in the league accounts for 15%. Income taxes are about 5%. Profits are 5.2% of the total $109,000,000.

This year's percentage analysis could be compared to the previous year's analysis to see if there are any significant changes. This is shown in Table 16–5. Ticket sales have taken a slight dip, but income from television has increased. Player costs have risen; other expenses have remained about the same. However, net profit has dropped from 7% to 3.0%, then risen to 5.2% of total revenues.

Percentage analysis is also useful in comparing two teams' financial performances. For example, the professional football league could compare the operating profits of the top eight teams with those of the middle ten or the bottom eight teams. This is shown in Table 16–6. It becomes apparent that those teams with the highest operating profits have the greatest income from enterprises such as concessions and postseason games. It is also apparent that player costs, team costs, stadium costs, and administrative costs are less for those teams with higher operating profits. The percentage analysis, when used to compare expenses, years, and teams, can be a valuable financial tool.

Table 16-5 Professional Football League: Percentage Analyses Three Years

Income	*This year*	*Last year*	*Previous year*
Ticket sales	56.8%	55.0%	62.1%
Television and radio	33.0	34.5	27.5
Postseason games	7.0	7.1	6.5
Concessions	1.9	2.0	2.0
Others	1.3	1.4	1.9
Total income	100.0	100.0	100.0
Operating expenses			
Player costs	42.4	45.4	39.2
Team expenses	17.4	16.9	16.9
Stadium costs	6.4	5.9	6.1
League costs	7.7	7.9	7.2
General administration	14.5	15.1	15.5
Other	1.2	1.8	1.1
Total operating expenses	89.6	94.0	86.0
Net income before taxes	10.4	6.0	14.0
Income taxes	5.2	3.0	7.0
Net income	5.2%	3.0%	7.0%

Table 16-6 Professional Football League: Percentage Analyses of Various Teams' Operating Profits for the Year

Income	*Top eight*	*Middle ten*	*Bottom eight*
Ticket sales	57.0%	56.4%	57.0%
TV and radio	30.6	34.0	34.4
Other income	12.4	9.6	8.6
Total income	100.0	100.0	100.0
Operating expenses			
Player costs	37.2	44.9	45.0
Team expenses	16.5	17.9	18.0
Stadium costs	5.0	5.1	9.7
Administrative	21.5	21.2	24.2
Total operating expenses	80.2	89.1	96.9
Operating profit	19.8%	10.9%	3.1%

RATIO ANALYSIS

Ratio analysis is one of the most common ways to evaluate financial operations. Rates of return are calculated by dividing the net income by any of several denominators: (1) total revenue, (2) total assets, (3) owners' equity. The rate of return on revenues indicates the portion of revenue that is profit. For example, a 5% rate of return on revenue indicates that the program made five cents for each dollar of revenue. This rate of return usually reveals a measure of operational productivity. If the program's operations are productive, the program will have a higher rate of return on revenues than a program that is relatively unproductive (see Table 16–6). However, a 5% rate of return on revenue for an athletic program may be small compared to the profits of a manufacturing firm. Consequently, similar programs must be compared, as shown in Table 16–6.

The rate of return on total assets is a measure of how efficiently the administrator is employing the program's total assets to produce a net income. This can be computed by dividing net income by total assets, and then comparing this figure to figures representing similar programs in previous years. For example, if one professional team had total assets of $5 million and a net income of $200,000, the rate of return on total assets would be 2.5%. Suppose another team had total assets of $6 million and a net income of $300,000. Its rate of return on total assets would be 5%, twice that of the first team.

The rate of return on owners' equity measures how much net profit is being made on the owners' investment. It shows the advisability of investing in an athletic program from the owners' point of view. Armed with the rate of return on equity, an owner or potential investor can compare investing in a particular program with other investment opportunities. For example, if the rate of return on owners' equity is 3%, an owner might wish to withdraw his equity and invest it in a savings and loan company, or in some other program at a higher rate of return.

An abbreviated income and expense statement and a statement of financial condition (balance sheet) for a professional basketball team are presented in Table 16–7.

The rates of return would be as follows:

	Last Year	*This Year*
Return on revenues	3.03%	5.26%
Return on total assets	2.00%	2.82%
Return on owners' equity	2.94%	5.71%

These rates must be interpreted with caution; they should be compared to the rates of similar teams, or to rates from different years to be meaningful.

The payback period is also used to determine the advisability of making a specific investment. It is calculated by dividing the cost of the investment by the expected annual return. The resulting figure is in terms of the number of years that will be required to recover the cost of the investment. This figure is often compared to what is considered an acceptable payback period for a particular type of investment. The ratio can be used to determine whether to buy a piece of equipment by using an annual savings figure instead of an annual return on investment. Usually minor equipment has a payback period of two to three years; larger equipment, five years; and major investments in facilities, ten to twenty years.

The current ratio indicates the financial status of an athletic program, whether the program can pay its current liabilities. The program's suppli-

Table 16-7 Financial Statements for a Professional Basketball Team

Financial condition statement
(Balance sheet as of May 31)

ASSETS	LAST YEAR	THIS YEAR
Current assets		
Cash	$ 175,000	$ 150,000
Marketable securities	1,825,000	1,740,000
Cash and investments	$2,000,000	$1,890,000
Player contracts, current	750,000	1,300,000
Other current assets	250,000	410,000
Total current assets	$3,000,000	$3,600,000
Long-term assets		
Player contracts, long term	500,000	1,750,000
League contracts	200,000	175,000
Fixed assets	75,000	125,000
Other long-term assets	125,000	350,000
Investments	1,100,000	1,100,000
Total	$2,000,000	$3,500,000
Total assets	$5,000,000	$7,100,000
LIABILITIES		
Current liabilities		
Player contracts payable	$ 740,000	$1,100,000
Other players	360,000	300,000
Total current liabilities	$1,100,000	$1,400,000
Long-term liabilities		
Player contracts, long term	$ 400,000	$1,900,000
Other long-term debts	100,000	300,000
Total liabilities	$1,600,000	$3,600,000
Owners' equity		
Capital stock	$2,700,000	$2,700,000
Retained earnings	700,000	800,000
Total equity	$3,400,000	$3,500,000
Total	$5,000,000	$7,100,000

Table 16-7 *(continued)*

Income and expense statement for the fiscal year	LAST YEAR	THIS YEAR
Revenues		
Ticket sales, regular games	$1,900,000	$1,800,000
Exhibition games	100,000	50,000
TV, radio	800,000	800,000
Playoffs	–	750,000
Concessions, net	70,000	80,000
Basketball camps	190,000	180,000
Investments	240,000	140,000
Total revenues	$3,300,000	$3,800,000
Expenses		
Basketball team and games	$2,000,000	$2,300,000
Basketball camps	170,000	150,000
Administration and promotion	600,000	750,000
Other costs	230,000	175,000
Total expenses	$3,000,000	$3,375,000
Net income before taxes	$ 300,000	$ 425,000
Income taxes	200,000	225,000
Net income	$ 100,000	$ 200,000
Additional information		
Earnings per share	$.22	$.42
Price per share	$2½–4½	$4–6
Dividends per share	$.23	$.15

	3 YRS AGO	4 YRS AGO	5 YRS AGO
Revenues	$3,400,000	$3,000,000	$3,100,000
Net income	260,000	122,000	370,000
Earnings per share	$.46	$.21	$.64
Dividends per share	$.23	$.15	$.15
Shareholders' equity	$3,300,000	$3,500,000	$3,500,000

ers, who wish to be paid on time, find this ratio highly significant. Computed by dividing the current assets by the current liabilities, the current ratio is normally considered sound if the ratio is two to one. In the case of the professional basketball team, their current assets for last year, $3,000,000, divided by their current liabilities, $1,100,000, equals a current ratio of 2.7 to 1. This year's current ratio ($3,600,000 ÷ $1,400,000) is 2.57 to 1, a slight drop in liquidity.

Another important indication of liquidity is the quick ratio or the acid test ratio. The primary advantage of this ratio is that it eliminates the less liquid current assets (like inventories and deferred expenses) from the total current assets. It is computed by dividing the total of cash and near-cash (accounts receivable and investments) by the current liabilities. A one-to-one ratio is considered to be financially sound. Last year, the pro team's quick ratio was 1.8 to 1 ($2,000,000 ÷ $1,100,000). This year's quick ratio is 1.35 to 1, a substantial decrease.

Various turnover ratios can be computed. The turnover of owners' equity is an indication of how efficiently the program is managing the equity. It is computed by dividing the total revenue by the owners' equity. Last year, the ratio for the pro basketball team was .97 to 1 ($3,300,000 ÷ $3,400,000). This year it is 1.08 to 1, a slight improvement.

Inventory turnover can be computed by dividing the cost of goods sold by the inventory. This turnover ratio is of particular significance in the case of concessions.

Accounts receivable turnover is a ratio used to evaluate the program's ability to collect its accounts receivable. It is computed by dividing the credit sales by accounts receivable.

Asset turnover indicates how efficiently the program's assets are being used to generate revenues. It is computed by dividing the total revenues by total assets. For the pro team, last year's asset turnover was .6 to 1 ($3,300,000 ÷ $5,000,000). This year it is .53 to 1, a decrease.

The earnings-per-share figure is important to the shareowners of the program. It shows the earning power of the capital stock, and is computed by dividing the net income by the number of shares outstanding. This is not the same figure as dividends per share, which is normally smaller since dividends per share are usually paid from the earnings per share. If the program's dividends are smaller than the earnings, the remainder of the net earnings are held in the retained earnings of the program. For last year, the earnings per share were $.22 while for this year they were $.42, approximately double. The dividends per share last year were $.23 while they were $.15 this year, down from last year when more dividends were paid than earnings.

The price-earnings ratio measures the market price of stock relative to the earnings of the program. From a potential owner's point of view, the price-earnings ratio is very important because it indicates other people's views about the relative worth of the stock. The price-earnings ratio for the pro team this year is from 9.5 to 1 to 14 to 1 ($4–6 per share ÷ $.42 per share).

These ratios must be evaluated by comparing them over time or by comparing them to similar programs. They can be useful in evaluating the financial affairs of an athletic program.

COMPARISON OF ACTUAL TO BUDGET

Probably the most common method of evaluating a financial situation is to compare the actual flow of funds to the budget. If an operating budget is prepared, it can be used to coordinate and evaluate the revenue and expenditure of a program. Variations between actual and budgeted can then

Westside High School

Revenues	Budgeted	Actual	Variance
Football	$ 40,000	$ 45,000	$5,000
Basketball	20,000	21,000	1,000
Other sports	7,000	7,000	-0-
Other income	10,000	11,000	1,000
Student fees	16,000	16,000	-0-
Concessions	20,000	22,000	2,000
Donations	18,000	18,000	-0-
Subsidy	25,000	25,000	
Total revenues	$156,000	$165,000	$9,000

be analyzed to determine the causes of the deviation. For example, when the Westside High School budget is compared to actual operations, the results are summarized as shown above.

A comparison shows that the program generated $9,000 over the amount of revenue estimated on the budget. Two winning seasons in basketball and football attracted more fans, resulting in an increase in other income (parking, most likely) and in concessions (more popcorn, candy, pop).

In similar fashion, the actual expenditures could be compared to budgeted expenditures, perhaps as shown below.

The comparison reveals an extra expense of $3,000 for football, probably associated with extra expenses involved in winning. Other sports and miscellaneous, however, did not spend as much as budgeted. More money ($1,000) was spent on concessions, but it was offset by $2,000 increase in revenues. Maintenance was $1,000 more than budgeted, probably caused by increased attendance.

Expenditures	Budgeted	Actual	Variance
Administration	$ 20,000	$ 20,000	-0-
Football	30,000	33,000	$3,000
Basketball	21,000	21,000	-0-
Other sports	38,000	37,000	(1,000)
Maintenance	9,000	10,000	1,000
Bond interest	6,000	6,000	-0-
Depreciation	10,000	10,000	-0-
Concessions	15,000	16,000	1,000
Miscellaneous	1,000	500	(500)
Total	$150,000	$153,500	$3,500

Objective: To Evaluate Financial Operations		
Analysis	**Strength**	**Weakness**
1. Does the athletic administrator actually use any of the following financial evaluation tools?		
1.1 Marginal analyses		
1.2 Break-even analyses		
1.3 Percentage analyses		
1.31 Over time		
1.32 With other programs		
1.4 Ratio analysis		
1.41 Over time		
1.42 With other programs		
1.5 Budget variances		
1.6 Others		
2. Does the program have:		
2.1 Double entry accounting		
2.2 Annual financial audit		
2.3 Financial statements		
Overall Evaluation:		

This simplified analysis of budget versus actual can be used in a variety of ways. Expenses and revenues can be controlled by comparing the actual situation with the budget and analyzing the resulting variations.

An athletic administrator should use a variety of financial analyses to administer a program.

CHAPTER SUMMARY

This chapter suggests the use of operating and capital budgets for planning the financial operations of an athletic program. It also suggests that various sources of capital may be used to acquire funds for long-term purposes: bonds/stocks, donations, booster clubs, student assessments, trust funds, reserve funds, joint funding, and private owners' capital. For short-term purposes, the following sources may be used: normal operating profits, financial subsidies, bank loans, and season ticket sales.

Various financial analyses can be used to evaluate the financial operations of an athletic program. This will help the administrator make decisions and take actions to accomplish financial objectives. These analyses include a double-entry accounting system, annual financial audits, and financial statements. Various tools can be used to evaluate the financial situation of an athletic program: marginal analyses, break-even analyses, percentage analyses, ratio analyses, and variance analyses.

Case 16-1 MSU'S FINANCIAL SITUATION*

Sid Davis, the athletic director of MSU, called a meeting of the athletic committee. At the meeting, he explained the situation facing MSU's athletic program. MSU had been placed on probation by the NCAA for at least two years. In addition the financial picture was bleak, the program having had a net loss of approximately $100,000 for each of the past three years. Revenue from football, the only profitable revenue-producing sport, was off significantly because of poor attendance. The President of MSU was giving Sid a bad time because alumni were pressing for better financial results.

MSU was a private school located in Metro City where two other major universities were located as well as a major professional team contending each year in the NFL. In addition there were a couple of smaller junior colleges. Within 100 miles there were three other major universities competing for attendance.

The costs for the athletic program were rising due to factors beyond MSU's control—financial aid costs were set by the fees of the institution, salaries and wages and travel costs were rising because of inflation, and if MSU planned to compete in the conference it would be unwise to have fewer players than the maximum set by the NCAA rules. The size of its coaching staff had increased, primarily because other schools in the conference also increased their staffs due to specialization in football. "What should we do?" was the question raised by Sid.

Dr. Black, an economics professor, was the first to raise a question. "How do we compare financially with other schools?"

Sid replied, "I have with me a table showing the revenues and expenses of other schools. As you know, we are a Class A school. Our financial results for the past three years show a $100,000–$150,000 loss for each year." He then passed out a xeroxed copy of the following table. (See Table 16–8)

Dr. Black pressed forward, "How do our revenues compare with other schools?"

"Well, last year our total revenues were approximately $1,250,000, most of which was from football receipts," replied Sid. "I also have two tables showing the revenues of other comparable schools," said Sid, as he passed out two papers to the committee members. (See Tables 16–9 and 16–10)

"Would it be possible to raise football ticket prices by one dollar per game?" asked Dr. Angell, an anthropology professor.

Dr. Black replied, "Well, public demand for football tickets is probably price elastic. Intercollegiate athletics competes for the marginal entertainment dollar. The price for a football ticket exceeds that of a movie, a play, and most musical events. It even compares with a professional football ticket which is by far the major competition which MSU faces. The price elasticity of demand would wipe us out in all probability. But there are some people who say that the price of college football tickets would not be price elastic, particularly if we were to have a winning season. As you know, "our last three football seasons were 4–6–1, 5–6, and 7–3–1."

Sid Davis interrupted, "As you know, we play our home games in Municipal Stadium which has a capacity of 60,000. Average attendance for

*The names, places, and events are disguised in this case.

Table 16-8 Comparative Averages for Total Revenues and Expenses (Thousands of Dollars)

Average operating results by respondent category	*10 years ago*	*9 years ago*	*8 years ago*	*7 years ago*	*6 years ago*	*5 years ago*	*4 years ago*	*3 years ago*	*2 years ago*	*1 year ago*
Class A institutions										
Average revenues	$672	$723	$749	$804	$853	$945	$1086	$1176	$1246	$1397
Average expenses	635	685	717	769	817	887	998	1094	1187	1322
Implied mean profit	$ 37	$ 38	$ 32	$ 35	$ 36	$ 58	$ 88	$ 82	$ 59	$ 75
Class B institutions										
Average revenues	$ 77	$ 85	$ 94	$104	$112	$123	$ 136	$ 146	$ 166	$ 185
Average expenses	90	99	108	116	130	148	168	192	226	247
Implied mean loss	$(13)	$(14)	$(14)	$(12)	$(18)	$(25)	$ (32)	$ (46)	$ (60)	$ (62)
Class C institutions										
Average revenues	$ 17	$ 17	$ 18	$ 18	$ 20	$ 21	$ 25	$ 26	$ 33	$ 37
Average expenses	47	49	51	56	59	63	70	77	88	102
Implied mean loss	$(30)	$(32)	$(33)	$(38)	$(39)	$(42)	$ (45)	$ (51)	$ (55)	$ (65)
Class D institutions										
Average revenues	$ 62	$ 60	$ 65	$ 76	$ 69	$ 69	$ 73	$ 82	$ 63	$ 69
Average expenses	128	135	140	151	156	170	176	190	183	196
Implied mean loss	$(66)	$(75)	$(75)	$(75)	$(87)	$(94)	$(103)	$(108)	$(120)	$(127)
Class E institutions										
Average revenues	$ 10	$ 10	$ 11	$ 11	$ 13	$ 14	$ 16	$ 18	$ 19	$ 22
Average expenses	25	26	29	33	36	39	43	48	51	54
Implied mean loss	$(15)	$(16)	$(18)	$(22)	$(23)	$(25)	$ (27)	$ (30)	$ (32)	$ (32)

Source: Mitchell H. Raiborn, "Financial Analysis of Intercollegiate Athletics," NCAA Study *(Shawnee Mission, Kansas, 1969)*.

Table 16-9 Mean and Median Total Revenues (Thousands of Dollars)

Revenues by respondent category	*10 years ago*	*9 years ago*	*8 years ago*	*7 years ago*	*6 years ago*	*5 years ago*	*4 years ago*	*3 years ago*	*2 years ago*	*1 year ago*
Class A institutions										
Mean total revenues	$672	$723	$749	$804	$853	$945	$1086	$1176	$1246	$1397
Median total revenues	593	704	728	760	861	869	969	1056	1217	1273
Class B institutions										
Mean total revenues	77	85	94	104	112	123	136	146	166	185
Median total revenues	58	62	65	72	78	83	97	106	120	148
Class C institutions										
Mean total revenues	17	17	18	20	20	21	25	26	33	37
Median total revenues	17	17	17	17	17	17	19	18	18	15
Class D institutions										
Mean total revenues	62	60	65	76	69	76	73	82	63	69
Median total revenues	45	39	43	58	61	63	54	51	49	43
Class E institutions										
Mean total revenues	10	10	11	11	13	14	16	18	19	22
Median total revenues	5	5	6	7	7	7	9	9	10	10

Source: Raiborn, "Financial Analysis of Intercollegiate Athletics."

Table 16-10 Analysis of Trends in Football Revenues (Thousands of Dollars)

Statistics measured by class	*10 years ago*	*9 years ago*	*8 years ago*	*7 years ago*	*6 years ago*	*5 years ago*	*4 years ago*	*3 years ago*	*2 years ago*	*1 year ago*
Class A respondents										
Average football revenues	$498	$527	$544	$585	$595	$697	$782	$855	$899	$960
Percentage of all revenues	72%	71%	71%	71%	69%	72%	71%	71%	70%	68%
Annual percentage change		6%	3%	8%	2%	17%	12%	9%	5%	7%
Class B respondents										
Average football revenues	$ 26	$ 31	$ 31	$ 35	$ 34	$ 38	$ 42	$ 39	$ 42	$ 45
Percentage of all revenues	40%	43%	41%	41%	38%	40%	39%	35%	35%	34%
Annual percentage change		19%	0	13%	−3%	12%	11%	−7%	8%	7%
Class C respondents										
Average football revenues	$ 7	$ 8	$ 8	$ 7	$ 8	$ 7	$ 8	$ 8	$ 8	$ 8
Percentage of all revenues	44%	51%	47%	45%	45%	37%	39%	38%	36%	33%
Annual percentage change		14%	0	−13%	14%	−13%	14%	0	0	0

Source: Raiborn, "Financial Analysis of Intercollegiate Athletics."

each of our five or six home games has been about 20,000 for the past three years. It's a shame to have a conference champ play here and draw anywhere from 16,000 to 24,000 people when we can go to their stadium and draw from 40,000 to 50,000 fans. In fact, if we were to drop one of our home games and play it away from home each year in Capitol City at Capitol University, we could probably make $75,000. Capitol City draws 50,-000 when Capitol University plays there against just about any other conference school."

Sid also said, "Here's another table showing the capacity utilization of stadium facilities of other schools. Incidentally, I've got another exhibit showing the effect of ticket pricing of professional teams." (See Tables 16–11 and 16–12)
compare to other schools?"

Sid again passed out another exhibit which he had xeroxed for the members of the athletic committee. (See Tables 16–13 and 16–14)

Sid continued, "Our expenses have been running about $1,350,000 a year."

"Hmm," frowned Dr. Black. "How can we cut some expenses?"

Dr. Zorba commented, "Would it be possible to put financial aid to athletes on a need basis? Athletes are generally granted financial aid (tuition, room and board, books, and miscellaneous personal expenses) by virtue of their athletic prowess—not because of financial need. I know, for example, that the Ivy League provided no financial aid to athletes. They recruit athletes who are granted financial aid by the university, not by the athletic department, on the same basis as other students. If we did the same, we could cut our expenses tremendously."

Sid responded, "Yes, we certainly could, but would we remain competitive with the other conference schools? By the way, I'm also passing out to you gentlemen another exhibit showing the composition of major expenses of other schools."

Another faculty member, Dr. Xanthus, raised a question, "Could we eliminate financial aid to nonrevenue-producing sports?"

Sid replied, "We could do so, but our swimming team, which is always ranked nationally, would certainly be hurt."

Dr. Xanthus continued, "Could we remove the nonrevenue-producing sports from our athletic budget? Football and basketball are generally the only sports which support themselves. Why should they carry the entire bag of other nonrevenue sports?"

Sid replied, "I suppose we could do so, and perhaps the institution could guarantee financial support of the nonrevenue producers."

Dr. Black asked, "Could we save money in recruiting? If we could save just half of the costs of recruiting, we could save two to three percent of our expenses. Why do we have to recruit twice—once prior to our conference deadlines and again when another conference deadline passes after ours?"

Sid responded, "You're right, but recruiting is such a minor expense compared to the total expenses. I'm not sure that it should be one that could be cut back. Competition for good athletes is so keen that we have to spend money just to stay even."

"Okay, then," Dr. Black continued, "could we cut back on travel and training tables?"

"We could, but again, every other school is going to travel and use training tables. We have to compete with them," Sid responded.

Table 16-11 Football and Basketball Capacity Utilization and Ticket Sales Composition (Class A Respondents Only)

	10 years ago	*9 years ago*	*8 years ago*	*7 years ago*	*6 years ago*	*5 years ago*	*4 years ago*	*3 years ago*	*2 years ago*	*1 year ago*
Varsity Football										
Average potential annual seating capacity for all home games (in thousands)	213	214	220	229	228	238	235	248	243	244
Average seating capacity per home game (in thousands)	41	42	42	44	43	45	45	47	46	47
Percentage of all paid attendance to potential annual seating capacity	53%	53%	53%	57%	56%	63%	66%	68%	69%	71%
Percentage of home game ticket revenues derived from public attendance	88%	89%	87%	88%	87%	88%	86%	87%	86%	87%

Source: Raiborn, "Financial Analysis of Intercollegiate Athletics."

Table 16-12 Effects of Professional Sports upon Intercollegiate Attendance and Ticket Pricing in Football and Basketball (For Respondents with Proximity to Professional Sports)

Influence upon attendance and pricing categorized by sport	*Positive effect*	*Adverse effect*	*No effect*	*No answer*
Effect on Varsity Football Attendance and Revenues				
For 134 applicable respondents	6%	24%	40%	30%
For 47 Class A	4	43	30	23
For 35 Class B	11	15	37	37
For 52 Class C	4	13	52	31
Facilitated Increased Prices				
For 134 applicable respondents	13%	3%	57%	27%
For 47 Class A	26	2	49	23
For 35 Class B	6	3	68	23
For 52 Class C	6	4	57	33
Effect on Varsity Basketball Attendance and Revenues				
For 194 applicable respondents	6%	11%	49%	34%
For 47 Class A	4	15	58	23
For 35 Class B	9	11	46	34
For 52 Class C	4	10	59	27
For 9 Class D	0	33	33	33
For 51 Class E	8	6	37	49
Facilitated Increased Prices				
For 194 applicable respondents	7%	2%	56%	35%
For 47 Class A	13	2	55	30
For 35 Class B	6	0	65	29
For 52 Class C	4	2	59	35
For 9 Class D	33	0	33	33
For 51 Class E	2	2	53	43

Source: Raiborn, "Financial Analysis of Intercollegiate Athletics."

Dr. Zorba again raised a question, "Is it possible to eliminate two-platoon football?"

"It's quite unlikely," Sid replied. "The influence of professional football in collegiate athletics is too strong."

Dr. Black again raised his hand, "Can we obtain institutional support for the athletic program? I do know that Class B and C and D colleges receive subsidies from their institutions. Your exhibits point this fact up to us. If intercollegiate athletics is a valued part of our university, then it should be offered some kind of support."

Dr. Zorba commented, "Yes, but the athletic program here is regarded as a self-supporting auxiliary enterprise. However, I do know that the following forms of indirect institutional support do take place:

(1) Some financial support is given for a portion of the operating costs of the physical plant.

Table 16-13 Mean and Median Total Expenses (Thousands of Dollars)

Expenses by respondent category	*10 years ago*	*9 years ago*	*8 years ago*	*7 years ago*	*6 years ago*	*5 years ago*	*4 years ago*	*3 years ago*	*2 years ago*	*1 year ago*
Class A institutions										
Mean total expenses	$635	$685	$717	$769	$817	$887	$998	$1094	$1187	$1322
Median total expenses	572	644	672	726	890	890	921	1076	1164	1299
Class B institutions										
Mean total expenses	99	99	108	116	130	148	168	192	226	247
Median total expenses	62	86	88	113	122	143	161	172	200	225
Class C institutions										
Mean total expenses	47	49	51	56	59	63	70	77	88	102
Median total expenses	40	38	40	44	48	51	57	64	70	76
Class D institutions										
Mean total expenses	128	135	140	151	156	170	176	190	183	196
Median total expenses	105	107	110	132	142	145	128	140	153	162
Class E institutions										
Mean total expenses	25	26	29	33	36	39	43	48	51	54
Median total expenses	16	19	22	24	25	25	28	31	43	43

Source: Raiborn, "Financial Analysis of Intercollegiate Athletics."

... by Object and Percentage of Total Expenses (Thousands of Dollars)

Expense classification	5 years ago		4 years ago		3 years ago		2 years ago		1 year ago	
	MEAN	PER CENT	MEAN	PER CENT	MEAN	PER CENT	MEAN	PER CENT	MEAN	PER CENT
Grants-in-aid										
Class A	$219	19%	$239	20%	$257	20%	$279	20%	$308	20%
Class B	63	29	71	28	78	27	96	30	115	31
Class C	35	13	37	12	39	12	47	13	55	13
Class D	61	31	67	32	73	32	74	33	76	32
Class E	26	23	29	24	32	24	40	26	40	24
Guarantees and options										
Class A	$181	15%	$210	16%	$217	15%	$227	15%	$247	14%
Class B	9	4	10	4	10	3	11	3	12	3
Class C	2	1	2	1	2	1	2	1	2	1
Class D	14	7	13	6	13	6	10	4	10	4
Class E	3	1	3	1	3	1	3	1	4	1
Salaries and wages										
Class A	$280	26%	$304	28%	$341	28%	$378	29%	$421	29%
Class B	48	24	53	24	66	25	83	29	94	29
Class C	29	36	32	36	36	37	40	36	46	37
Class D	59	30	64	31	69	31	71	31	77	32
Class E	26	38	28	37	30	36	34	36	36	36
All travel expenses										
Class A	$106	10%	$118	11%	$131	11%	$144	11%	$155	11%
Class B	28	14	32	14	39	15	44	15	47	14
Class C	14	18	15	17	16	16	18	16	20	16
Class D	25	14	25	13	28	14	28	14	31	14
Class E	11	16	12	16	14	17	17	18	19	19

Table 16-14 *(continued)*

Expense classification	*5 years ago*		*4 years ago*		*3 years ago*		*2 years ago*		*1 year ago*	
	MEAN	PER CENT	MEAN	PER CENT	MEAN	PER CENT	MEAN	PER CENT	MEAN	PER CENT
Equipment and uniforms										
Class A	$ 45	4%	$ 49	4%	$ 55	4%	$ 58	4%	$ 64	4%
Class B	17	8	18	7	22	7	25	8	24	6
Class C	12	15	14	16	15	15	17	15	17	14
Class D	12	7	12	7	12	6	16	8	16	7
Class E	9	10	11	11	13	12	13	11	12	9

Source: Raiborn, "Financial Analysis of Intercollegiate Athletics."

(2) A fee is required of students, all or a portion of which goes for athletics.
(3) Financial aid costs such as fee remissions are absorbed by the institution.
(4) Financial deficits are absorbed by the institution when the need arises.

I should think that subtle forms of athletic subsidy would have more appeal to our university administration than line item appropriations. These certainly might stimulate considerable faculty and student opposition."

Sid said, "Ok, we'll look into that possibility."

"Could we raise more private funds?" asked Dr. Xanthus. "I know that state institutions have not been as aggressive as private schools."

Sid responded, "It's my general impression that private fund raising for annual budgets has been pressed as far as we can go."

Dr. Black stated, "Well, we know what the general problem is. I wonder if other schools in our conference are facing the same one. If so, perhaps the President of our University could get together with other presidents to develop a conference-wide strategy for approaching the financial problem. I should think that only on a conference-wide approach could our problem be solved. It's just not politically feasible for one institution within a conference to cut back on its program because it would put us at a competitive disadvantage."

Case 16-2 MIDWESTERN STATE UNIVERSITY'S FINANCIAL ANALYSIS

The Midwestern State University's Faculty Athletic Committee had posed some questions about the financial operations of its athletic program to its athletic director.

Corky Straws, the athletic director of Midwestern State University, approached his business manager, Dud Dudley, and asked, "Dud, what percentage of our total revenues come from our football ticket sales? What percentage of our expenses are spent for football? What percentage of total revenues is the amount allocated to us from student fees? What percentage of our expenses is spent for debt service (repayment of principal and interest on bonds)?"

Dud replied, "I don't know exactly, but I can make a percentage analysis of our income and expenses for the past three or four years to see if there is a constant pattern of percentages. Should I do so?"

"Yes, I think it might be helpful. It might reveal some interesting trends. Go ahead and do so!" Corky responded. "And could you tell me whether we are going to break even on basketball this year? As you know, when we hired our basketball coach three years ago, he stated that he could turn our basketball program around from a 'financial loser' to at least a 'break-even level.' Have we accomplished this level yet?"

Dud replied, "Boy, that would take some doing to allocate the various revenues and expenses to basketball, but I think I could do so."

"Good," Corky said, "and could we determine whether football is pay-

Revenues and Expenditures This Year

*Revenues**	*Actual*	*Next year's estimate*
Ticket sales (net)		
Football	$1,410,881	$1,581,000
Basketball	245,390	260,000
Other Sports	2,681	2,800
TOTAL TICKET SALES	$1,658,952	$1,843,800
Conference Pool Division	260,000	200,000
Television	95,289	?
Radio	35,300	35,300
Programs and Concessions	100,000	120,000
Other Sources (Parking, etc.)	5,000	5,000
Sales Tax Refund	53,820	53,800
Investment Earnings	80,780	82,500
Gifts and Donations	148,272	233,000
Stadium Rental	85,240	95,000
Student Fees	165,000	180,000
Recovery of Indirect Costs	50,000	50,000
TOTAL REVENUE	$2,737,653	$2,898,400
*Expenditures**		
Administration and general	$ 424,603	$ 446,336
Buildings and grounds	103,096	105,482
Publicity (net after allocation)	74,032	76,000
Football	1,023,893	1,062,606
Basketball	237,843	258,547
Baseball	60,928	66,280
Track	78,037	88,053
Golf	24,739	25,659
Swimming	37,191	42,675
Tennis	27,271	29,297
Radio and TV	10,000	10,000
Concessions	45,000	55,000
Scholarships (included with sports of $406,000)		
Band	7,520	7,500
Cheerleaders	2,350	2,450
Pom-pom Girls	1,540	1,750
Plant Improvement		50,000
Debt Service	568,971	568,321
TOTAL EXPENDITURES	$2,727,014	$2,895,956
NET CHANGE	$ 10,639	$ 2,444

* *On a Cash Basis—No Accruals*

ᐧomparison of Budget versus Revenues and Expenditures Two Years Ago

*Revenues**	*Budgeted*	*Actual*
icket Sales (net after guarantees)		
Football	$1,368,000	$1,257,013
Football Bowl Game	—	146,843
Basketball	60,000	146,504
Other Sports	2,500	1,407
TOTAL TICKET SALES	$1,430,500	$1,551,767
onference Pool Division	160,000	250,000
elevision	—	96,163
adio	17,500	46,772
rograms and Concessions	100,000	95,103
rking Lot	—	1,798
les Tax Refund	50,000	53,820
vestment Earnings	88,000	68,915
ifts and Donations	215,000	358,691
ther Revenue Items	5,000	13,952
udent Fees	165,000	165,000
ecovery of Indirect Costs	—	—
TOTAL REVENUES	$2,231,000	$2,701,961
*Expenditures**		
dministration and General	$ 380,903	$ 385,838
uildings and Grounds	57,344	86,244
ıblicity, net after allocation	56,328	37,977
raining, net after allocation	—	2,356
ootball	974,528	1,189,689
ootball Bowl Game	—	77,084
asketball	181,936	226,690
aseball	50,223	61,749
rack	74,590	74,354
olf	25,615	21,406
vimming	36,362	36,716
ennis	21,749	31,191
adio and TV	—	602
oncessions	50,000	40,120
and	7,200	2,466
holarships (included with sports of $408,646)		
ebt Service	300,000	341,029
and Scholarships	5,000	5,000
jury Claims	—	249
ther Expenses	—	12,295
TOTAL EXPENDITURES	$2,221,778	$2,633,055
ET CHANGE	$ 9,212	$ 68,906

*On a Cash Basis—No Accruals

Comparison of Budget versus Revenues and Expenditures Three Years Ag

*Revenues**	*Budgeted*	*Actual*
Ticket Sales (net after guarantees)		
Football	$1,326,985	$1,208,65
Basketball	60,000	54,50
Other Sports	1,500	1,26
TOTAL TICKET SALES	$1,388,485	$1,264,43
Conference Pool Division	160,000	220,00
Radio and Television	17,500	80,55
Programs and Concessions	100,000	83,73
Parking Lot		49
Sales Tax Refund		49,84
Investment Earnings	70,000	69,95
Gifts and Donations	120,000	400,24
Other Revenue Items	18,000	17,18
Student Fees	157,500	157,50
Recovery of Indirect Costs	37,000	42,98
TOTAL REVENUES	$2,063,485	$2,386,93
*Expenditures**		
Administration and General	$ 368,688	$ 375,79
Buildings and Grounds	52,640	58,72
Publicity, net after allocation	47,956	32,65
Football	952,954	1,055,31
Basketball	171,272	193,97
Baseball	46,432	59,83
Track	71,038	73,04
Golf, Swimming, Tennis	81,762	76,04
Band	7,100	1,71
Radio and Television		27,29
Concessions	50,000	37,54
Scholarships (included with sports of $388,981)		
Debt Service	200,000	329,95
Band Scholarships	(5,000)	
Employee Injury Claim		7
TOTAL EXPENDITURES	$2,049,842	$2,321,97
NET CHANGE	$ 13,643	$ 64,95

* *On a Cash Basis—No Accruals*

omparison of Budget versus Revenues and Expenditures Four Years Ago

*Revenues**	*Budgeted*	*Actual*
icket Sales (net after guarantees)		
Football	$1,047,000	$1,087,898
Basketball	40,480	35,702
Other Sports	1,500	1,482
TOTAL TICKET SALES	$1,088,980	$1,125,082
onference Pool Division	165,000	180,000
adio and Television	17,500	109,456
rograms and Concessions	100,000	77,305
arking Lot		2,483
ifts and Donations	120,000	120,000
ther Revenue Items	93,000	133,215
tudent Fees	166,500	166,500
ecovery of Indirect Costs	37,000	59,500
TOTAL REVENUES	$1,787,980	$1,973,541
*Expenditures**		
dministration and General	$ 313,202	$ 309,697
uildings and Grounds	65,044	65,195
raining Room and Publicity, net	30,754	25,474
ootball	892,605	1,005,092
asketball	149,220	143,197
aseball	43,915	52,920
rack	70,695	75,794
olf, Swimming, Tennis	79,651	83,494
and	1,200	1,710
adio and Television		36,753
oncessions	40,000	39,507
cholarships (included with sports of $403,233)		
lant Additions		797
ebt Service	52,600	37,689
and Scholarships	5,000	5,000
ther Non-Recurring Costs		1,685
TOTAL EXPENDITURES	$1,743,866	$1,884,004
ET CHANGE	$ 44,114	$ 89,537

On a Cash Basis—No Accruals

ing for itself and for all the other sports? A marginal analysis for this year could provide an interesting picture for our athletic committee's benefit."

"Further, let's take a look at how well our yearly budgeting system works. How good are we at budgeting our yearly revenues and expenses?" Corky asked.

"Okay," Dud replied, "but as you know, budgeting and allocating our revenues and expenses are fairly difficult. I can budget our football ticket sales fairly accurately, but I have very little knowledge about the television revenues because I do not know ahead of time what games will be televised. Sometimes we have appeared on television three times a year and other years we have not been on TV at all. Further, our conference pool division from television and radio is difficult to predict because we do not know whether teams from our conference will be on national or regional television next year. It depends on ABC's whims."

"Yes, I'm aware of this problem," Corky said.

Dud continued, "I would estimate that 85% of all TV and radio income is derived from football and 15% from basketball."

"That's a good estimate," Corky said.

"All scholarship donations are spent for football, basketball, and other sports (baseball, track, golf, swimming, tennis). About 60% of all donations and earnings from donations go for football, 8% for basketball, and 32% goes for other sports," Dud stated.

"I didn't know, but that sounds right," Corky said.

"Our sales of programs and concessions are approximately 80% from football, 15% from basketball, and 5% from other sports," Dud said. "The sales tax refund, which we consider as income, is 87% from football tickets and 13% from basketball," Dud continued.

"Our student fees, h'mm. Well, regular football tickets sell for $49 a season and basketball season tickets are $42. That's a 55–45 split. We could allocate our student fee income that way," said Dud.

"Our recovery from indirect costs is what is transferred to us from the scholarship program. So we could allocate it 60–8–32%."

"All right, that sounds okay for allocation purposes," commented Corky Straws. "Now, what about allocation of expenses?"

"We could allocate the administrative, buildings and grounds, publicity, concessions, and debt service on the basis of total revenue generated by football, basketball, and other sports. That's approximately 80–15–5%. The band, cheerleaders, and pom-pom could be split 85–15 because they are used only at football and basketball games. How does that sound?" asked Dud.

"Okay," replied Corky. "I assume that you have already allocated the scholarships, training and medical, equipment, and some publicity directly to each sport, haven't you?"

"Yes, I have," replied Dud.

"All right, then," continued Corky, "Let's review our percentage analysis, our budgeting effectiveness, and our allocation and marginal analysis next week. Will you be ready to discuss your financial analyses with me by then?" asked Corky.

"Yes, I'll give you a call," responded Dud, as he pulled the last three or four years of financial data from his files.

QUESTIONS:

1. What does the percentage analysis of the financial statements point up?
2. How effective is the budget compared to actual?
3. What does the allocation of revenue and expenses point up?
4. What does a marginal analysis of football, basketball, and other sports profits point to?

Part VI

The Organizational Structure of an Athletic Program

Once objectives and strategies have been formulated, an organizational structure must be designed to function accordingly. The organization must carry out strategies and accomplish objectives. The principles involved are discussed in this section.

17

ORGANIZING THE FORMAL STRUCTURE OF AN ATHLETIC PROGRAM

Strategies and related objectives are carried out in the formal organization structure. It is the relationship of the specialized job functions, their objectives, the authority, responsibility, and accountability, and personnel who perform the specialized job functions to reach the athletic program objectives. The rationale for organizing the structure is similar to the following: (1) fans need the entertainment provided by sports; (2) to create a sports program requires various strategies; (3) these strategies help to determine specific athletic program objectives; (4) individuals must perform specialized functions so the program can reach its objectives; (5) these functions must be grouped together in coordinated fashion to reach the objectives of satisfying the needs of fans and other interested people; (6) delegation of authority, responsibility, and accountability has to be entrusted to personnel in order to perform the functions needed to reach program and personal objectives. The rationale for a formal organization structure is based on needs, services, strategies, objectives, functions, and delegation—usually in that order.

There are four fundamental steps in organizing the structure of an athletic program.

1. Determine the objectives, both organizational and personal.
2. Analyze the specialized operative and managerial functions necessary to accomplish the objectives.
3. Group these specialized operative and managerial functions into some meaningful relationship to become efficient.

4. Delegate the objectives, functions, and related authority, responsibility, accountability, to personnel to perform the specialized functions to accomplish the objectives—both organizational and personal.

The following is a more detailed account of these basic concepts and their effect on the athletic program.

FUNCTIONAL EMERGENCE IN GROWING HIGH SCHOOL ATHLETIC PROGRAMS

Each sport in an athletic program has to be coached, marketed, financed, staffed, and administered. When the high school or college athletic program consists of several sports, these functions are usually performed by the athletic director and assistant athletic directors, depending on the size of the institution. Regardless of the program's size, however, these duties must be performed.

When an athletic program grows in size, then certain functions emerge and become separately administered. A coach may handle three sports in a very small high school, but as the program grows, he/she will usually coach only one sport, and perhaps add some assistant coaches for that sport. Perhaps the principal of a small high school can handle such duties as purchasing, financing, ticket selling, staffing, and so on, while the coach handles all the coaching. In any event, with organizational growth in the athletic program, the functions will emerge as separate functions to be administered by someone to whom the necessary authority, responsibility, accountability, will have to be delegated. This concept of functional emergence or functional evolution may be illustrated by showing the formal or-

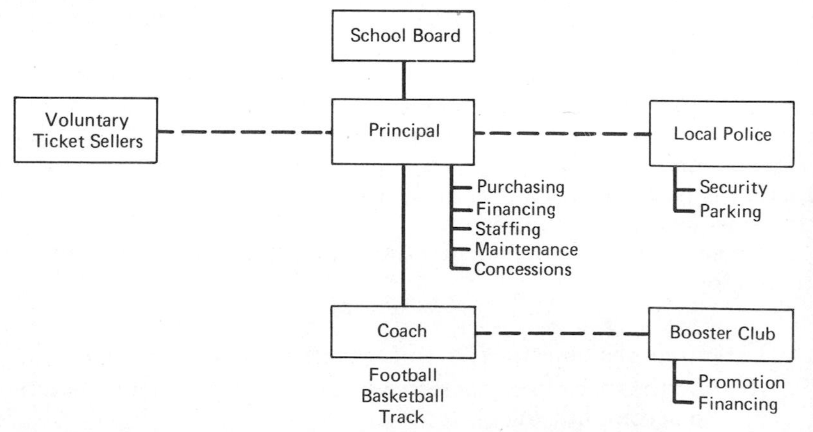

Figure 17-1 Stage I: Small High School Athletic Program Formal Organizational Structure

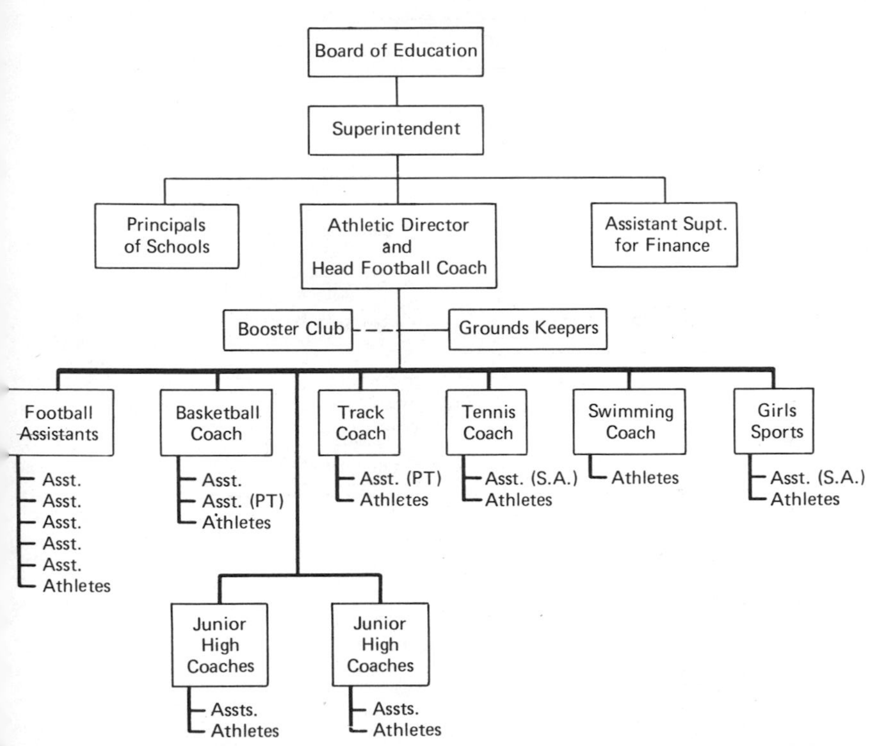

'igure 17–2 Stage II: Medium Size High School Athletic Program Formal Organizational Structure

ganizational structure of a very small high school, a medium-sized high school, and a large public school system. The various stages of growth will show a pattern of various functions which will emerge as separate organizational functions.

In the small high school, volunteers are called upon to promote and finance the program, to sell tickets, to maintain and to oversee security, parking, and so forth. The principal is usually the chief administrator; the coach handles all the sports (see Figure 17-1).

In the medium-sized high school system, there are now several separate administrators—separate coaches for different sports, each with assistants; a financial assistant superintendent; groundskeepers; an athletic director in charge of all high school and junior high athletics, reporting directly to the superintendent of schools. Principals of the various elementary and secondary schools have little to do with the administration of athletic programs (see Figure 17-2).

In Stage III we see separate functions emerge as to finance, building services, and athletic administration. Athletic councils, game officials, and coaches for boys' and girls' sports at high schools and junior highs are some additions to the staff (see Figure 17-3).

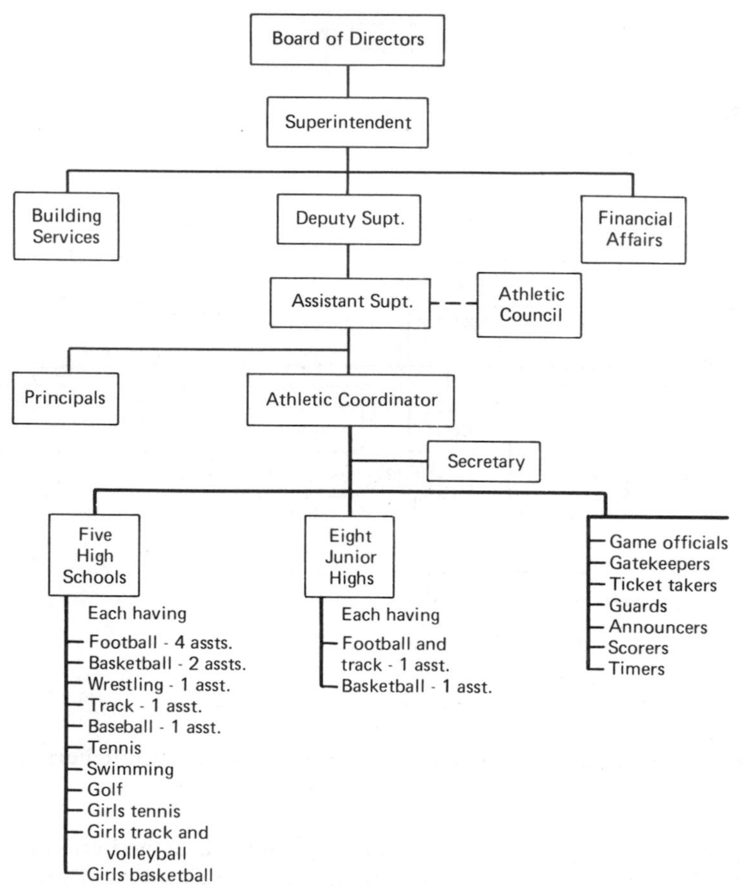

Figure 17-3 Stage III: Large Size School System Athletic Program Forma[l] Organizational Structure

FUNCTIONAL GROWTH IN COLLEGIATE PROGRAMS

One organizational objective of most collegiate athletic programs i[s] growth. Growth indicates the public's positive opinion of the program an[d] provides an increasing financial flow. The collegiate athletic program at [a] small college is usually combined with the physical education department both are under one department head who reports to the dean of instruc tion. The coaches also teach; functions such as marketing and financing th[e] athletic program are provided by the established collegiate system. I[n] Stage I the organizational structure would be similar to that shown in Fig ure 17–4.

In Stage II, as the college expands its enrollment, a division of athletic separate from the physical education department is established. An athleti[c]

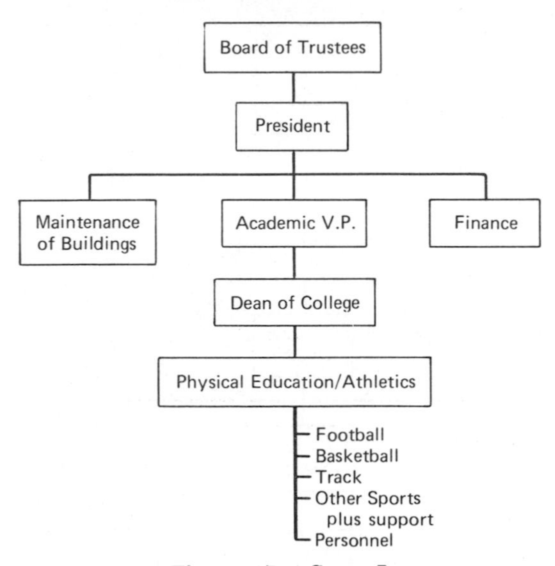

Figure 17-4 Stage I

director responsible for the function of intercollegiate athletics is hired. A faculty athletic committee helps to formulate policies. The athletic director usually reports to the president. In addition to the coaches, a sports information director appears on the scene. Ticket selling and financing are beginning to separate from the regular functions of the college. A Stage II organizational structure appears in Figure 17–5.

In Stage III (Figure 17-6), assistant athletic directors appear on the scene. One assistant might be in charge of nonrevenue spring sports; another, in charge of tickets, promotion, stadium rental, and related market-

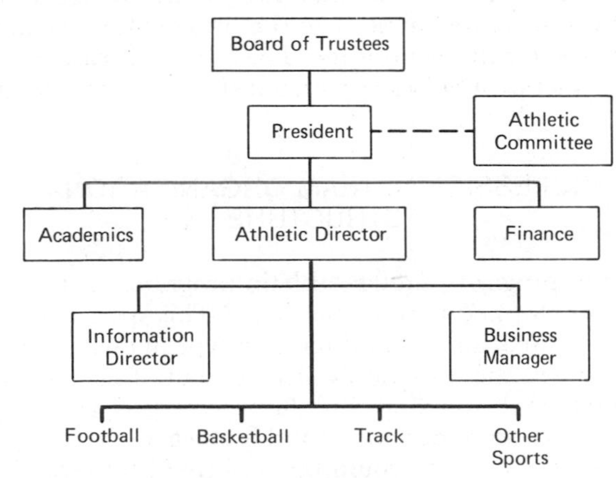

Figure 17-5 Stage II

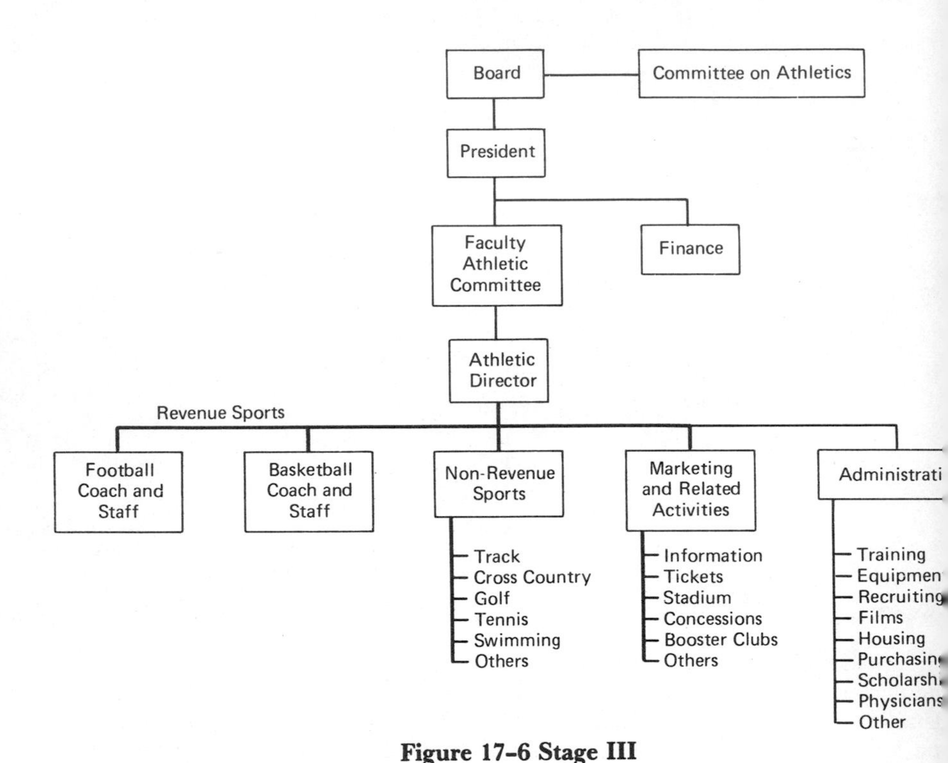

Figure 17-6 Stage III

ing functions; another may be in charge of administrative matters and related activities. Normally the football and basketball coaches have their own separate staffs. In Stage III, separate positions have emerged for trainers and recruiters, and for individuals to look after equipment, films, and housing. The finances can still be handled by the college. Sometimes the athletic director may report directly to the president, other times he could report through the faculty committee. The board of trustees usually has a committee on athletics. The organizational structure may be shown in Figure 17–6.

PROFESSIONAL TEAM ORGANIZATIONAL STRUCTURE

A professional program, unlike athletic programs in high schools and colleges, is usually formed around one sport. This sport is produced, marketed, financed, staffed, and administered in typical business fashion. However, depending on the program's size, certain functions such as the coaching (production) function will have emerged as a separate one. Others, such as marketing, personnel, and finance might not emerge as separate, distinct functions; they could be performed by several individuals. For example, in Figure 17–7 the organizational structure for a professional NFL football team appears.

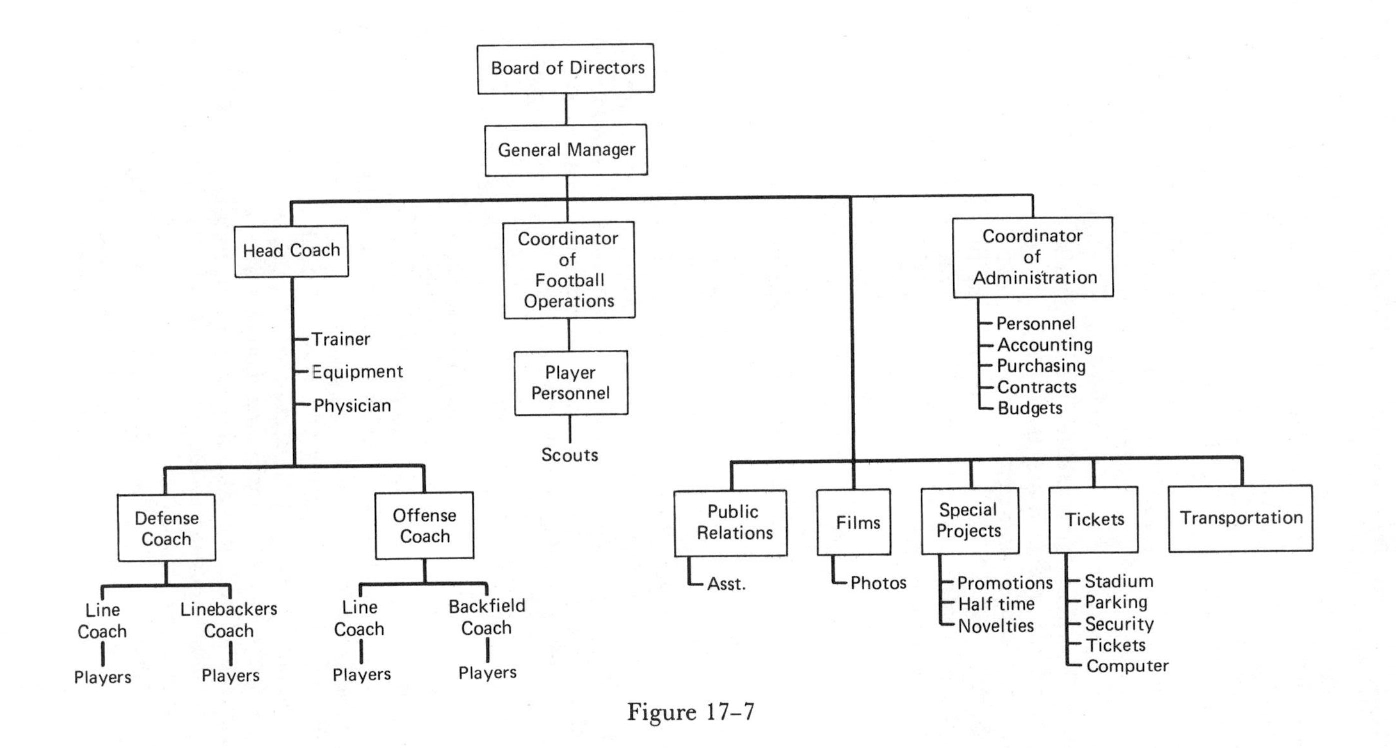
Board of Directors
General Manager
Head Coach
Trainer
Equipment
Physician
Defense Coach
Line Coach
Players
Linebackers Coach
Players
Offense Coach
Line Coach
Players
Backfield Coach
Players
Coordinator of Football Operations
Player Personnel
Scouts
Coordinator of Administration
Personnel
Accounting
Purchasing
Contracts
Budgets
Public Relations
Asst.
Films
Photos
Special Projects
Promotions
Half time
Novelties
Tickets
Stadium
Parking
Security
Tickets
Computer
Transportation

Figure 17–7

Line functions (usually indicated by heavy lines) are concerned with directly producing and marketing customer utilities (form, time, place, possession) which fans are willing to pay for. *Service functions* supplement the line functions. These include the functions of the trainer and the physician, which serve the coaching function. The proper equipment is also essential for effective coaching. Personnel and finance are also classified as service functions since they are not directly involved in providing customer utilities. *Staff* functions are advisory in nature. Those who perform them include consultants, lawyers, and tax experts.

The line functions can make or break the athletic program. The coaching (production) function creates the form utility paid for by fans. The marketing function determines the time, place, and possession utilities. The athletic program is organized around these two line functions. The other two—personnel and finance—supplement the line functions. The same is true of the administrative function. All of the functions are necessary, but they are not of equal importance.

Grouping of Related Functions

Normally, a sport serves as a base for organizing activities in which similar functions are grouped around the sport. On a football team, related functions are grouped around the football coaching function. Those who perform the related functions are the trainer, the equipment man, and the physicians. Game films may be used as well. Grouping activities in this way results in efficient coordination of similar functions (see Figure 17-7).

If, however, an athletic program is comprised of several sports, the training, equipment, physicians, and films can be grouped together to serve all the different sports. Such is the case in many large college programs (see Figure 17-6).

In the case of a large program, the marketing activities—promotion (SID), tickets, stadium operations, concessions, and booster clubs—should also be grouped together, preferably under one supervisor. If not, then the athletic administrator will have to perform these tasks.

Financial functions should be grouped together in the same way. One person usually works with accounts, deposits, bonds, investments, scholarships, and donations, if the program is large enough to support these activities. If not, the athletic administrator must work with finances, with the assistance of the local scholastic financial operations.

The personnel functions also should be grouped together. If size permits, one person should engage in recruiting and selection, and work with contracts and athletes' salaries.

The bases for grouping these functions are varied. The sport is the most common base for grouping related functions, particularly in scholastic programs comprised of several sports. The coaching function is based on sports; coaching may be broken down into specialized functions such as offensive coaching, defensive coaching, backfield, line, and kicking. These functional bases are usually at the lower supervisory level of the organizational structure.

Groupings of various functions are usually found at the middle management echelons of an organization structure. Scouting functions are grouped around territorial bases. Booster clubs are also based on territory if the program is large. These bases—sports, functions, territories, and sometimes special project bases—serve as the foundation for grouping related functions.

SPAN OF SUPERVISION AND RELATED FACTORS

The number of subordinates reporting to a superior can be referred to as the span of supervision. If too many employees report to one supervisor, then lost time, wasted effort, misspent money, personal frustrations, and inefficiencies creep into the organizational structure. What factors determine whether a wide span or a narrow span of supervision is most efficient in an organization?

The first factor is the similarity or dissimilarity of activities. If the activities to be supervised are similar, then a wide span of supervision can be easily designed into the organization structure. Coordination and supervision would be simpler than if dissimilar activities were supervised. Dissimilar activities would suggest a narrow span of supervision.

The physical distance between functions is another factor that affects the span of supervision. If there is a great distance between activities, a narrow span of supervision is advisable. A short distance between activities is conducive to a wide span of supervision.

Stability of operations is another. If an athletic program has a degree of stability, then a wide span can be maintained. In a constantly changing organization, a narrow span of supervision is the best strategy.

Complexity of functions is another factor affecting the size of a supervisor's span. If duties within an organization are complex, then a narrow span is necessary. If duties are routine, then a wide span can be used.

A constant onslaught of new problems would suggest the use of a narrow span of supervision. If new problems are not a part of the supervisor's responsibility, then a wide span can be suggested.

The types of employees would be another. If subordinates are well-educated, knowledgeable, and responsible, a supervisor can maintain a wide span of supervision. Otherwise, a narrow span becomes necessary.

An athletic program's span of supervision can be designed or evaluated for each supervisory position by comparing the theory of a span to an actual situation, and evaluating the consequent strengths and weaknesses.

Objective: To Determine the Span of Supervision for Organizational Efficiency

Factors →	**Theory →**		**Compared to →**	**Actual Situation →**		**Evaluation**	
	Wide Span	*Narrow Span*		*Wide*	*Narrow*	*Strong*	*Weak*
1. Activities							
1.1 Similar	X						
1.2 Dissimilar		X					
2. Distance between activities							
2.1 Short	X						
2.2 Long		X					
3. Stability of operations							
3.1 Stable	X						
3.2 Unstable		X					
4. Complexity of activities							
4.1 Routine	X						
4.2 Complex		X					
5. New problems							
5.1 Infrequent	X						
5.2 Frequent		X					
6. Employees							
6.1 Responsible	X						
6.2 Not responsible		X					
7. Others							
Overall Evalution							

SPECIALIZATION OF FUNCTIONS

Most athletic functions have become specialized because administrators have found that specialization increases efficiency. As athletic programs grow, duties become specialized. New employees who answer to the administrator must be hired. However, specialization improves the quality and increases the quantity of the goods and services that help the organization achieve its objectives. Specialization, to a certain extent, produces better athletes and better employees. Without specialization, several unrelated functions must be performed by a single person. At the lower levels of the organizational structure, specialization is fairly common. However, as a person progresses upward in the organization, less and less specialization is required. An effective and efficient athletic administrator must be able to perform diverse functions competently.

The athletic administrator can evaluate the organizational functions by using the chart on the next page. In addition, administrators can determine the effectiveness of their own programs by comparing theory to the actual situation.

DELEGATION OF OBJECTIVES, FUNCTIONS, AUTHORITY, RESPONSIBILITY, AND ACCOUNTABILITY

Most athletic administrators have been forced to delegate some of their activities to other people. The reason is obvious: the administrator cannot possibly perform all the administrative and operative functions necessary to accomplish organizational objectives. Consequently, several operative functions are usually entrusted to subordinates. The first one is usually the coaching function. This is especially true when several sports are involved. Several coaches are hired and entrusted with the responsibility of overseeing coaching activities. For effective delegation, several principles must be practiced.

The first principle is clarity of delegation. The functions entrusted to another must be clearly understood by both the delegator and the subordinate. There are usually three ways to ensure that the new duties are understood: (1)devise an organization chart, (2) compose job descriptions and specifications, and (3) compile organization manuals. These three methods are classical ways to guarantee clarity of delegation in the formal organizational structure.

Another principle of delegation is known as the coincidence of authority and responsibility: authority and responsibility must be delegated simultaneously. If only responsibility is delegated, the subordinate will not have the authority to perform necessary duties. This is a common fault in delegation. As a result, the subordinate must obtain permission from the delegator for practically every action performed, resulting in lost time,

Objective: To Design an Organization's Functions for Efficiency

Factors	Strength	Weakness
1. Have the objectives been determined?		
1.1 Organizational		
1.2 Personal		
2. Have the functions been determined?		
2.1 Operative		
2.11 Coaching		
2.12 Marketing		
2.13 Financial		
2.14 Personnel		
2.2 Managerial		
2.21 Planning		
2.22 Acquiring		
2.23 Organizing		
2.24 Leading		
2.25 Coordinating		
2.26 Evaluating		
3. Has a distinction been made of:		
3.1 Line functions		
3.2 Service functions		
3.3 Staff functions		
4. Have functions become specialized?		
4.1 About right		
4.2 Too much		
4.3 Not enough		
5. Have operative functions been properly grouped?		
5.1 Coaching		
5.2 Marketing		
5.3 Finance		
5.4 Personnel		
6. Is the span of supervision proper for each supervisory function?		
7. Has functional growth and emergence been planned for?		
Overall Evaluation:		

frustrations on the part of both, wasted energy, high costs, and inefficiencies.

Another organizational principle is called unity of command. There should be one boss for each separate activity delegated to each individual. When two or more supervisors are telling a subordinate how, what and when to perform a function, obviously there will be conflicts in their orders. When that happens, what will the subordinate do? He will probably wait until the situation is straightened out, thus losing time, money, feelings, and the like, all causing organizational inefficiencies.

A further principle of delegation is having a clearly defined chain of command. Subordinates must know their superiors. When problems arise, where does a person turn? Each person should have a clear notion of who the boss is and how to communicate with the management. Otherwise, several problems can arise. For example, if a trainer goes directly to the athletic director to solve a problem, without going through the proper channels, what happens? The trainer's immediate boss does not know about the problem; once he/she does find out about it, embarrassment and frustration result. Bypassing the formal chain of command causes all sorts of inefficiencies. The same is true in downward bypassing, when an athletic administrator goes directly to an employee without going through his/her immediate supervisor. Probably, the chief ways of establishing a clear chain of command are through organization charts and procedure manuals written to give detailed instructions as to who does what, when and through what channels.

Fixed responsibility is another principle of delegation. Efficiency is more likely to be achieved when responsibility (the obligation to perform a function) is clearly fixed on a person. Sometimes that obligation should be clearly fixed on a group of persons (committee or board). When accountability arises for the performance of a function, it can be easily measured if responsibility is fixed ahead of time.

Feedback of some sort becomes necessary to insure that proper delegation is working effectively. When objectives have been delegated, feedback should come in the form of written reports or actual observation of results. Sometimes this feedback may be called accountability, or the measure of how well the objectives and functions with corresponding authority and responsibility have been carried out. Feedback or accountability is a basic principle of delegation.

Delegation can be more efficiently performed if the preceding principles—clarity of delegation, coincidence of authority and responsibility, unity of command, clearly defined chain of command, fixed responsibility, and feedback—are followed. If responsibility (the obligation to perform a function) and accountability (the measurement of how well the function is performed) and authority (the right to perform a function) are understood, chances are good that delegation can be efficiently performed.

An administrator can evaluate the delegation process by using the following analysis:

Objective: Delegation to Achieve Organizational Efficiency

Factors	Strength	Weakness
1. Has delegation in actuality (not lip service) taken place?		
1.1 Objectives		
1.2 Functions		
1.3 Authority		
1.4 Responsibility		
1.5 Accountability		
2. Has each delegation been clear?		
2.1 Organization charts		
2.2 Job descriptions		
2.3 Authority–responsibility–accountability manuals		
2.4 Others		
3. Has unity of command been observed?		
4. Is there a clearly defined and observed chain of command?		
4.1 Organization chart		
4.2 Written procedures		
4.3 Others		
5. Is responsibility fixed and clearly established for each function?		
6. Is there adequate feedback (accountability) on the functions delegated?		
6.1 Written reports		
6.2 Actual observation		
Overall Evaluation:		

Centralization versus Decentralization of Functions

One of the key decisions facing an athletic administrator concerns the centralization or decentralization of various functions. When the managerial functions (mainly planning, acquiring, coordinating, and evaluating) are concentrated at the top levels of the organizational structure, there is centralization. When the managerial functions are dispersed to lower levels

Objective: To Determine the Degree of Centralization or Decentralization for Each Function

Factors →	**Theory →**	**Compared to →**	**Actual Situation →**	**Evaluation**	
				Strength	*Weakness*
1. Competent personnel	Decentralize				
2. Large size and growth	Decentralize				
3. Wide geographic dispersion	Decentralize				
4. Well understood philosophy of management	Decentralize				
5. Find trouble spots	Decentralize				
6. Minimize financial risks	Decentralize				
7. Local market conditions	Decentralize				
8. Participation in decision making	Decentralize				
9. Standardized products and services	Centralize				
10. Uniform policies	Centralize				
11. Communications effectiveness	Centralize				
12. High personnel turnover	Centralize				
Overall Evaluation:					

in the organizational structure, it is known as decentralization. The problem arises when the administrator must determine the degree of concentration or dispersion of managerial functions for his program. How much administrative decision making is to take place at the bottom (decentralization) levels and how much at the top (centralization)? What are the deciding factors?

The first is competent personnel. If competent employees are available then decentralization can take place. If the athletic program is large and growing, a certain amount of decentralization would seem appropriate. Geographic dispersion is another factor. If there is a wide degree of geographic dispersion for the various activities, decentralization is advisable. Another factor is the philosophy of management. If the various managers have a consistent and well-understood philosophy of administration, then it becomes much easier to decentralize.

Decentralizing the functions can be used to find trouble spots in the organization. When functions are centralized, trouble spots are very difficult to find. Minimizing financial risks is also made possible through decentralization. When functions are concentrated at the top, financial risks are much heavier.

If participation in decision making is to occur, then decentralization has to follow. Rather than all decisions being made at the top (the essence of centralization), decentralization encourages the participation and training of key personnel.

Decentralization helps the organization to take advantage of local market conditions. However, if the products and services offered to people are highly standardized, such a factor would suggest a high degree of centralization.

If uniform policies are prevalent in all the organizational functions, such a factor would suggest a high degree of centralization. If communications equipment and communications ability is very effective within and from without the organization, such would suggest a degree of centralization. If a high rate of personnel turnover exists, such a factor would suggest a more highly concentrated effort to forestall key people leaving, thus favoring centralization. If constant turnover is a problem, it is best that decisions be made at the top.

These factors may be evaluated by an athletic administrator to determine the degree of concentration or dispersion for each separate function within the organization structure.

Relationship of Managerial and Operative Functions

Functions are synonymous with work, both mental and physical. Hard work is absolutely necessary to accomplish the objective of producing a winning team to satisfy fans. This hard work must be broken down into specialized functions; a coordinated effort (or a team effort) is necessary if the program is to accomplish its objectives. The major specialized functions for an athletic program may be analyzed and evaluated as follows.

Managerial functions	Operative functions COACHING	MARKETING	FINANCIAL	PERSONNEL	Overall
Planning	A	B	C	A	B
Acquiring	A	A	A	A	A
Organizing	B	C	C	C	C
Leading	A	B	C	B	B
Coordinating	A	B	C	A	B
Evaluating	A	B	D	A	B
Overall	A	B	C	A	B+

The coaching (or production) function is needed to *produce* a winning team. The marketing function is needed to *sell* the team to fans. The finance function is needed to *acquire* the financial resources for both long-term and short-term needs. The personnel function is needed to *staff* the program with top-notch athletes and other employees. The administrative function is needed to provide the *leadership* for planning, acquiring, and organizing the resources, as well as for leading, coordinating, and evaluating the whole program or parts of it. A matrix may explain the relationship of all these functions, sometimes classified into two types: operative and managerial.

The preceding matrix may also serve as a "report card" for how well an athletic program is performing its functions, based on a management audit. For example, coaching receives an overall A, marketing a B, financial a C, and personnel an A. Collectively, all four would receive a B+.

In a similar fashion, the planning functions deserve a B, the acquiring an A, the organizing a C, leading a B, coordinating a B, and evaluating a B, for an overall rating of B+.

This matrix also shows the basic organization functions of any athletic program, whether it be large, medium, or small. Regardless of size, all the functions must be performed by someone, somehow, at some time.

CHAPTER SUMMARY

The administrative functions of planning, acquiring, organizing, leading, coordinating, and evaluating have to be performed through the operative functions of coaching, marketing, and financing. This is the case for all the sports of any athletic program. All of these functions must be handled by someone, somehow, sometime, regardless of size if an athletic organizational structure is to be effective. These functions—both managerial and operative—are the foundation on which organizational structure is built. They may be performed by one person with voluntary assistance from others, or they may be performed by several people in a large athletic program. If a program grows, then these functions emerge as separate and apart from other functions and must be grouped into a logical sequence. Individuals are delegated the necessary authority, responsibility, and accountability to accomplish the objectives by performing the specific functions. This functional growth and emergence is illustrated in the organizational structures of high schools, colleges, and professional teams (see Figures 17-1 through 17-7). Line, service, and staff functions are also shown.

These functions are logically grouped around a specific sport that forms the base of the organizational structure. However, other bases may be used—territory, special projects, and similar functions.

The span of supervision is affected by various factors. The administrator must determine whether to design a wide or narrow span for each supervisory position.

Functions are specialized to attain greater organizational efficiency, up to a point.

The delegation of functions is enhanced if various principles are followed; for the best results, clarity of delegation, the coincidence of authority and responsibility, unity of command, a clearly defined chain of command, fixed responsibility, and assessment of feedback for accountability purposes are extremely important.

A key decision facing athletic administrators is whether to centralize or decentralize the managerial functions of coaching, marketing, finance, and personnel. Various factors should be considered in this strategic decision.

Finally, all managerial and operative functions may be evaluated by the use of a matrix, assigning grades in report card fashion based on a management audit of the athletic program.

Case 17-1 KANSAS CITY STARS*

When Paul Winchell was hired as head football coach of The Kansas City Stars, a professional football team, the organizational structure of the coaching function (not the entire organization) appeared somewhat as shown in Figure 17–8.

Recently a newspaper article reported the following:

> Coach Paul Winchell of the Stars laid the final brick in a remodeling job of his staff today. Winchell's staff revamping, begun about a month ago, was completed today. Winchell decided on the restructuring in order to take a larger role in the overall coaching duties.
>
> Evidence that Winchell was restructuring his staff surfaced 26 days ago when one coach resigned rather than step aside as defensive coordinator. In the revamping, Winchell decided to eliminate both the defensive and offensive coordinator positions, but the coach considered the move a demotion.
>
> "The restructuring had to do with philosophy, not people," Winchell said. "Whenever you have a hierarchy situation your lines of communication are sometimes shut off. You have to go through an empire to com-

* The people and places in this case have been disguised.

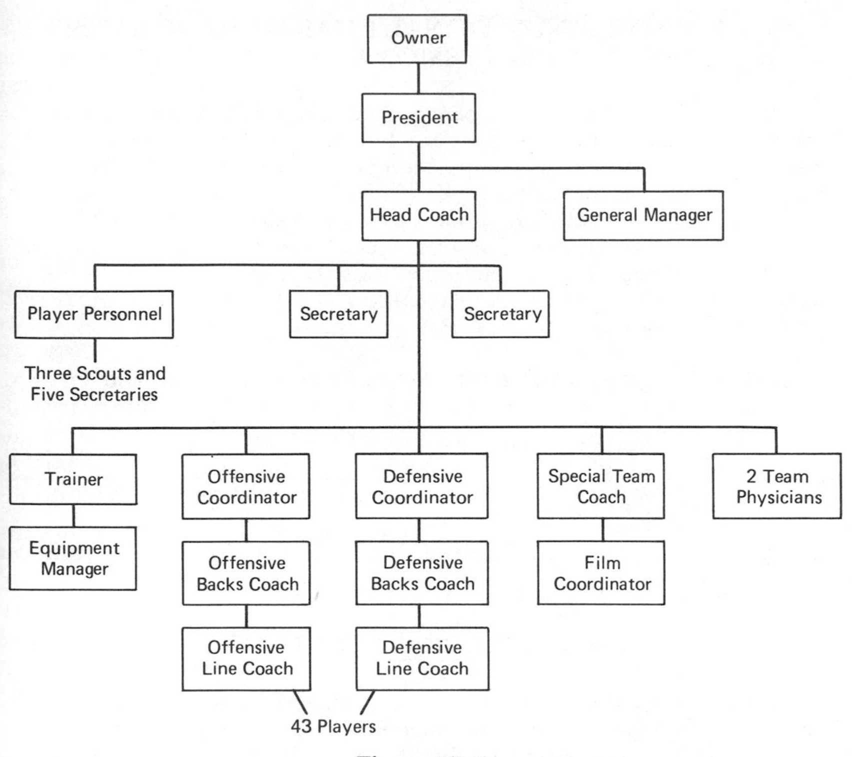

Figure 17-8

municate with people, and sometimes things get lost in the translation or watered down.

"Maybe it was a selfish decision, but I was beginning to feel like I wasn't a coach anymore. I was getting farther away from the football team. That wasn't fair to the people who hired me, the fans, or the media. I'm banking on my personality helping our football team a little more."

When he finished restructuring, Winchell had six coaches, plus a special team's coach. He kept the training, equipment, two physicians, and film coordinator functions. The player personnel function was separated from his command.

QUESTIONS:

1. Comment on Winchell's remarks about the restructuring.
2. Redraw the organization chart after Winchell's restructuring.
   a. Comment on the "line" and "service" functions.
   b. Comment on the size of the span of supervision.
   c. Why do you think that the player personnel function was separated from the coaching function?

Case 17-2 ORGANIZATIONAL CHARACTERISTICS OF SELECTED NFL PROFESSIONAL FOOTBALL TEAMS

Does the front office organization structure of a NFL professional team affect its win-loss record? Are there any formal organization characteristics associated with a team's winning percentage? Let us take a look at four teams' organization structures to see if some hypotheses could be formulated that might partially explain a team's win-loss percentage.

Personal interviews were conducted with four teams. Two (team M and team K) have been winners and two (team H and team N) have been losers. Their respective win-loss percentages for the past several years are presented in Table 17-1.

Table 17-1 Win-Loss Percentages of Selected Football Teams

Winners		*Losers*	
TEAM M	TEAM K	TEAM H	TEAM N
57% in 15 years	60% in 16 years	44% in 16 years	27% in last 10 years

ORGANIZATIONAL FUNCTIONS

All four teams alike performed both managerial and operative functions. The dominant operative production function of coaching prevailed in all four teams. The personnel function (both player and nonplayer) was also recognizable as well as a financial function. The various functions and their relationships are presented in Table 17-2 which compares the four teams' similarities and dissimilarities.

Functions Performed by the Head Coach

Since the head coach is the most influential executive of any professional football team, it is necessary to analyze the various functions he performs. A glance at Table 17-3 shows the head coach's functions.

Span of Supervision for Head Coach

A further refinement of the responsibilities of the head coach is shown in Table 17-4, which reveals the total span of supervision for the head coach of winning and losing teams. The total span includes all the people reporting either directly or indirectly to the head coach, including the 43 players and nonplayers. Obviously, the assistant coaches have a more direct relationship with the players they coach, but the head coach also has direct and indirect relationships with players as well as other support personnel.

It is interesting to note from Table 17-6 the turnover of head coaches of both winning and losing teams.

Table 17-2 Organizational Functions and Relationships

Team K	*Team M*
Owner and President	Board of Directors
Executive Vice President	Chairman of the Board
General Manager	President
2 Secretaries	Senior Vice President and Treasurer
Assistant General Manager	Vice President
Secretary	Secretary
Secretary-Treasurer	General Manager
Secretary	Coordinator of Administration
Data Processing	Accounting
3 Assistants	Non-player Personnel
Chief Accountant	Public Relations
Assistant	Assistant
2 Clerks	Film Director
Public Relations	Special Projects
Assistant	Ticket and Stadium
Promotions–Advertising	Transportation
2 Secretaries	Coordinator of Operations
Ticket Operations	Player Personnel
1 Assistant	Head Coach
1 Accountant	4 Trainers
2 Secretaries	Equipment
Construction and Maintenance	Physician
3 Assistants	Defensive Coordinator
Stadium Operations	Defensive Line Coach
5 Assistants	Players
Head Coach	Linebacker Coach
2 Secretaries	Players
Trainer	Offensive Coordinator
Equipment	Offensive Line Coach
2 Physicians	Players
Player Personnel	Offensive Backfield Coach
2 Assistants	Players
Defensive Linebacker	
Players	
Defensive Backs	
Players	
Defensive Line	
Players	
Offensive End	
Players	
Offensive Backs	
Players	
Defensive Line	
Players	

Table 17-2 *(continued)*

Team N	*Team H*
Owners (Multiple)	President
President	Senior Vice President/Secretary-Treasure
Assistant to President	Assistant to the President, a Legal Couns
Business Manager-Treasurer	Head Coach and General Manager
Assistant	Secretary
V. P. Administration	Assistant General Manager
Entertainment Director	Public Relations
Promotion Director	2 Assistants
Public Relations	Ticket Office
P. R. Consultant	3 Assistants
Statistics	Controller
Executive Vice President	2 Assistants
Ticket Manager	Head Coach/General Manager*
Assistant	2 Trainers
Head Coach	Equipment
Special Assistant	Assistants
Administrative Assistant	Maintenance, Equipment
4 Team Physicians	Defensive Coordinator
Strength & Conditioning	Linebacker Coach
Trainer	Players
Assistant	Defensive Line
Equipment	Players
Assistant	Defensive Back
Professional Personnel	Players
Player Personnel	Special Teams
6 Assistant Scouts	Players
Photography	Offensive Coordinator
Still Photo	Receiver Coach
Quarterback Coach	Players
Players	Offensive Line
Receivers Coach	Players
Players	Offensive Back
Offensive Line	Players
Players	Photo Services
Offensive Backfield	Secretary
Players	
Special Teams	
Players	
Defensive Line	
Players	
Linebackers	
Players	
Offensive Backfield	
Players	

* *Two positions combined.*

Table 17-3 Functions Performed Directly or Indirectly by the Head Coach

Winners		*Losers*	
TEAM M	TEAM K*	TEAM H	TEAM N
Coaching	Coaching	Coaching	Coaching
Training	Training	Training	Training
Equipment	Equipment	Equipment	Equipment
Physicians	Physicians	Physicians	Physicians
Clerical	Films	Films	Films
	Clerical	Marketing	Personnel
		PR	Clerical
		Tickets	
		Accounting	
		Personnel	
		Clerical	

* *The player personnel function was also included as part of the previous coach's duties.*

Table 17-4 Total Span of Supervision for the Head Coach

WINNERS		LOSERS	
Team M	*Team K*	*Team H*	*Team N*
Trainers	Trainer	2 Trainers	3 Trainers
quipment	Equipment	3 Equipment	2 Equipment
hysician	3 Physicians	9 Coaches	8 Coaches
Coaches	2 Secretaries	Photography	2 Photography
Secretary	7 Coaches	2 Secretaries	7 Player Personnel
	Film Coordinator	Asst. Gen. Mgr.	1 Pro Personnel
		3 Public Relations	4 Physicians
		4 Ticket Office	2 Assistants
		3 Accounting	1 Secretary
		6 Personnel	
		Non-Players	
3	14	32	30
		Players	
3	43	43	43
5	57	75	73

Table 17-5 Types and Numbers of Employees of Selected Professional Football Teams

	Team M	*Team K*	*Team N*	*Team*
OWNERS	5	1	23	1
EMPLOYEES				
Top Management	2	2	1	1
Middle Management	3	2	6	3
Supervisory Management	7	11	9	5
Assistant Coaches	6	7	8	9
Operative Personnel Full-Time	15	29	34	21
Total Full-Time Employees	33	51	58	39
Operative Personnel Part-Time	25	11–13	0	0
Players, active	43	43	43	43

Table 17-6 Turnover of Head Coaches of Selected Football Teams

Team M	*Team K*	*Team H*	*Team N*
2 coaches in 16 years	2 coaches in 16 years	10 coaches in 16 years	4 coaches in 10 yea
8 years average tenure	8 years average tenure	1.6 years average tenure	2.5 years average tenure

Objectives of the Teams

Table 17-7 shows the organizational objectives as perceived by the managements of the four teams. All of the teams recognize the following objectives:

1. Providing a team to satisfy the entertainment needs of the fans
2. Producing a winning team
3. Making the playoffs
4. Growing in attendance
5. Making a profit
6. Improving the team image
7. Obtaining a share of the entertainment market
8. Improving the image of professional football
9. Maintaining survival in its present location
10. Satisfying some needs of those who contribute to the team—customers, athletes, employees, creditors, owners, managers, suppliers, government, community, and the NFL

When each team management was asked to rank the top three objectives, the most obvious one was winning. However, entertainment and profit were also mentioned quite often as well as employee needs. Table 17-7 shows an analysis of organizational objectives of the four teams.

Table 17-7 Objectives of Selected Football Teams and Their Importance

	Team M	*Team K*	*Team N*	*Team H*
1. Providing a team to satisfy the entertainment needs of the fans	Important	Major	Important	Major
2. Producing a winning team	Major	Major	Major	Major
3. Making the playoffs	Minor	Important	Major	Major
4. Growing in attendance	Major	Major	Major	Major
5. Making a profit	Major	Major	Important	Major
6. Improving the team image	Important	Important	Major	Major
7. Improving the image of professional football	Important	Important	Minor	Minor
8. Obtaining a share of the entertainment market	Minor	Important	Minor	Important
9. Maintaining survival in present location	Minor	Important	Major	Minor
10. Satisfying the needs of contributors				
Customers	Important	Important	Important	Major
Athletes	Major	Important	Major	Minor
Employees	Important	Important	Major	Minor
Creditors	Important	Important	Important	Minor
Owners	Important	Important	Important	Important
Managers	Important	Important	Important	Important
Suppliers	Important	Important	Important	Minor
Government	Important	Important	Important	Important
Community	Important	Important	Important	Major
NFL	Important	Important	Major	Important
Ranking of three most important objectives				
1.	Profit	Winning	Winning	Winning
2.	Player needs	Entertain	Entertain	Playoffs
3.	Winning	Profit	Employee needs	Profit

Similarities in the Structure of Organizations

Although teams are not totally similar, there are quite a few consistencies as shown in Table 17-8.

Table 17-8 Similarities in Organizational Structural Characteristics of Selected Professional Football Teams

	Team M	*Team K*	*Team N*	*Team H*
1. Major objective of winning	Yes	Yes	Yes	Yes
2. Dominant production (coaching) function	Yes	Yes	Yes	Yes
3. Existence of marketing functions	Yes	Yes	Yes	Yes
4. Recognition of player personnel function	Yes	Yes	Yes	Yes
5. Minor finance function	Yes	Yes	Yes	Yes
6. Degree of specialization of functions	High	High	High	High
7. Recognition of line/service/staff functions	No	No	No	No
8. Existence of formal personnel organization chart	No	No	No	Yes
9. Existence of informal organization	Yes	Yes	Yes	Yes
10. Span of supervision of head coaches	Wide	Wide	Wide	Wide
11. Authority and responsibility delegated to head coach	Yes	Yes	Yes	Yes
12. Degree of centralization in decision making	High	High	High	High
13. Levels of organization structure				
Top	Yes	Yes	Yes	Yes
Middle	Yes	Yes	Yes	Yes
Supervisory	Yes	Yes	Yes	Yes

QUESTIONS:

1. Are there any hypotheses that may be suggested concerning:
   a. Head coaching functions and win-loss records?
   b. Span of supervision of head coaches and win-loss records?
   c. Number of assistant coaches and win-loss records?
   d. Number of total employees and win-loss records?
   e. Professional player personnel function and win-loss records?
2. Comment on the functional growth and emergence of the following functions:
   a. Coaching (production)
   b. Marketing
   c. Finance
   d. Personnel
3. Comment on any other organizational concepts and principles.

18

ADMINISTERING WOMEN'S SPORTS

THE NATURE OF WOMEN'S SPORTS

In the past ten years most high school and collegiate athletic programs ave added a line of women's sports to their original male line. In theory, ıtroducing women's basketball, track, and golf should present only those dministrative problems associated with any growing athletic program. Iowever, there are some problems unique to women's sports; these must be ecognized and dealt with by the administrator. There are four major facors that influence women's sports at the present time: (1) the role of vomen as perceived by members of society; (2) the physiological differnces between men and women; (3) the introductory stage of the life cycle f women's sports; (4) the impact of Title IX on women's and men's sports.

The Role of Women's Sports as Viewed by Society

Sports reflect the society's cultural and social values. Some beliefs rearding the roles of men and women have been held for centuries. Men ave often been characterized as strong and aggressive, while women have een considered weak and passive. Until recently, women have not been ncouraged to participate in sports since the values associated with excelnce in sports—achievement, aggressiveness, strength, and swiftness—ave been considered contradictory to the role of women in society.

These values are hard to dislodge; the culture of Western civilization is ounded on such beliefs and stereotypes. Despite the passage of Title IX, hich legally states the equality of men and women, the roles played by men and women in society are still considered somewhat different. Society's disposition toward women in sports continues to influence the administrative practices of women's athletics. The sports engaged in; the quality of facilities and equipment; the marketing procedures; the employment opportunities for women athletes, coaches, and administrators; and the funding of women's sports are all affected.

Traditionally, women's sports are based on physical education instruction in lifetime sports. The tradition for men's sports has grown out of competitive athletic programs. If women's sports are to become as competitive as men's sports, society's orientation toward women and women's athletics must continue to change. The change will not be rapid, but it must be far reaching. The passage of Title IX of the Education Amendments of 1972 should improve society's opinion of women in sports. It reads in part:

> No person in the United States shall, on the basis of sex, be excluded from participation in, or be denied the benefit of, or be subjected to discrimination under any educational program or activity receiving federal financial assistance.

Since most schools receive federal money, each school's athletic administrator must ensure that equal opportunities in sports exist for both males and females. This is a difficult responsibility, especially for athletic administrators who still hesitate on the subject of women's sports.

Despite the fact that males and females are legally equal, suggestions of inequality still exist in some aspects of our culture. In the United States some individuals still consider a woman's place to be in the home. These people certainly frown on competitive athletics for women. Some people may feel that women engaging in competitive athletics with males conflicts with their religious values. Although a woman's role in politics must be condoned, women are not always encouraged to engage in competitive political activity. The ERA movement is helping to improve women's political position, yet the position of the woman athlete remains dubious.

Unless these beliefs change radically, they will continue to inhibit the growth of women's athletics. However, the legal implications of Title IX should make gradual growth possible.

THE PHYSIOLOGICAL DIFFERENCES BETWEEN MALES AND FEMALES

The physiological differences between males and females must be considered by the administrator of athletic programs. Those who engage in competitive athletics (athletic teams) are selected on the basis of competitive skills—usually physical skills. Studies have proved that males and females do not perform equally in athletic contests. Comparisons of swimming times, track and field times, basketball performances, and practically all forms of athletic activity indicate that males often do better than females. Most adult males are considerably stronger than females, posses greater muscular and cardiovascular endurance, and can outshine females in most motor skills. Such physiological differences suggest several administrative practices.

An athletic program can provide comparable sports for men and women; unfortunately, providing a large number of sports for both sexes may not be practical or financially possible. When there is a vast difference in the performance of males and females, separate athletic programs should be made available.

There is a danger of going to extremes in separate programs. It is not necessary to have separate rules; this would cause frustrations and tensions similar to those experienced by colleges when the NCAA and Association of Intercollegiate Athletics for Women fought for control of women's intercollegiate athletics. Doubling personnel and services to accommodate male and female programs would be wasteful. However, there will continue to be imbalances between the veteran male and newly introduced female athletic programs.

Women's and men's athletics cannot achieve total equality overnight. Women's athletics will not grow if men's athletics are severely limited. Experience has shown that where women's athletics have grown, men's athletic programs have also grown and have provided technical, financial, and spectator support for the women's program.

Many women would love to play and compete if it were not for the cultural forces against them. However, these forces do exist. Although women's sports are constantly increasing in popularity, it will be a long time before they elicit nationwide approval.

Competitors, both male and female, must maintain a winning philosophy. Although women's athletic programs are going through difficult times, a stalwart attitude could make the difference between success and failure.

When money is spent on a program and when spectators support a team, there is pressure—whether the competitors are women or men—to realize the objectives of winning, growing, and providing entertainment. It is inevitable that women's and men's teams will eventually strive for the same goals.

At present, men know more about athletics than women. They have had extensive experience administering and participating in athletics; most women find competitive athletics rather new. Today, clear understanding must be shown by both men and women administrators as more women's athletic programs are introduced to the system.

THE INTRODUCTORY STAGE OF WOMEN'S SPORTS LIFE CYCLE

Women's sports are at the introductory stage of the product-service life cycle. This is significant to the administrator who devises strategies for the women's program.

Often, the major objective of a women's program in the introductory

stage is to develop the character of the female athletes. In this case, littl
emphasis is placed on growth, profits, image and other male athletic pro
gram objectives. However, attempts should be made to attract fans. Th
major sports strategy should be to introduce sports suited to women's phys
iological interests. Perhaps basketball, track, swimming, tennis, golf, vol
leyball, and gymnastics are the logical ones to introduce. After this, th
administrator can either introduce a revenue-producing sport or follow th
lead of other schools in nonrevenue sports.

In the case of team sports, the emphasis should be placed on winning
particularly if the athletic program is to raise money by selling tickets an
eventually work toward financial independence.

The promotion strategy for women's sports in the introductory stage i
to use a pioneering approach, to try to get potential fans to attend a gam
by supplying location, time, and general information. The best medi
would be newspapers, radio, perhaps TV, and handbills.

The pricing strategy would be either one of the following: (1) to ente
the market quickly, a below-the-market price would be suitable to encour
age attendance; or (2) to skim the market of hard-core women's sports fans
a high price would be advisable; in this case, the number of paying custom
ers might be limited.

The scheduling strategy would be to play games at popular times and a
convenient places. Perhaps a women's game could precede or follow
men's athletic event. During the introductory stage, it is difficult to attrac
spectators unless some sort of special compensation is involved.

The personnel strategy would be to use creative salespeople and aggres
sive ticket sellers. A new women's sport is often difficult to sell. Conse
quently, just sitting back and hoping to sell tickets is not an effectiv
strategy.

During the introductory stage of any athletic program, the administra
tion must be willing to lose money. This is true in the case of women's ath
letics. Financial subsidies must be available to finance that portion of th
athletic program. Having plenty of liquid financial reserves would be a
appropriate strategy.

Until a winning tradition is established, the proposed target marke
would be the parents of players and their friends. It would probably tak
five to ten years before any substantial change could be noticed in the ta
get market characteristics. It is wise to find out specifically who attends b
name, how many attend, when they come, where they live, and what cha
acteristics they possess.

The product-service life cycle concept should be adapted to eac
women's sport. Some sports, like basketball, grow faster than others. If a
exciting revenue-producer like basketball were nourished, perhaps it coul
provide the profits necessary to support other women's sports. The point is
though, that the introductory stage of women's sports is characterized b
lack of fan attendance, a high financial risk, possible failure, and high cos
and expenses in relation to revenues. The administrator must work out th
bugs in the program. Hopefully, there will be a gradual rise in attendanc

esulting in increased revenues; this would enable the program to become elf-supporting and to work toward the goals of male athletic programs.

THE IMPACT OF TITLE IX ON WOMEN'S AND MEN'S PROGRAMS

Since the 1972 Educational Act was passed, there has been issued by IEW a special supplement to Title IX concerning athletics (June 4, 1975). ts text directly affects the administration of women's and men's programs.

Section 86.41 Athletics

a) *General.* No person shall, on the basis of sex, be excluded from participation in, be denied the benefits of, be treated differently from another person or otherwise be discriminated against in any interscholastic, intercollegiate, club, or intramural athletics offered by recipient, and no recipient shall provide any such athletics separately on such basis.

b) *Separate Teams.* Notwithstanding the requirements of paragraph (a) of this section, a recipient may operate or sponsor separate teams for members of each sex where selection for such teams is based on competitive skill or the activity involved is a contact sport. However, where a recipient operates or sponsors a team in a particular sport for members of one sex but operates or sponsors no such team for members of the other sex, and athletic opportunities for members of that sex have previously been limited, members of the excluded sex must be allowed to try out for the team offered unless the sport involved is a contact sport. For the purpose of this part, contact sports include boxing, wrestling, rugby, ice hockey, football, basketball, and other sports the purpose or major activity of which involves bodily contact.

c) *Equal Opportunity.* A recipient which operates or sponsors interscholastic, intercollegiate, club, or intramural athletics shall provide equal athletic opportunity for members of both sexes. In determining whether equal opportunities are available the director will consider, among other factors:

i whether the selection of sports and levels of competition effectively accommodate the interests and abilities of members of both sexes
ii the provision of equipment and supplies
iii the scheduling of games and practice times
iv travel and per diem allowance
v opportunity to receive coaching and academic tutoring
vi assignment and compensation of coaches and tutors
vii provision of locker rooms, practice and competitive facilities
viii provision of medical and training facilities and services
ix provision of housing and dining facilities and services
x publicity

Unequal aggregate expenditures for members of each sex or unequal expenditures for male and female teams if a recipient operates or sponsors separate teams will not constitute non-compliance with this section, but the director may consider the failure to provide necessary funds for teams for one sex in assessing equality of opportunity for members of each sex.

d) *Adjustment Period* . . . A recipient . . . shall fully comply with this section as expeditiously as possible but in no event later than three years from the effective date of this regulation.

Analysis

Paragraph 86.41(b) permits separate teams for members of each se where selection for the team is based on competitive skill, or the activit involved is a contact sport. If, however, a team in a noncontact sport, th membership of which is based in skill, is offered for members of one sex an not for members of the other sex, and athletic opportunities for the sex fo whom no team is available have previously been limited, individuals o that sex must be allowed to compete for the team offered. For example, i tennis is offered for men and not for women, and a woman wishes to pla on the tennis team, if women's sports have previously been limited at th institution in question, that woman may compete for a place on the men' team. However, this provision does not alter the responsibility unde 86.41(c) with regard to the provision of equal opportunity. Under 86.41(c recipients are required to select "sports and levels of competition which ef fectively accommodate the interests and abilities of members of bot sexes." Thus an institution would be required to provide separate teams fo men and women in situations where the provision of only one team woul not "accommodate the interests and abilities of members of both sexes. This provision, of course, applies whether sports are contact or noncontac As in the section of physical education, a contact sport is defined by usin some examples and leaving the status of other sports to be determined o the basis of whether their purpose or major activity involves bodily contac

As provided in the proposed regulation, the department will not con sider unequal aggregate expenditures for members of each sex or unequa expenditures for male and female teams if such separate teams are offere or sponsored. Clearly it is possible for equality of opportunity to be pro vided without exact equality of expenditure. However, any failure to pro vide necessary funds for women's teams may be considered by th department in assessing equality of opportunity for members of each sex

The department will construe this section (86.41(d)) as requiring recip ents to comply before the end of the adjustment period wherever possibl

Section 86.53 Recruitment

(a) Non-discrimination Recruitment and Hiring. A recipient shall not discriminate on the basis of sex in the recruitment and hiring of employees . . .

Section 86.54 Compensation

A recipient shall not make or enforce any policy or practice which, on the basis of sex:

(a) Makes distinction in rates of pay or other compensation.

(b) Results in the payment of wages to employees of one sex at a rate less than that paid to employees of the opposite sex for equal work on jobs the performance of which requires equal skill, effort, and responsibility, and which are performed under similar working conditions.

Section 86.55 Job Classification and Structure

A recipient shall not:

(a) Classify a job as being for males or females.

(b) Maintain or establish separate lines of progression, seniority lists, career ladders, or tenure systems based on sex.

(c) Maintain or establish separate lines of progression, seniority systems, career ladders, or tenure systems for similar jobs, position descriptions, or job requirements which classify persons on the basis of sex, unless sex is a bona fide occupational qualification for the positions in question as set forth in 86.51.

ADDITIONAL HEW GUIDELINES FOR ATHLETICS (published September 24, 1975)

These sections apply to each segment of the athletic program of a federally assisted educational institution whether or not that segment is the subject of direct financial support through the department. Thus, the fact that a particular segment of an athletic program is supported by funds received from various other sources (such as student fees, general revenues, gate receipts, alumni donations, booster clubs, and non-profit foundations) does not remove it from the reach of the statute and hence of the regulatory requirements. However, drill teams, cheerleaders, and the like, which are covered more generally as extracurricular activities under Section 86.31, are not a part of the institution's "athletic program" within the meaning of the regulation.

Section 86.41 does not address the administrative structure(s) which are used by educational institutions for athletic programs. Accordingly, institutions are not precluded from employing separate administrative structures for men's and women's sports (if separate teams exist) or a unitary structure . . .

If by opening a team to both sexes in a contact sport an educational institution does not effectively accommodate the abilities of members of both sexes (see Section 86.41(i)), separate teams in that sport will be required if both men and women express interest in the sport and the interests of both sexes are not otherwise accommodated. For example, an institution would not be effectively accommodating the interests and abilities of women if it abolished all of its women's teams and opened up its men's teams to women, but only a few women were able to qualify for the men's team.

CHAPTER SUMMARY

Theoretically, the administration of women's and men's sports should be similar. However, there are some differences in women's sports that affect their administration.

In our society, women's sports are not viewed in the same light as men's sports. Various social, religious, and political values held by people suggest that women's sports will not make rapid strides in fan attendance. However, Title IX should help women's sports to grow gradually.

The physiological differences between women and men suggest that at the present time separate sports should be provided for both men and women.

Since women's sports are not at the introductory stage of the product life cycle, various strategies may be suggested for promotion, pricing, winning, scheduling, choosing personnel, financing the program, and determining the target market.

The impact of Title IX is so pervasive that its effect on men's and women's sports—in particular, regarding discrimination and equal opportunities in the areas of equipment, schedules, travel, tutoring, coaching, facilities, medical services, housing, publicity, and finance—should be fully understood.

Case 18-1 WOMEN'S EQUALITY IN NONCOMPETITIVE ATHLETICS?

The following are real life situations at educational institutions whose names are not mentioned.[1]

At a private school the women's and men's physical education departments are separate. Instructional courses between men and women vary. For example, women cannot take wrestling and men cannot take self-defense or volleyball.

At a southern state university female students could not take coaching courses for credit, with the result that they were not "qualified" to coach teams.

At a liberal arts school women majoring in physical education must take a service course each term. There is no similar requirement for men.

At another college women must show proficiency in two sports in order to graduate. Men need show proficiency in one sport.

Men, not women, may be able to exempt required physical education courses by taking a skills test.

Male, but not female, varsity athletes may be exempted from physical education classes.

Men, but not women, may receive credit for participating in intercollegiate athletics.

At a major state university women were prohibited from participating

[1] These real life situations were drawn from the paper, "*What Constitutes Equality for Women in Sport?*" prepared by the Project on the Status and Education of Women, Association of American Colleges, 1818 R Street, N. W., Washington, D.C., 1974.

in any of the five intramural team sports in the "all campus division program." They could only compete in the individual or dual sports.

At one institution a woman could not use the handball courts unless a male signed up for her.

At a large midwestern university, the intramural pool was specifically reserved for "faculty, administrative staff, and male students" two hours each day. That is, this was a time for men only.

Recently, the Education Amendments Act of 1972, Title IX, was passed. The key section reads:

No person in the United States shall, on the basis of sex, be excluded from participation in, be denied the benefits of, or be subjected to discrimination under any educational program or activity receiving federal financial assistance.

Title IX allows the government to withdraw funds, debar institutions from eligibility for future funds, and to bring suit against institutions that discriminate against students or employees on the basis of sex. Since practically all colleges receive federal money, they would be subject to the law.

QUESTIONS:

1. Do athletics have an educational value?
2. What is the traditional attitude toward women in athletics?
3. Can an educational institution successfully use the argument their athletic conferences do not allow women in athletics?
4. Can lack of duplicate facilities be successfully used as an argument for not having women engage in athletics?
5. What reaction do you have regarding the examples cited of women's participation in noncompetitive athletics?

Case 18-2 WOMEN'S ATHLETICS IN HIGH SCHOOL? PART I

Dr. Harry Vandergriff, Superintendent of Public Schools for Fayetteville, was surprised by a request that he had received concerning the women's physical education courses at Fayetteville High School. In the year 1970, he instituted a program to obtain course improvement suggestions from teachers. Right away, Dr. Vandergriff received a proposal from Mrs. Bill Brunner, women's physical education teacher, and Mr. Joe Holt, Supervisor of Physical Education to (1) redesign the high school's women's physical education program around individual sports and (2) to develop a women's varsity athletic team in varied sports.

During 1970 there was not a varsity program available to women students. Women's physical education classes covered several sports during the year. The classes were designed to give the girl students as much exposure as possible to different sports and acquaint them with the rules and the skills associated with each of the sports. Not enough time was spent on each sport to develop a very high skill level in any one sport.

Dr. Vandergriff remembered that in 1949 a study had been made concluding that girls should not participate in competitive athletics because it was harmful to their health. He never had given the idea of a women's varsity athletic team much thought. He just took it for granted that women did not want to participate in competitive athletics. So the Brunner proposal took him by surprise.

Various reasons for not having women's varsity athletics in the past, according to Dr. Vandergriff, were that

1. Not enough interest existed among women students.
2. A women's program would lose money.
3. Personnel were not available to carry the extra work load required by women's varsity teams.

None of the schools in Fayetteville's conference had women's varsity athletics, and only a very few schools in Fayetteville's region had women's varsity teams. Some of the smaller school systems in the area had women's basketball and track teams; however, these schools generally did not develop teams in other sports such as gymnastics, tennis, golf, and so forth.

In her proposal, Mrs. Brunner cited the following objectives which could be accomplished by the development of a women's athletic program:

For the total athletic program

1. Help women to appreciate athletics
2. Involve more parents and friends of the athletes in the Fayetteville Booster Club
3. Make fuller use of existing facilities

For the woman athlete

1. Increase her self-confidence
2. Develop sportsmanship and respect for other athletes
3. Learn discipline
4. Improve health and physical appearance
5. Improve relationships between the sexes

For the woman coach

1. Receive professional recognition and treatment
2. Improve coach and student interaction
3. Achieve some degree of self-fulfillment

Mrs. Brunner did not mention the objective of developing a winning team to provide entertainment for fans. Nor did she mention making a profit, growing, improving an image. She was concerned with development of women athletes and women's coaches. She felt that financially the women's athletic program would not be self-supporting; however, initially there appeared to be sufficient funds available to implement the program if there were some volunteer help to coach the teams. Mr. and Mrs. Brunner were willing to donate their time to coach the girls' teams in their beginning stages.

A need for additional facilities and equipment appeared to be minimal. If the women's program grew, there would be a demand for additional facilities; however, this problem did not appear to be very important in the near future. The primary need would first be in the nature of additional equipment and additional staff.

Dr. Vandergriff guessed that there was no significant religious pressure against women's athletics. He did recall that two preachers called him one time to object to girls wearing shorts in public.

In 1970 he did not know about the women's liberation movement, nor was there any pressure about the equal rights amendment. As far as he knew, there were no legal problems involved in starting a women's athletic team. His main concerns were economic and technological in nature.

Several problems were foreseen initially. The men's and women's teams would oftentimes be competing for the use of the same facilities along with teams from the two junior high schools. Scheduling of games and meets would present another problem. When men's and women's teams were scheduled together, there would exist problems with providing adequate dressing rooms, uniforms, equipment, and practice times. Problems would also result from the inability to schedule exactly the same opponents. A major economic factor was the existence of a strong major university athletic program near the high school which always affected negatively attendance at Fayetteville's athletic events.

Another major factor in scheduling the women's athletic events and practices was the traditional activities that involved the potential female athlete. Pep squad, cheerleading, drill team, band, and academics all competed for the abilities and talents of each girl.

A major task for the new program would be to inform the public about the program and its benefits. This would be necessary to gain acceptance of the program among the community members, school officials and teachers, male athletes and coaches, students, and parents.

Some of the other questions to be answered involved the pay of coaches, the inherent financial losses of the total athletic program, equal treatment for both girls and boys, especially regarding equipment and travel expenses in attending away-from-home games. What about the band director who might be forced to play four nights a week if both girls and boys played on separate nights, twice a week?

With any degree of success, however, the women's program would succeed in changing the public's stereotyping of the woman athlete. Their view of her as somewhat offbeat would be replaced by appreciation and support.

Dr. Vandergriff had to decide whether the new women's program had merit. He was trying to make a decision and formulate his reasoning in order to include it in his annual report and recommendations to the Fayetteville School Board.

Case 18-3 WOMEN'S ATHLETICS IN HIGH SCHOOL? PART II

The Fayetteville High School's women's athletic program was entering its sixth year of interscholastic competition. What initially started as a revision of the high school's physical education courses was now a growing, competitive, and dynamic women's athletic program. Today the program included girls' gymnastics, track, basketball, tennis, golf, and swimming.

Dr. Vandergriff received a recent Sunday issue of one of the state's two leading state capitol newspapers (on the front page) which read in part:

FAYETTEVILLE—Male chauvinism has suffered a painful setback at Fayetteville High School.

Most coaches, particularly those who must worry about their own purse strings, long have feared the day when girls' sports might be more heavily emphasized. That could only mean draining the budget for boys' sports.

"I'll have to admit it, I felt the same way," said Fayetteville athletic director Doyne Davis. "I mean the money for girls' sports would have to come from somewhere. That means cutting into the overall athletic budget."

The natural conclusion was that someday boys' sports would surely decline and suffer hard financial times. And all because the "weaker" sex spent the money from the athletic funds.

Somewhere there has to be a middle ground. From all indications, Fayetteville appears to have found it.

During the past school year, Fayetteville won six different athletic state championships, twice finished third in Class AAA state competition and sent both boys' and girls' basketball teams to the state tournament quarterfinals.

Those state titles came in two groups. In cross country, golf and tennis, Fayetteville teams captured Class AAA state championships. In boys' swimming, and girls' track and swimming, the state titles were won against competition from every classification—including the higher classification, AAAA.

Those third places came in boys' track and girls' gymnastics.

"We are extremely proud of that overall record," Davis said. "We did well in every girls' sport. They (girls' sports) got more money than in the past. But the school wound up with its most state titles ever in one year."

Davis said he thought that proved that a school can have successful programs in both girls' and boys' sports and still spend money on each.

Ironically, the only Fayetteville High School athletic team with a losing record was varsity football. And Davis' rebuilding program is on the verge of providing a return to prosperity there, too.

Davis isn't a male chauvinist. His change of heart and resultant conclusions are a strong comment against the anti-women sports' chauvinist's cause.

However, one characteristic of Fayetteville's banner year is even more stunning than the mere disapproving of old-fashioned money-spending fears.

Usually, when such a truckload of state titles goes to one school, the reasons are obvious. Almost every time, the school so blessed is enjoying the fruits of a good run of athletes who excel in two or even more sports.

At Fayetteville, such is not the case. Multisport competitors are the exception—not the rule.

One might understand that in swimming and tennis, plus golf and cross country to a slightly lesser degree. All of these require demanding practice time and usually attract specialists who don't have time to devote to another sport.

Girls sports, however, are a different story, beyond swimming and gymnastics. Since girls' basketball long has been established in Arkansas, the same girls usually pass their springtime away by running track against each other in different parts of the state.

Instead, Fayetteville had only two girls—Kathy Morgan and Betsy Broyles—who excelled in both sports. The other track standouts either didn't play girls' basketball or didn't make the starting lineup.

"This wasn't just a bunch of seniors, either," Davis said. "The tennis and swimming programs have been on top for years and will stay that way. The same is true in cross country, where we only lost two seniors. And Sue Carol Brunner (the girls' basketball coach) told me she's only losing a few of her players.' "

Of course, one of those is Kathy Morgan, likely the single most outstanding senior athlete this year at Fayetteville. Only two weeks ago, she played well in the state high school All-Star game at Conway. In track, she won the shot put and discus events at the state meet. She also had a state record distance in the discus.

Fayetteville's girls' relay teams also set three state records. The foursome of Vicki Williams, Paula Fairess, Debbie McLain and Kathy McLain ran 50.0 in the 440-yard relay, 1:44.5 in the 880-yard relay and 1:55.4 in the 880-yard medley relay.

The boys' track team pleased coach Whit Fowlkes by placing third in Class AAA. The key to that was shot putter Jim Elliot, who became the state's best high schooler in that event by winning the Meet of Champions as a junior.

The original goals and objectives of the program that Mrs. Brunner had outlined appeared to be met. The Fayetteville teams were competitive; they had done well in their season play as well as in district and state competition. Mrs. Brunner had received recognition for her coaching efforts as volunteer and was now receiving salary compensation for her added work.

Despite their original timidity and skepticism, the male athletes and coaches had accepted the women's athletic program. As originally predicted at the program's inception, the male and female athletes had increased interaction because of the increased mutual interest which centered around athletics. It was found that the male athletes were willing to offer pointers and suggestions to the women as they developed their skills and methods.

Because of the early entrance which Fayetteville High School had made into women's athletics, it had avoided many of the disappointments and growing pains which a majority of the schools had recently experienced since the passage of Title IX federal legislation concerning women. Although most high school systems were still struggling with their women's programs, the future looked good for the continued growth and development of women's athletics. With this future growth potential, it was felt that the Fayetteville public schools should plan for the future growth and development of its women's athletic program.

Dr. Vandergriff remarked, "When Title IX legislation was passed in 1971, we were already in 'good faith' compliance with it. We were already performing Title IX activities and had no person designated as Title IX director. Mrs. Brunner had asked our administrative staff to plan for women's athletics before any pressure from the Federal Government existed in legislative form. As a result of our planning, we avoided many problems arising at the last moment. Any time that pressures are put on us by any outside agency (whatever external force it might be), we tend to say no and rationalize our decisions in some way or another. We did not have to do that in the case of women's athletics."

Dr. Vandergriff went on to say, "The State Activities Association had been a problem for us because it was difficult for them to adapt to women's athletics. For example, during football season, no girls were allowed to participate in girls' sports. As a result, all girls' activities had to be played during the winter or spring. In addition, we had to persuade them to consider girls' gymnastics as a proper activity. However, with Mrs. Brunner's leadership, the Association is now very cooperative."

One of the problems to be faced was that of staffing. Mr. Brunner was faced with increased demand from his regular duties which had resulted in a diminished ability to coach the women's teams. Since the program's inception, the number of sports, as well as the number of women participants had grown, which resulted in a greater coaching manpower strain.

In response to the success of the women's program, it was felt that the women merited their own uniforms, equipment, and to a certain extent, their own facilities. Previously the women had to share with the men's teams or use old men's equipment and uniforms. It was felt that such things as new uniforms would enhance the athletes' play as well as improve the program's image.

Also the women were forced to share dressing rooms and such equipment as the whirlpool. Hopefully, resources could be provided to alleviate this problem.

Low attendance at women's athletic events was a major concern. Mr. Brunner felt that this was a result of primarily two factors:

1. Women's events were generally scheduled at less popular times than men's events (weekday nights vs. weekend nights).
2. The standards for women's athletics were constantly compared to the standards for men.

Expanding on the last point, he noted that one of his tracksters ran the hurdles in a time which would probably rank in the top ten of the nation; however, because her time is compared with men's records, she does not get the local recognition she deserves. A comment at a basketball game like "she shoots just like a boy" is indicative of the general comparisons made between the men's and women's performances.

The question which administrators and coaches had to face was how to maintain the growth and capitalize upon Fayetteville's early entrance into women's athletics, especially since increased emphasis had been placed upon the program as a result of Title IX.

Case 18-4 NORTHSIDE, SOUTHSIDE!

Approximately 1000 students and faculty from each of two schools were asked to give their attitudes about various sports that make up the athletic programs. Both schools have a student population of about 1400. Northside High is the oldest school composed of both white and black students with an excellent win-loss record in both football and basketball during the past 15 years. Southside has approximately 99% white students; they started their athletic program about 10 years ago. Students and faculty in several home rooms were asked to complete the semantic differential concerning their views about the overall athletic program. In addition, they were asked their views about football, track, tennis, and golf—those sports activities engaged in by both schools. Further, they were asked their views about ticket prices.

Girls' sports were being introduced for the first time on a great scale. Consequently, some attempt was made to get faculty and student attitudes about girls' sports. A modification of the semantic differential was used to determine whether male or female coaches should be coaching boys or girls. Also an attempt was made to determine attitudes of whether boys' and girls' athletic events (in basketball, tennis, golf, and track) should be played at the same time and place and whether boys and girls should travel together to the athletic events.

QUESTION:

1. How would you interpret Charts 1 through 3?

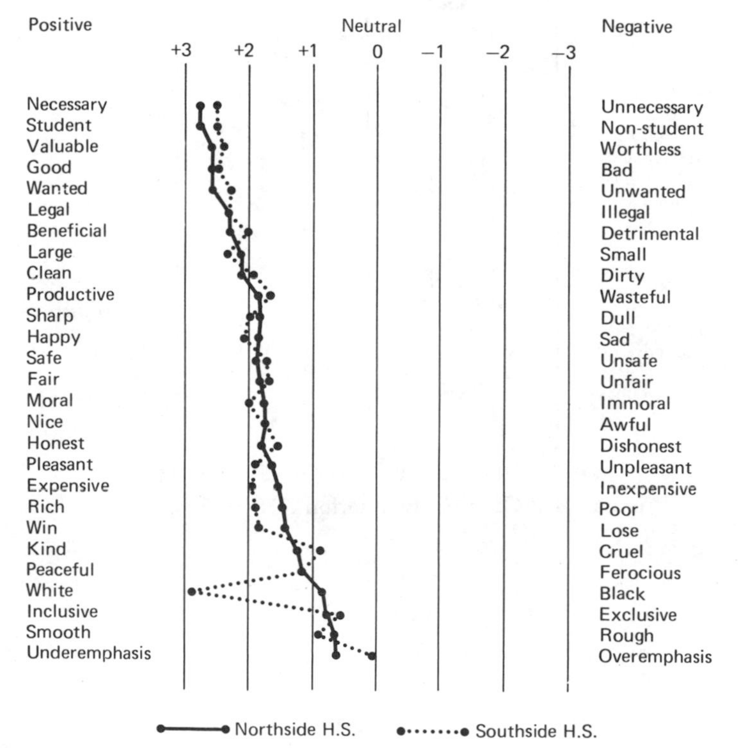

Figure 18–1 Chart 1: Comparative Evaluation of Athletic Programs

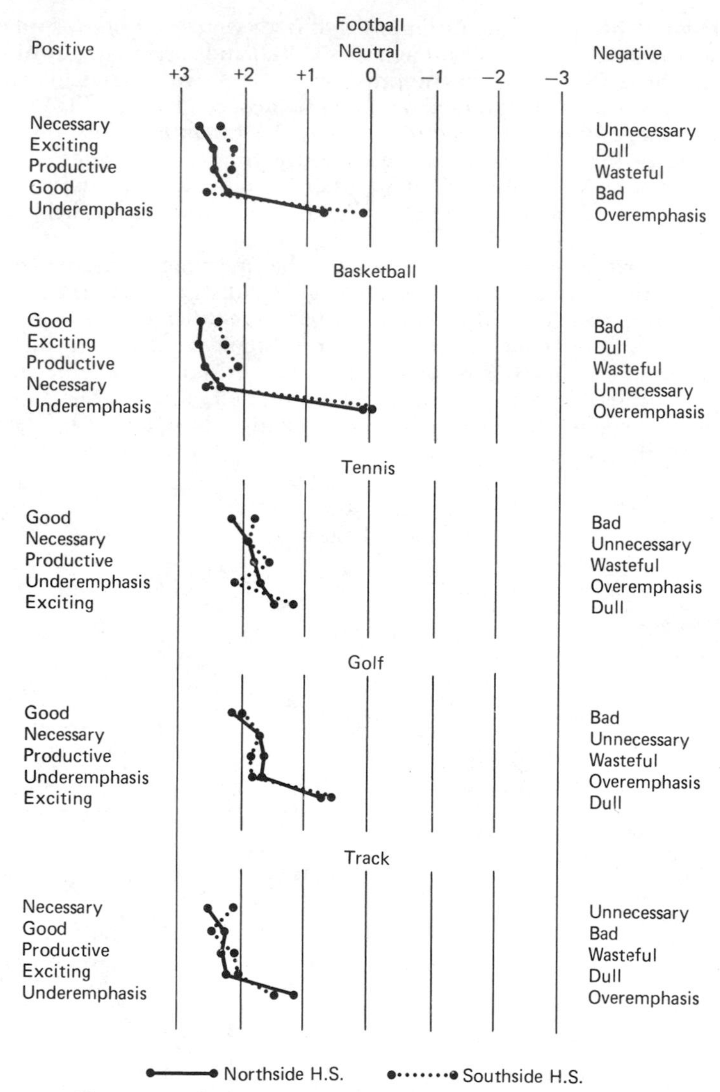

Figure 18–2 Chart 2: Evaluation of Five Boys' Sports

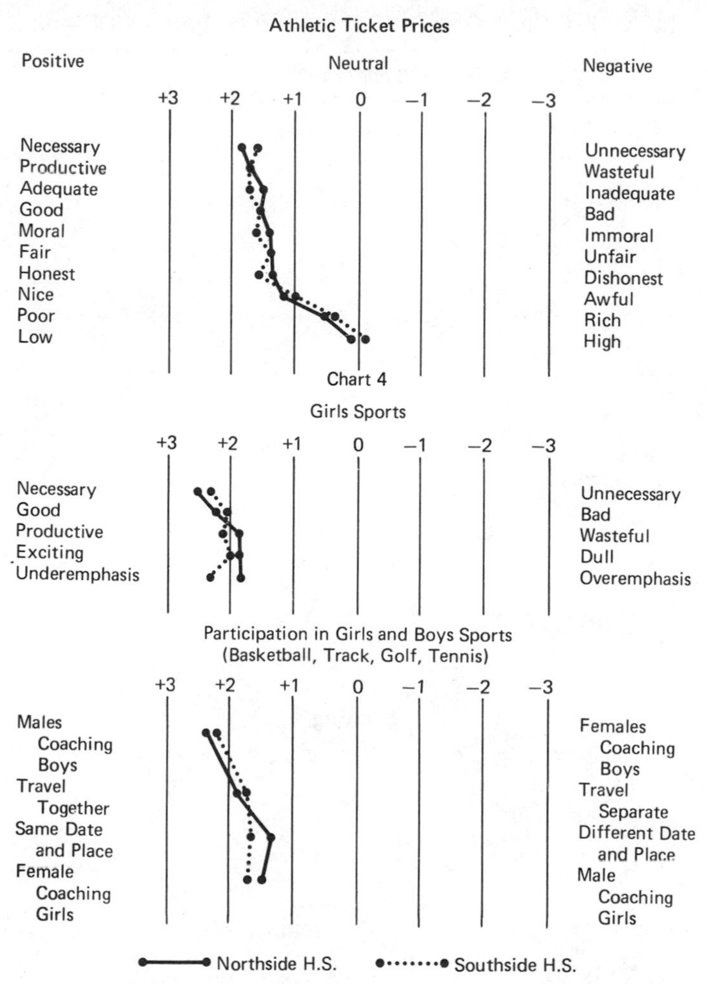

Figure 18–3 Chart 3: Athletic Ticket Prices

Table 18-1 Rank Order of Each Sport by Various Criteria

Rank Order		
	Necessary	
Northside		*Southside*
1. Football		1. Basketball
2. Basketball		2. Football
3. Track		3. Girls Sport
4. Girls Sports		4. Track
5. Tennis		5. Tennis
6. Golf		6. Golf
	Good	
1. Basketball		1. Football
2. Football		2. Basketball
3. Track		3. Track
4. Girls Sports		4. Girls Sport
5. Tennis		5. Golf
6. Golf		6. Tennis
	Productive	
1. Basketball		1. Football
2. Football		2. Basketball
3. Track		3. Girls Sport
4. Girls Sports		4. Track
5. Tennis		5. Golf
6. Golf		6. Tennis
	Exciting	
1. Basketball		1. Basketball
2. Football		2. Football
3. Track		3. Track
4. Girls Sports		4. Girls Sport
5. Tennis		5. Tennis
6. Golf		6. Golf
	Overemphasis	
1. Football		1. Football
2. Golf		2. Basketball
3. Basketball		3. Track
4. Track		4. Golf
5. Tennis		5. Tennis
6. Girls Sports		6. Girls Spor

INDEX

A

B

F

G

H

I

J

L

W